ASCENDANCE OF A BOOKWORM

I'll do anything to become a librarian!

Part 1 **If there aren't any books, I'll just have to make some!**

Volume 7

Author: **Miya Kazuki** / Artist: **Suzuka**

Character Designer: **You Shiina**

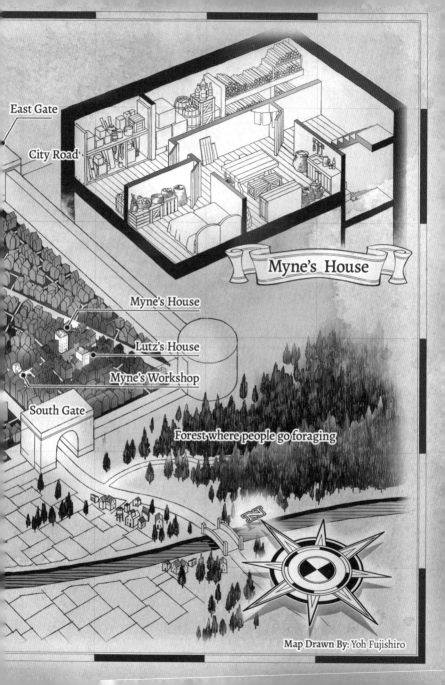

East Gate

City Road

Myne's House

Myne's House

Lutz's House

Myne's Workshop

South Gate

Forest where people go foraging

Map Drawn By: Yoh Fujishiro

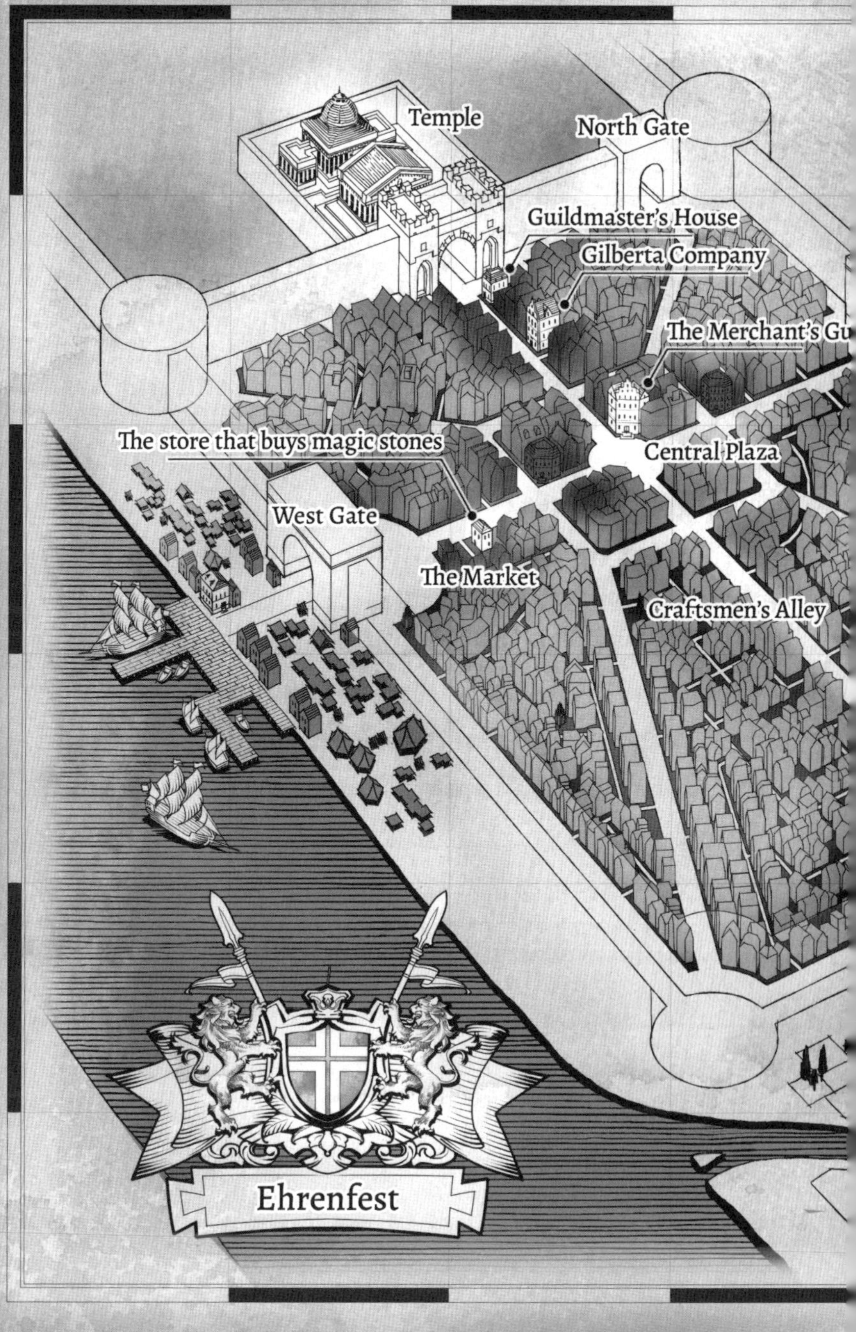
Temple
North Gate
Guildmaster's House
Gilberta Company
The Merchant's Gu
The store that buys magic stones
Central Plaza
West Gate
The Market
Craftsmen's Alley
Ehrenfest

ASCENDANCE OF A BOOKWORM
I'll do anything to become a librarian!

Part 1 If there aren't any books,
I'll just have to make some!
Volume VII

Ch.30 Freida's Contract and the Baptism Ceremony

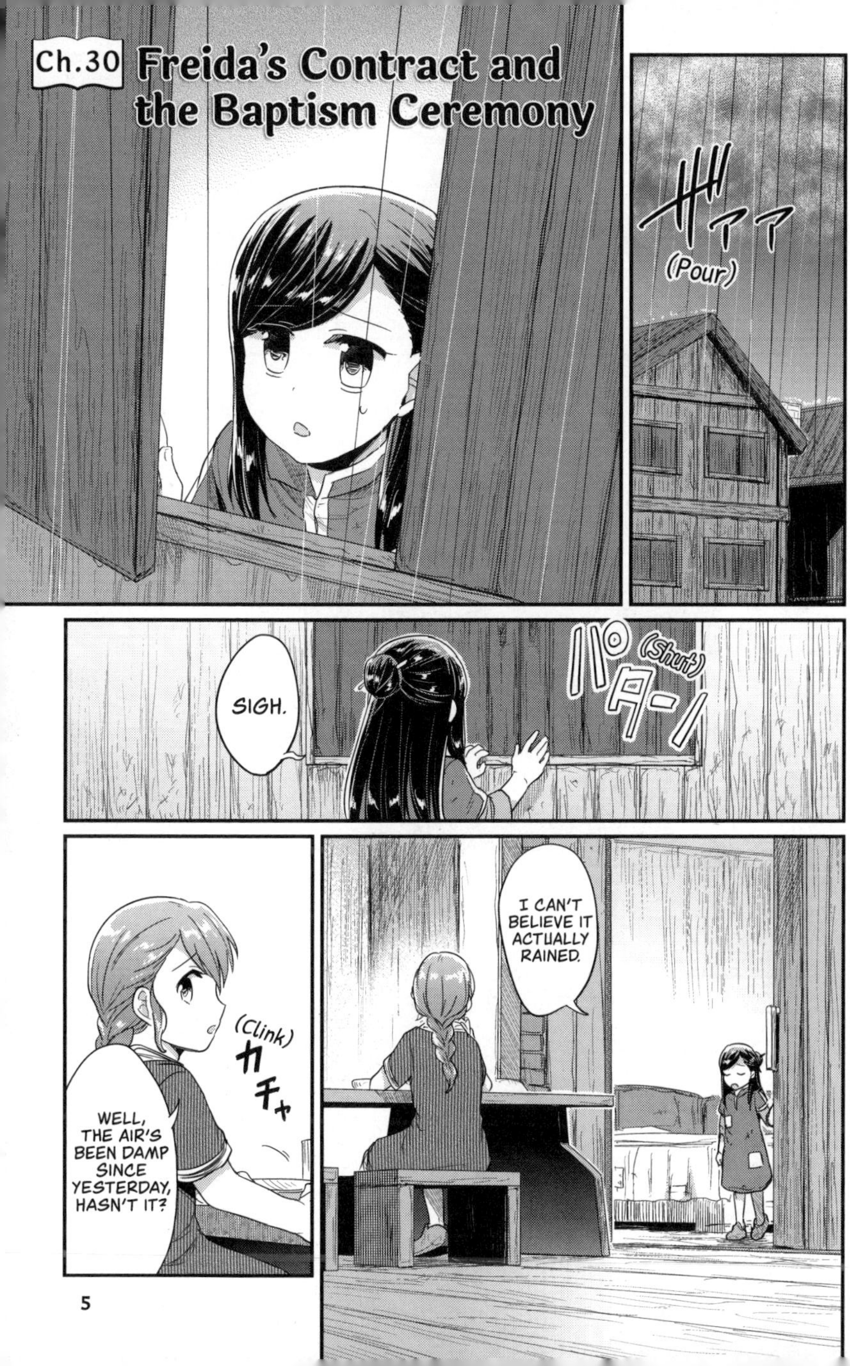

ザァア
(Pour)
パターン
(Shut)
SIGH.
I CAN'T BELIEVE IT ACTUALLY RAINED.
(Clink)
カチャ
WELL, THE AIR'S BEEN DAMP SINCE YESTERDAY, HASN'T IT?

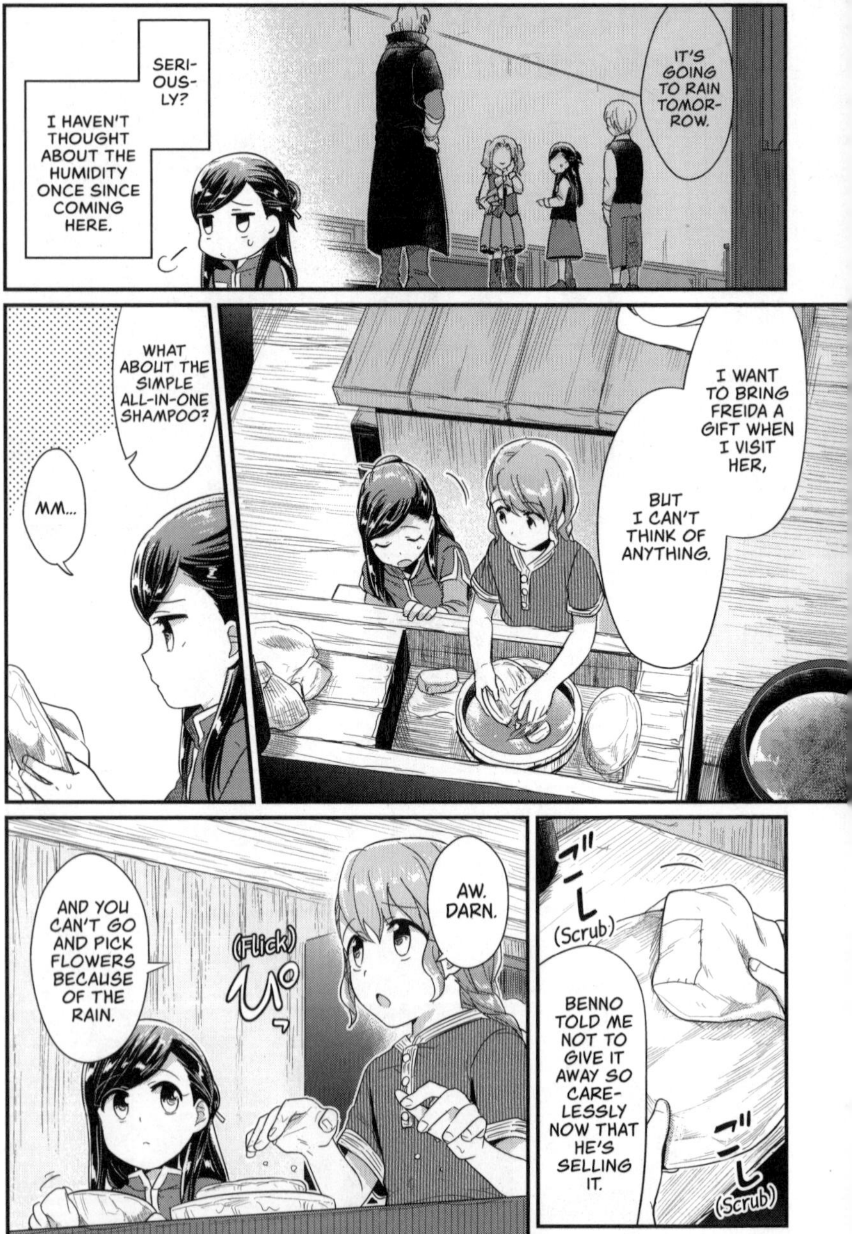
IT'S GOING TO RAIN TOMORROW.
SERIOUSLY?
I HAVEN'T THOUGHT ABOUT THE HUMIDITY ONCE SINCE COMING HERE.
I WANT TO BRING FREIDA A GIFT WHEN I VISIT HER,
BUT I CAN'T THINK OF ANYTHING.
WHAT ABOUT THE SIMPLE ALL-IN-ONE SHAMPOO?
MM...
(Scrub)
BENNO TOLD ME NOT TO GIVE IT AWAY SO CARELESSLY NOW THAT HE'S SELLING IT.
(Scrub)
AW. DARN.
AND YOU CAN'T GO AND PICK FLOWERS BECAUSE OF THE RAIN.
(Flick)

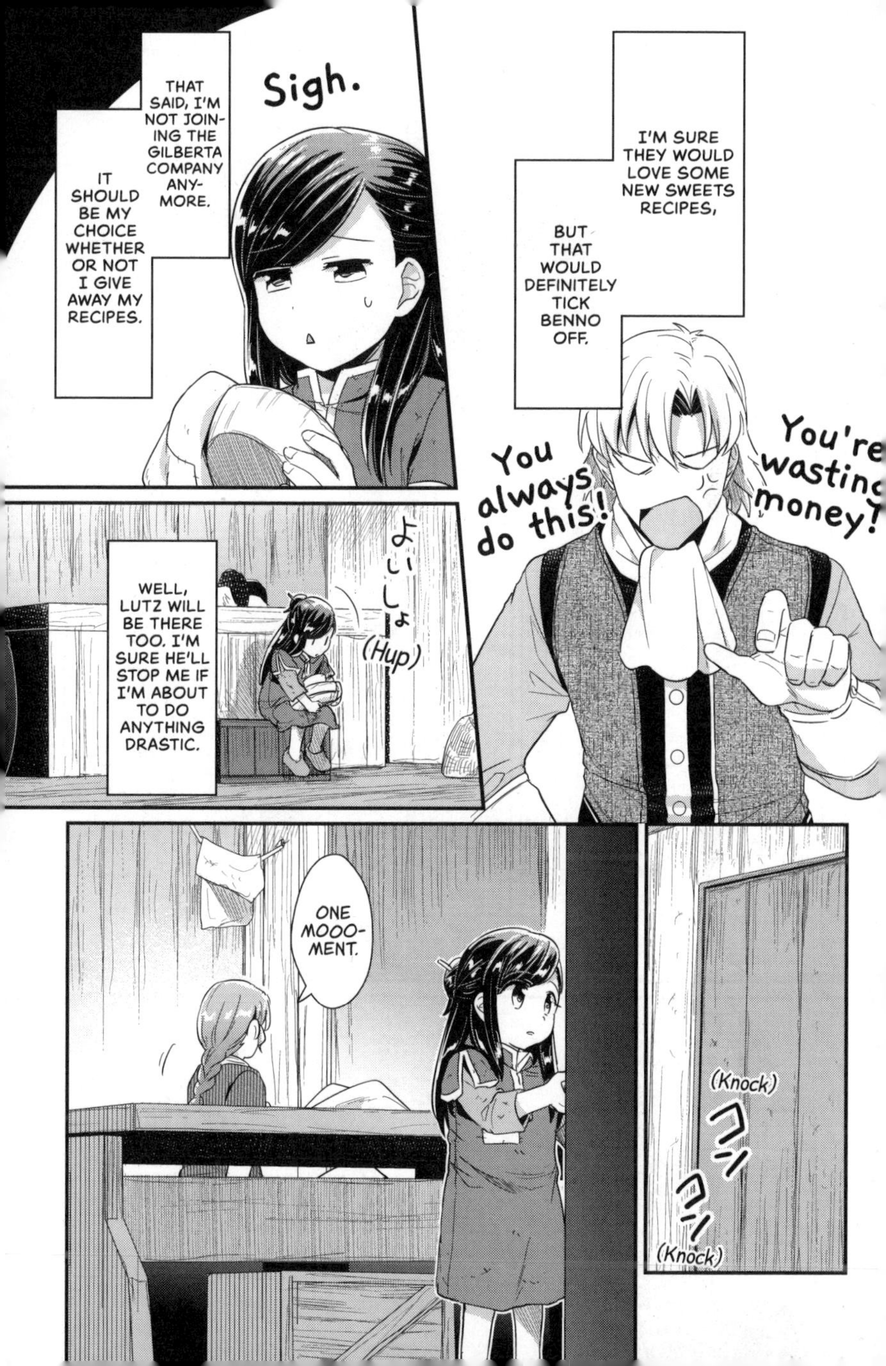
I'M SURE THEY WOULD LOVE SOME NEW SWEETS RECIPES,
BUT THAT WOULD DEFINITELY TICK BENNO OFF.
You're wasting money!
You always do this!
Sigh.
THAT SAID, I'M NOT JOIN-ING THE GILBERTA COMPANY ANY-MORE.
IT SHOULD BE MY CHOICE WHETHER OR NOT I GIVE AWAY MY RECIPES.
よいしょ
(Hup)
WELL, LUTZ WILL BE THERE TOO. I'M SURE HE'LL STOP ME IF I'M ABOUT TO DO ANYTHING DRASTIC.
(Knock)
コン
コン
(Knock)
ONE MOOOO-MENT.

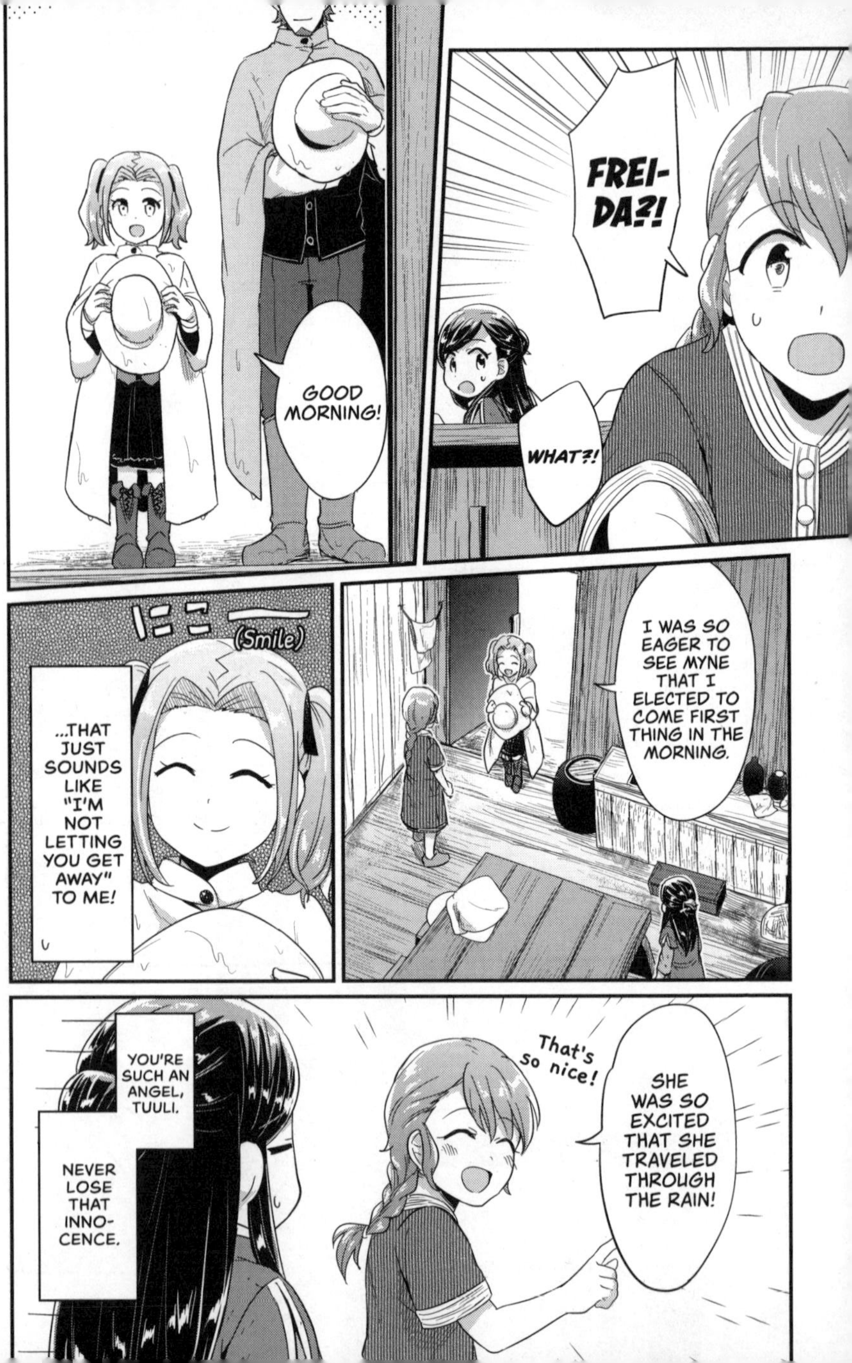
FREI-DA?!
WHAT?!
GOOD MORNING!
I WAS SO EAGER TO SEE MYNE THAT I ELECTED TO COME FIRST THING IN THE MORNING.
にこー
(Smile)
...THAT JUST SOUNDS LIKE "I'M NOT LETTING YOU GET AWAY" TO ME!
That's so nice!
SHE WAS SO EXCITED THAT SHE TRAVELED THROUGH THE RAIN!
YOU'RE SUCH AN ANGEL, TUULI.
NEVER LOSE THAT INNOCENCE.

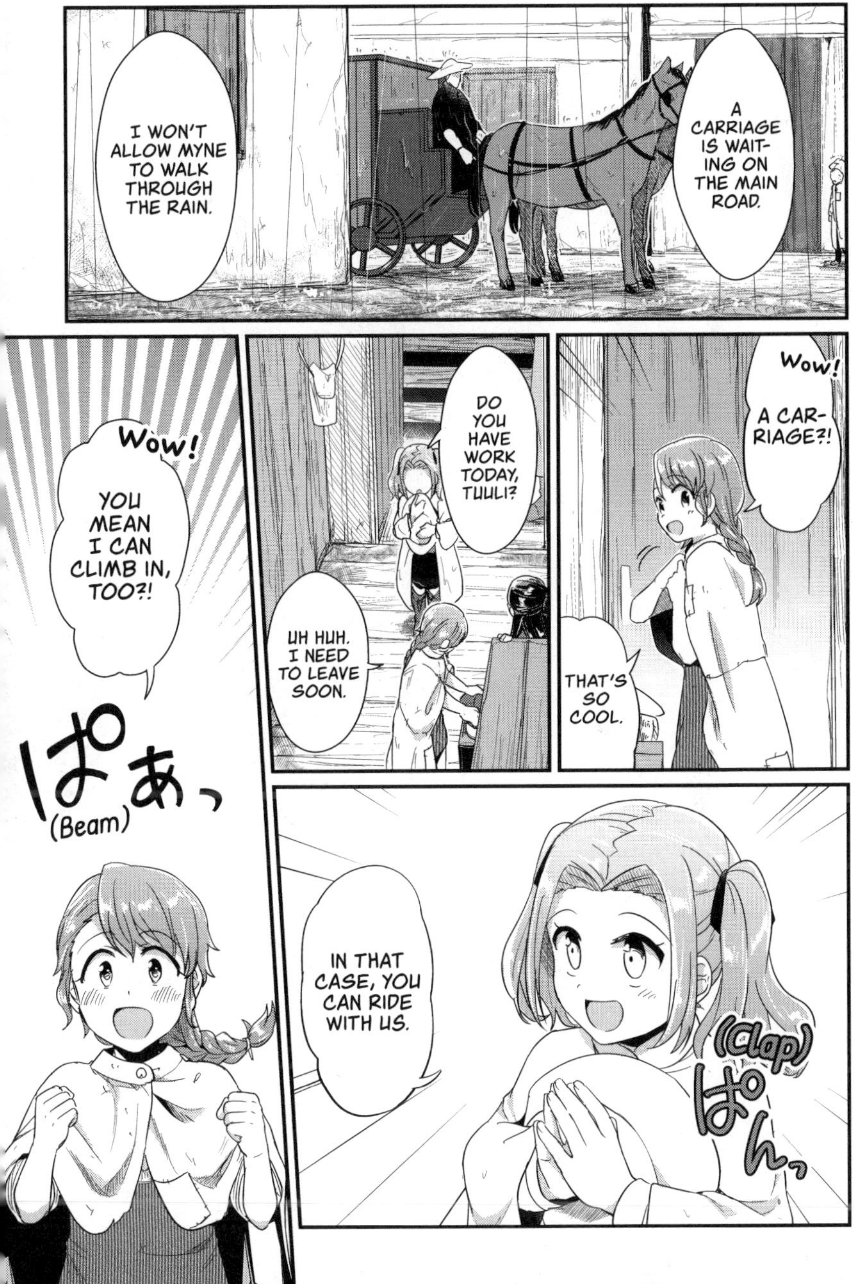
A CARRIAGE IS WAITING ON THE MAIN ROAD.
I WON'T ALLOW MYNE TO WALK THROUGH THE RAIN.
Wow!
A CARRIAGE?!
THAT'S SO COOL.
DO YOU HAVE WORK TODAY, TUULI?
UH HUH. I NEED TO LEAVE SOON.
IN THAT CASE, YOU CAN RIDE WITH US.
ぱんっ
(Clap)
Wow!
YOU MEAN I CAN CLIMB IN, TOO?!
ぱあっ
(Beam)

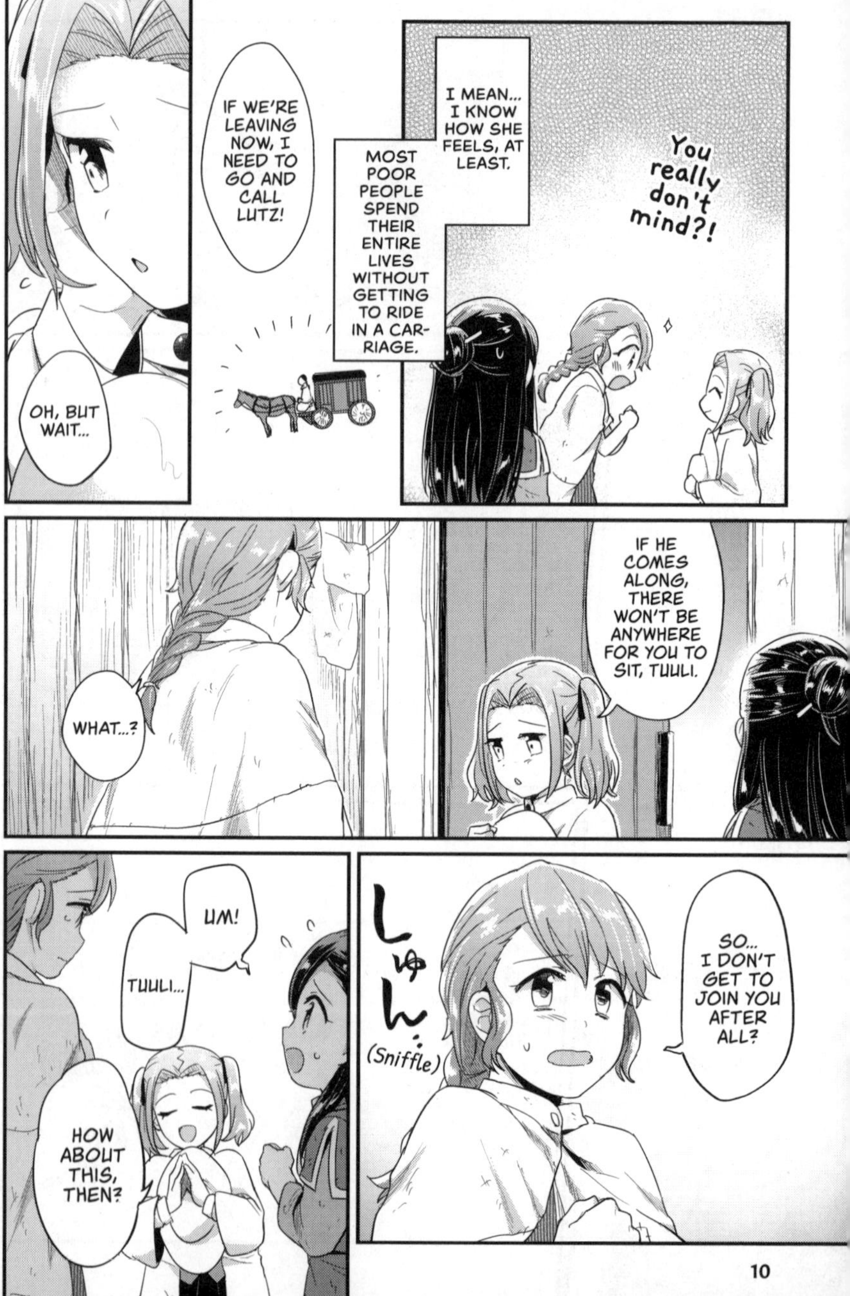
You really don't mind?!
I MEAN... I KNOW HOW SHE FEELS, AT LEAST.
MOST POOR PEOPLE SPEND THEIR ENTIRE LIVES WITHOUT GETTING TO RIDE IN A CAR-RIAGE.
IF WE'RE LEAVING NOW, I NEED TO GO AND CALL LUTZ!
OH, BUT WAIT...
IF HE COMES ALONG, THERE WON'T BE ANYWHERE FOR YOU TO SIT, TUULI.
WHAT...?
しゅん
(Sniffle)
SO... I DON'T GET TO JOIN YOU AFTER ALL?
UM!
TUULI...
HOW ABOUT THIS, THEN?

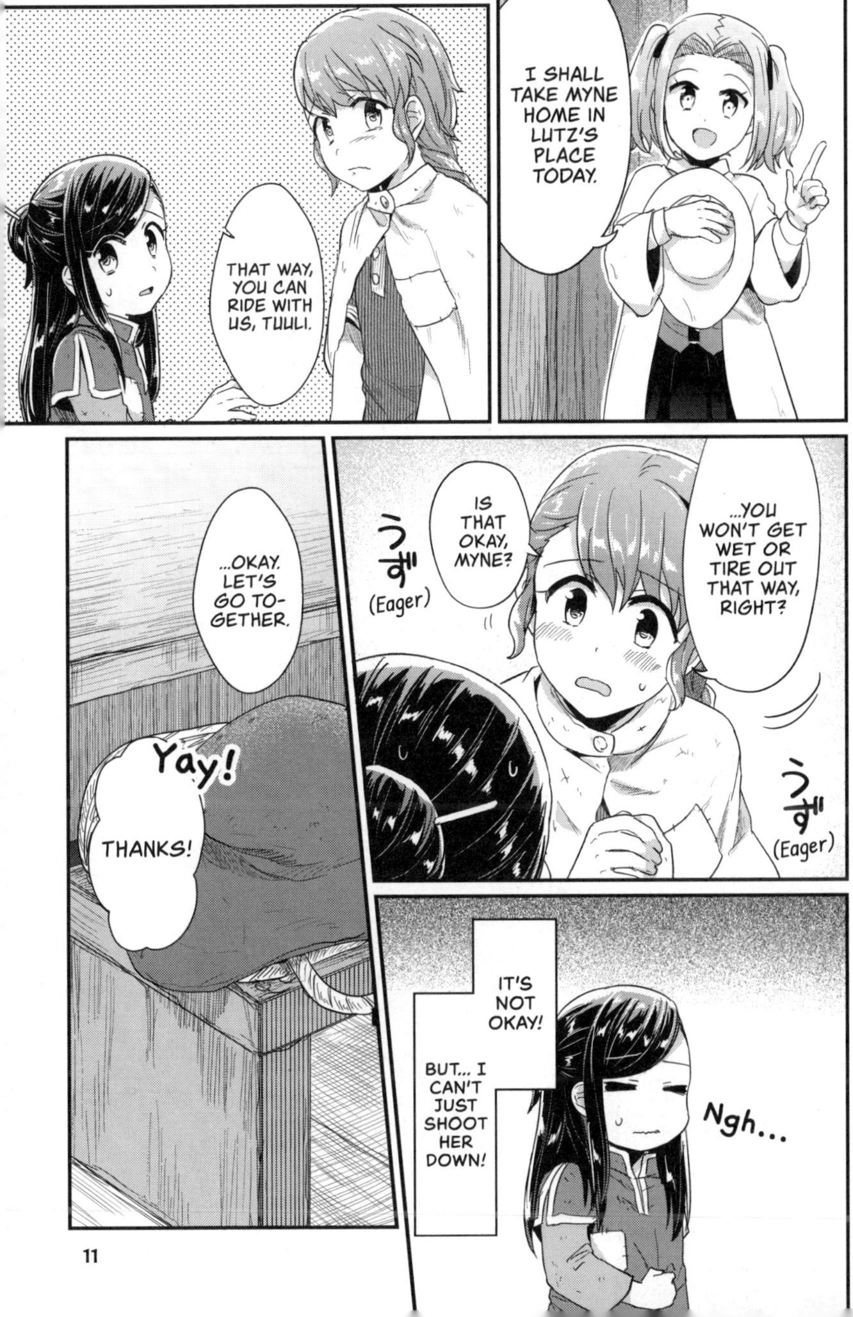
I SHALL TAKE MYNE HOME IN LUTZ'S PLACE TODAY.
THAT WAY, YOU CAN RIDE WITH US, TUULI.
...YOU WON'T GET WET OR TIRE OUT THAT WAY, RIGHT?
うず
(Eager)
IS THAT OKAY, MYNE?
うず
(Eager)
IT'S NOT OKAY!
BUT... I CAN'T JUST SHOOT HER DOWN!
Ngh...
...OKAY. LET'S GO TO-GETHER.
Yay!
THANKS!

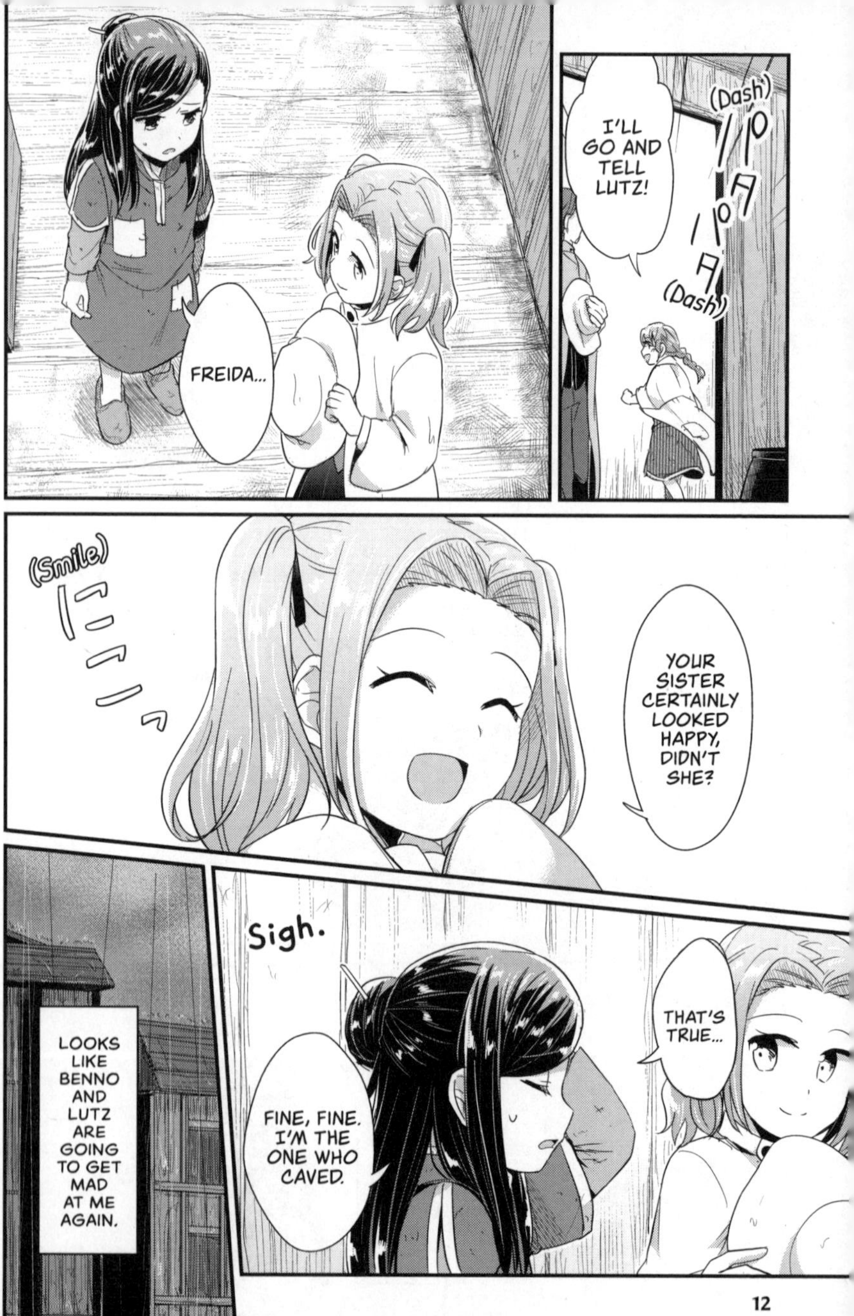
I'LL GO AND TELL LUTZ!
(Dash)
(Dash)
FREIDA...
(Smile)
YOUR SISTER CERTAINLY LOOKED HAPPY, DIDN'T SHE?
THAT'S TRUE...
Sigh.
FINE, FINE. I'M THE ONE WHO CAVED.
LOOKS LIKE BENNO AND LUTZ ARE GOING TO GET MAD AT ME AGAIN.

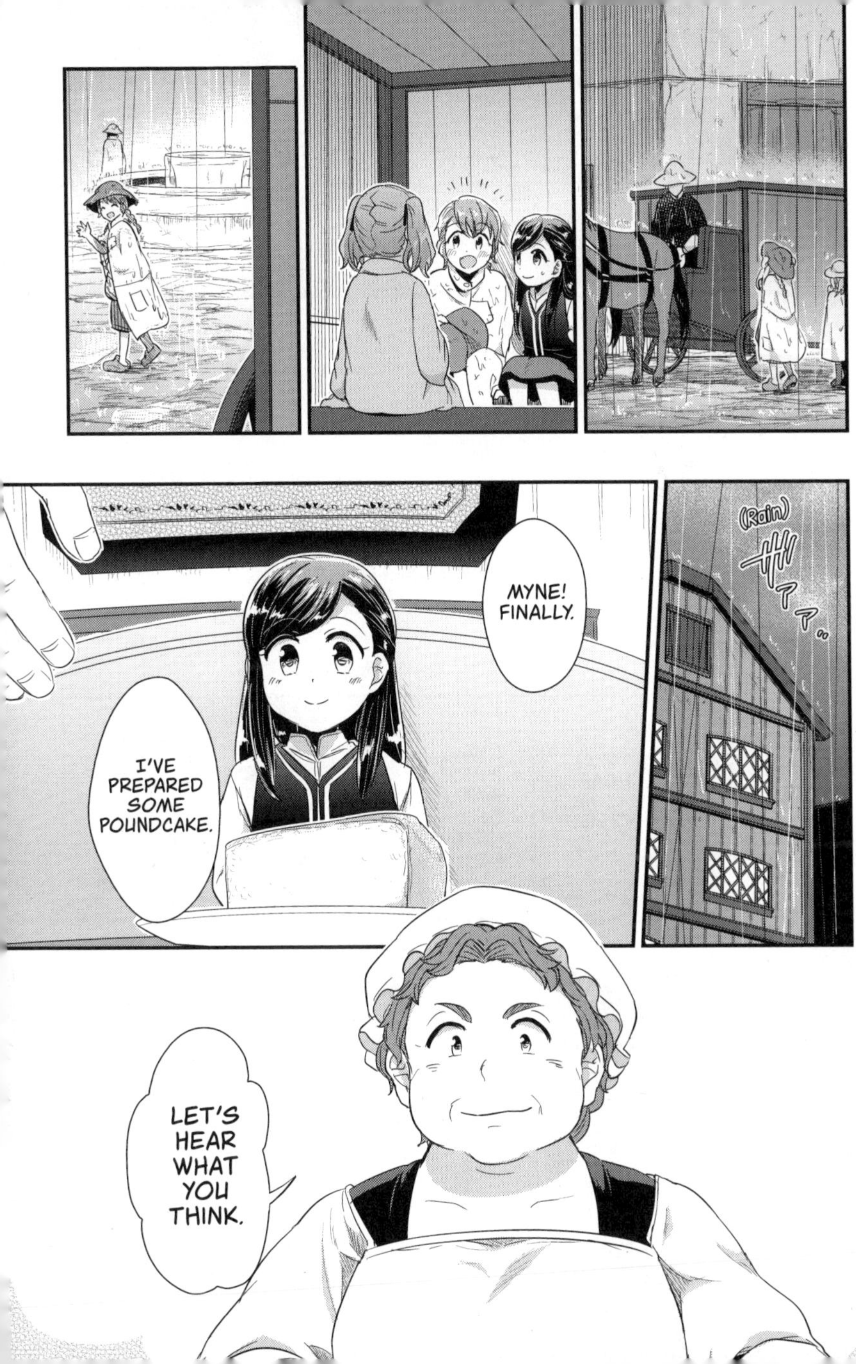
(Rain)
ザアア..
MYNE! FINALLY.
I'VE PREPARED SOME POUNDCAKE.
LET'S HEAR WHAT YOU THINK.

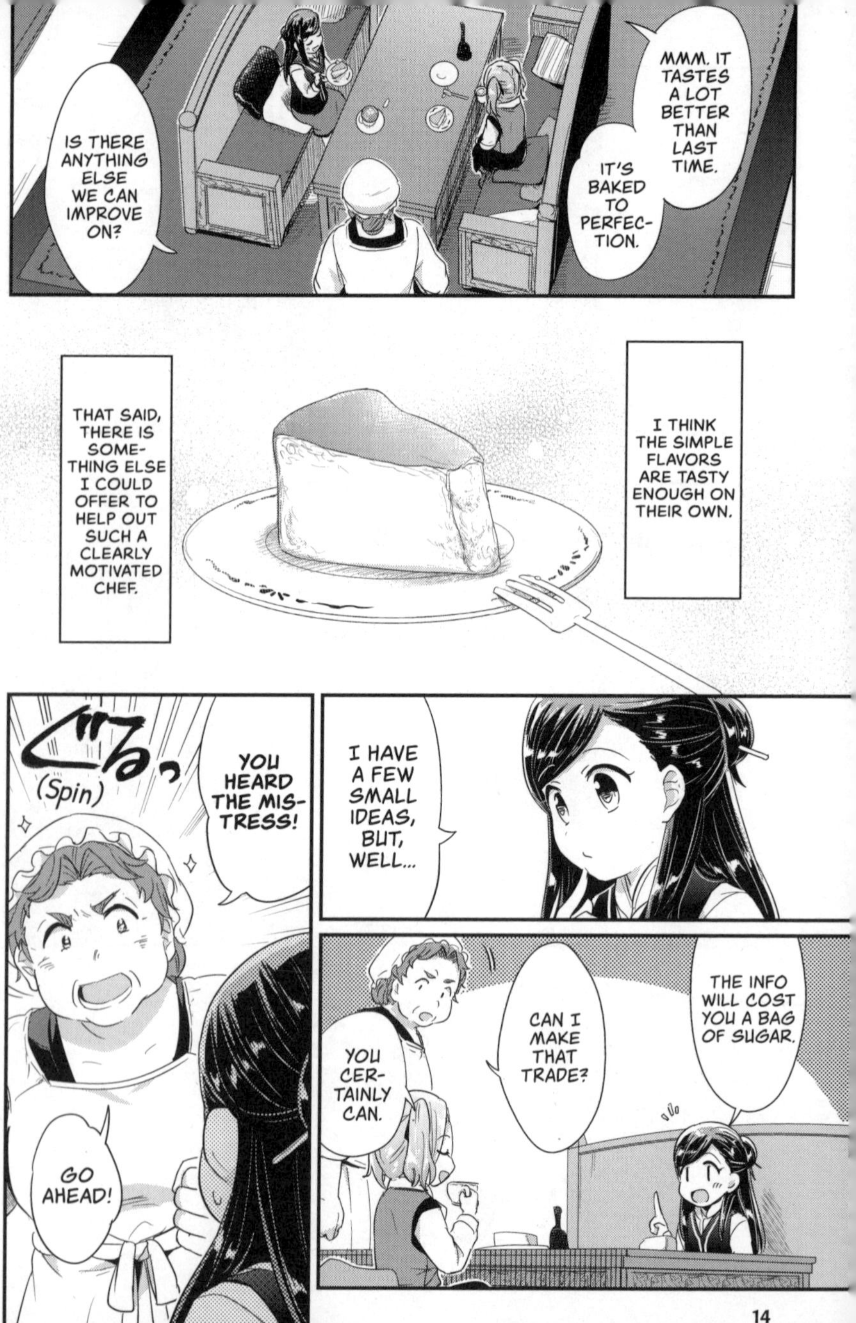
MMM. IT TASTES A LOT BETTER THAN LAST TIME.
IT'S BAKED TO PERFEC-TION.
IS THERE ANYTHING ELSE WE CAN IMPROVE ON?
I THINK THE SIMPLE FLAVORS ARE TASTY ENOUGH ON THEIR OWN.
THAT SAID, THERE IS SOME-THING ELSE I COULD OFFER TO HELP OUT SUCH A CLEARLY MOTIVATED CHEF.
I HAVE A FEW SMALL IDEAS, BUT, WELL...
THE INFO WILL COST YOU A BAG OF SUGAR.
CAN I MAKE THAT TRADE?
YOU CER-TAINLY CAN.
(Spin)
YOU HEARD THE MIS-TRESS!
GO AHEAD!

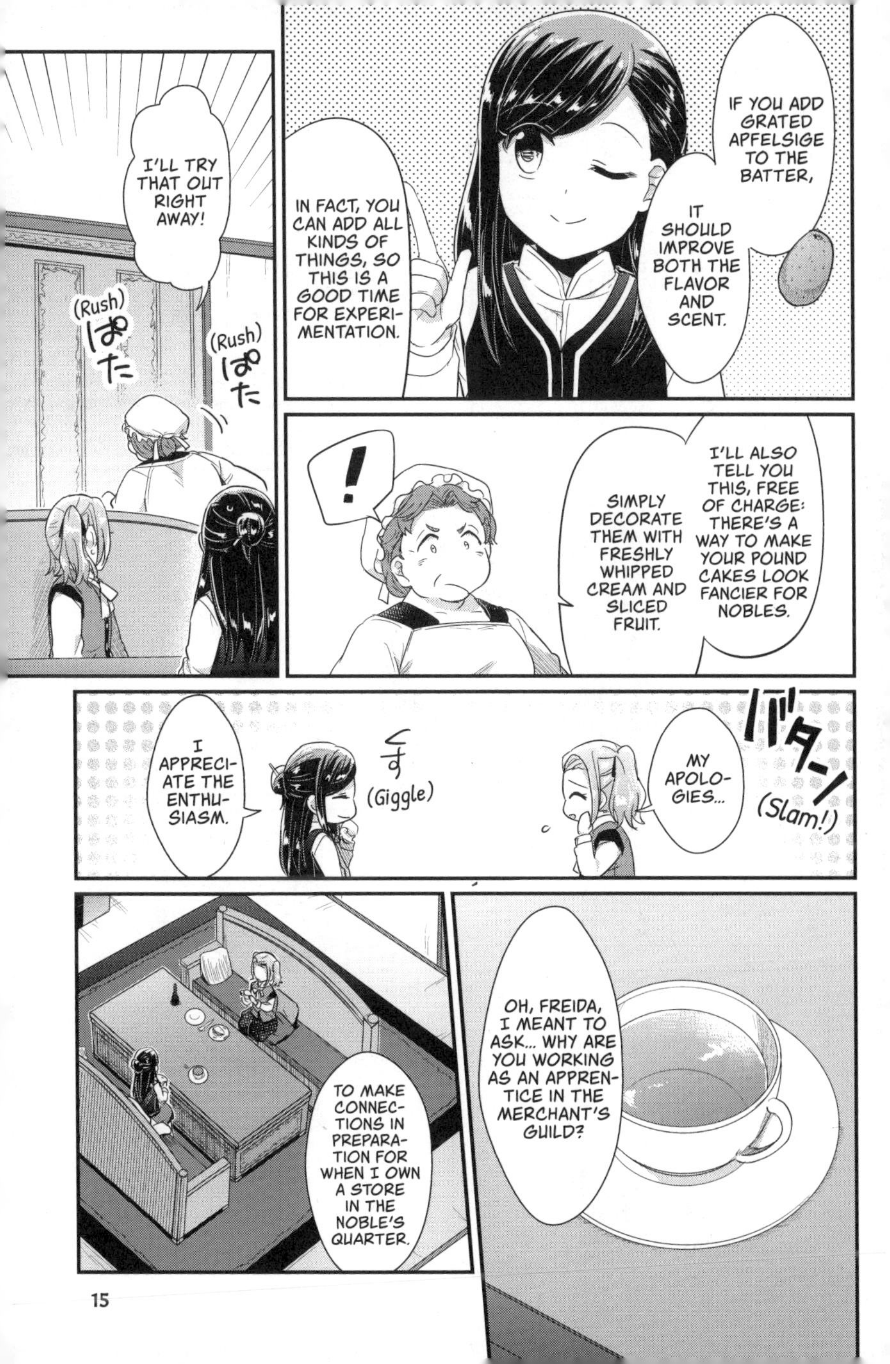
IF YOU ADD GRATED APFELSIGE TO THE BATTER,
IT SHOULD IMPROVE BOTH THE FLAVOR AND SCENT.
IN FACT, YOU CAN ADD ALL KINDS OF THINGS, SO THIS IS A GOOD TIME FOR EXPERIMENTATION.
I'LL ALSO TELL YOU THIS, FREE OF CHARGE: THERE'S A WAY TO MAKE YOUR POUND CAKES LOOK FANCIER FOR NOBLES.
SIMPLY DECORATE THEM WITH FRESHLY WHIPPED CREAM AND SLICED FRUIT.
!
I'LL TRY THAT OUT RIGHT AWAY!
(Rush) ぱた
(Rush) ぱた
バタン (Slam!)
MY APOLOGIES...
くす (Giggle)
I APPRECIATE THE ENTHUSIASM.
OH, FREIDA, I MEANT TO ASK... WHY ARE YOU WORKING AS AN APPRENTICE IN THE MERCHANT'S GUILD?
TO MAKE CONNECTIONS IN PREPARATION FOR WHEN I OWN A STORE IN THE NOBLE'S QUARTER.

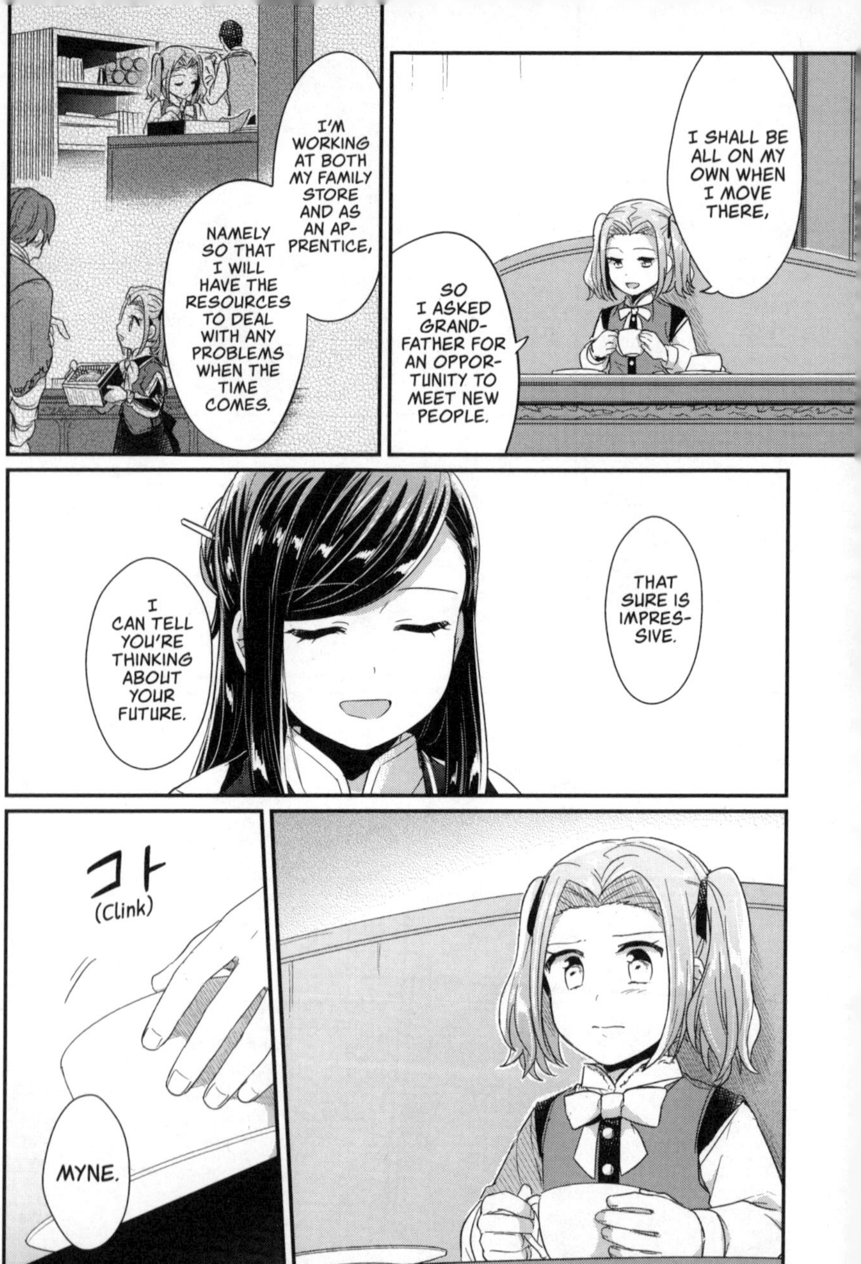
I SHALL BE ALL ON MY OWN WHEN I MOVE THERE,
SO I ASKED GRAND-FATHER FOR AN OPPOR-TUNITY TO MEET NEW PEOPLE.
I'M WORKING AT BOTH MY FAMILY STORE AND AS AN AP-PRENTICE,
NAMELY SO THAT I WILL HAVE THE RESOURCES TO DEAL WITH ANY PROBLEMS WHEN THE TIME COMES.
THAT SURE IS IMPRES-SIVE.
I CAN TELL YOU'RE THINKING ABOUT YOUR FUTURE.
コト
(Clink)
MYNE.

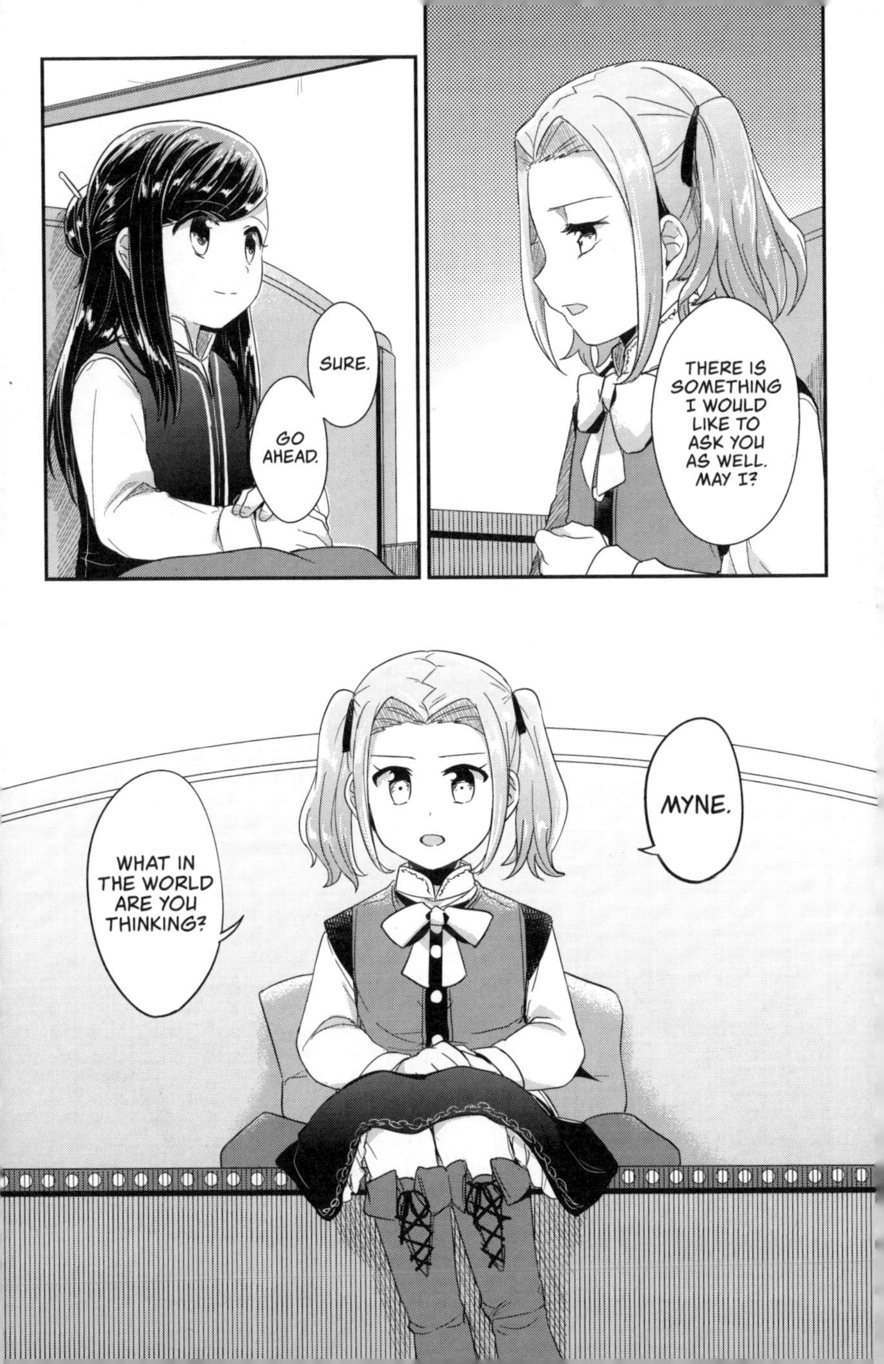
THERE IS SOMETHING I WOULD LIKE TO ASK YOU AS WELL. MAY I?
SURE.
GO AHEAD.
MYNE.
WHAT IN THE WORLD ARE YOU THINKING?

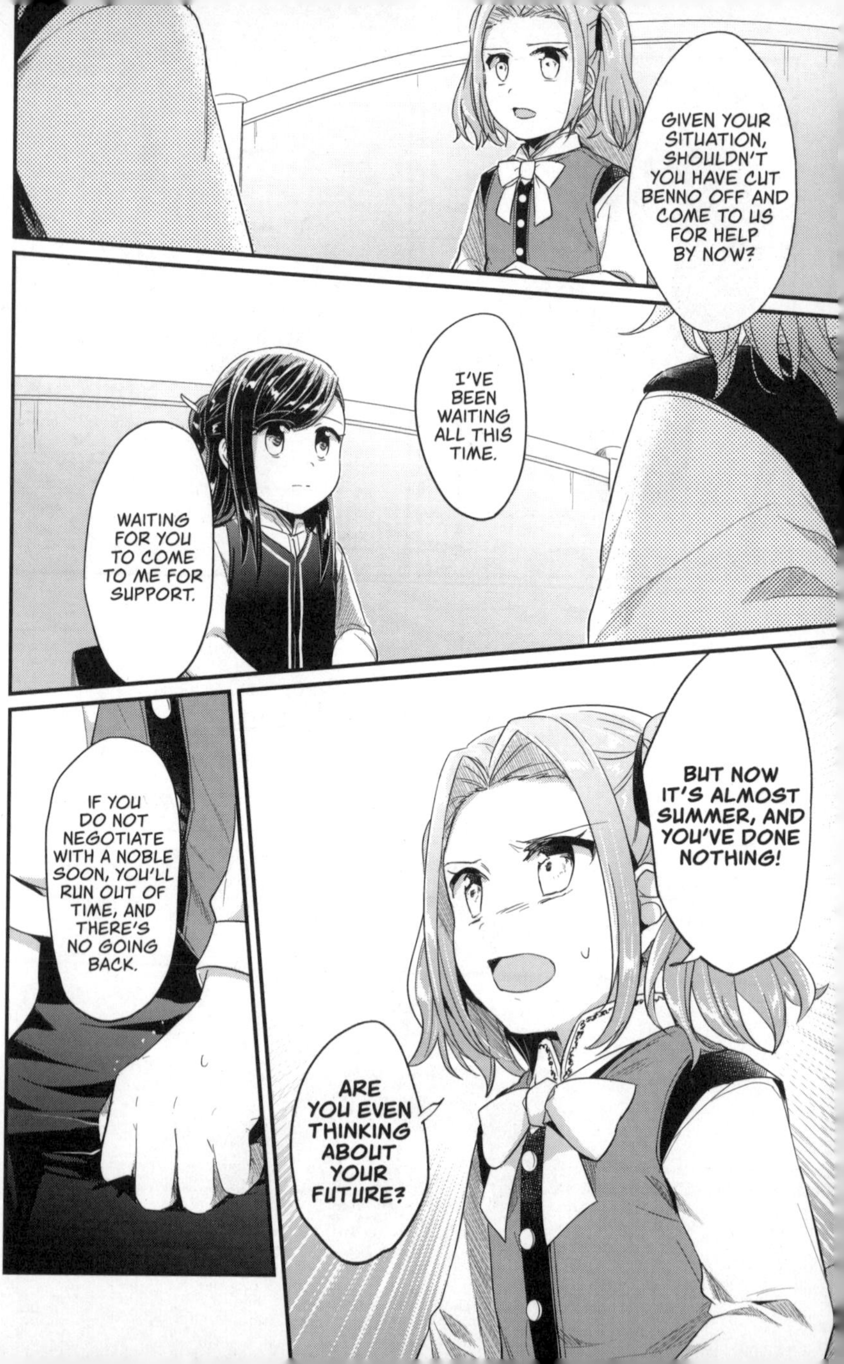
GIVEN YOUR SITUATION, SHOULDN'T YOU HAVE CUT BENNO OFF AND COME TO US FOR HELP BY NOW?
I'VE BEEN WAITING ALL THIS TIME.
WAITING FOR YOU TO COME TO ME FOR SUPPORT.
BUT NOW IT'S ALMOST SUMMER, AND YOU'VE DONE NOTHING!
ARE YOU EVEN THINKING ABOUT YOUR FUTURE?
IF YOU DO NOT NEGOTIATE WITH A NOBLE SOON, YOU'LL RUN OUT OF TIME, AND THERE'S NO GOING BACK.

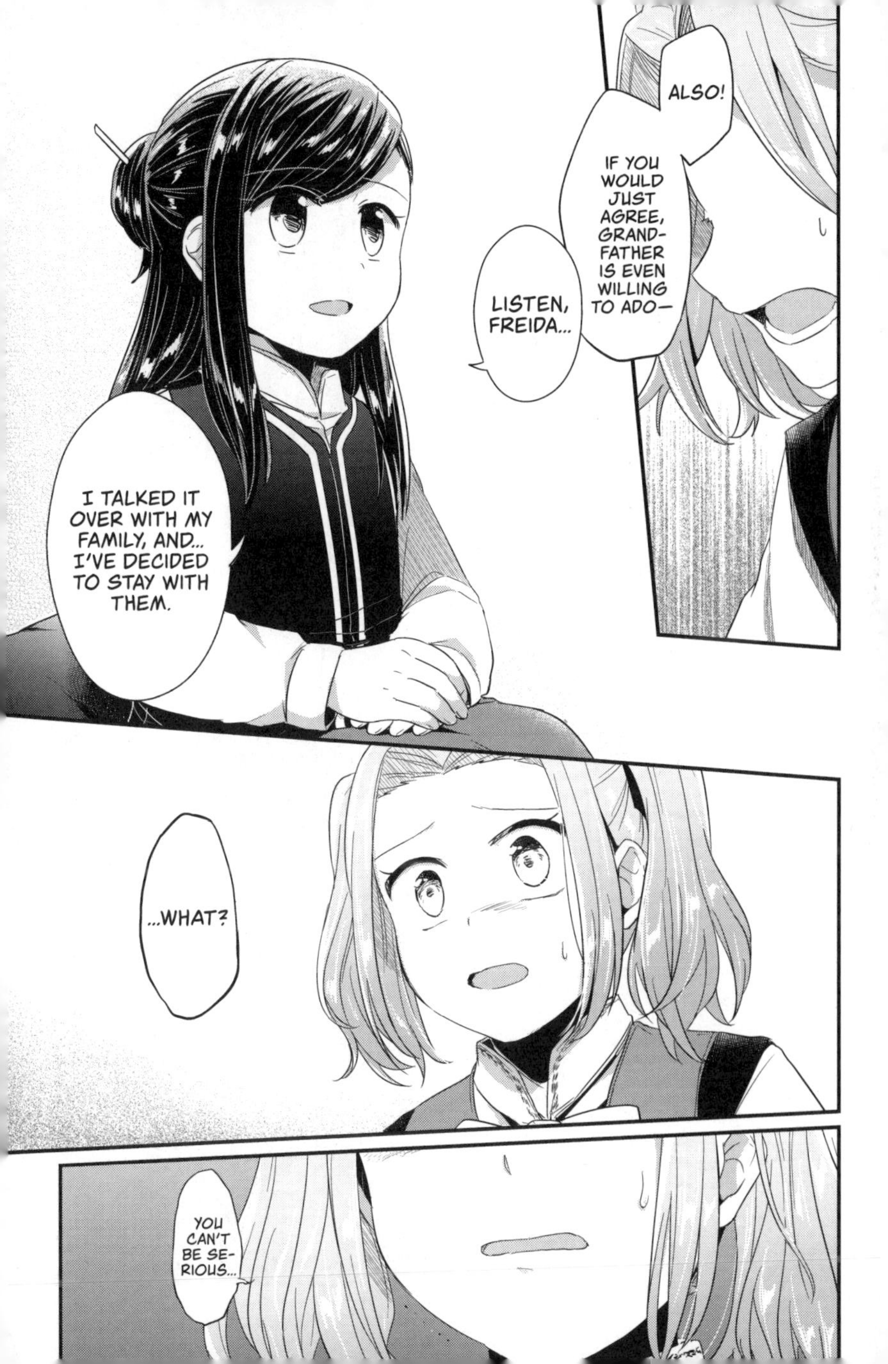
ALSO!
IF YOU WOULD JUST AGREE, GRAND-FATHER IS EVEN WILLING TO ADO—
LISTEN, FREIDA...
I TALKED IT OVER WITH MY FAMILY, AND... I'VE DECIDED TO STAY WITH THEM.
...WHAT?
YOU CAN'T BE SE-RIOUS...

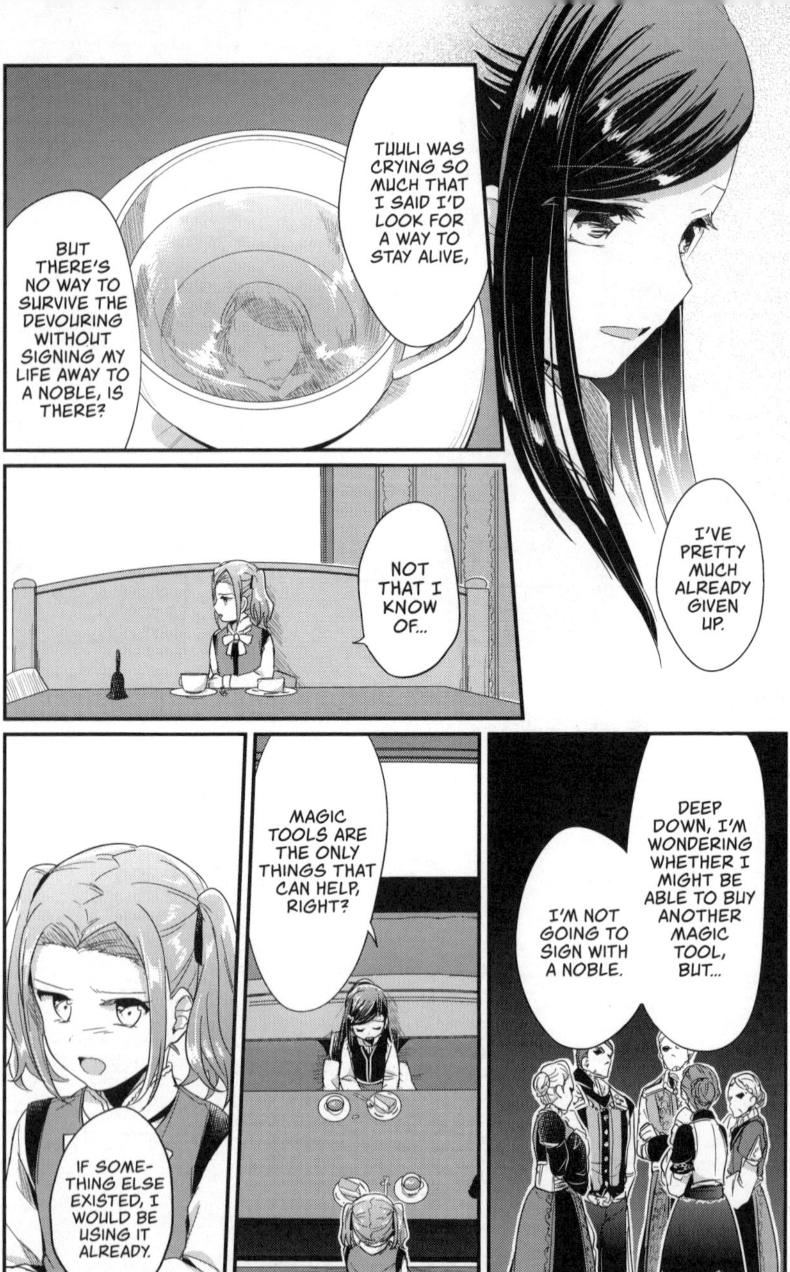

TUULI WAS CRYING SO MUCH THAT I SAID I'D LOOK FOR A WAY TO STAY ALIVE,
BUT THERE'S NO WAY TO SURVIVE THE DEVOURING WITHOUT SIGNING MY LIFE AWAY TO A NOBLE, IS THERE?
I'VE PRETTY MUCH ALREADY GIVEN UP.
NOT THAT I KNOW OF...
DEEP DOWN, I'M WONDERING WHETHER I MIGHT BE ABLE TO BUY ANOTHER MAGIC TOOL, BUT...
I'M NOT GOING TO SIGN WITH A NOBLE.
MAGIC TOOLS ARE THE ONLY THINGS THAT CAN HELP, RIGHT?
IF SOME-THING ELSE EXISTED, I WOULD BE USING IT ALREADY.

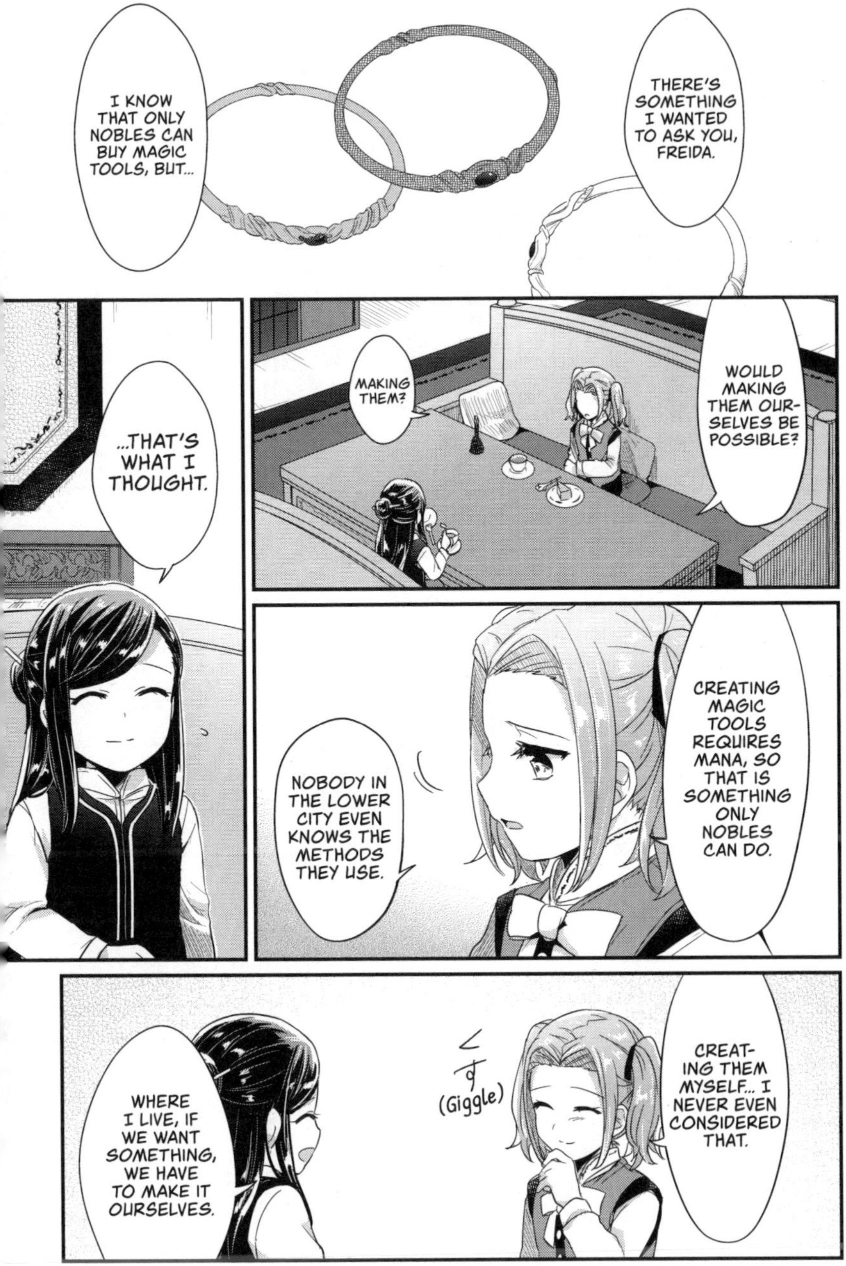
THERE'S SOMETHING I WANTED TO ASK YOU, FREIDA.
I KNOW THAT ONLY NOBLES CAN BUY MAGIC TOOLS, BUT...
WOULD MAKING THEM OURSELVES BE POSSIBLE?
MAKING THEM?
CREATING MAGIC TOOLS REQUIRES MANA, SO THAT IS SOMETHING ONLY NOBLES CAN DO.
NOBODY IN THE LOWER CITY EVEN KNOWS THE METHODS THEY USE.
...THAT'S WHAT I THOUGHT.
CREATING THEM MYSELF... I NEVER EVEN CONSIDERED THAT.
くす
(Giggle)
WHERE I LIVE, IF WE WANT SOMETHING, WE HAVE TO MAKE IT OURSELVES.

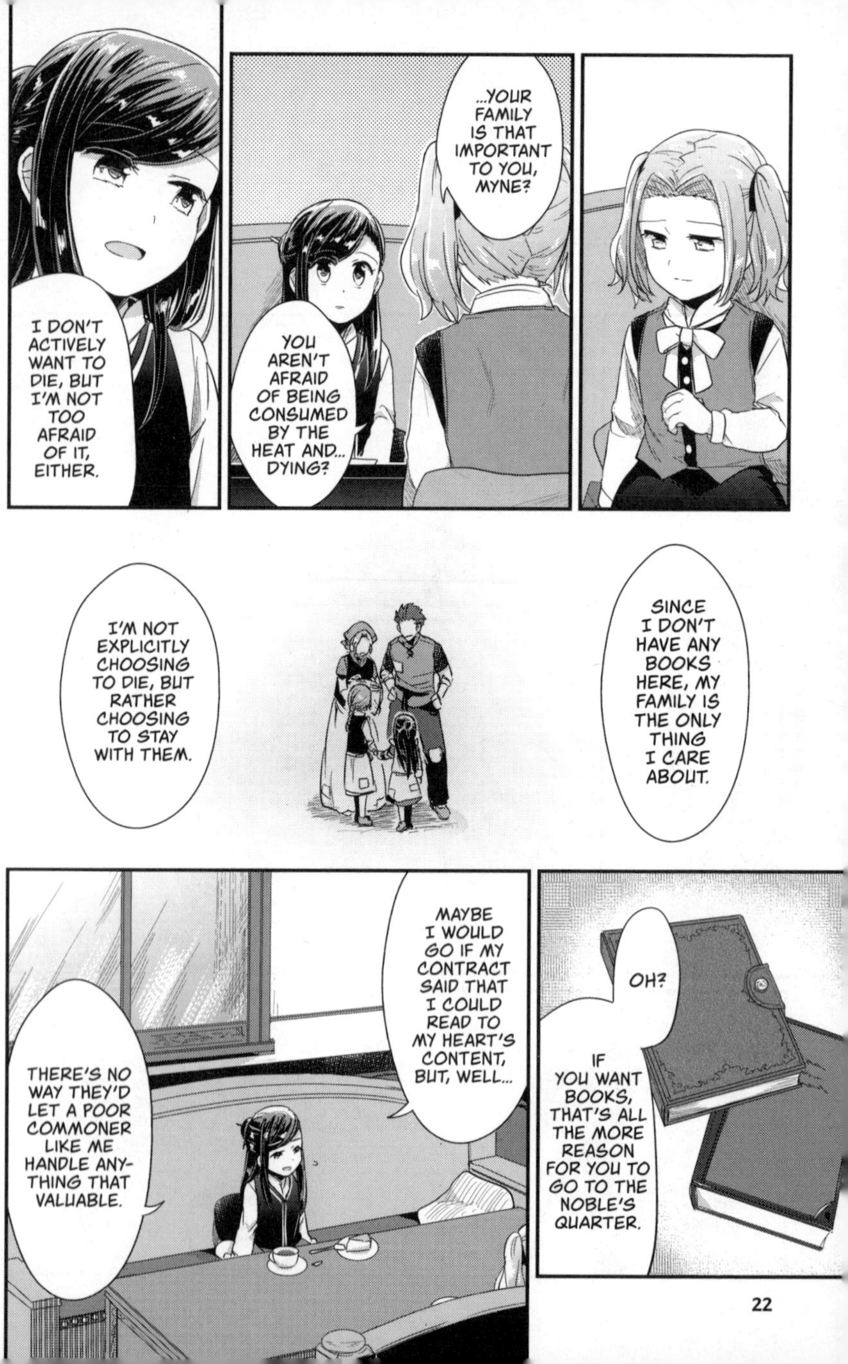
...YOUR FAMILY IS THAT IMPORTANT TO YOU, MYNE?
YOU AREN'T AFRAID OF BEING CONSUMED BY THE HEAT AND... DYING?
I DON'T ACTIVELY WANT TO DIE, BUT I'M NOT TOO AFRAID OF IT, EITHER.
SINCE I DON'T HAVE ANY BOOKS HERE, MY FAMILY IS THE ONLY THING I CARE ABOUT.
I'M NOT EXPLICITLY CHOOSING TO DIE, BUT RATHER CHOOSING TO STAY WITH THEM.
OH?
IF YOU WANT BOOKS, THAT'S ALL THE MORE REASON FOR YOU TO GO TO THE NOBLE'S QUARTER.
MAYBE I WOULD GO IF MY CONTRACT SAID THAT I COULD READ TO MY HEART'S CONTENT, BUT, WELL...
THERE'S NO WAY THEY'D LET A POOR COMMONER LIKE ME HANDLE ANY-THING THAT VALUABLE.

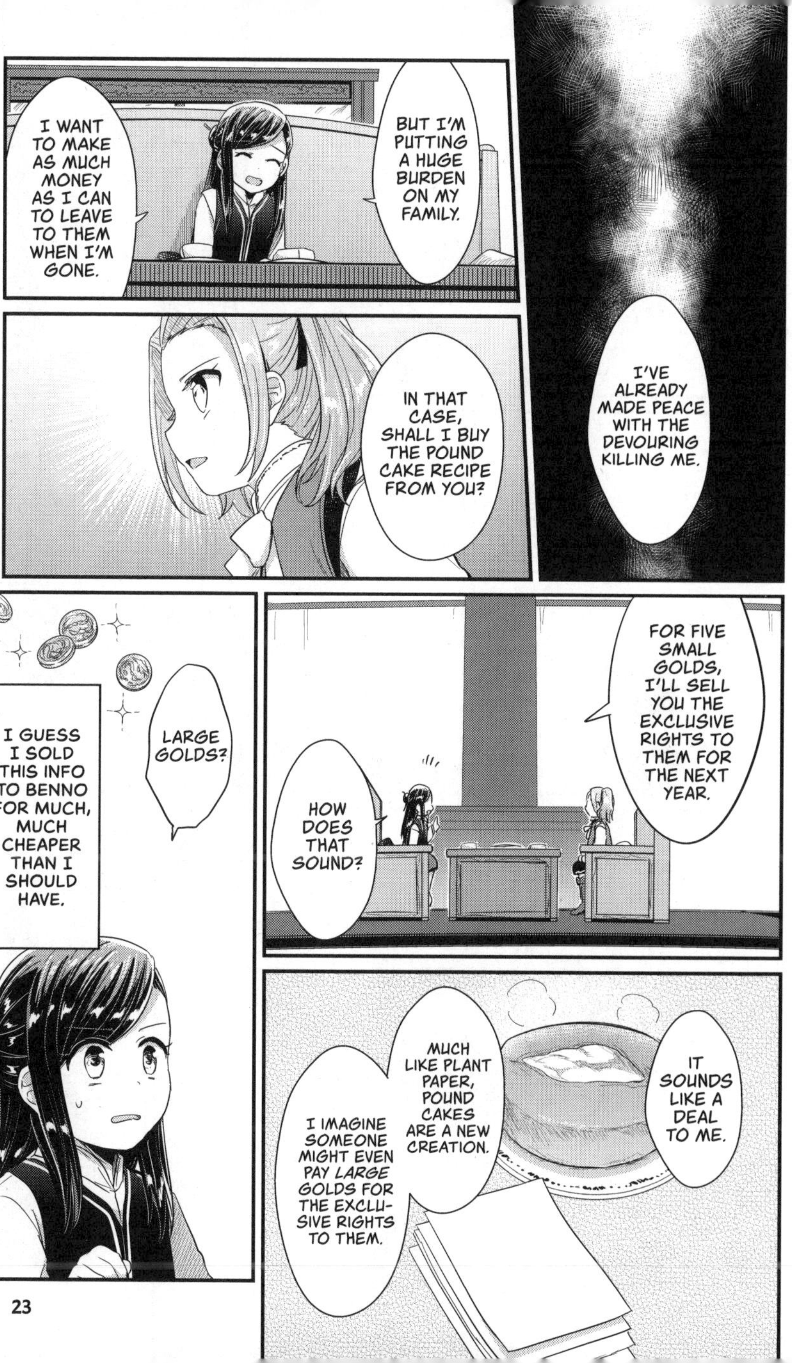
I'VE ALREADY MADE PEACE WITH THE DEVOURING KILLING ME.
BUT I'M PUTTING A HUGE BURDEN ON MY FAMILY.
I WANT TO MAKE AS MUCH MONEY AS I CAN TO LEAVE TO THEM WHEN I'M GONE.
IN THAT CASE, SHALL I BUY THE POUND CAKE RECIPE FROM YOU?
FOR FIVE SMALL GOLDS, I'LL SELL YOU THE EXCLUSIVE RIGHTS TO THEM FOR THE NEXT YEAR.
HOW DOES THAT SOUND?
IT SOUNDS LIKE A DEAL TO ME.
MUCH LIKE PLANT PAPER, POUND CAKES ARE A NEW CREATION.
I IMAGINE SOMEONE MIGHT EVEN PAY *LARGE* GOLDS FOR THE EXCLUSIVE RIGHTS TO THEM.
LARGE GOLDS?
I GUESS I SOLD THIS INFO TO BENNO FOR MUCH, MUCH CHEAPER THAN I SHOULD HAVE.

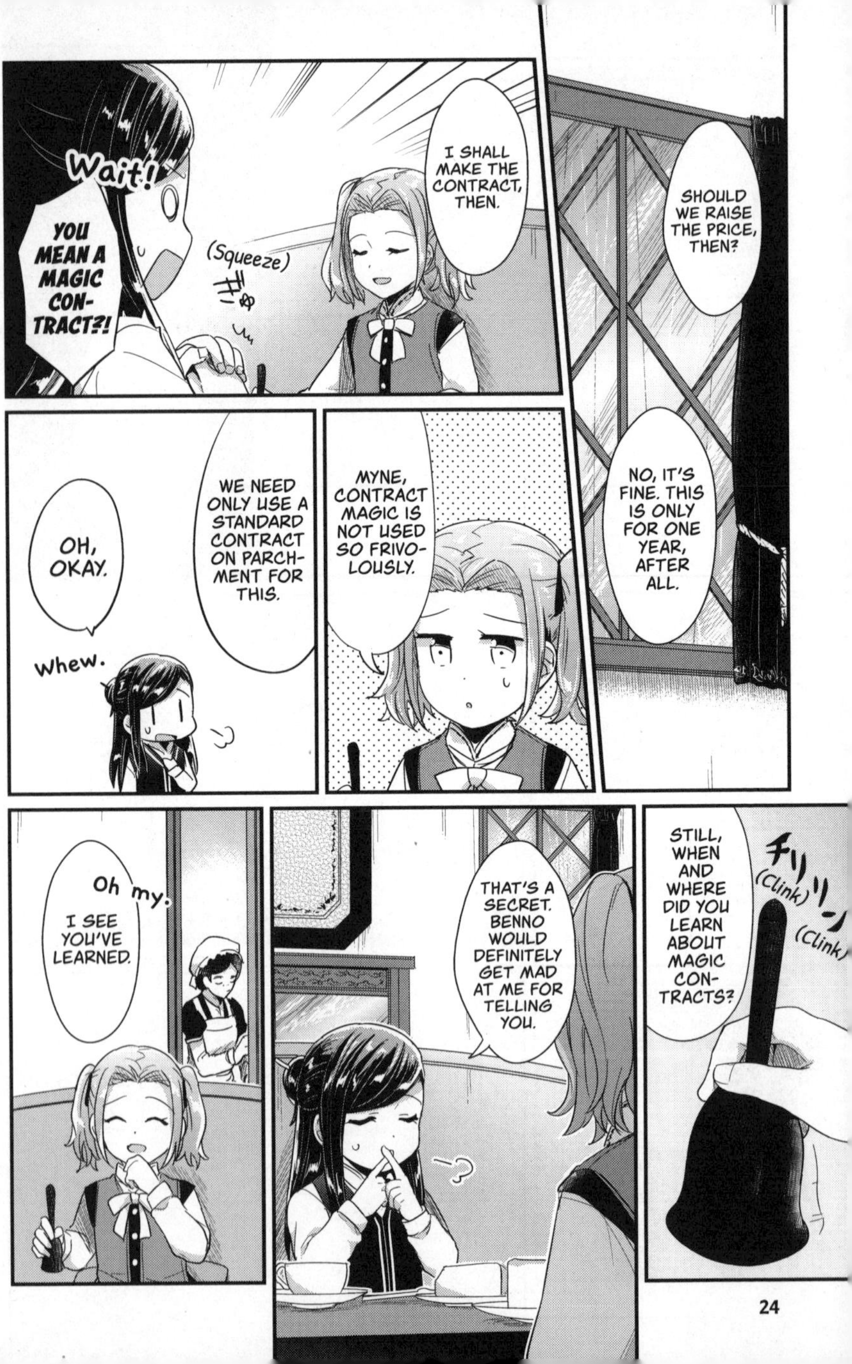
SHOULD WE RAISE THE PRICE, THEN?
NO, IT'S FINE. THIS IS ONLY FOR ONE YEAR, AFTER ALL.
I SHALL MAKE THE CONTRACT, THEN.
(Squeeze)
Wait!
YOU MEAN A MAGIC CONTRACT?!
MYNE, CONTRACT MAGIC IS NOT USED SO FRIVOLOUSLY.
WE NEED ONLY USE A STANDARD CONTRACT ON PARCHMENT FOR THIS.
OH, OKAY.
Whew.
STILL, WHEN AND WHERE DID YOU LEARN ABOUT MAGIC CONTRACTS?
チリ
(Clink)
リン
(Clink)
THAT'S A SECRET. BENNO WOULD DEFINITELY GET MAD AT ME FOR TELLING YOU.
—?
Oh my.
I SEE YOU'VE LEARNED.

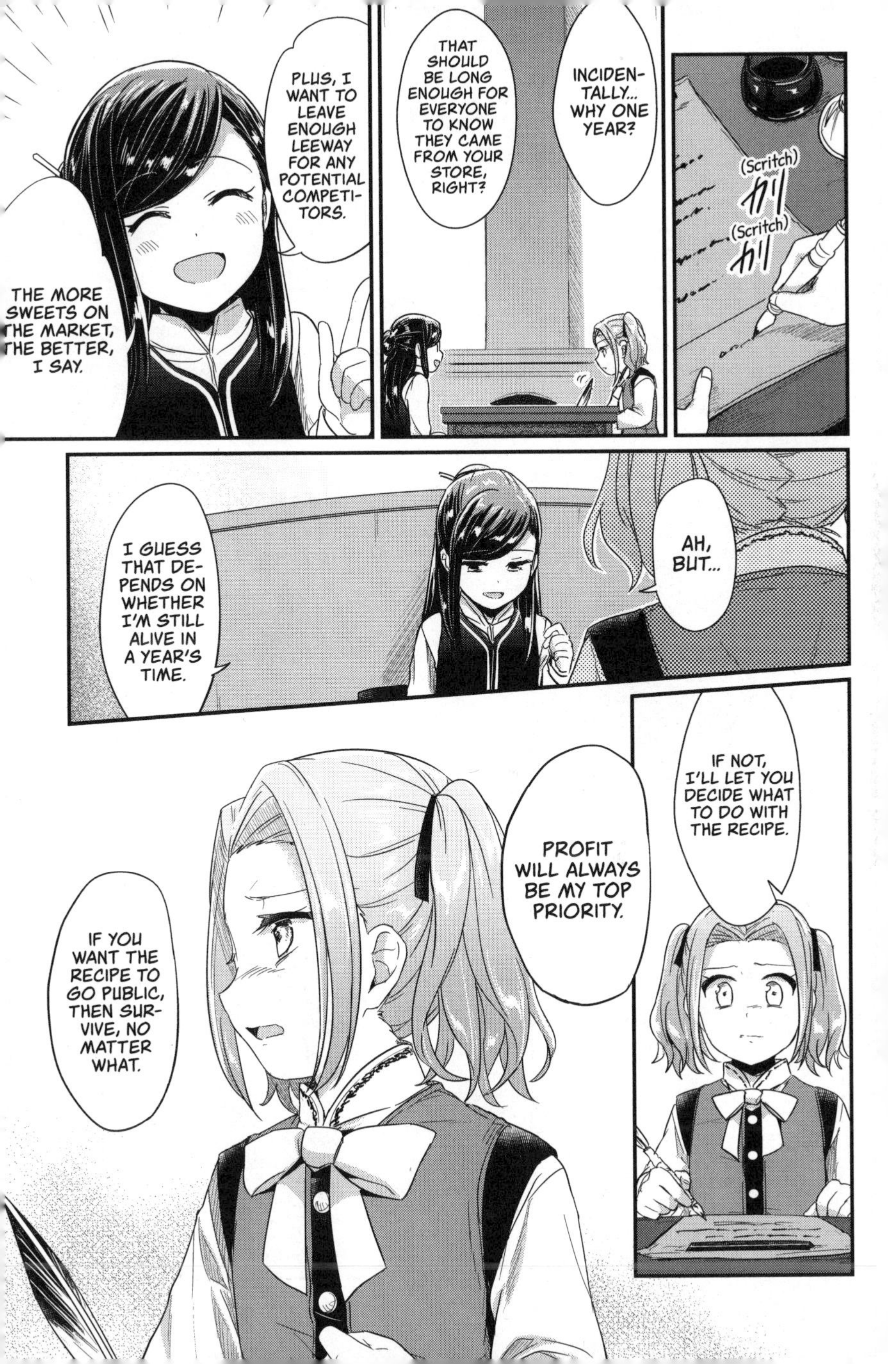
(Scritch) カリ
(Scritch) カリ
INCIDENTALLY... WHY ONE YEAR?
THAT SHOULD BE LONG ENOUGH FOR EVERYONE TO KNOW THEY CAME FROM YOUR STORE, RIGHT?
PLUS, I WANT TO LEAVE ENOUGH LEEWAY FOR ANY POTENTIAL COMPETITORS.
THE MORE SWEETS ON THE MARKET, THE BETTER, I SAY.
AH, BUT...
I GUESS THAT DEPENDS ON WHETHER I'M STILL ALIVE IN A YEAR'S TIME.
IF NOT, I'LL LET YOU DECIDE WHAT TO DO WITH THE RECIPE.
PROFIT WILL ALWAYS BE MY TOP PRIORITY.
IF YOU WANT THE RECIPE TO GO PUBLIC, THEN SURVIVE, NO MATTER WHAT.

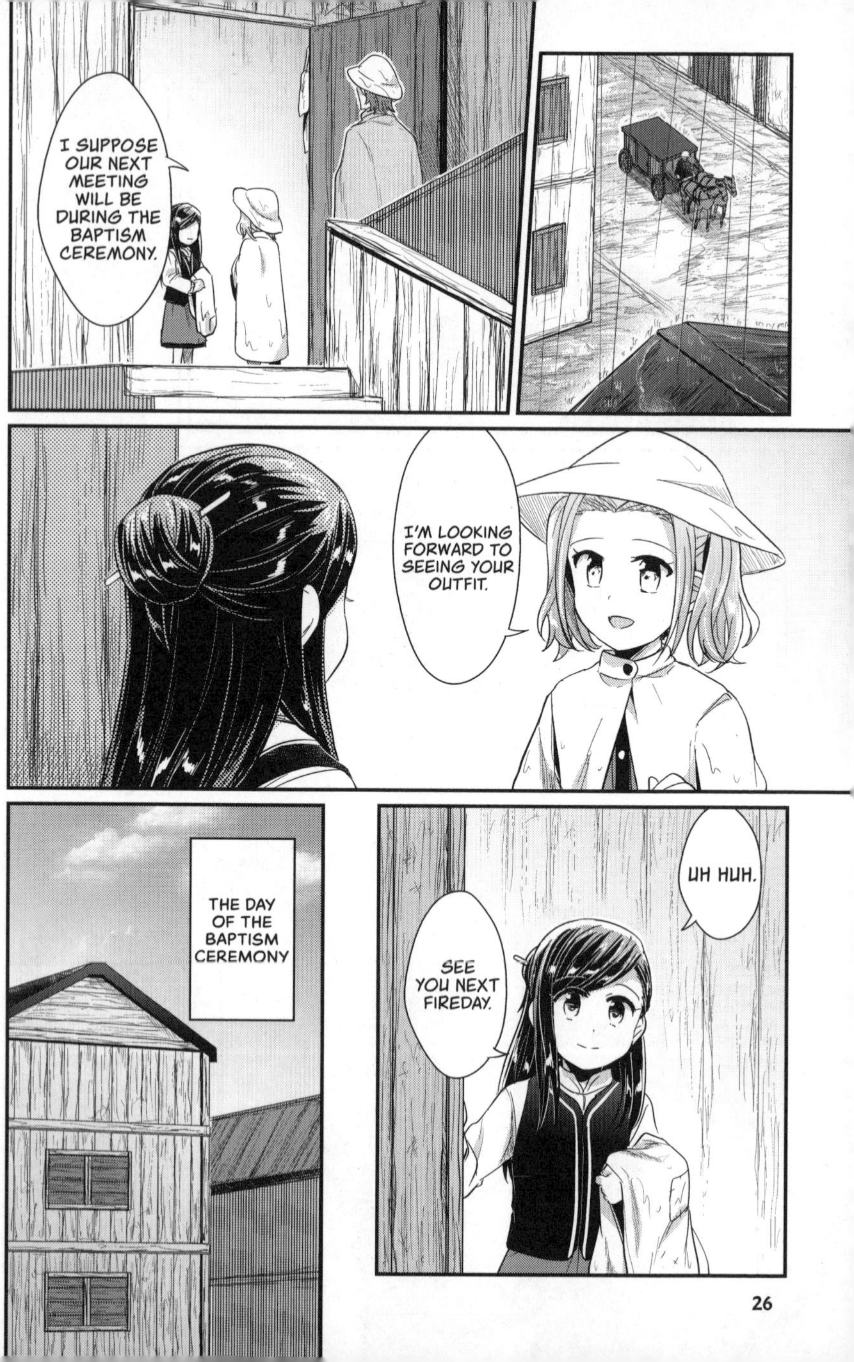
I SUPPOSE OUR NEXT MEETING WILL BE DURING THE BAPTISM CEREMONY.
I'M LOOKING FORWARD TO SEEING YOUR OUTFIT.
UH HUH.
SEE YOU NEXT FIREDAY.
THE DAY OF THE BAPTISM CEREMONY

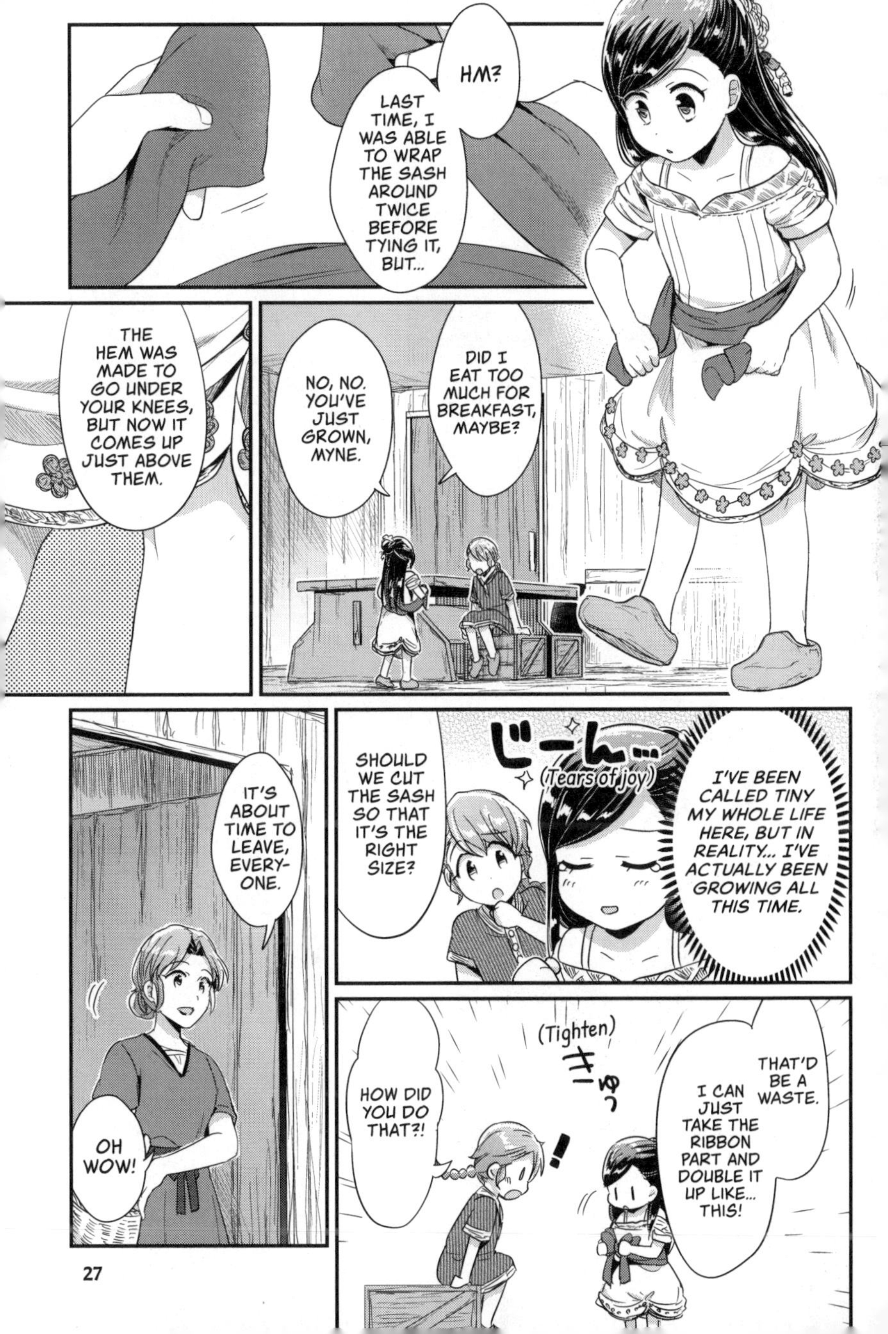
HM?
LAST TIME, I WAS ABLE TO WRAP THE SASH AROUND TWICE BEFORE TYING IT, BUT...
DID I EAT TOO MUCH FOR BREAKFAST, MAYBE?
NO, NO. YOU'VE JUST GROWN, MYNE.
THE HEM WAS MADE TO GO UNDER YOUR KNEES, BUT NOW IT COMES UP JUST ABOVE THEM.
I'VE BEEN CALLED TINY MY WHOLE LIFE HERE, BUT IN REALITY... I'VE ACTUALLY BEEN GROWING ALL THIS TIME.
じーん…
(Tears of joy)
SHOULD WE CUT THE SASH SO THAT IT'S THE RIGHT SIZE?
THAT'D BE A WASTE.
I CAN JUST TAKE THE RIBBON PART AND DOUBLE IT UP LIKE... THIS!
キュッ
(Tighten)
HOW DID YOU DO THAT?!
IT'S ABOUT TIME TO LEAVE, EVERY-ONE.
OH WOW!

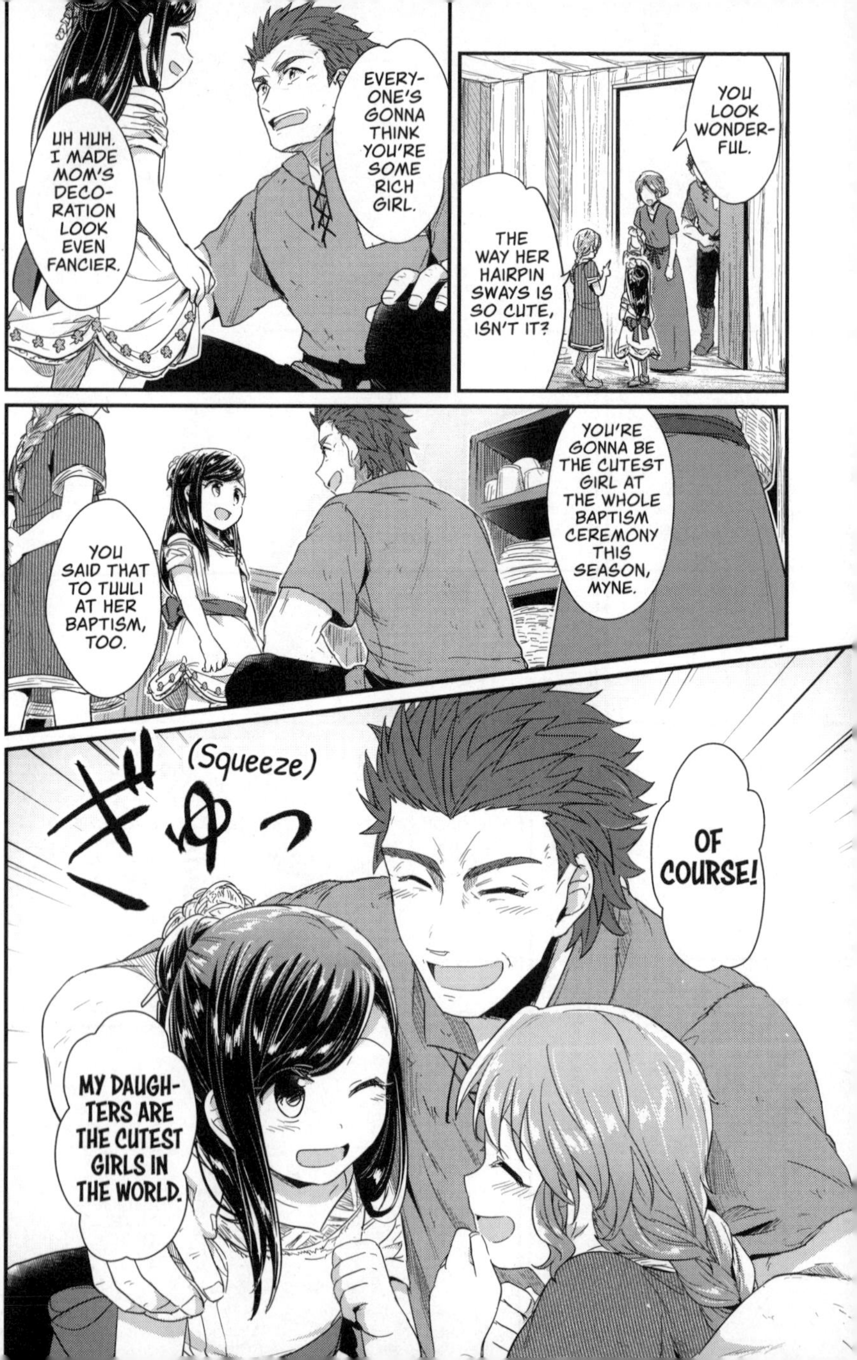
YOU LOOK WONDERFUL.
THE WAY HER HAIRPIN SWAYS IS SO CUTE, ISN'T IT?
EVERYONE'S GONNA THINK YOU'RE SOME RICH GIRL.
UH HUH. I MADE MOM'S DECORATION LOOK EVEN FANCIER.
YOU'RE GONNA BE THE CUTEST GIRL AT THE WHOLE BAPTISM CEREMONY THIS SEASON, MYNE.
YOU SAID THAT TO TUULI AT HER BAPTISM, TOO.
OF COURSE!
ぎゅっ
(Squeeze)
MY DAUGHTERS ARE THE CUTEST GIRLS IN THE WORLD.

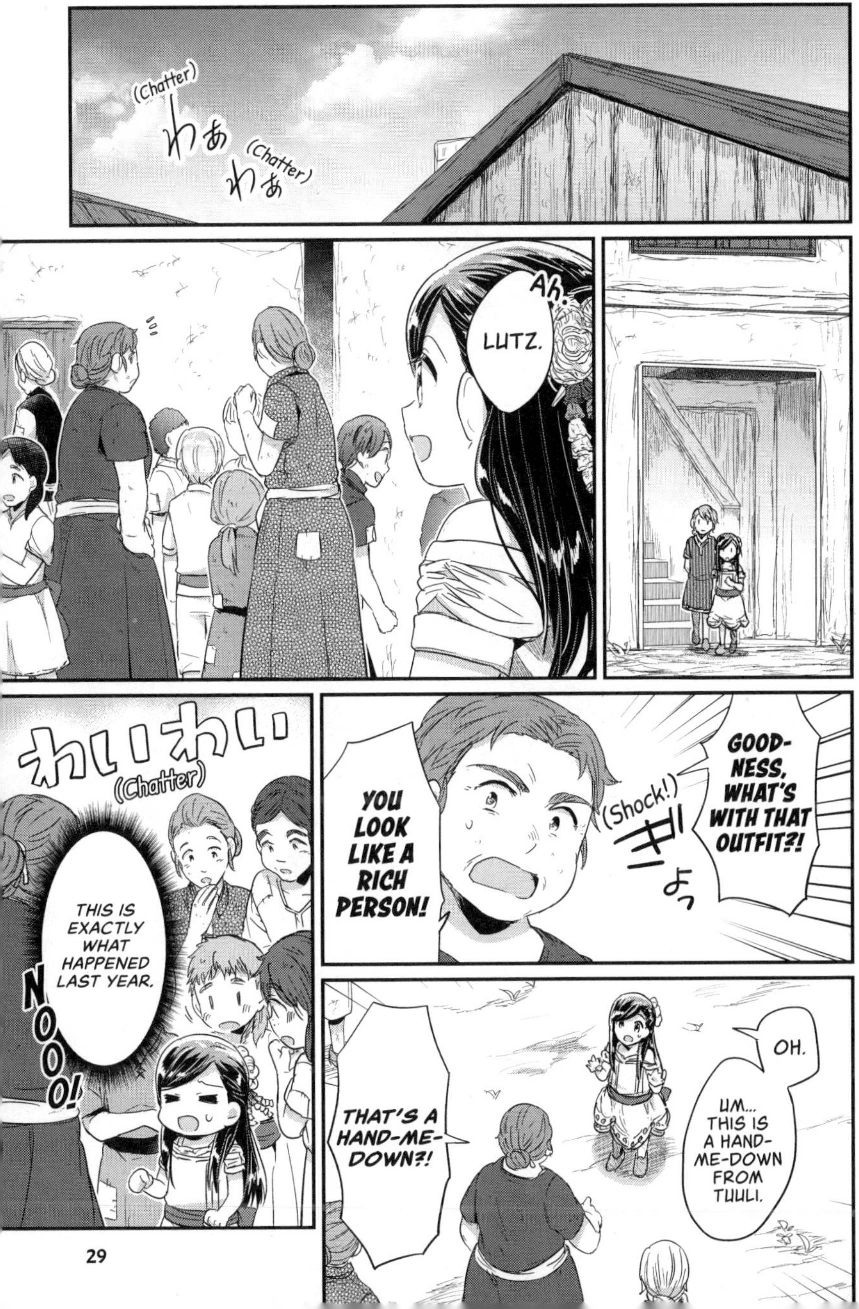
(Chatter)
わぁ
(Chatter)
わぁ
Ah.
LUTZ.
GOOD-NESS, WHAT'S WITH THAT OUTFIT?!
(Shock!)
ぎょっ
YOU LOOK LIKE A RICH PERSON!
OH.
UM... THIS IS A HAND-ME-DOWN FROM TUULI.
THAT'S A HAND-ME-DOWN?!
わいわい
(Chatter)
THIS IS EXACTLY WHAT HAPPENED LAST YEAR.
NOOOO!

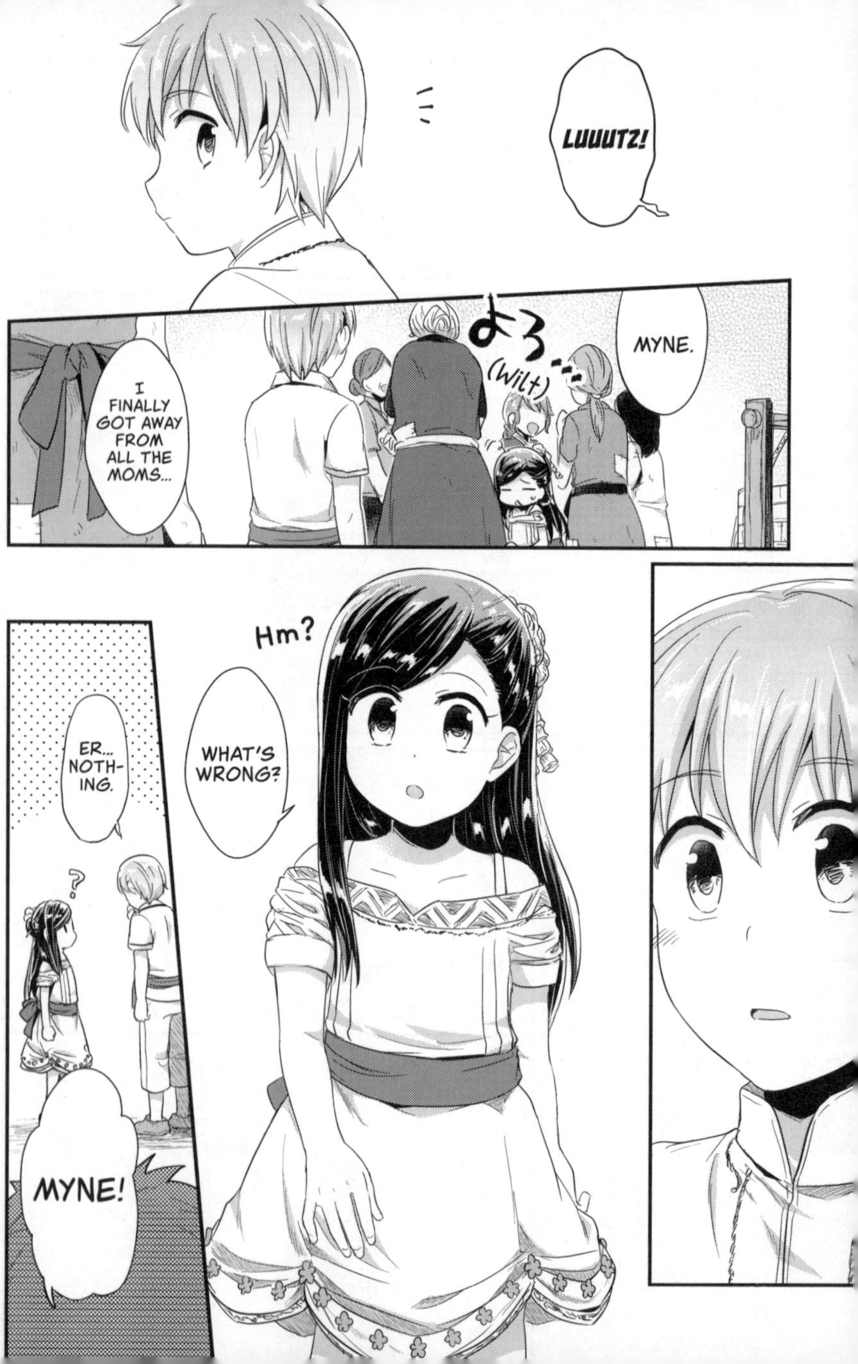
LUUUTZ!
MYNE.
よろ
(Wilt)
I FINALLY GOT AWAY FROM ALL THE MOMS...
Hm?
WHAT'S WRONG?
ER... NOTHING.
MYNE!

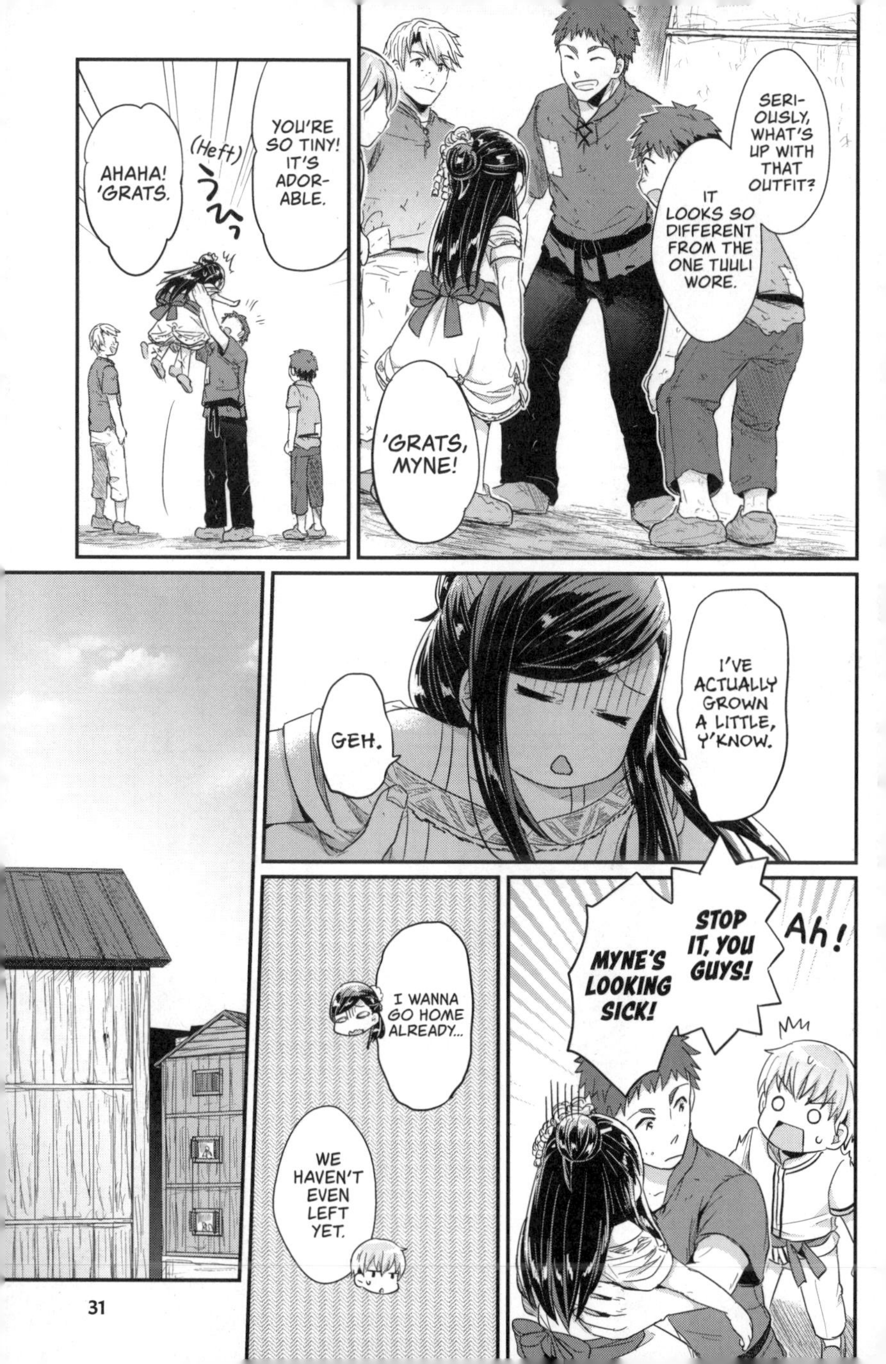
SERIOUSLY, WHAT'S UP WITH THAT OUTFIT?
IT LOOKS SO DIFFERENT FROM THE ONE TUULI WORE.
'GRATS, MYNE!
YOU'RE SO TINY! IT'S ADORABLE.
(Heft)
うひっ
AHAHA! 'GRATS.
I'VE ACTUALLY GROWN A LITTLE, Y'KNOW.
GEH.
Ah!
STOP IT, YOU GUYS!
MYNE'S LOOKING SICK!
I WANNA GO HOME ALREADY...
WE HAVEN'T EVEN LEFT YET.

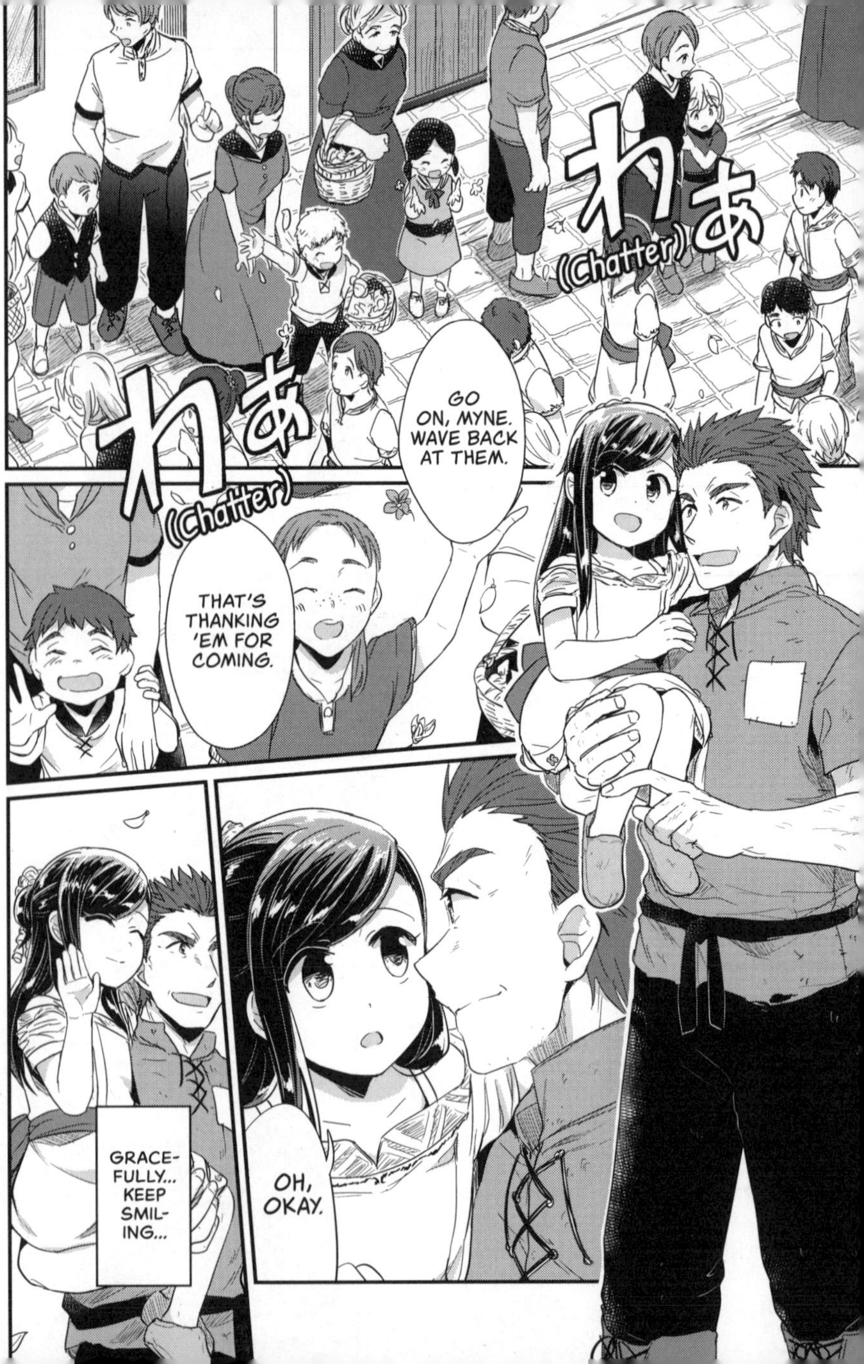
わあ
(Chatter)
わあ
(Chatter)
GO ON, MYNE. WAVE BACK AT THEM.
THAT'S THANKING 'EM FOR COMING.
OH, OKAY.
GRACE-FULLY... KEEP SMIL-ING...

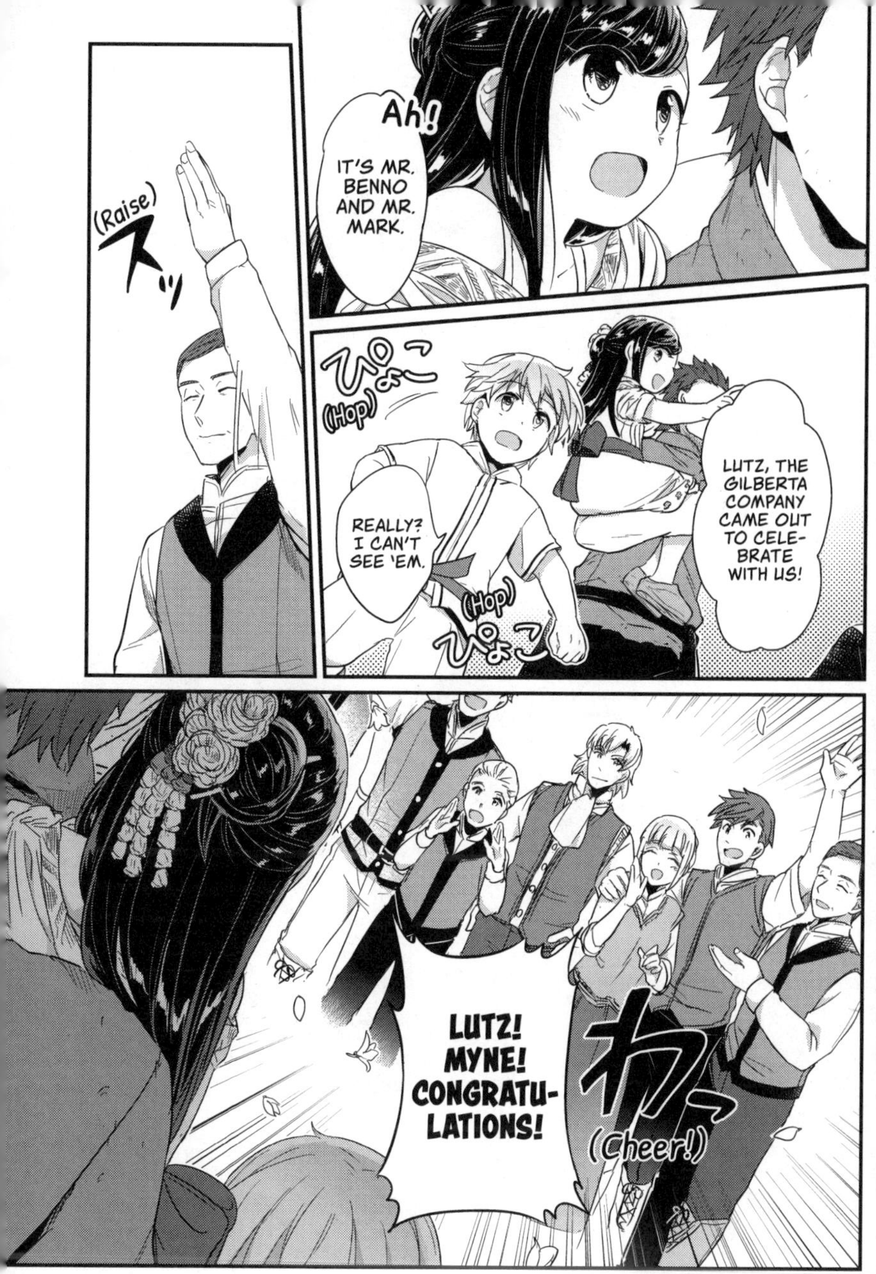
Ah!
IT'S MR. BENNO AND MR. MARK.
LUTZ, THE GILBERTA COMPANY CAME OUT TO CELEBRATE WITH US!
ぴょこ
(Hop)
REALLY? I CAN'T SEE 'EM.
(Hop)
ぴょこ
(Raise)
スッ
LUTZ! MYNE! CONGRATULATIONS!
わーっ
(Cheer!)

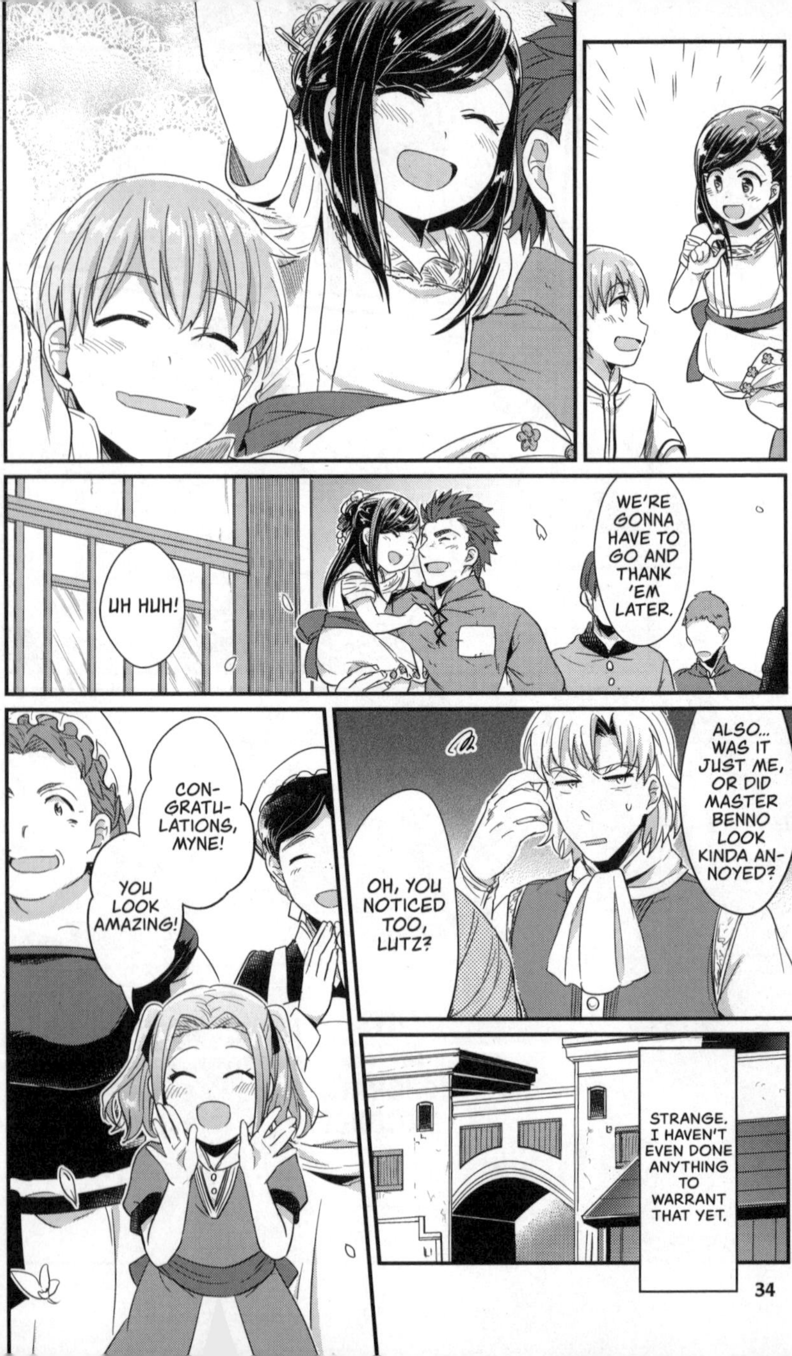
WE'RE GONNA HAVE TO GO AND THANK 'EM LATER.
UH HUH!
ALSO... WAS IT JUST ME, OR DID MASTER BENNO LOOK KINDA AN-NOYED?
OH, YOU NOTICED TOO, LUTZ?
STRANGE. I HAVEN'T EVEN DONE ANYTHING TO WARRANT THAT YET.
CON-GRATU-LATIONS, MYNE!
YOU LOOK AMAZING!

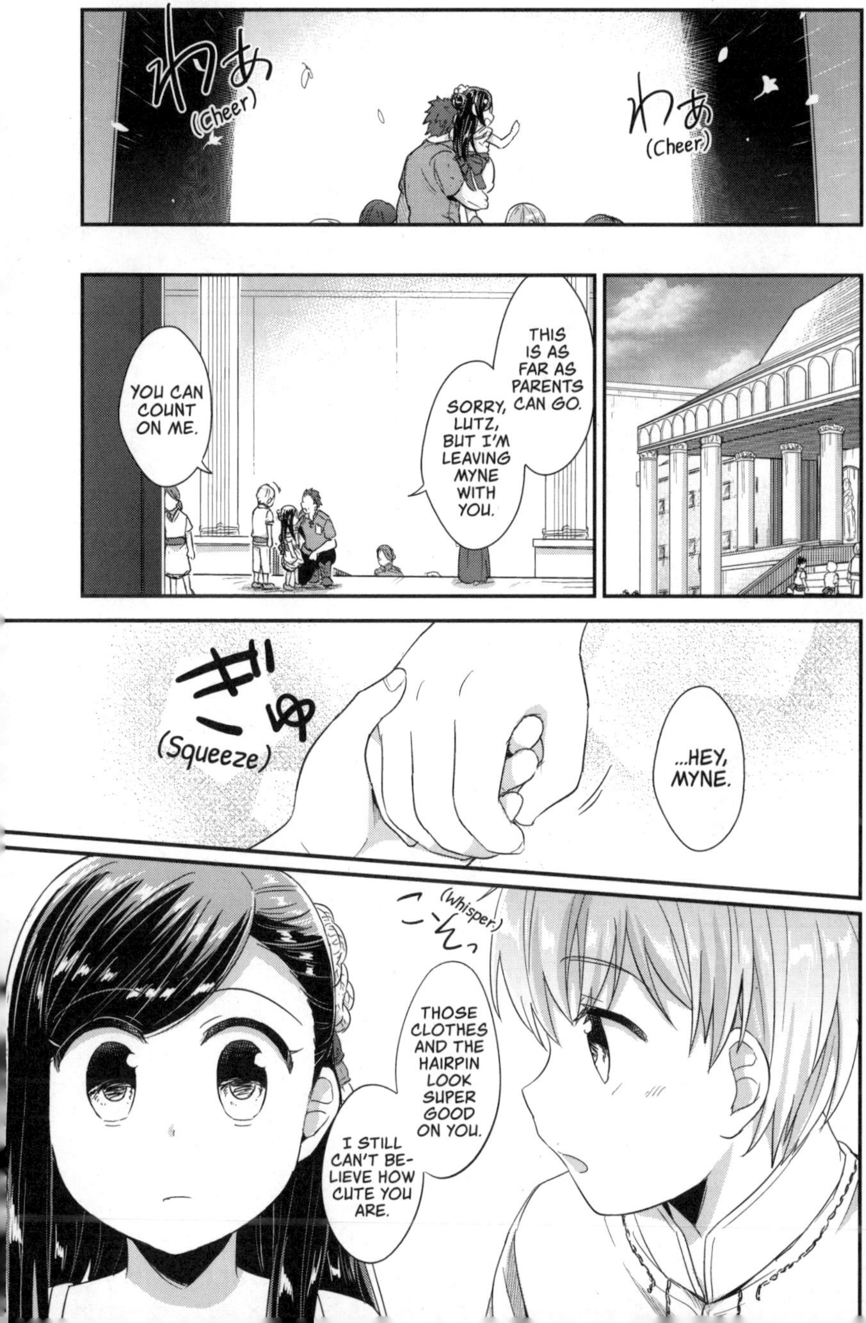
わあ
(Cheer)
わあ
(Cheer)
THIS IS AS FAR AS PARENTS CAN GO.
SORRY, LUTZ, BUT I'M LEAVING MYNE WITH YOU.
YOU CAN COUNT ON ME.
...HEY, MYNE.
ぎゅ
(Squeeze)
こそっ
(Whisper)
THOSE CLOTHES AND THE HAIRPIN LOOK SUPER GOOD ON YOU.
I STILL CAN'T BE-LIEVE HOW CUTE YOU ARE.

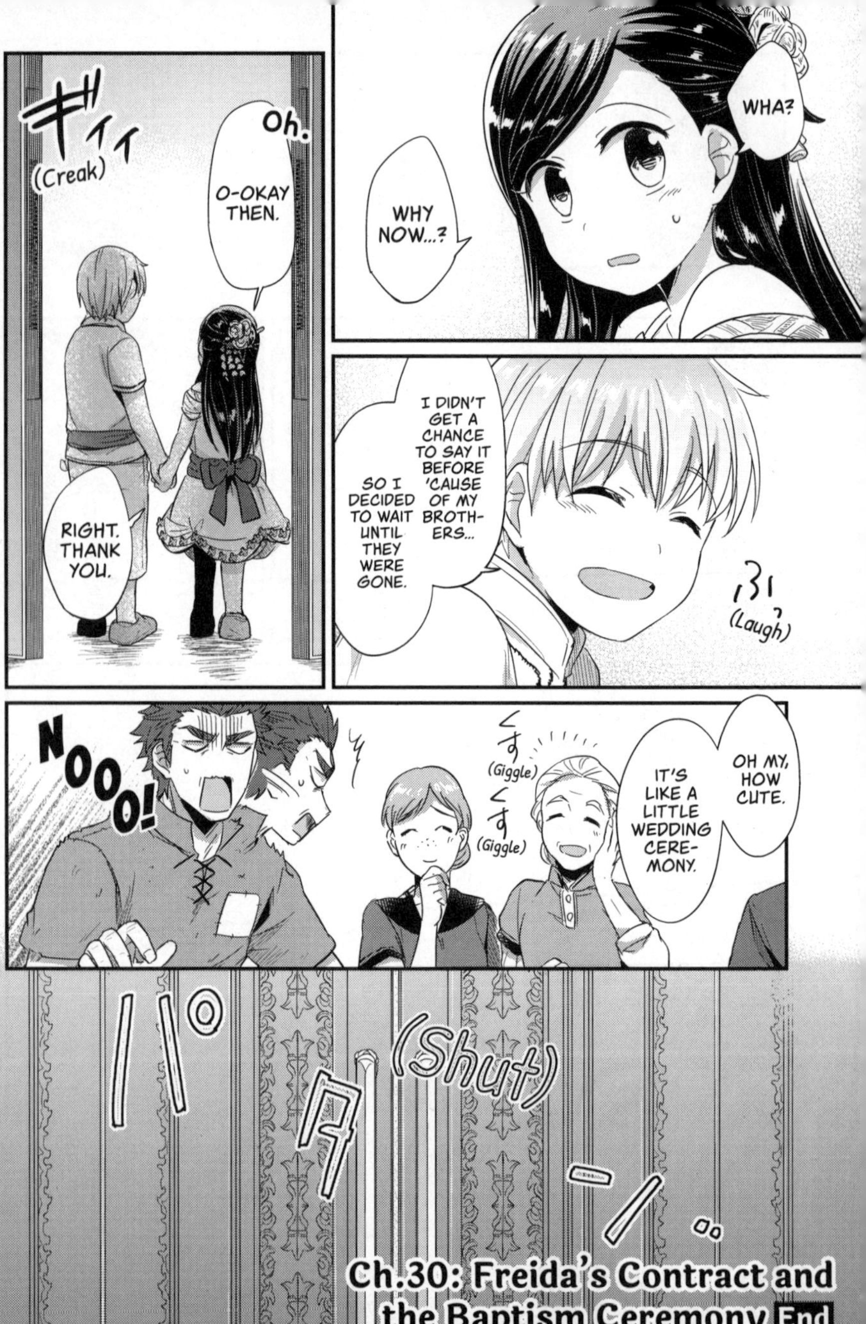
WHA?
WHY NOW...?
I DIDN'T GET A CHANCE TO SAY IT BEFORE 'CAUSE OF MY BROTHERS...
SO I DECIDED TO WAIT UNTIL THEY WERE GONE.
(Laugh)
(Creak)
Oh.
O-OKAY THEN.
RIGHT. THANK YOU.
OH MY, HOW CUTE.
IT'S LIKE A LITTLE WEDDING CEREMONY.
(Giggle)
(Giggle)
NOOOO!
(Shut)
Ch.30: Freida's Contract and the Baptism Ceremony End

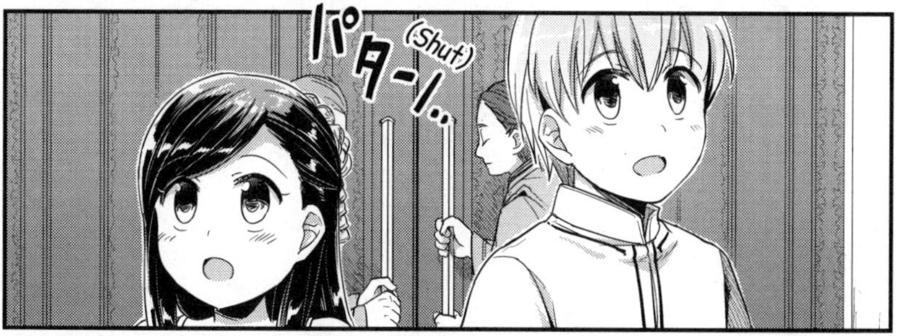
パターン..
(Shut)

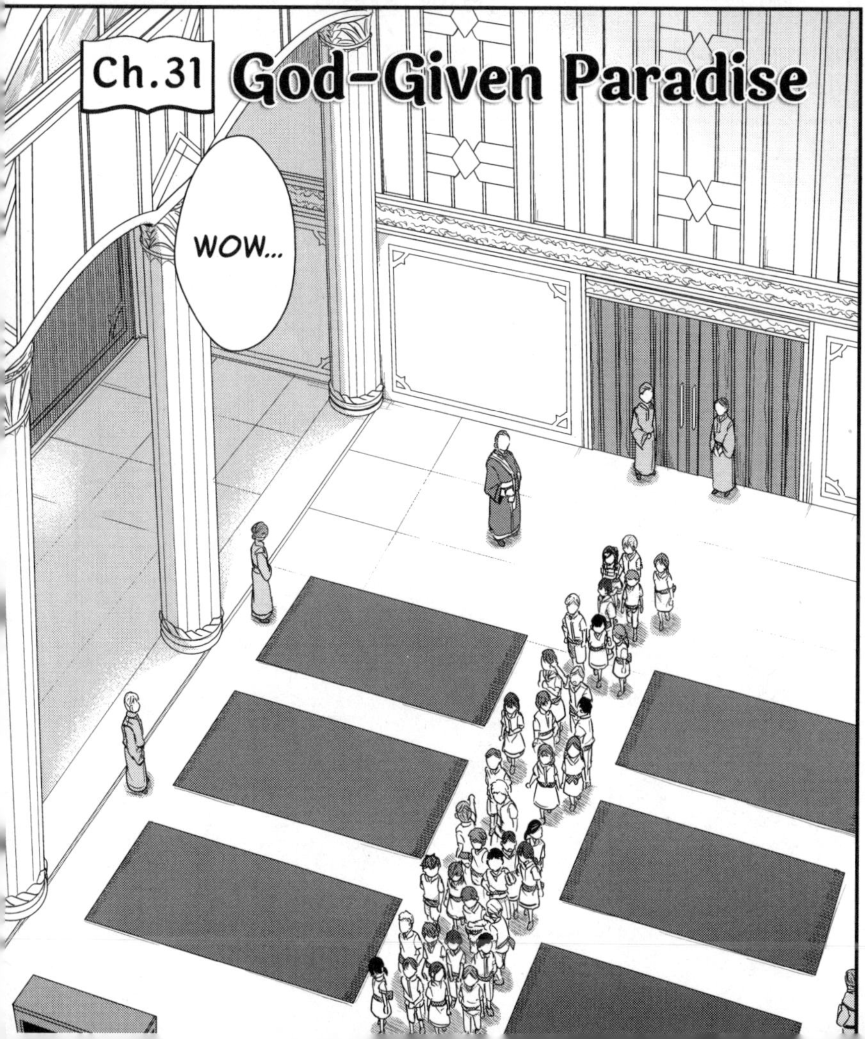
Ch.31 God-Given Paradise
WOW...

チリーン
(Ring)

ス (Step)
ブッ

THIS PLACE IS HUGE.

チリーン
(Ring)

!

THE HECK?

チリーン
(Ring)

THE BELL THAT MAN JUST RANG...

IT MUST BE A MAGIC TOOL THAT KEEPS OUR VOICES DOWN.

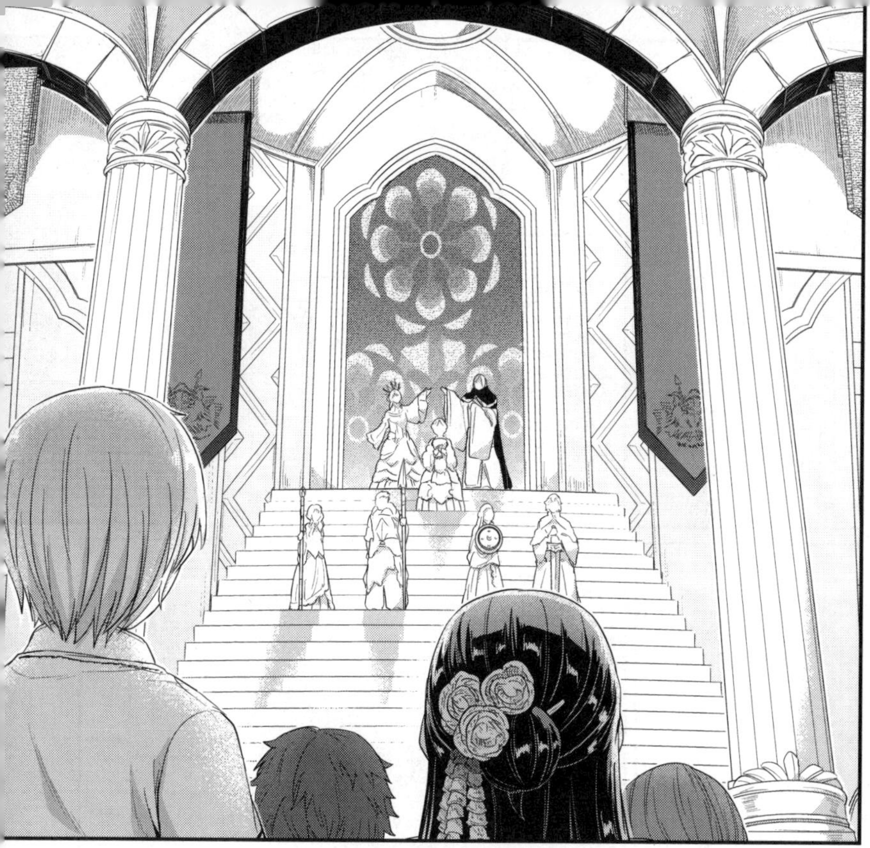

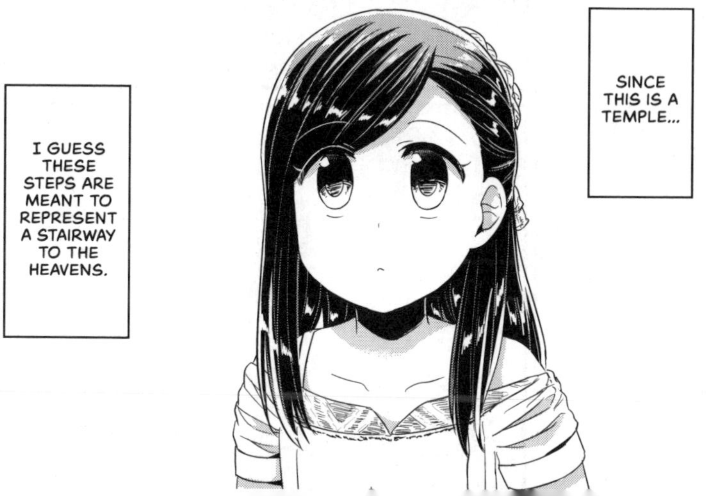
SINCE THIS IS A TEMPLE...
I GUESS THESE STEPS ARE MEANT TO REPRESENT A STAIRWAY TO THE HEAVENS.

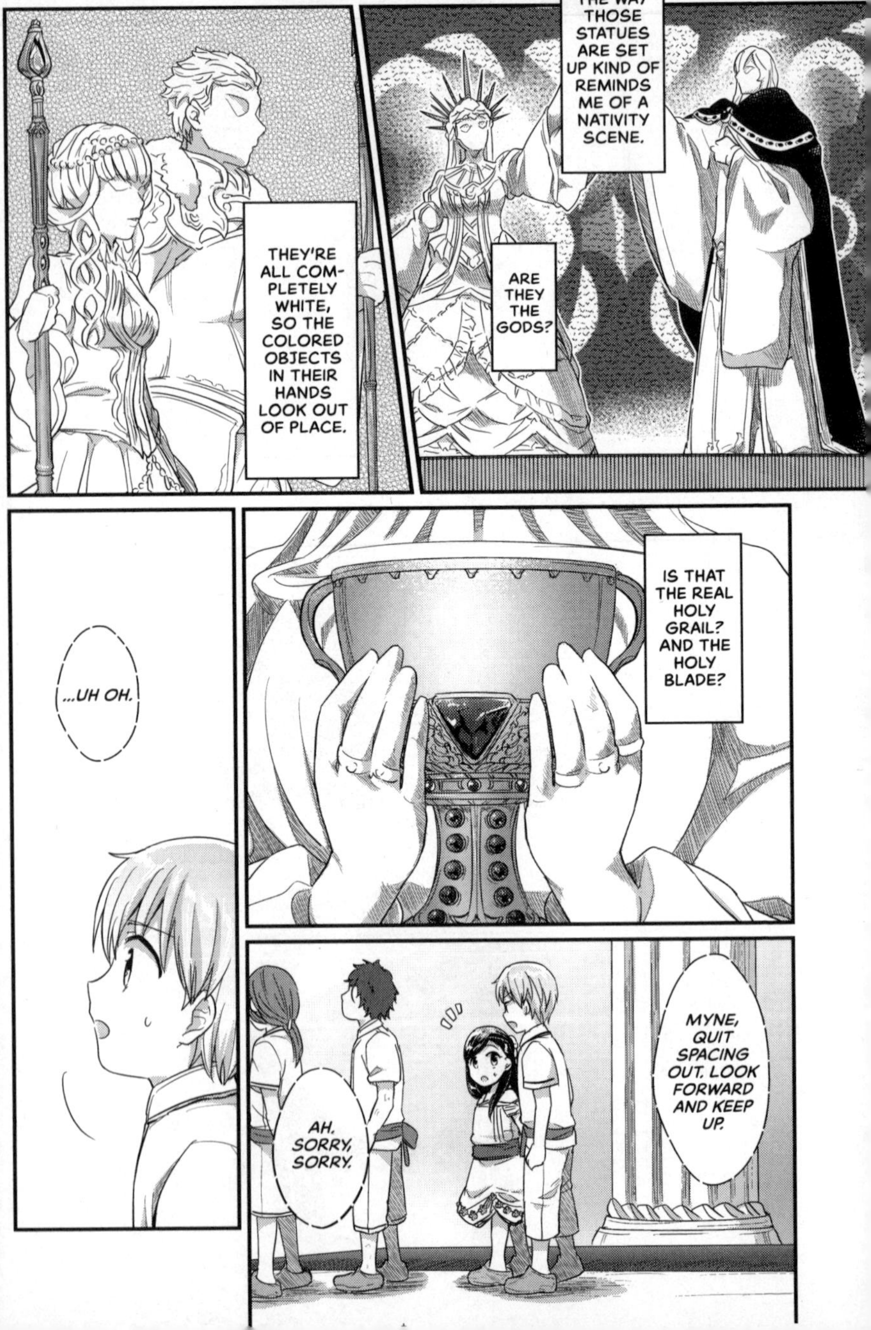
THE WAY THOSE STATUES ARE SET UP KIND OF REMINDS ME OF A NATIVITY SCENE.
ARE THEY THE GODS?
THEY'RE ALL COM-PLETELY WHITE, SO THE COLORED OBJECTS IN THEIR HANDS LOOK OUT OF PLACE.
IS THAT THE REAL HOLY GRAIL? AND THE HOLY BLADE?
MYNE, QUIT SPACING OUT. LOOK FORWARD AND KEEP UP.
AH. SORRY, SORRY.
...UH OH.

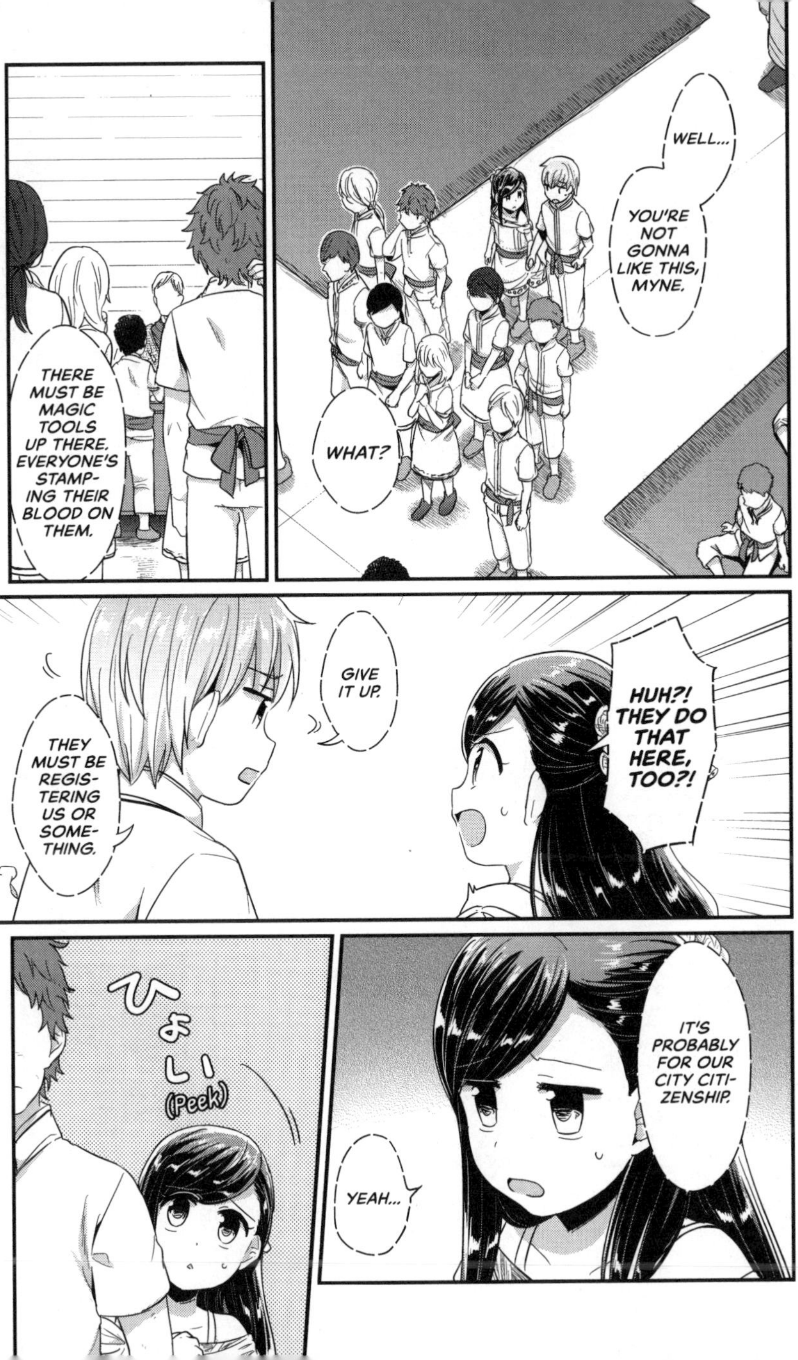
WELL...
YOU'RE NOT GONNA LIKE THIS, MYNE.
WHAT?
THERE MUST BE MAGIC TOOLS UP THERE. EVERYONE'S STAMPING THEIR BLOOD ON THEM.
HUH?! THEY DO THAT HERE, TOO?!
GIVE IT UP.
THEY MUST BE REGISTERING US OR SOMETHING.
IT'S PROBABLY FOR OUR CITY CITIZENSHIP.
YEAH...
ひょい
(Peek)

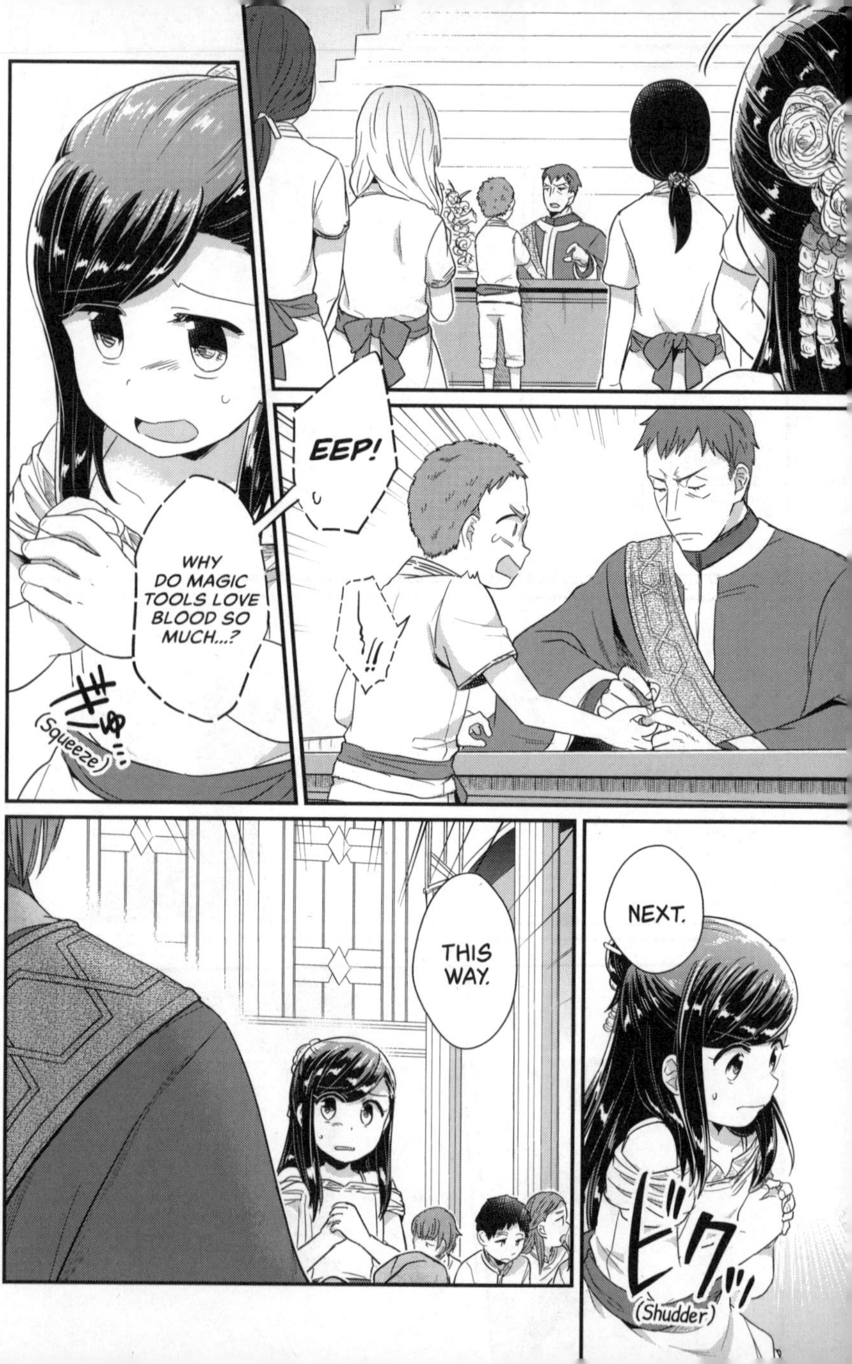
EEP!
!!
WHY DO MAGIC TOOLS LOVE BLOOD SO MUCH...?
(Squeeze)
NEXT.
(Shudder)
THIS WAY.

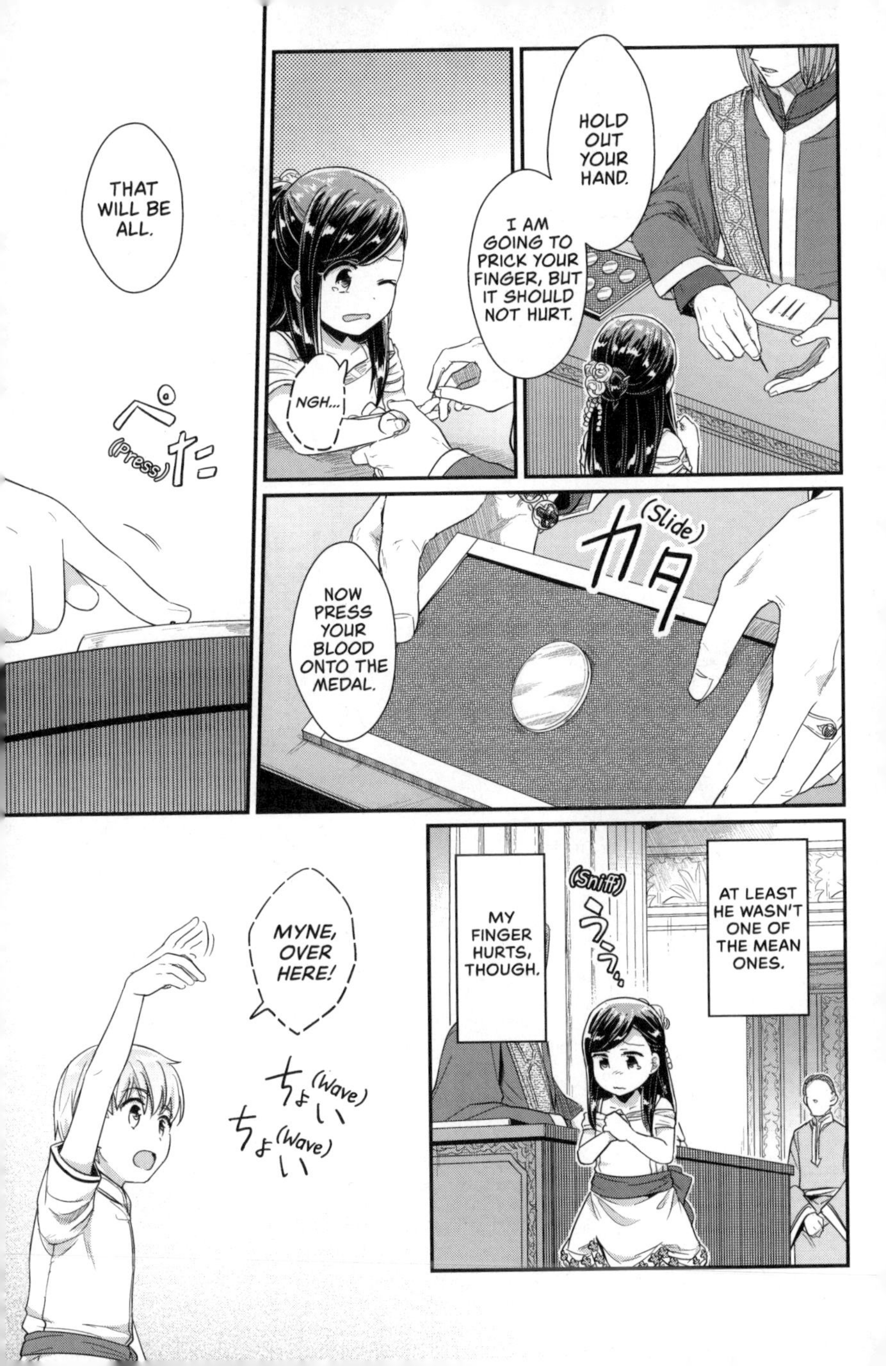
HOLD OUT YOUR HAND.
I AM GOING TO PRICK YOUR FINGER, BUT IT SHOULD NOT HURT.
NGH...
(Slide) カタ
NOW PRESS YOUR BLOOD ONTO THE MEDAL.
THAT WILL BE ALL.
(Press) ぺた
AT LEAST HE WASN'T ONE OF THE MEAN ONES.
MY FINGER HURTS, THOUGH.
(Sniff) うぅ
MYNE, OVER HERE!
(Wave) ちょい
(Wave) ちょい

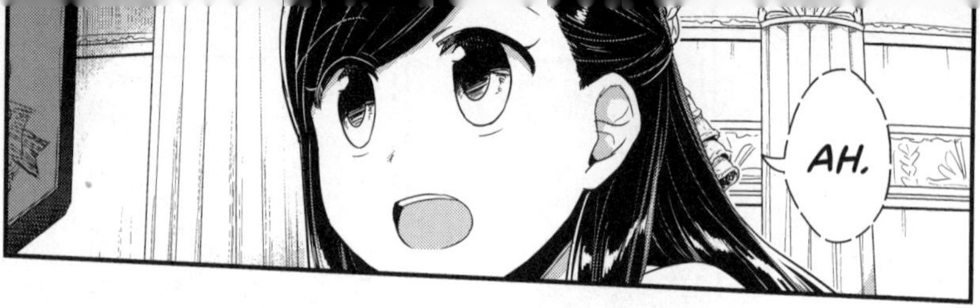
AH.

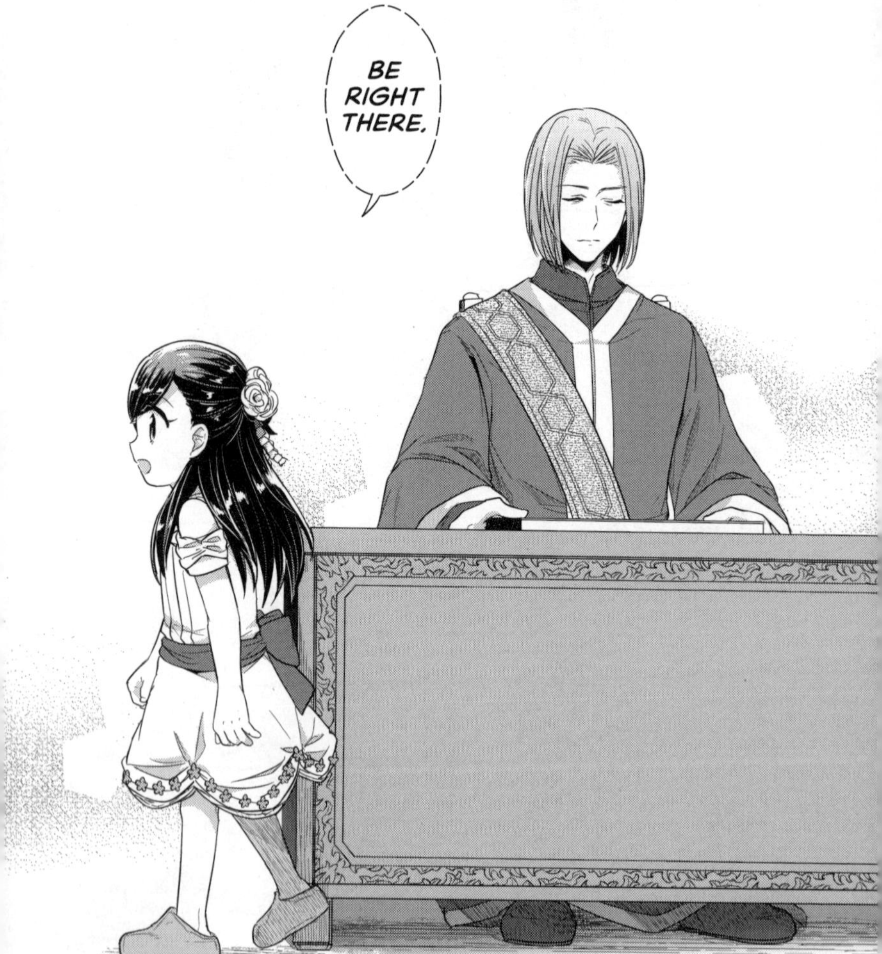
BE RIGHT THERE.

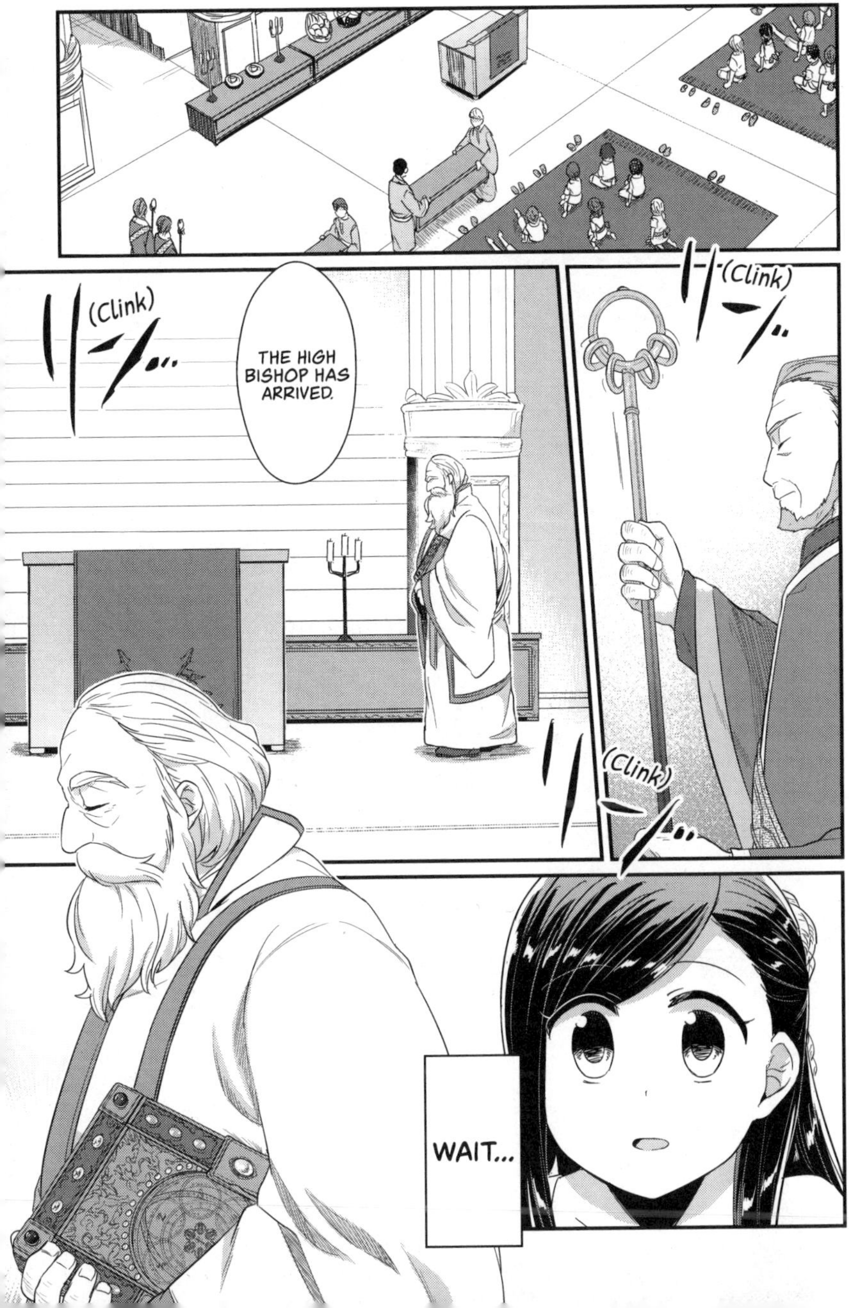
(Clink)
(Clink)
THE HIGH BISHOP HAS ARRIVED.
(Clink)
WAIT...

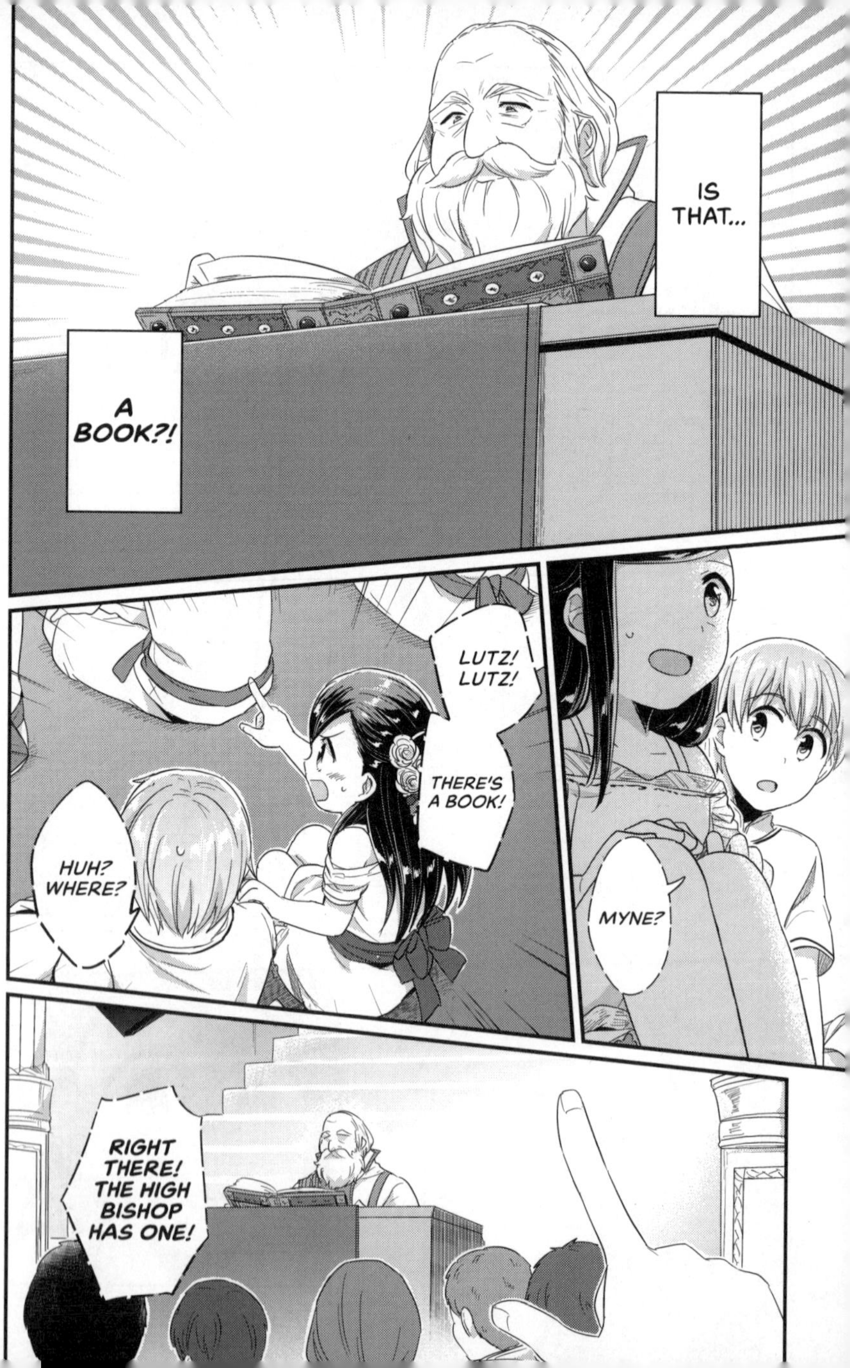
IS THAT...
A BOOK?!
MYNE?
LUTZ! LUTZ!
THERE'S A BOOK!
HUH? WHERE?
RIGHT THERE! THE HIGH BISHOP HAS ONE!

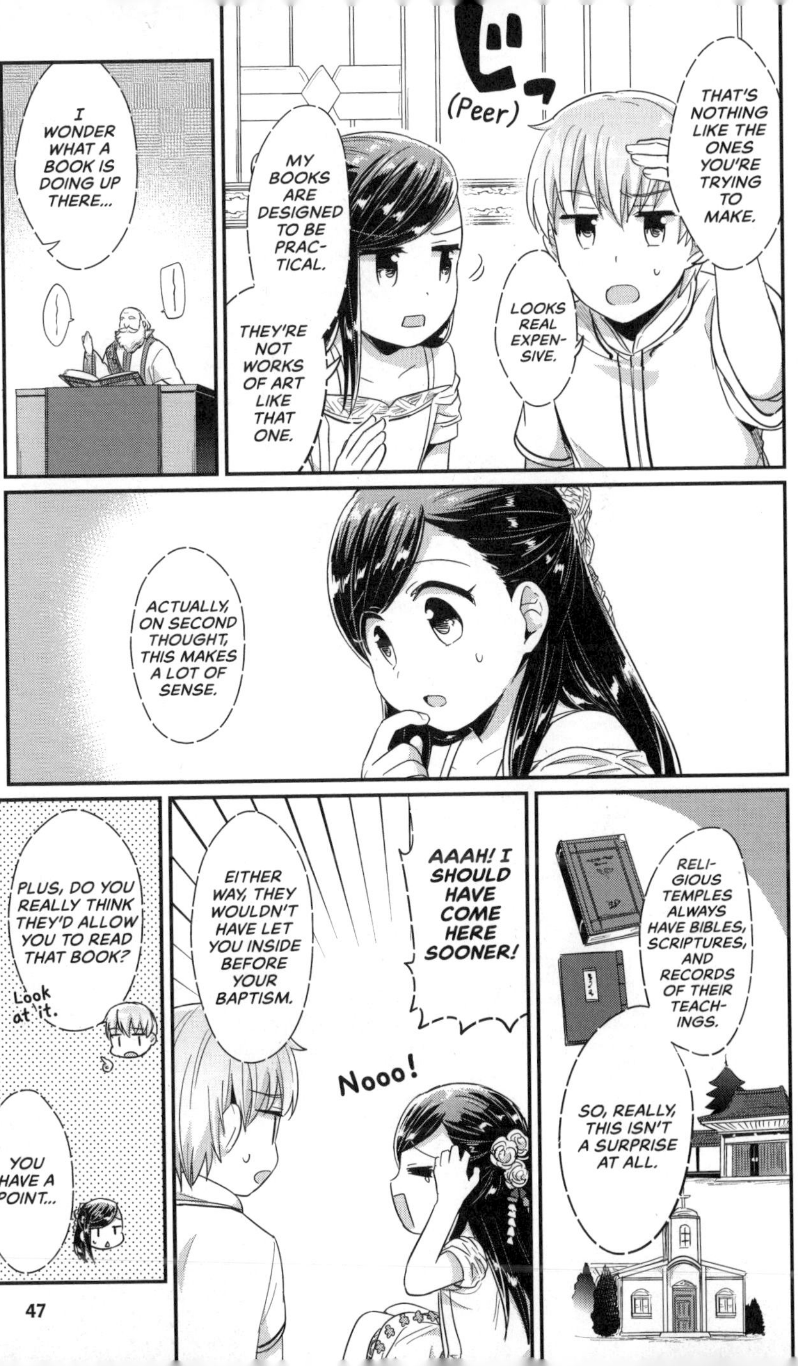

(Peer)
THAT'S NOTHING LIKE THE ONES YOU'RE TRYING TO MAKE.
LOOKS REAL EXPENSIVE.
MY BOOKS ARE DESIGNED TO BE PRAC-TICAL.
THEY'RE NOT WORKS OF ART LIKE THAT ONE.
I WONDER WHAT A BOOK IS DOING UP THERE...
ACTUALLY, ON SECOND THOUGHT, THIS MAKES A LOT OF SENSE.
RELI-GIOUS TEMPLES ALWAYS HAVE BIBLES, SCRIPTURES, AND RECORDS OF THEIR TEACH-INGS.
SO, REALLY, THIS ISN'T A SURPRISE AT ALL.
AAAH! I SHOULD HAVE COME HERE SOONER!
Nooo!
EITHER WAY, THEY WOULDN'T HAVE LET YOU INSIDE BEFORE YOUR BAPTISM.
PLUS, DO YOU REALLY THINK THEY'D ALLOW YOU TO READ THAT BOOK?
Look at it.
YOU HAVE A POINT...

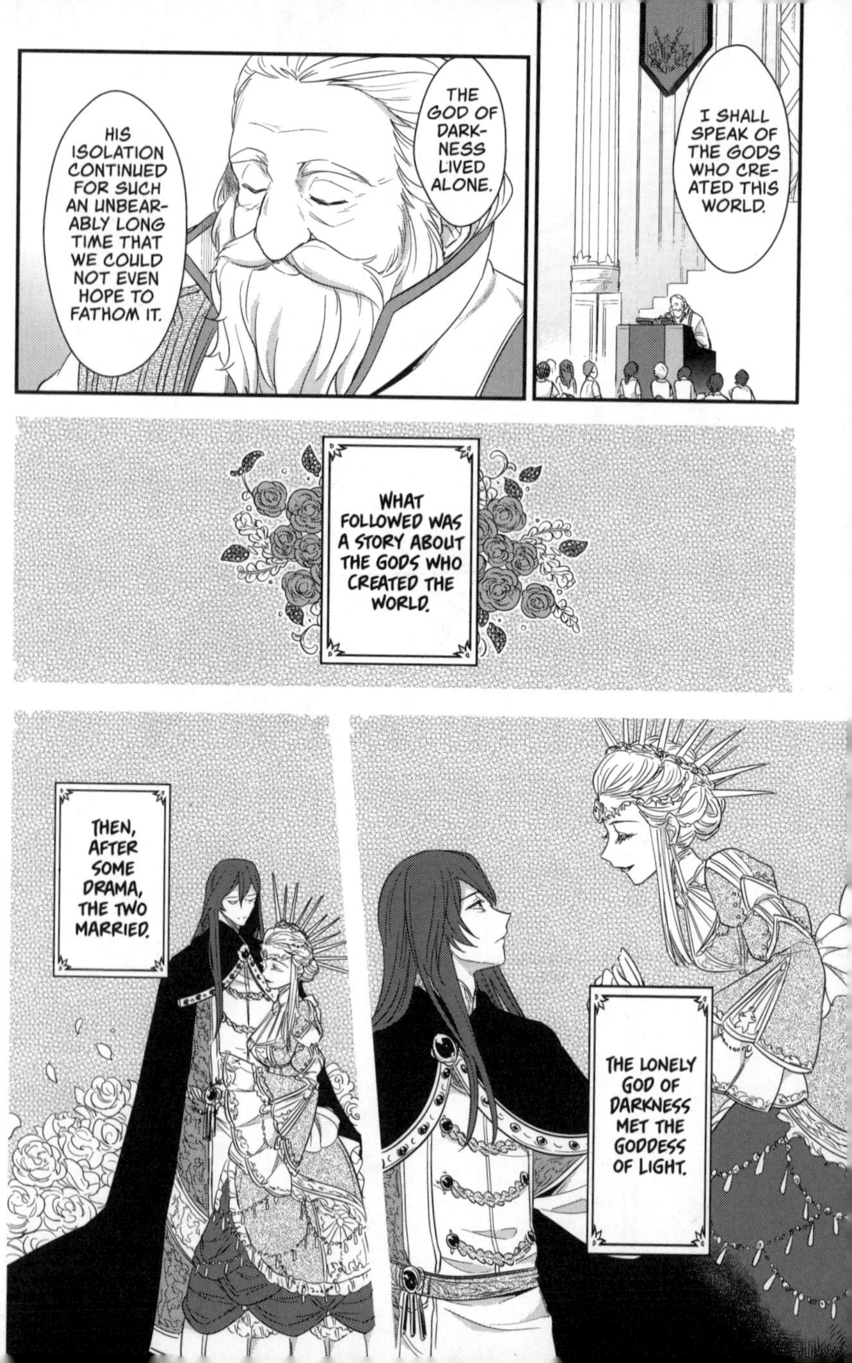
I SHALL SPEAK OF THE GODS WHO CREATED THIS WORLD.
THE GOD OF DARKNESS LIVED ALONE.
HIS ISOLATION CONTINUED FOR SUCH AN UNBEARABLY LONG TIME THAT WE COULD NOT EVEN HOPE TO FATHOM IT.
WHAT FOLLOWED WAS A STORY ABOUT THE GODS WHO CREATED THE WORLD.
THE LONELY GOD OF DARKNESS MET THE GODDESS OF LIGHT.
THEN, AFTER SOME DRAMA, THE TWO MARRIED.

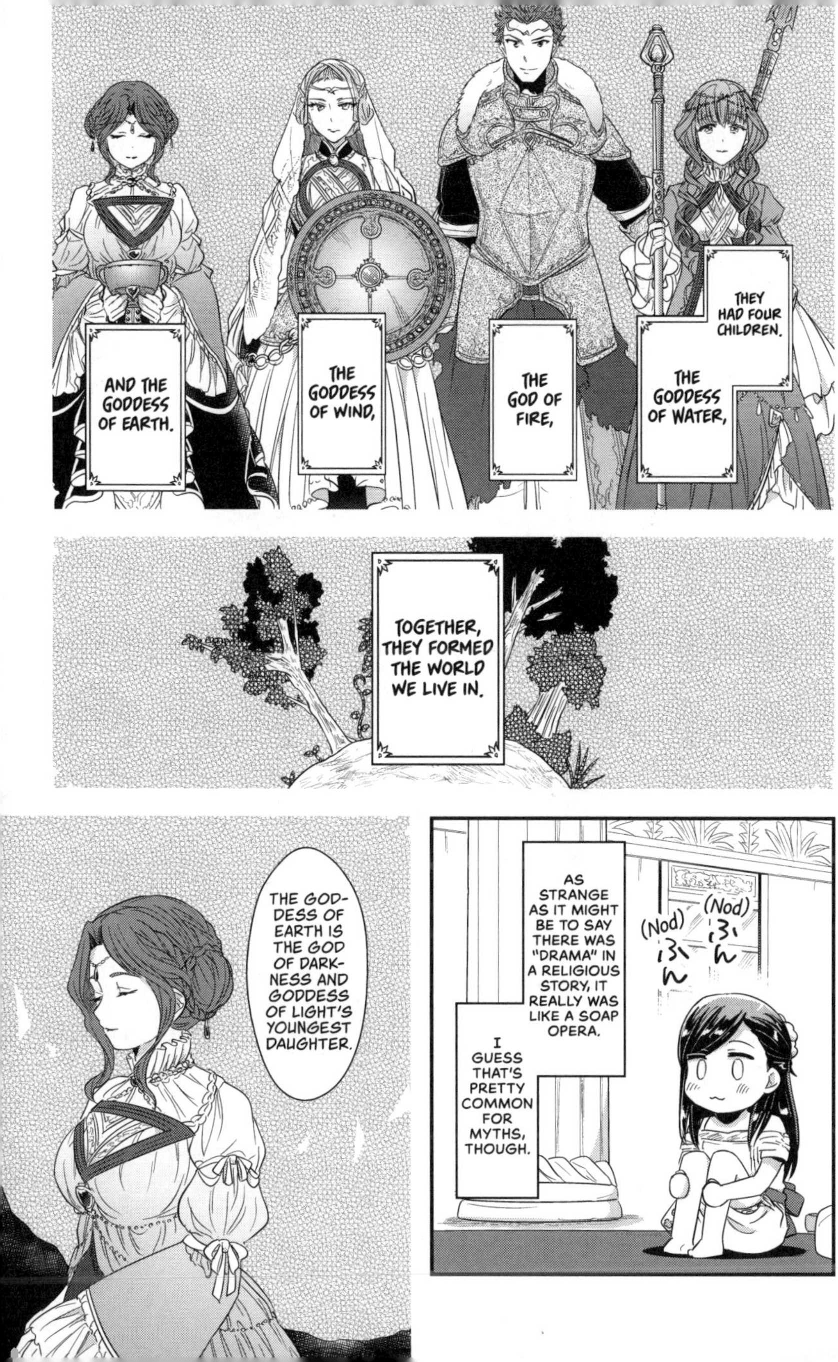
THEY HAD FOUR CHILDREN.
THE GODDESS OF WATER,
THE GOD OF FIRE,
THE GODDESS OF WIND,
AND THE GODDESS OF EARTH.
TOGETHER, THEY FORMED THE WORLD WE LIVE IN.
AS STRANGE AS IT MIGHT BE TO SAY THERE WAS "DRAMA" IN A RELIGIOUS STORY, IT REALLY WAS LIKE A SOAP OPERA.
(Nod) ふん
(Nod) ふん
I GUESS THAT'S PRETTY COMMON FOR MYTHS, THOUGH.
THE GOD-DESS OF EARTH IS THE GOD OF DARK-NESS AND GODDESS OF LIGHT'S YOUNGEST DAUGHTER.

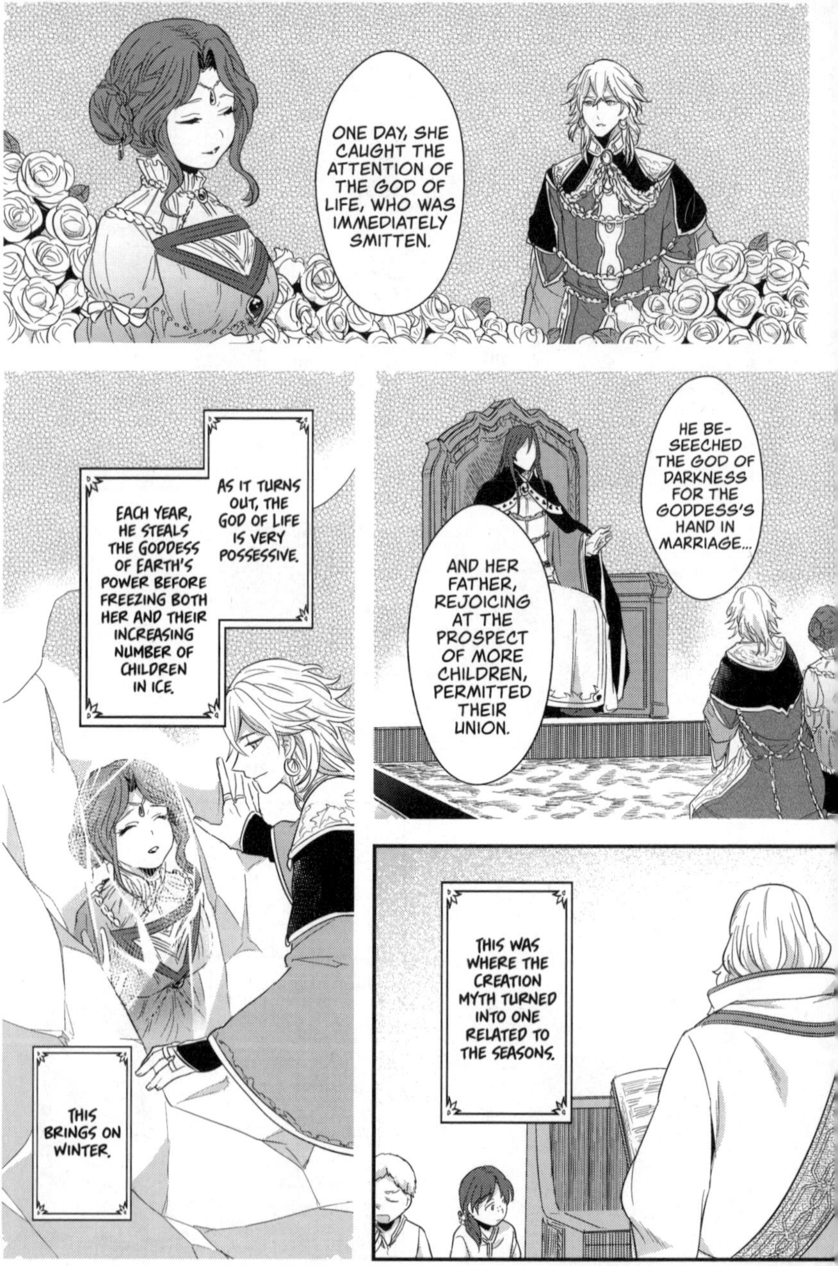
ONE DAY, SHE CAUGHT THE ATTENTION OF THE GOD OF LIFE, WHO WAS IMMEDIATELY SMITTEN.
HE BE-SEECHED THE GOD OF DARKNESS FOR THE GODDESS'S HAND IN MARRIAGE...
AND HER FATHER, REJOICING AT THE PROSPECT OF MORE CHILDREN, PERMITTED THEIR UNION.
THIS WAS WHERE THE CREATION MYTH TURNED INTO ONE RELATED TO THE SEASONS.
AS IT TURNS OUT, THE GOD OF LIFE IS VERY POSSESSIVE.
EACH YEAR, HE STEALS THE GODDESS OF EARTH'S POWER BEFORE FREEZING BOTH HER AND THEIR INCREASING NUMBER OF CHILDREN IN ICE.
THIS BRINGS ON WINTER.

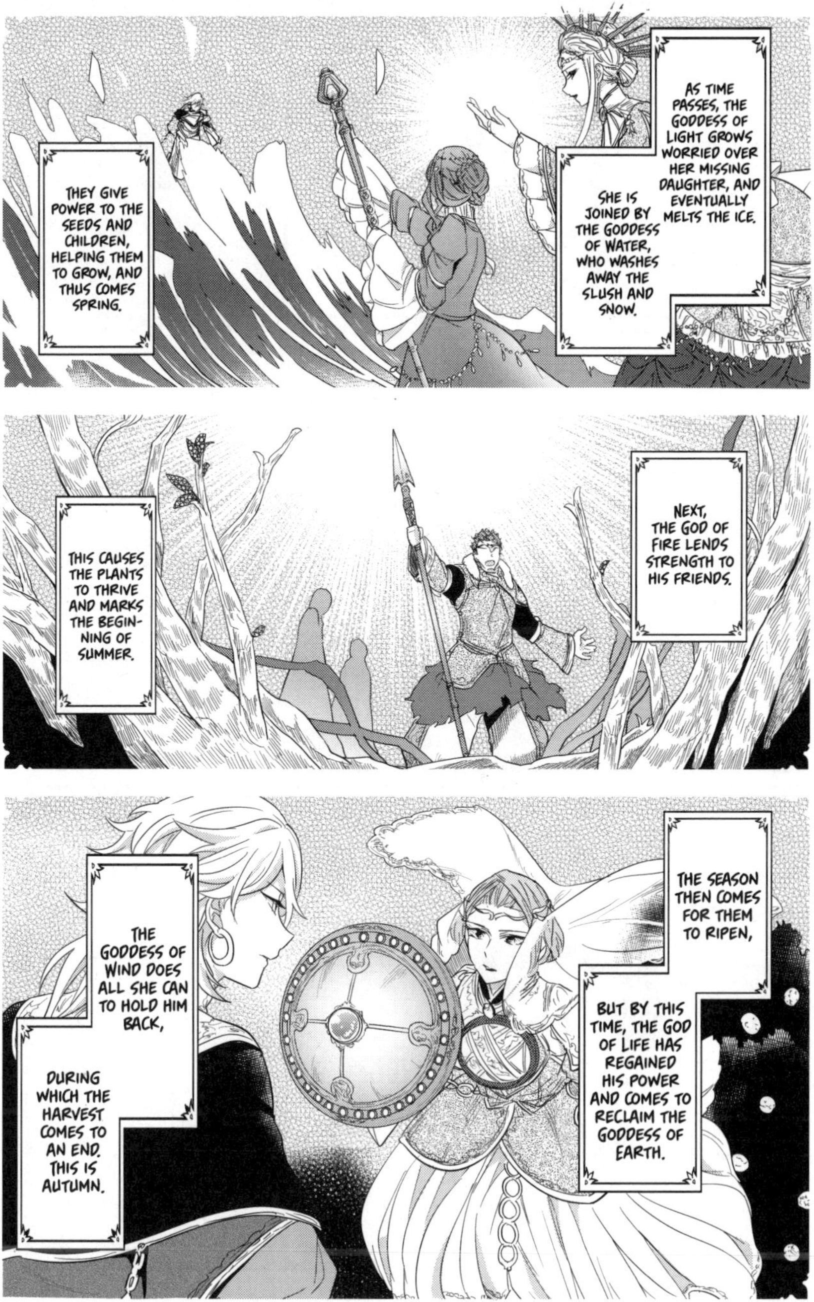
AS TIME PASSES, THE GODDESS OF LIGHT GROWS WORRIED OVER HER MISSING DAUGHTER, AND EVENTUALLY MELTS THE ICE.
SHE IS JOINED BY THE GODDESS OF WATER, WHO WASHES AWAY THE SLUSH AND SNOW.
THEY GIVE POWER TO THE SEEDS AND CHILDREN, HELPING THEM TO GROW, AND THUS COMES SPRING.
NEXT, THE GOD OF FIRE LENDS STRENGTH TO HIS FRIENDS.
THIS CAUSES THE PLANTS TO THRIVE AND MARKS THE BEGINNING OF SUMMER.
THE SEASON THEN COMES FOR THEM TO RIPEN,
BUT BY THIS TIME, THE GOD OF LIFE HAS REGAINED HIS POWER AND COMES TO RECLAIM THE GODDESS OF EARTH.
THE GODDESS OF WIND DOES ALL SHE CAN TO HOLD HIM BACK,
DURING WHICH THE HARVEST COMES TO AN END. THIS IS AUTUMN.

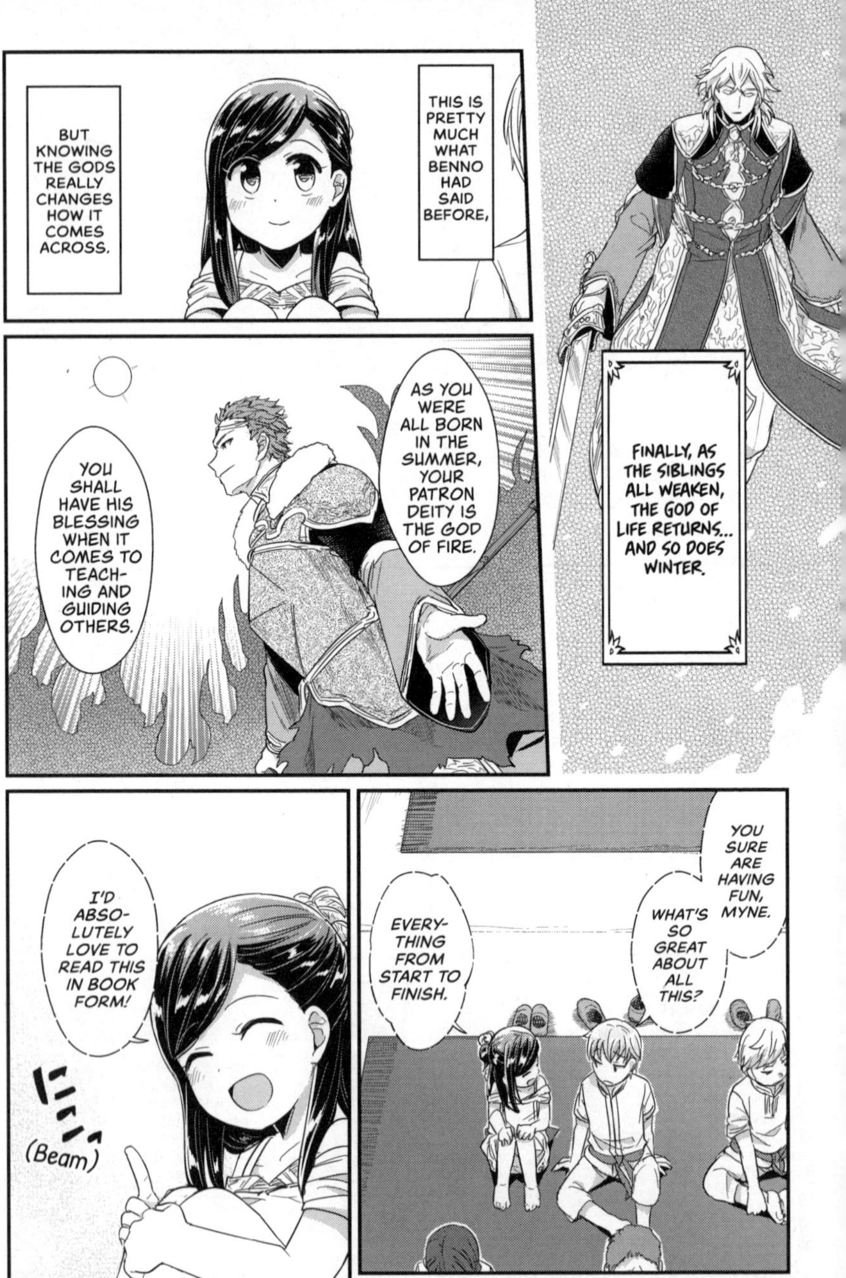
FINALLY, AS THE SIBLINGS ALL WEAKEN, THE GOD OF LIFE RETURNS... AND SO DOES WINTER.
THIS IS PRETTY MUCH WHAT BENNO HAD SAID BEFORE,
BUT KNOWING THE GODS REALLY CHANGES HOW IT COMES ACROSS.
AS YOU WERE ALL BORN IN THE SUMMER, YOUR PATRON DEITY IS THE GOD OF FIRE.
YOU SHALL HAVE HIS BLESSING WHEN IT COMES TO TEACHING AND GUIDING OTHERS.
YOU SURE ARE HAVING FUN, MYNE.
WHAT'S SO GREAT ABOUT ALL THIS?
EVERYTHING FROM START TO FINISH.
I'D ABSOLUTELY LOVE TO READ THIS IN BOOK FORM!
(Beam)

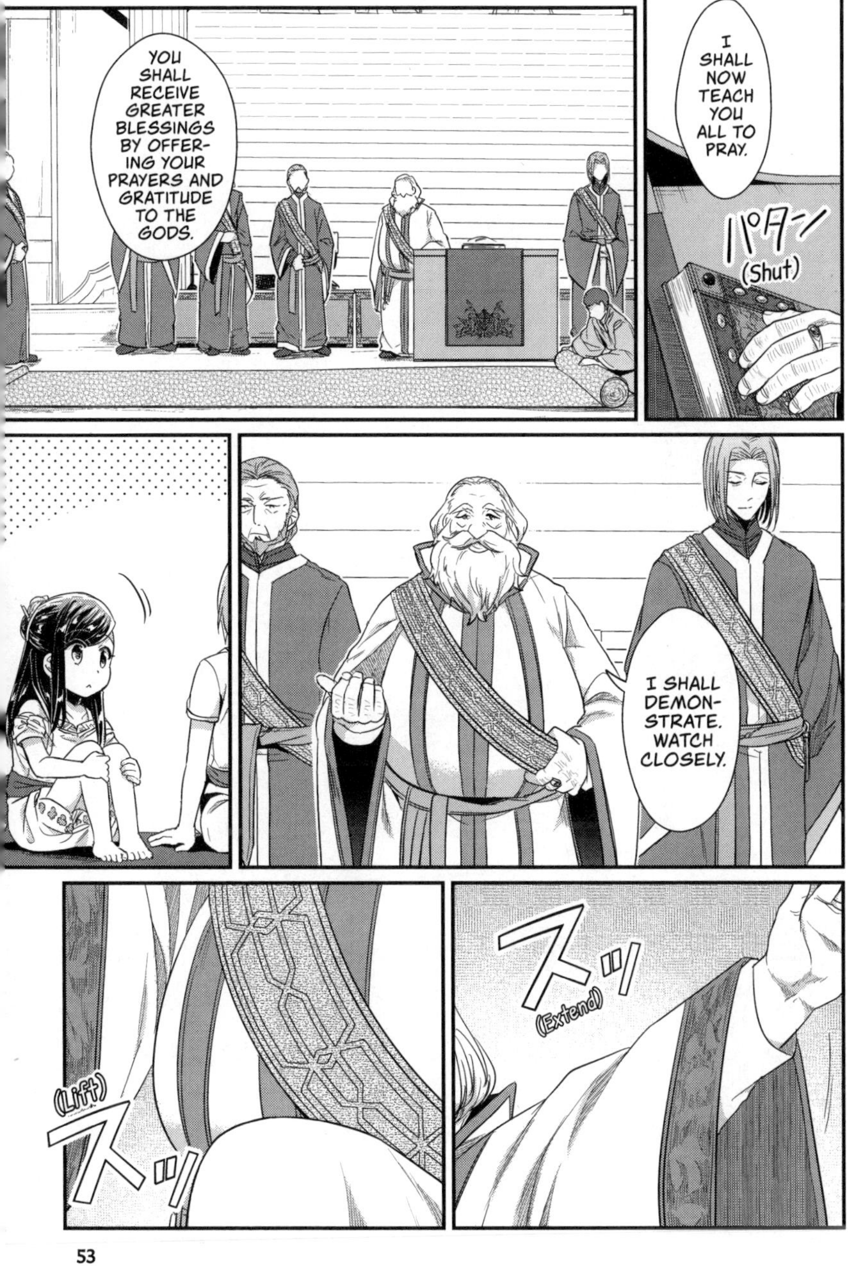
I SHALL NOW TEACH YOU ALL TO PRAY.
パタン
(Shut)
YOU SHALL RECEIVE GREATER BLESSINGS BY OFFERING YOUR PRAYERS AND GRATITUDE TO THE GODS.
I SHALL DEMONSTRATE. WATCH CLOSELY.
スッ
(Extend)
(Lift)
スッ

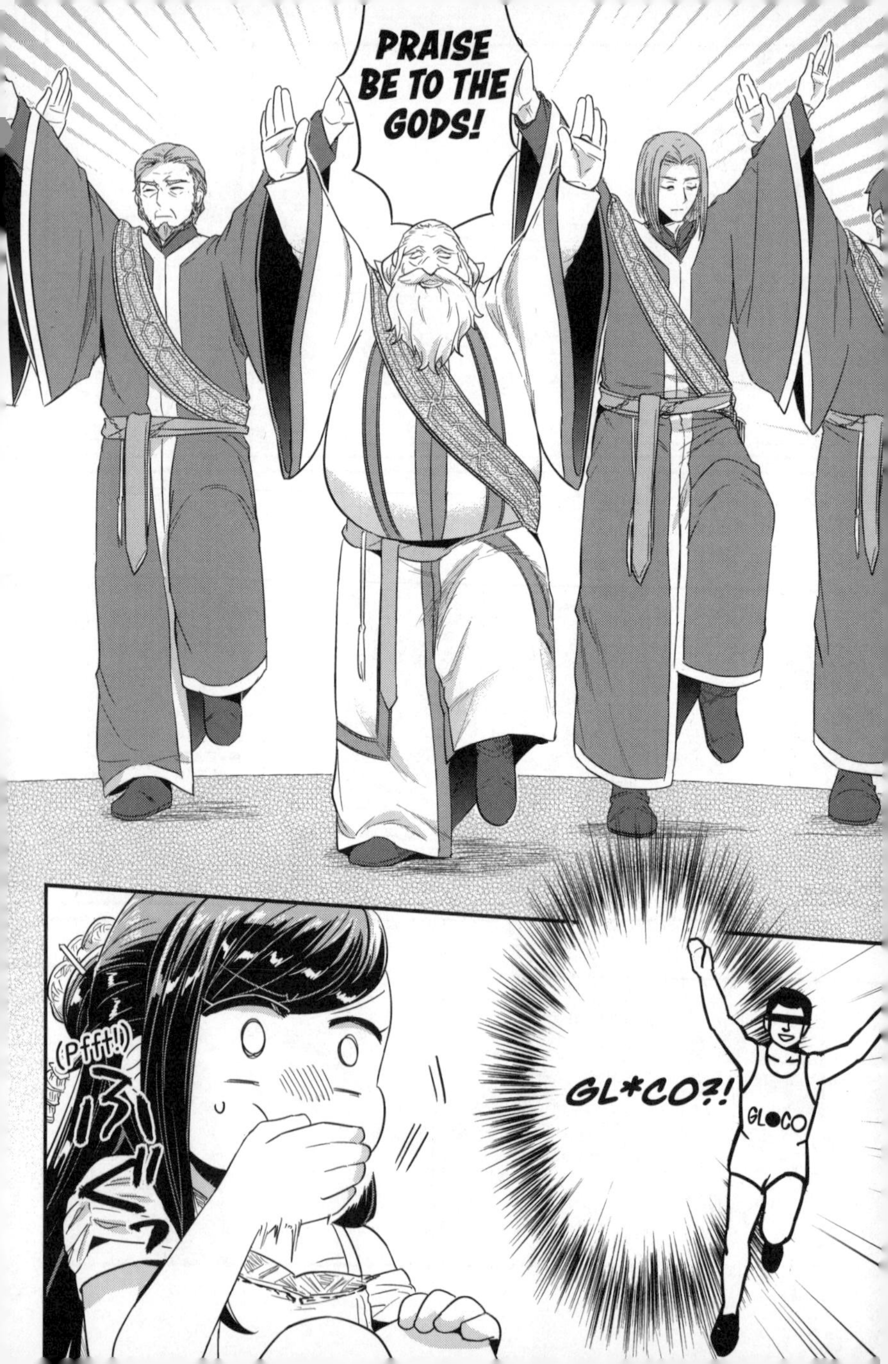
PRAISE BE TO THE GODS!
GL*CO?!
GL●CO
(Pffft!)

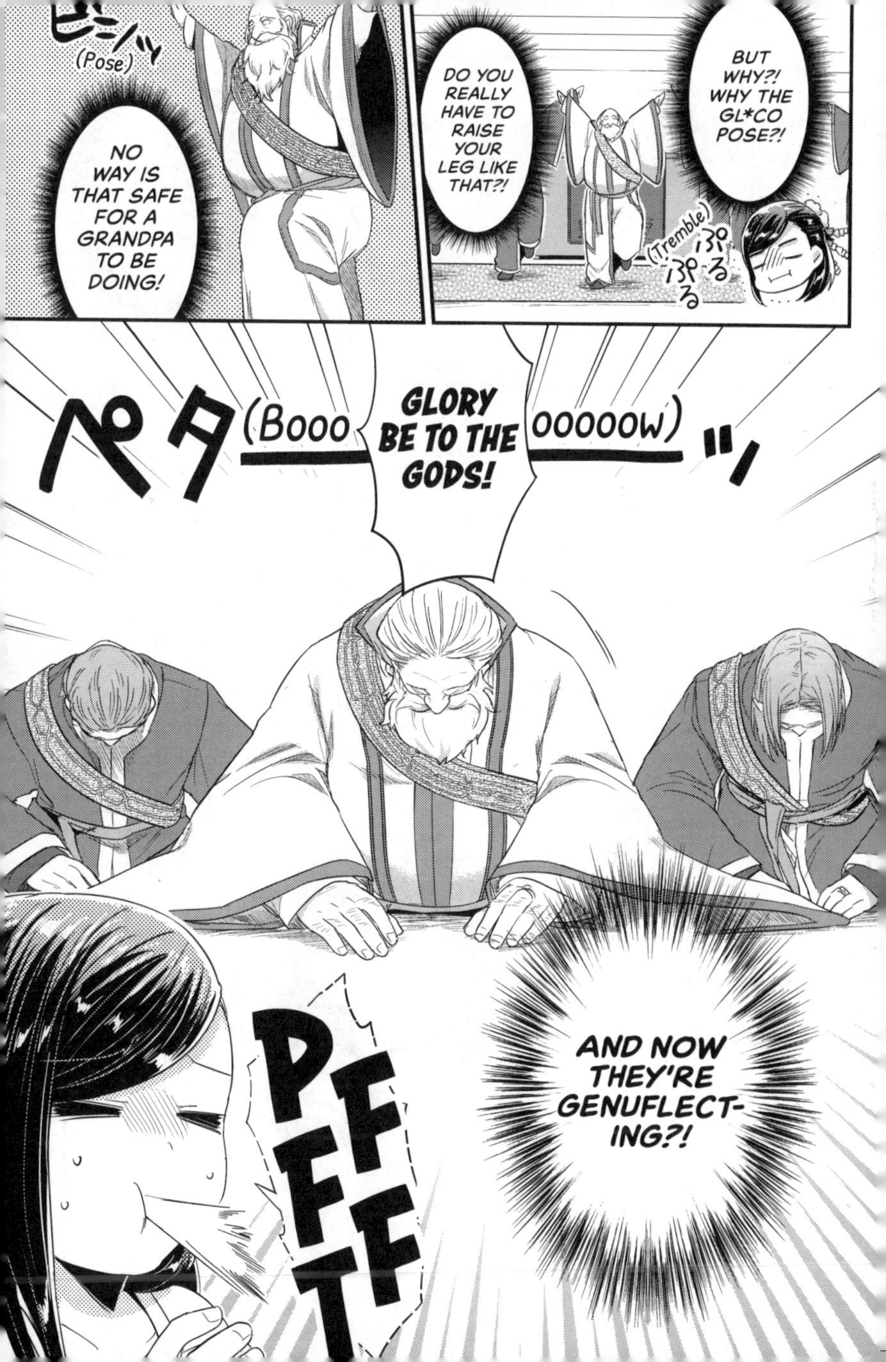
BUT WHY?! WHY THE GL*CO POSE?!
DO YOU REALLY HAVE TO RAISE YOUR LEG LIKE THAT?!
ぷるぷる (Tremble)
ビシッ (Pose)
NO WAY IS THAT SAFE FOR A GRANDPA TO BE DOING!
ペタッ (Boooooooow)
GLORY BE TO THE GODS!
AND NOW THEY'RE GENUFLECT-ING?!
PFFFT

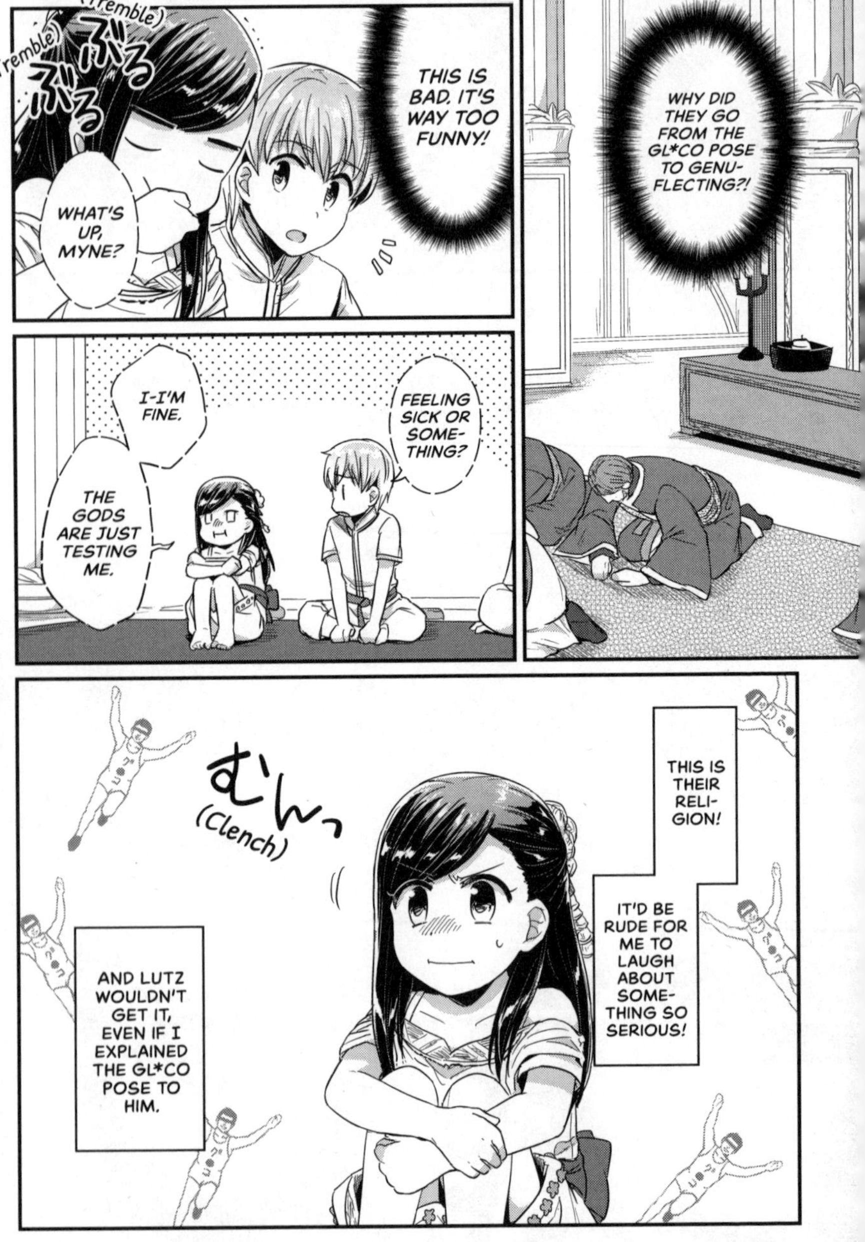
WHY DID THEY GO FROM THE GL*CO POSE TO GENU-FLECTING?!
ぶる ぶる (Tremble) (Tremble)
THIS IS BAD. IT'S WAY TOO FUNNY!
WHAT'S UP, MYNE?
FEELING SICK OR SOME-THING?
I-I'M FINE.
THE GODS ARE JUST TESTING ME.
THIS IS THEIR RELI-GION!
IT'D BE RUDE FOR ME TO LAUGH ABOUT SOME-THING SO SERIOUS!
むんっ (Clench)
AND LUTZ WOULDN'T GET IT, EVEN IF I EXPLAINED THE GL*CO POSE TO HIM.

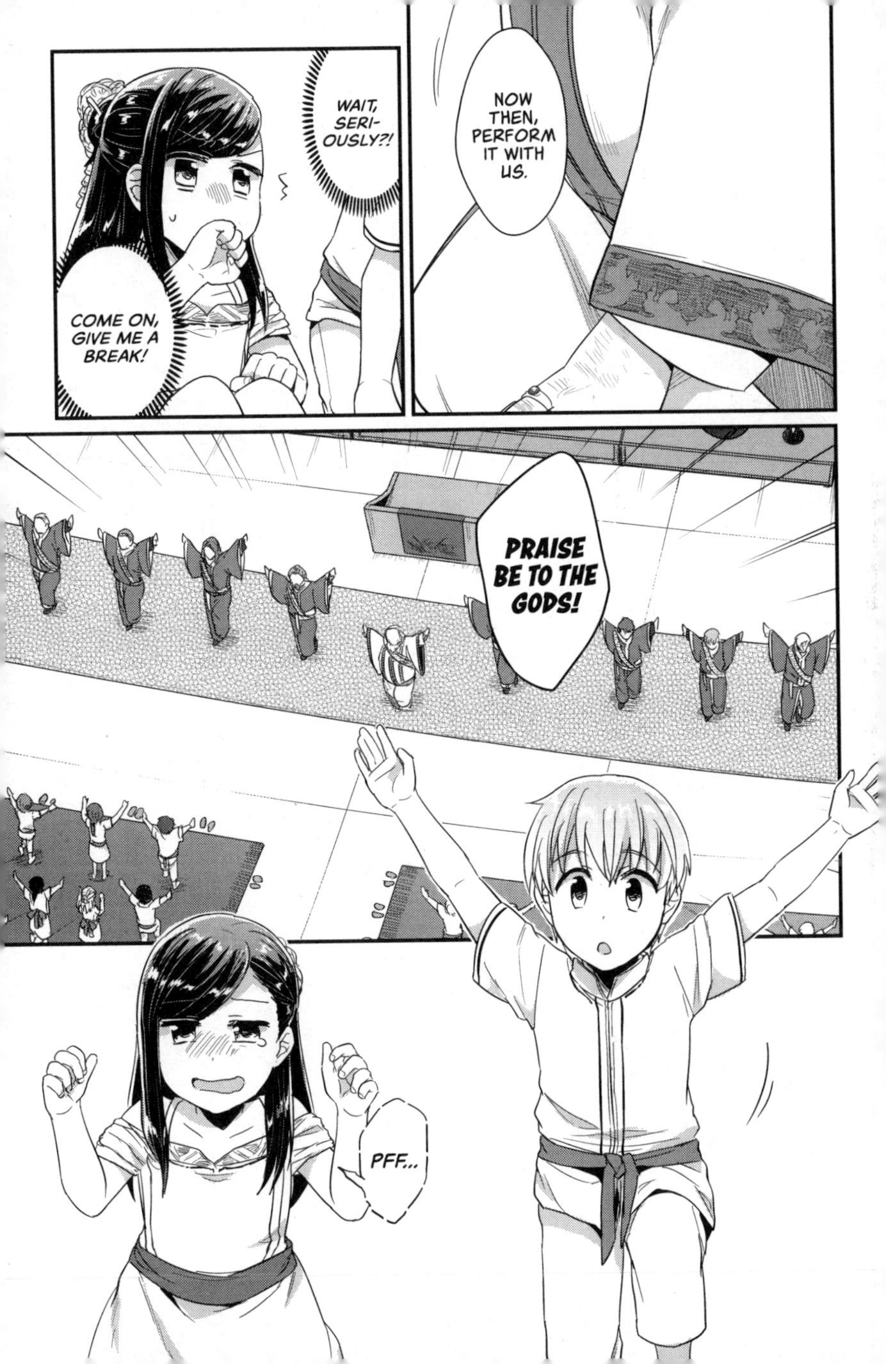
NOW THEN, PERFORM IT WITH US.
WAIT, SERIOUSLY?!
COME ON, GIVE ME A BREAK!
PRAISE BE TO THE GODS!
PFF...

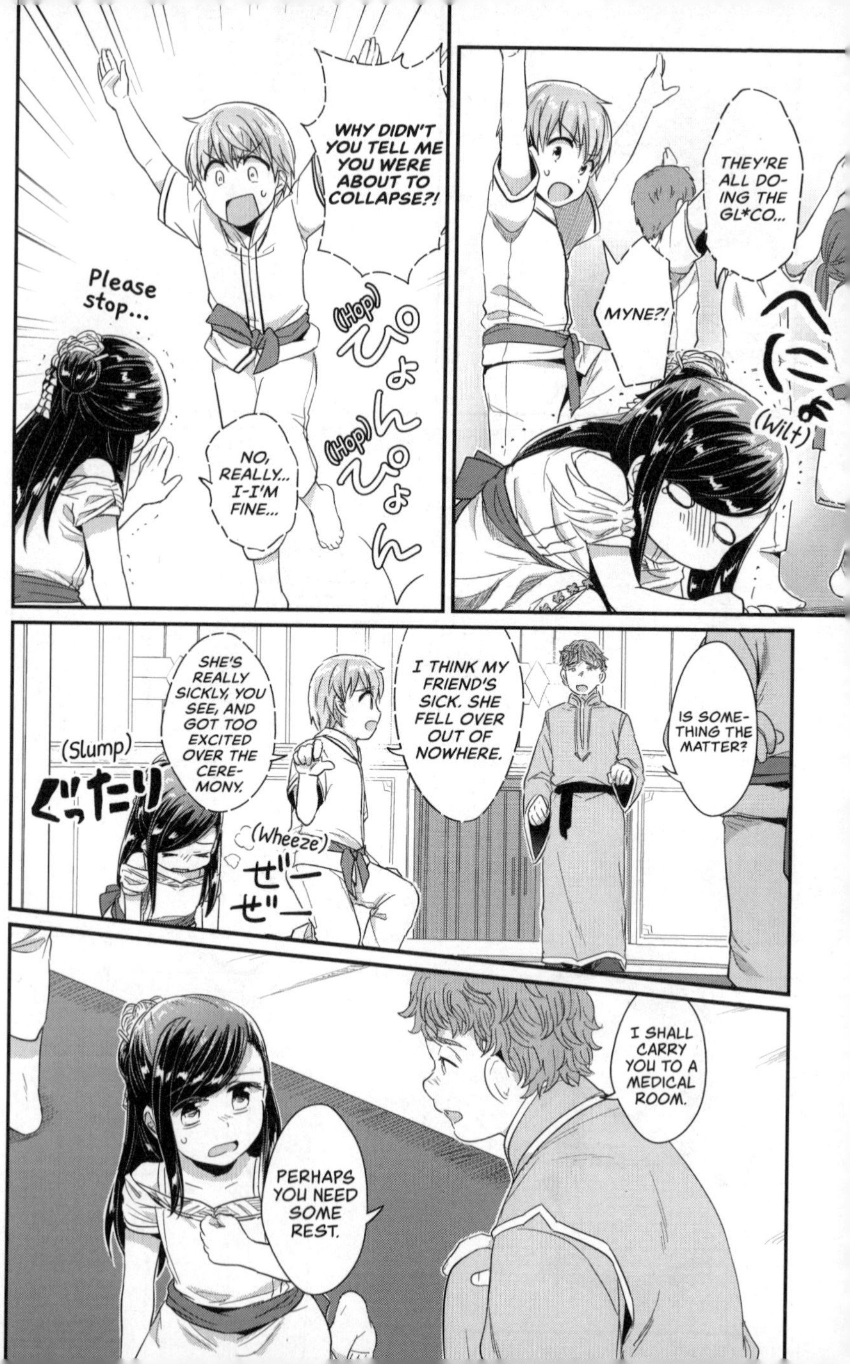
THEY'RE ALL DOING THE GL*CO...
MYNE?!
へにょ
(Wilt)
WHY DIDN'T YOU TELL ME YOU WERE ABOUT TO COLLAPSE?!
ぴょんぴょん
(Hop)
(Hop)
Please stop...
NO, REALLY... I-I'M FINE...
IS SOMETHING THE MATTER?
I THINK MY FRIEND'S SICK. SHE FELL OVER OUT OF NOWHERE.
SHE'S REALLY SICKLY, YOU SEE, AND GOT TOO EXCITED OVER THE CEREMONY.
(Slump)
ぐったり
(Wheeze)
ゼーゼー
I SHALL CARRY YOU TO A MEDICAL ROOM.
PERHAPS YOU NEED SOME REST.

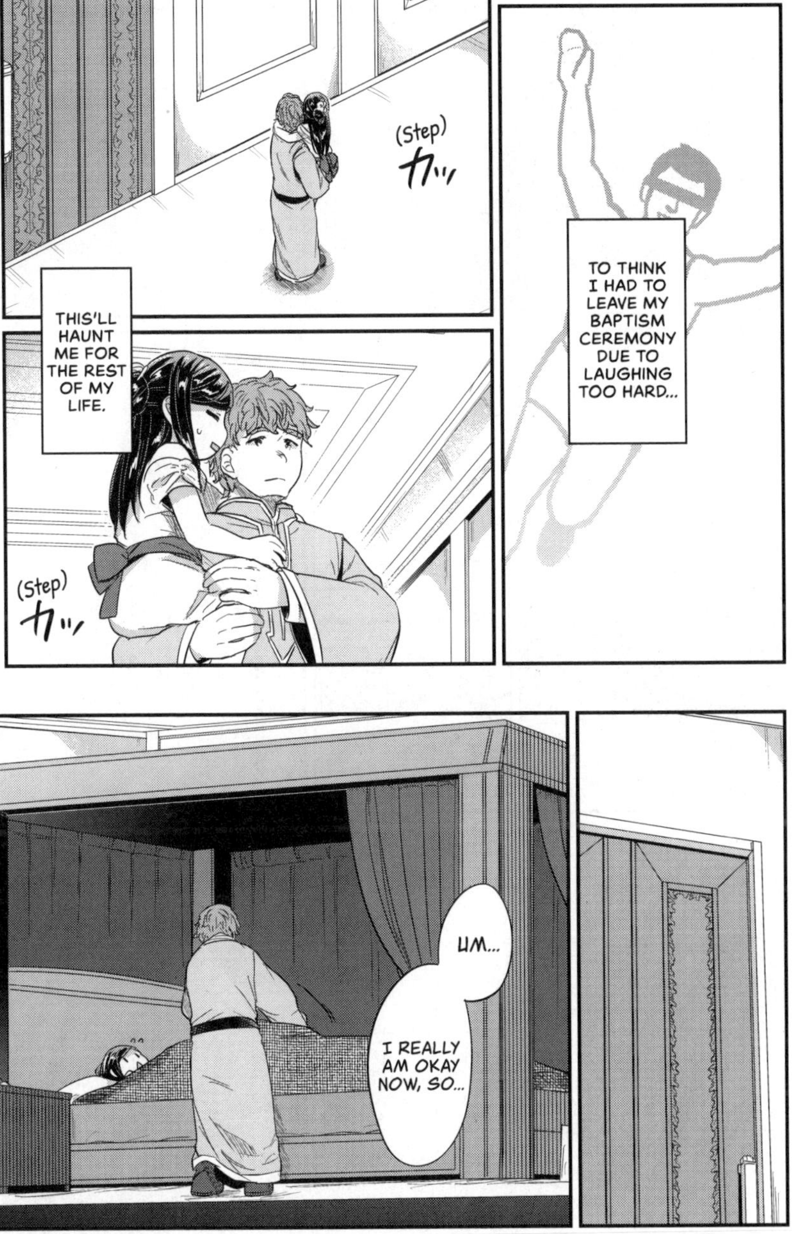
TO THINK I HAD TO LEAVE MY BAPTISM CEREMONY DUE TO LAUGHING TOO HARD...
(Step)
カッ
THIS'LL HAUNT ME FOR THE REST OF MY LIFE.
(Step)
カッ
UM...
I REALLY AM OKAY NOW, SO...

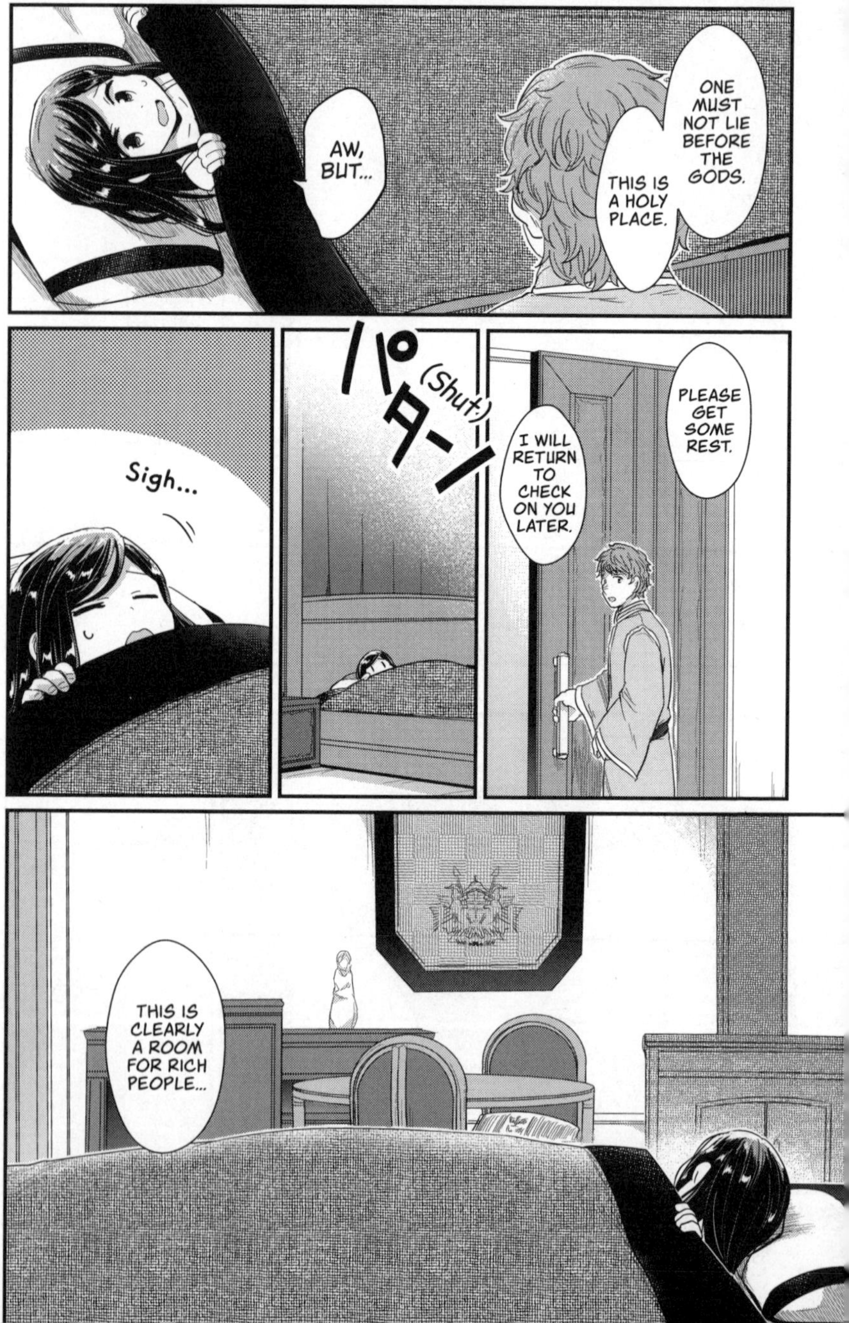
ONE MUST NOT LIE BEFORE THE GODS.
THIS IS A HOLY PLACE.
AW, BUT...
PLEASE GET SOME REST.
I WILL RETURN TO CHECK ON YOU LATER.
パターン
(Shut)
Sigh...
THIS IS CLEARLY A ROOM FOR RICH PEOPLE...

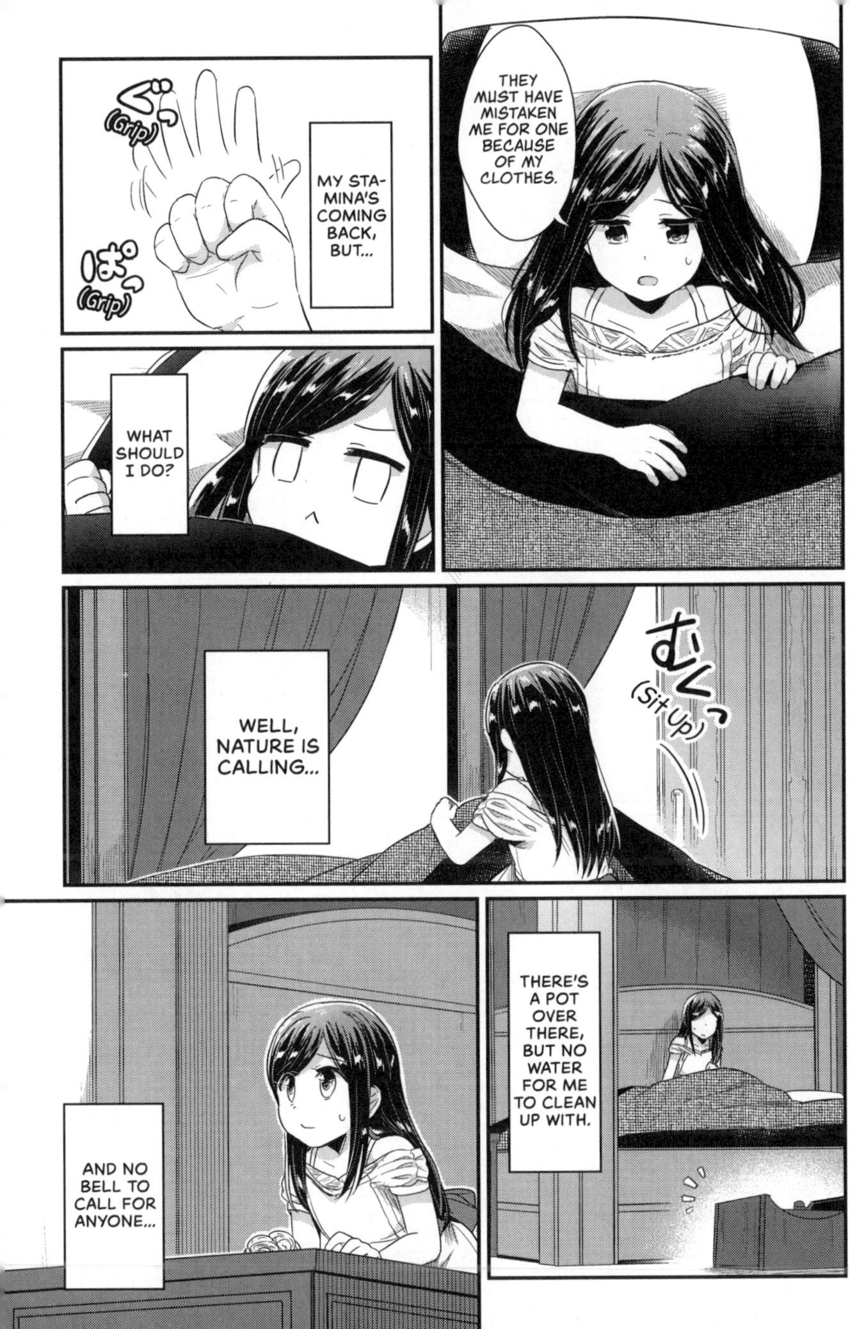
THEY MUST HAVE MISTAKEN ME FOR ONE BECAUSE OF MY CLOTHES.
(Grip)
(Grip)
MY STA-MINA'S COMING BACK, BUT...
WHAT SHOULD I DO?
(Sit Up)
WELL, NATURE IS CALLING...
THERE'S A POT OVER THERE, BUT NO WATER FOR ME TO CLEAN UP WITH.
AND NO BELL TO CALL FOR ANYONE...

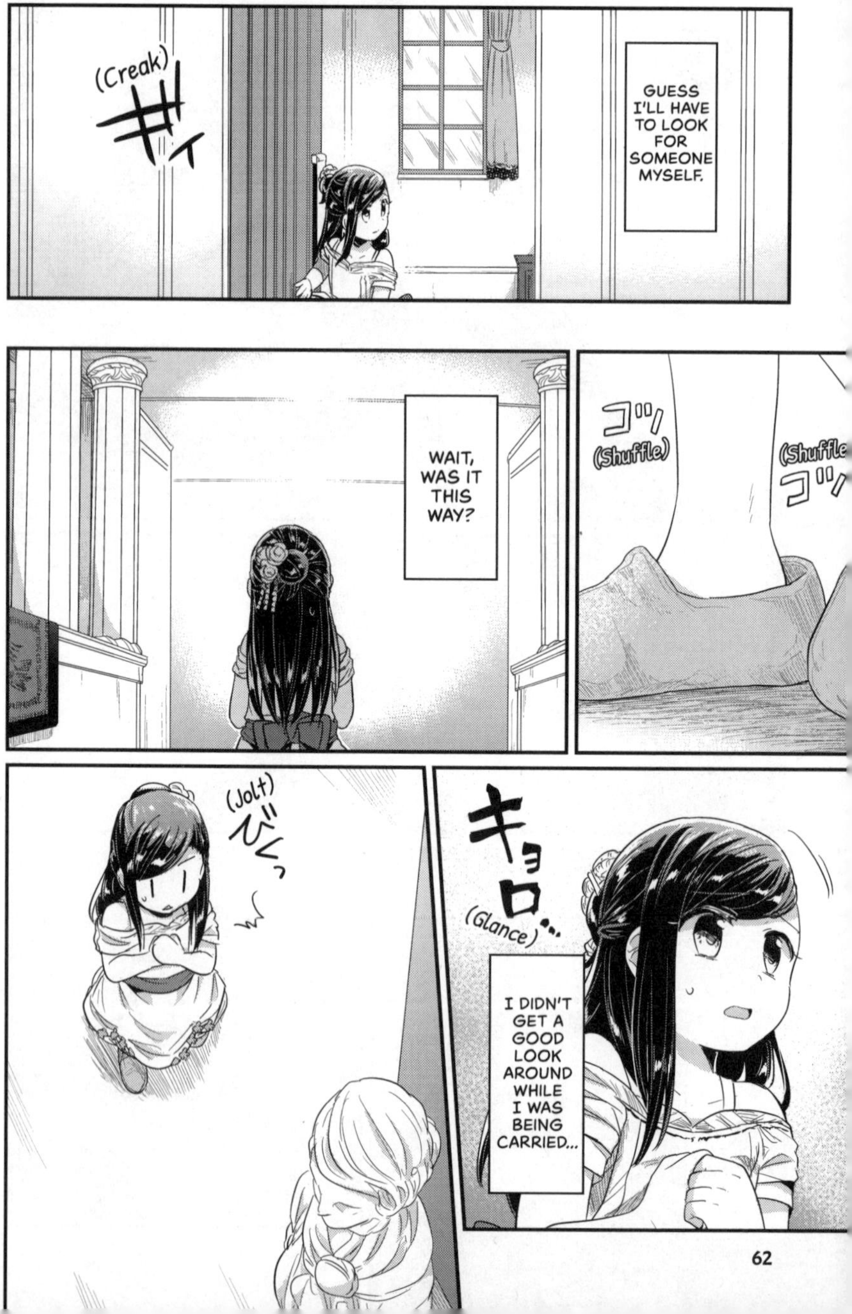
GUESS I'LL HAVE TO LOOK FOR SOMEONE MYSELF.
ギィ
(Creak)
(Shuffle
コツ
コツ
(Shuffle)
WAIT, WAS IT THIS WAY?
キョロ
(Glance)
I DIDN'T GET A GOOD LOOK AROUND WHILE I WAS BEING CARRIED...
びくっ
(Jolt)

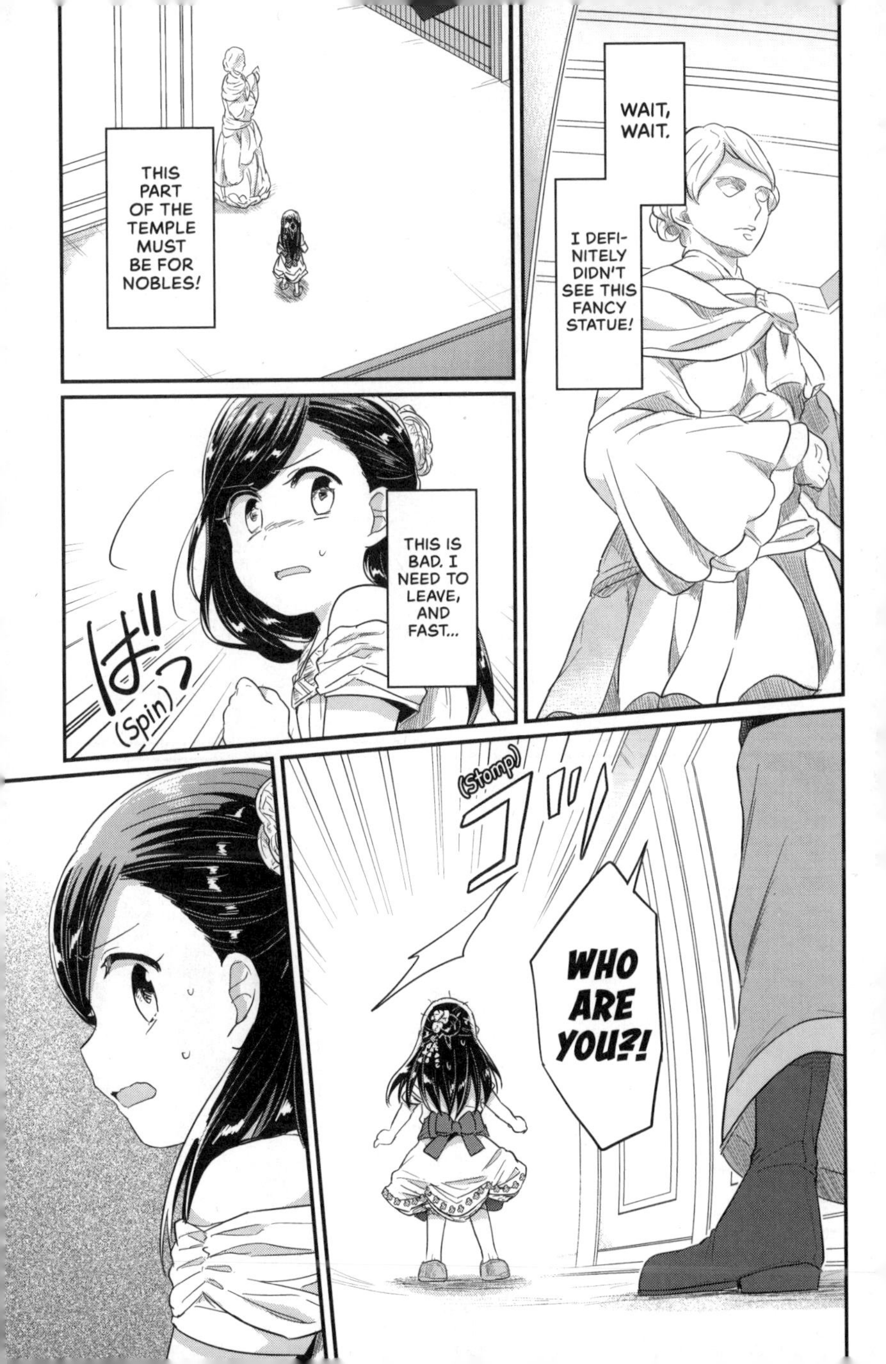
WAIT, WAIT.
I DEFINITELY DIDN'T SEE THIS FANCY STATUE!
THIS PART OF THE TEMPLE MUST BE FOR NOBLES!
THIS IS BAD. I NEED TO LEAVE, AND FAST...
ばっ
(Spin)
(Stomp)
ゴッ
WHO ARE YOU?!

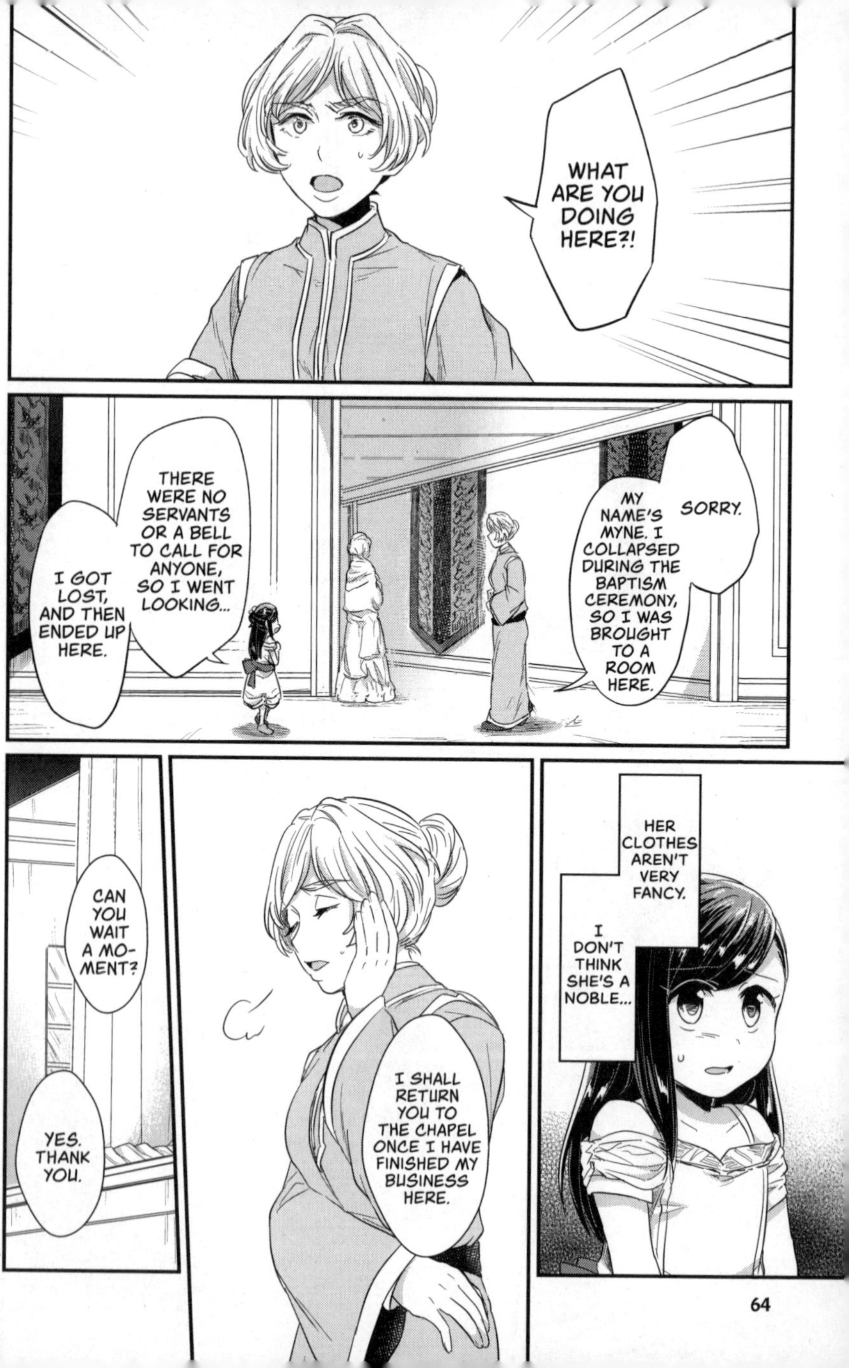
WHAT ARE YOU DOING HERE?!
SORRY.
MY NAME'S MYNE. I COLLAPSED DURING THE BAPTISM CEREMONY, SO I WAS BROUGHT TO A ROOM HERE.
THERE WERE NO SERVANTS OR A BELL TO CALL FOR ANYONE, SO I WENT LOOKING...
I GOT LOST, AND THEN ENDED UP HERE.
HER CLOTHES AREN'T VERY FANCY.
I DON'T THINK SHE'S A NOBLE...
I SHALL RETURN YOU TO THE CHAPEL ONCE I HAVE FINISHED MY BUSINESS HERE.
CAN YOU WAIT A MO-MENT?
YES. THANK YOU.

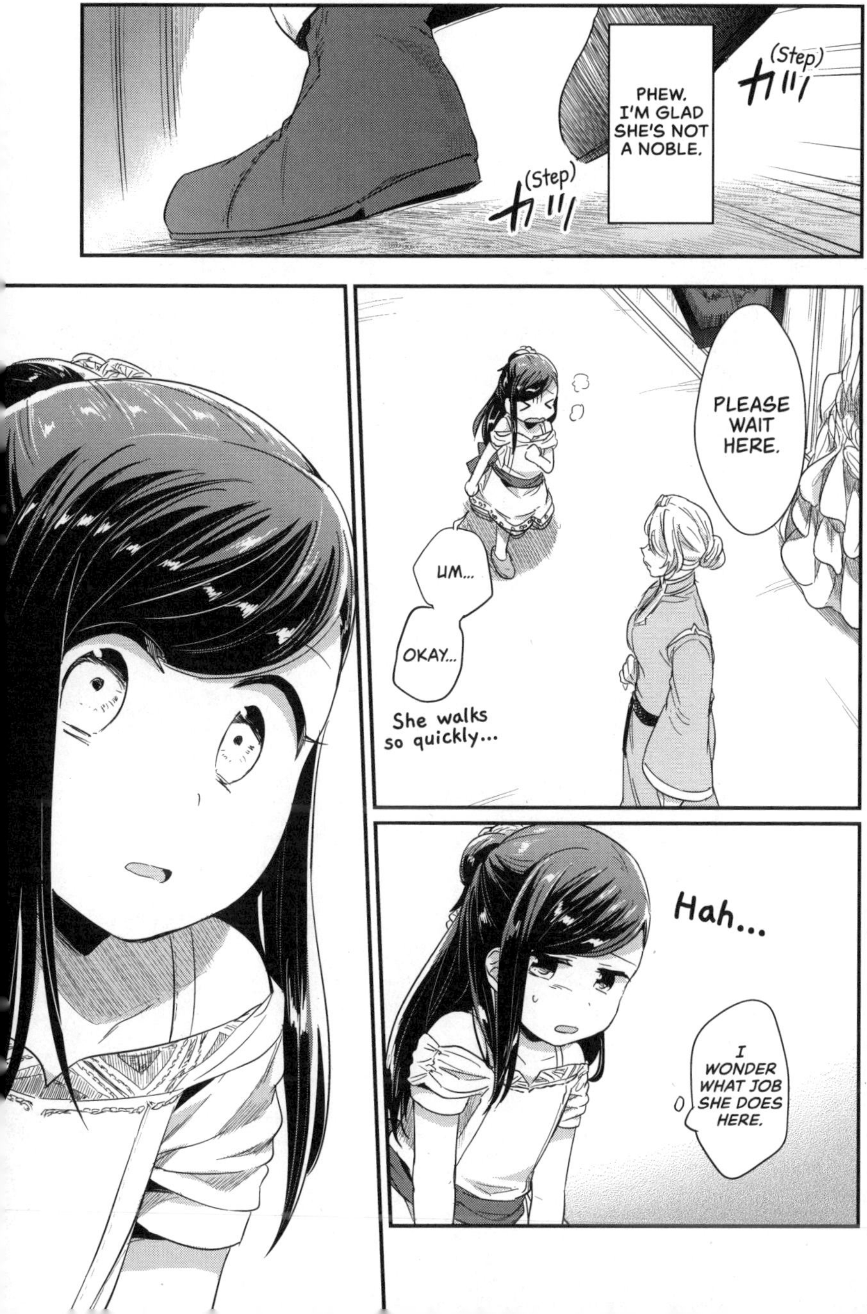
(Step)
PHEW. I'M GLAD SHE'S NOT A NOBLE.
(Step)
PLEASE WAIT HERE.
UM...
OKAY...
She walks so quickly...
Hah...
I WONDER WHAT JOB SHE DOES HERE.

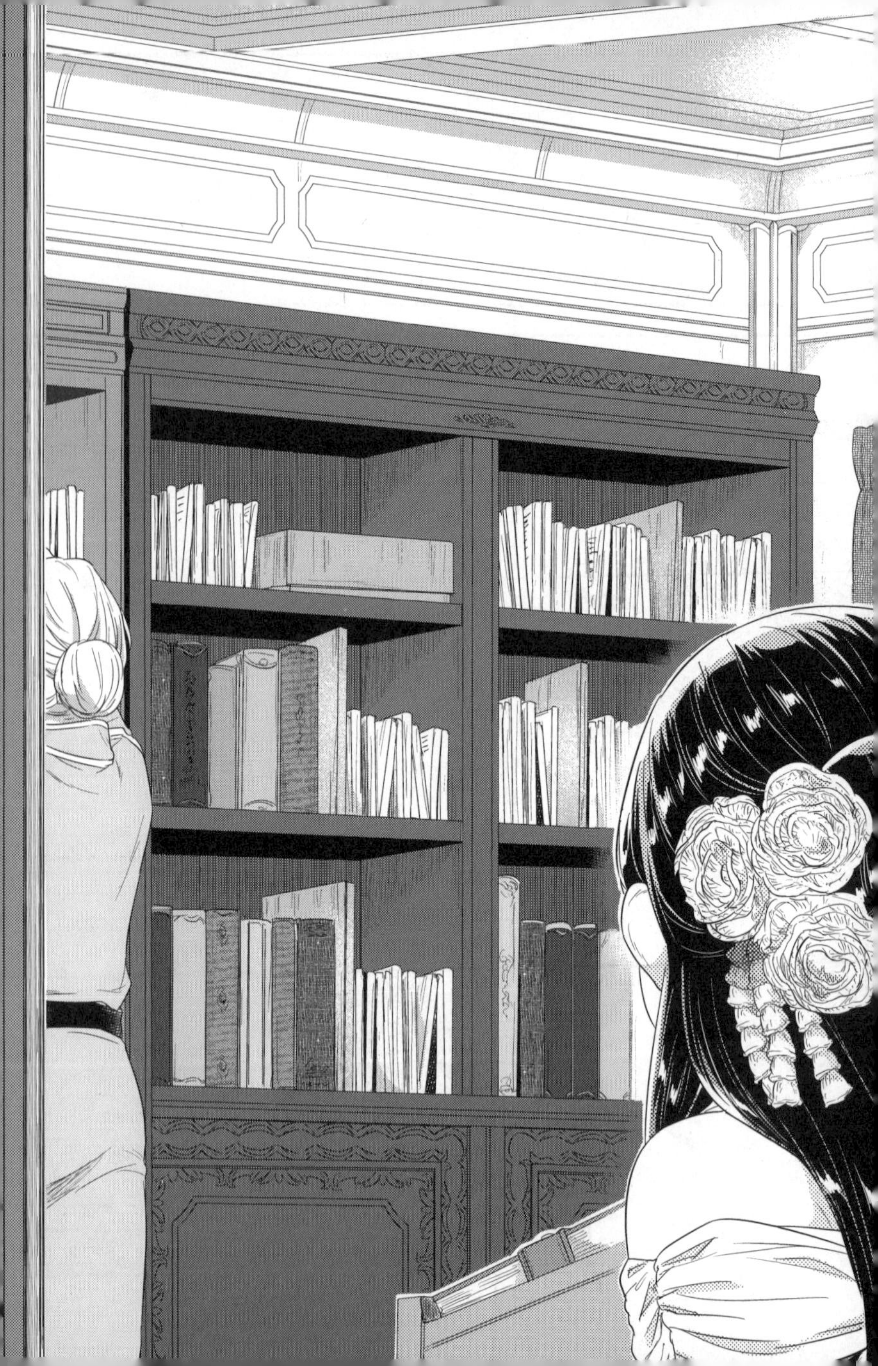

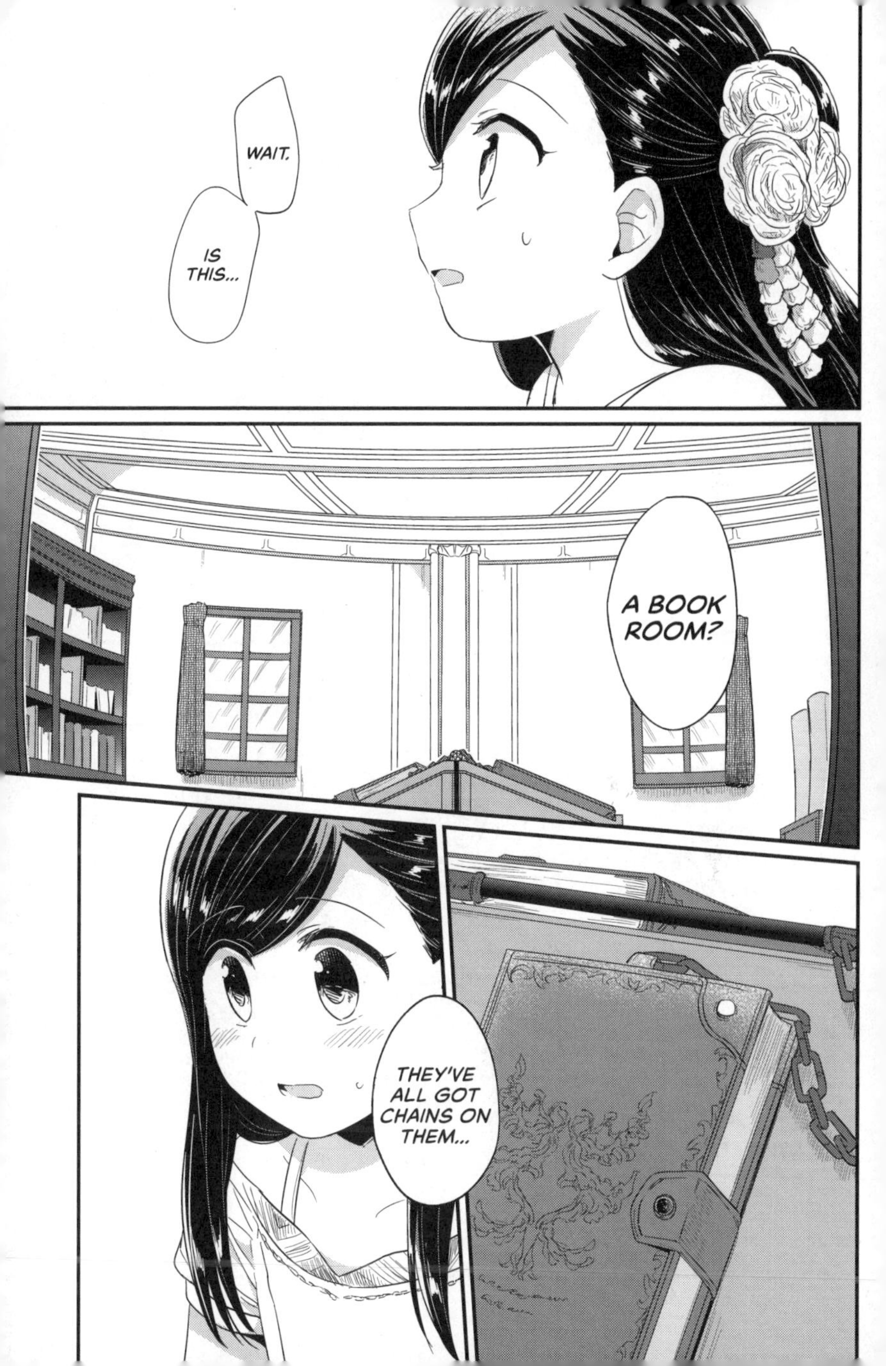
WAIT.
IS THIS...
A BOOK ROOM?
THEY'VE ALL GOT CHAINS ON THEM...

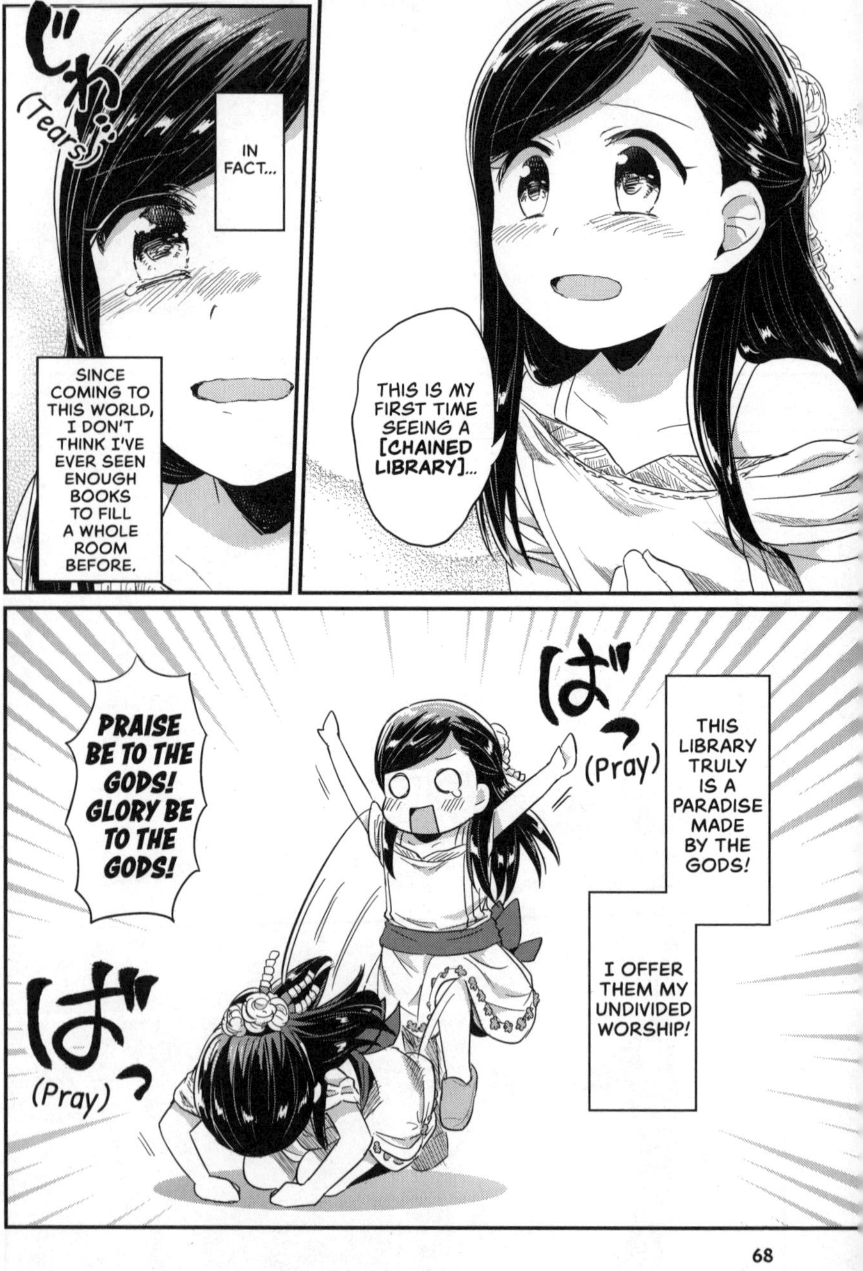
THIS IS MY FIRST TIME SEEING A [CHAINED LIBRARY]...
じわ
(Tears)
IN FACT...
SINCE COMING TO THIS WORLD, I DON'T THINK I'VE EVER SEEN ENOUGH BOOKS TO FILL A WHOLE ROOM BEFORE.
ばっ
(Pray)
THIS LIBRARY TRULY IS A PARADISE MADE BY THE GODS!
I OFFER THEM MY UNDIVIDED WORSHIP!
PRAISE BE TO THE GODS! GLORY BE TO THE GODS!
ばっ
(Pray)

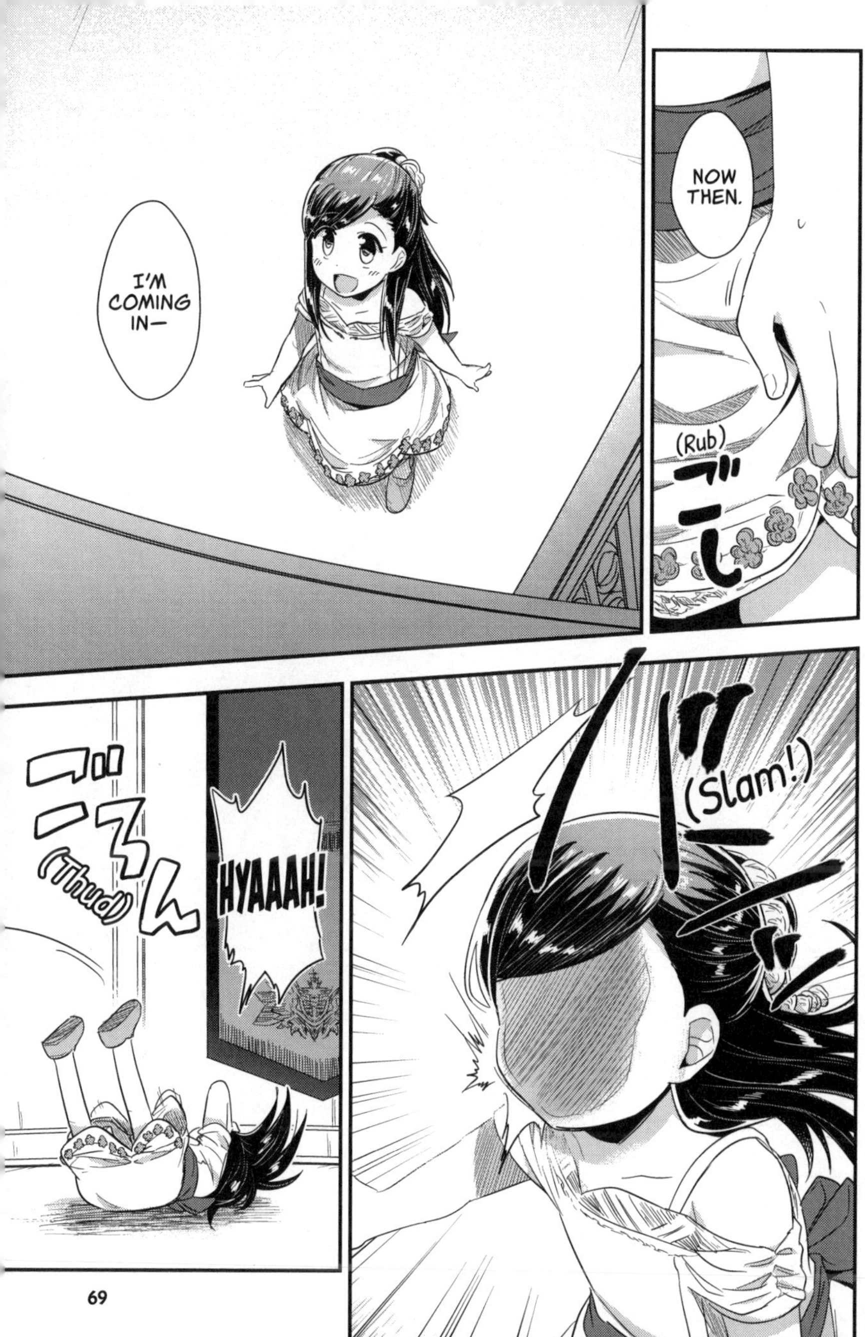
NOW THEN.
(Rub)
I'M COMING IN—
(Slam!)
HYAAAH!
(Thud)

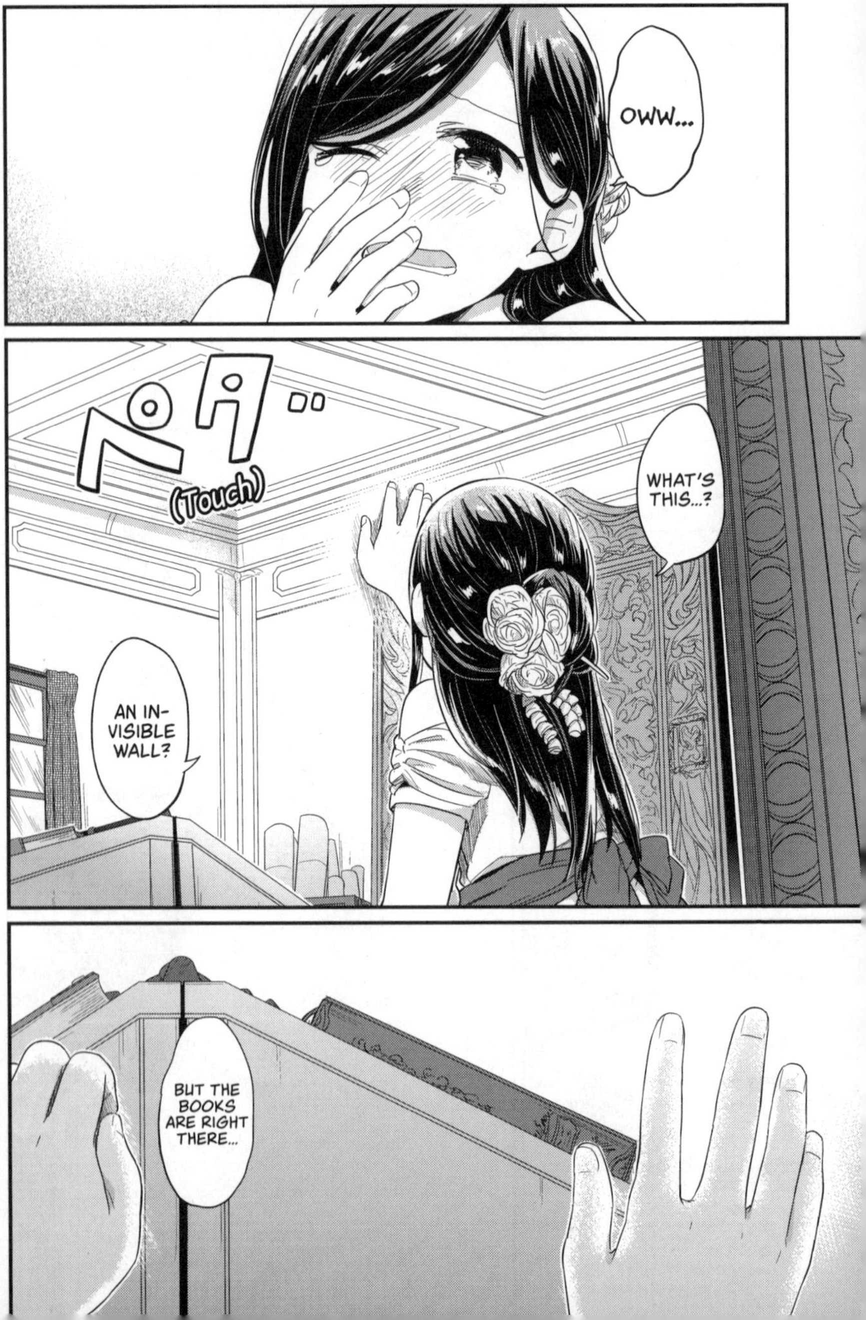
OWW...
ペタ
(Touch)
WHAT'S THIS...?
AN IN-VISIBLE WALL?
BUT THE BOOKS ARE RIGHT THERE...

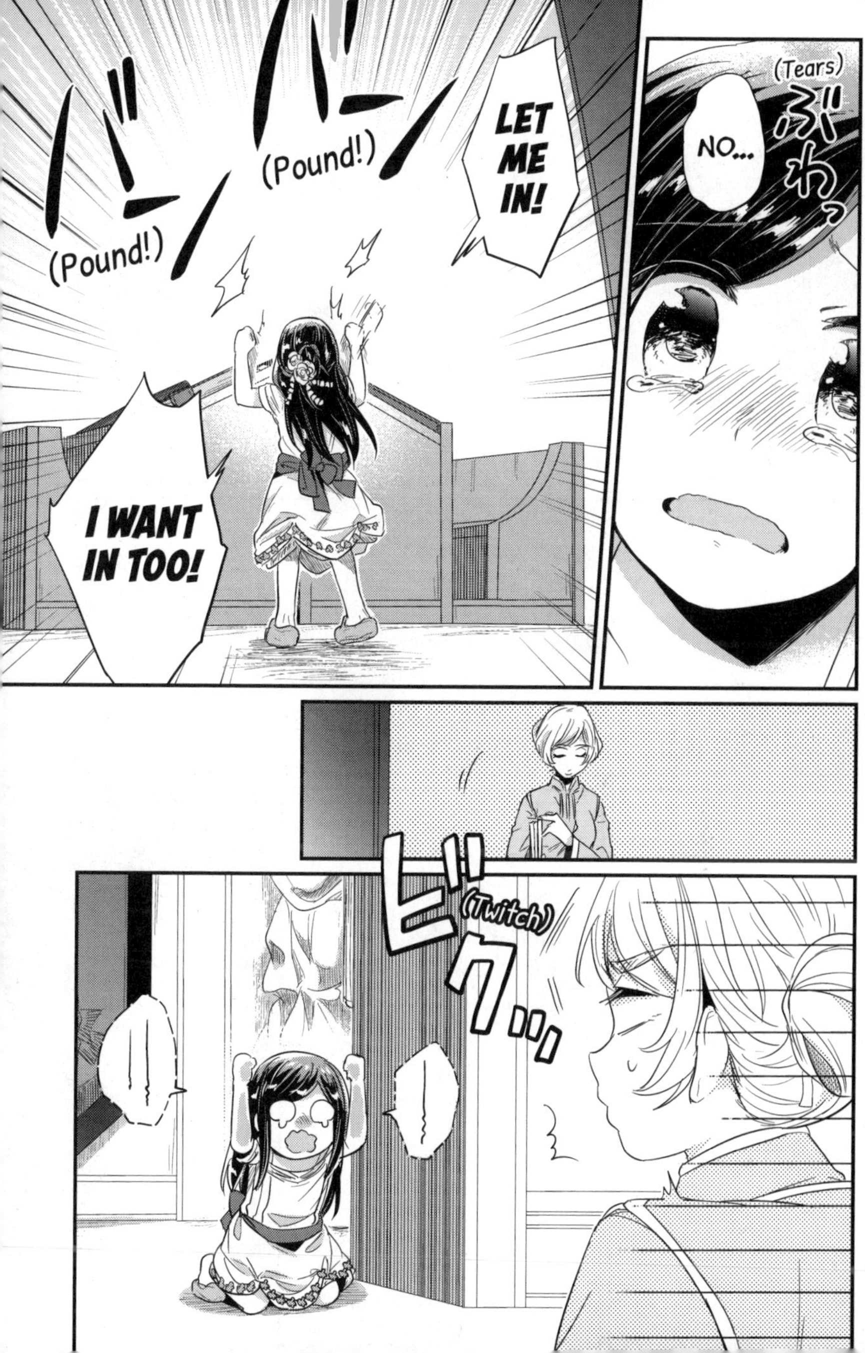

(Tears)
ぶわっ
NO...
LET ME IN!
(Pound!)
(Pound!)
I WANT IN TOO!
ビクッ
(Twitch)

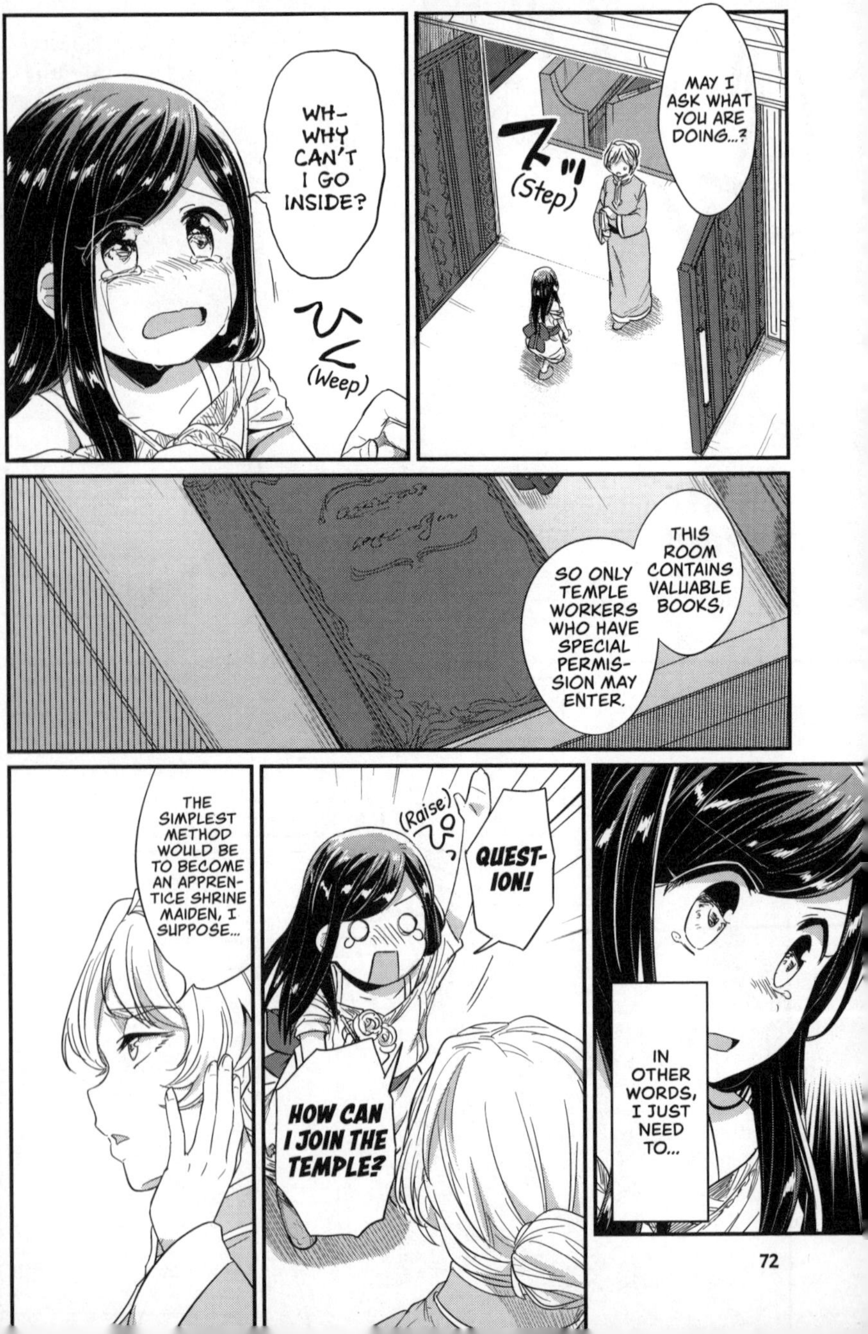
MAY I ASK WHAT YOU ARE DOING...?
ズッ
(Step)
WH-WHY CAN'T I GO INSIDE?
ひく
(Weep)
THIS ROOM CONTAINS VALUABLE BOOKS,
SO ONLY TEMPLE WORKERS WHO HAVE SPECIAL PERMISSION MAY ENTER.
IN OTHER WORDS, I JUST NEED TO...
QUESTION!
ぴっ
(Raise)
HOW CAN I JOIN THE TEMPLE?
THE SIMPLEST METHOD WOULD BE TO BECOME AN APPRENTICE SHRINE MAIDEN, I SUPPOSE...

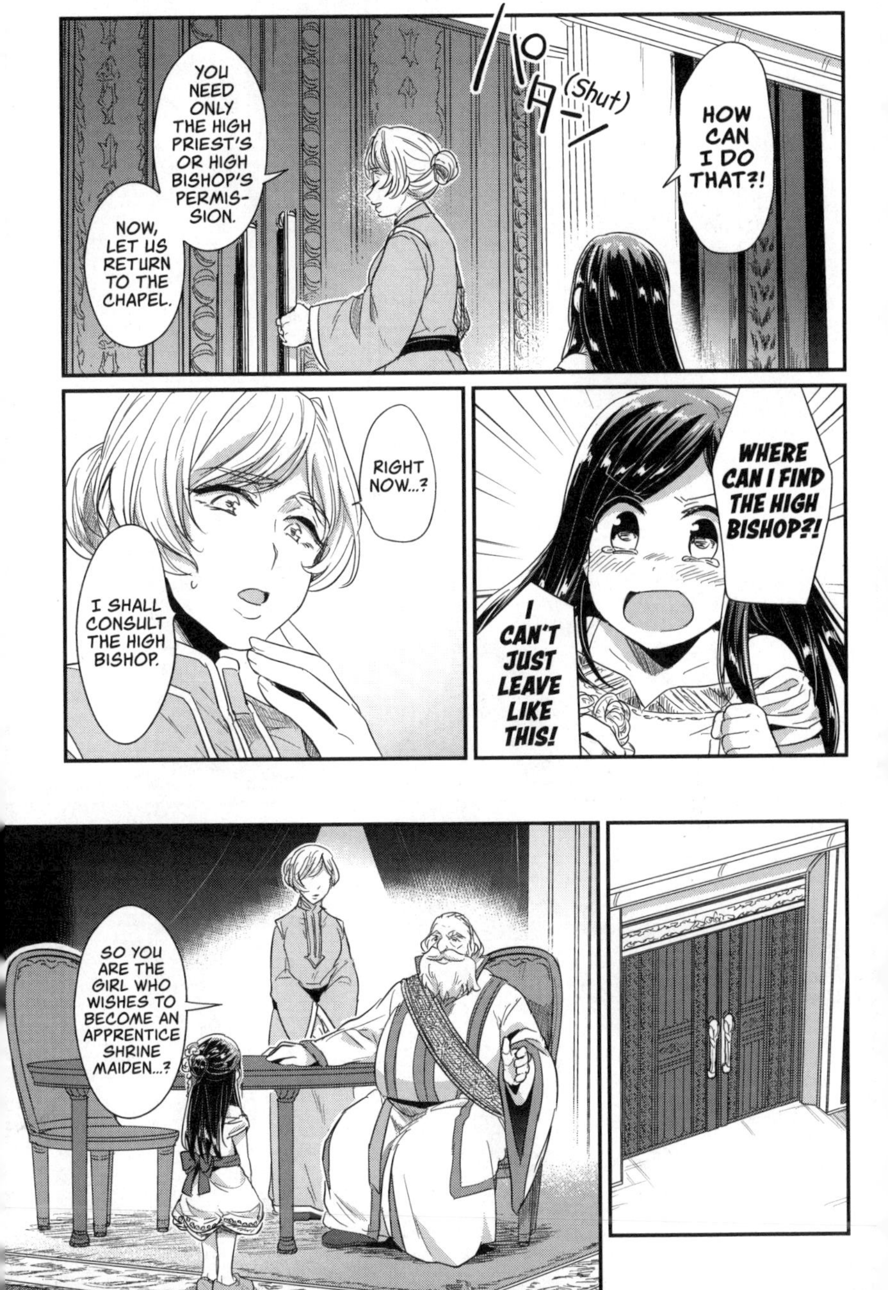
(Shut)
HOW CAN I DO THAT?!
YOU NEED ONLY THE HIGH PRIEST'S OR HIGH BISHOP'S PERMISSION.
NOW, LET US RETURN TO THE CHAPEL.
WHERE CAN I FIND THE HIGH BISHOP?!
I CAN'T JUST LEAVE LIKE THIS!
RIGHT NOW...?
I SHALL CONSULT THE HIGH BISHOP.
SO YOU ARE THE GIRL WHO WISHES TO BECOME AN APPRENTICE SHRINE MAIDEN...?

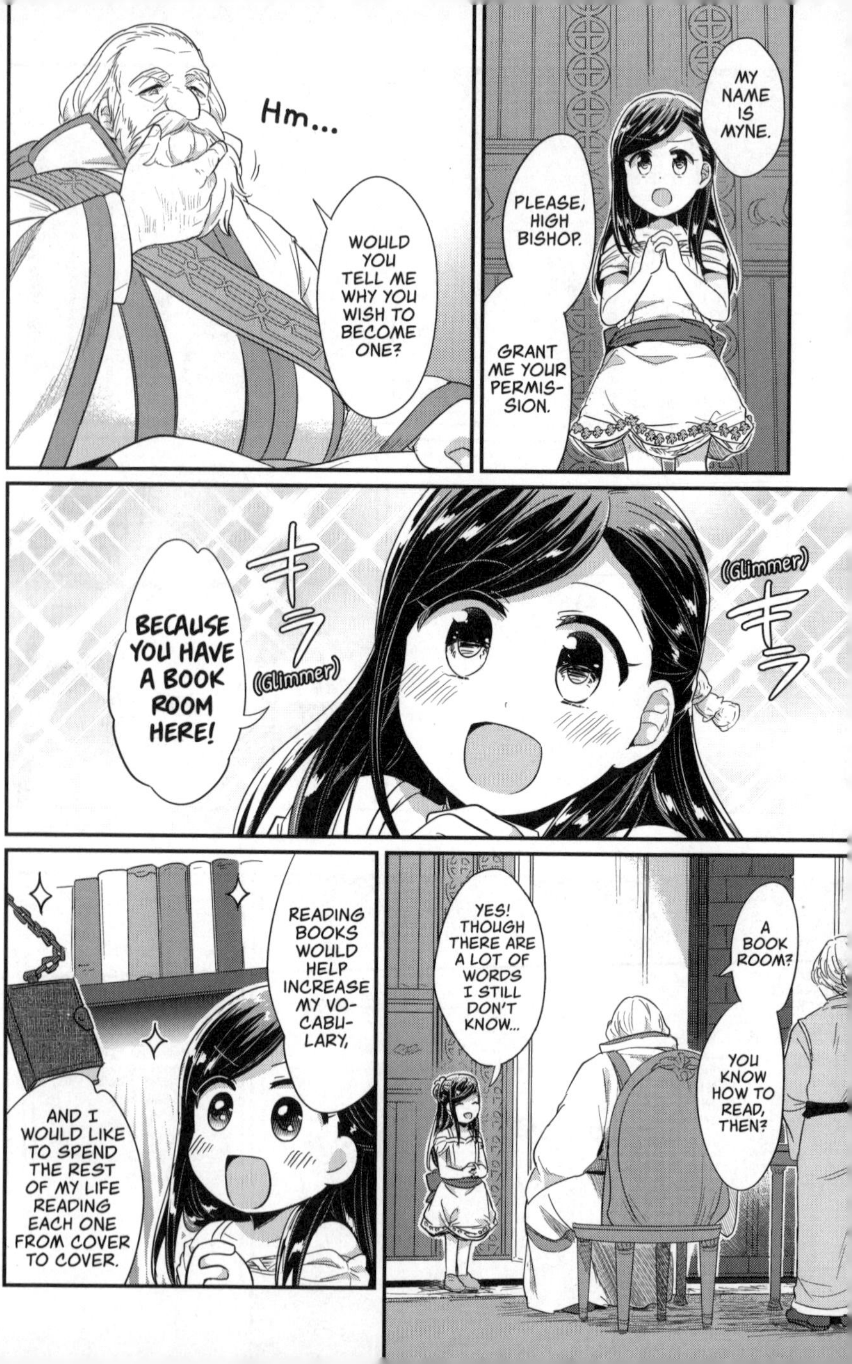
MY NAME IS MYNE.
PLEASE, HIGH BISHOP.
GRANT ME YOUR PERMISSION.
Hm...
WOULD YOU TELL ME WHY YOU WISH TO BECOME ONE?
キラ
(Glimmer)
BECAUSE YOU HAVE A BOOK ROOM HERE!
キラ
(Glimmer)
A BOOK ROOM?
YOU KNOW HOW TO READ, THEN?
YES! THOUGH THERE ARE A LOT OF WORDS I STILL DON'T KNOW...
READING BOOKS WOULD HELP INCREASE MY VOCABULARY,
AND I WOULD LIKE TO SPEND THE REST OF MY LIFE READING EACH ONE FROM COVER TO COVER.

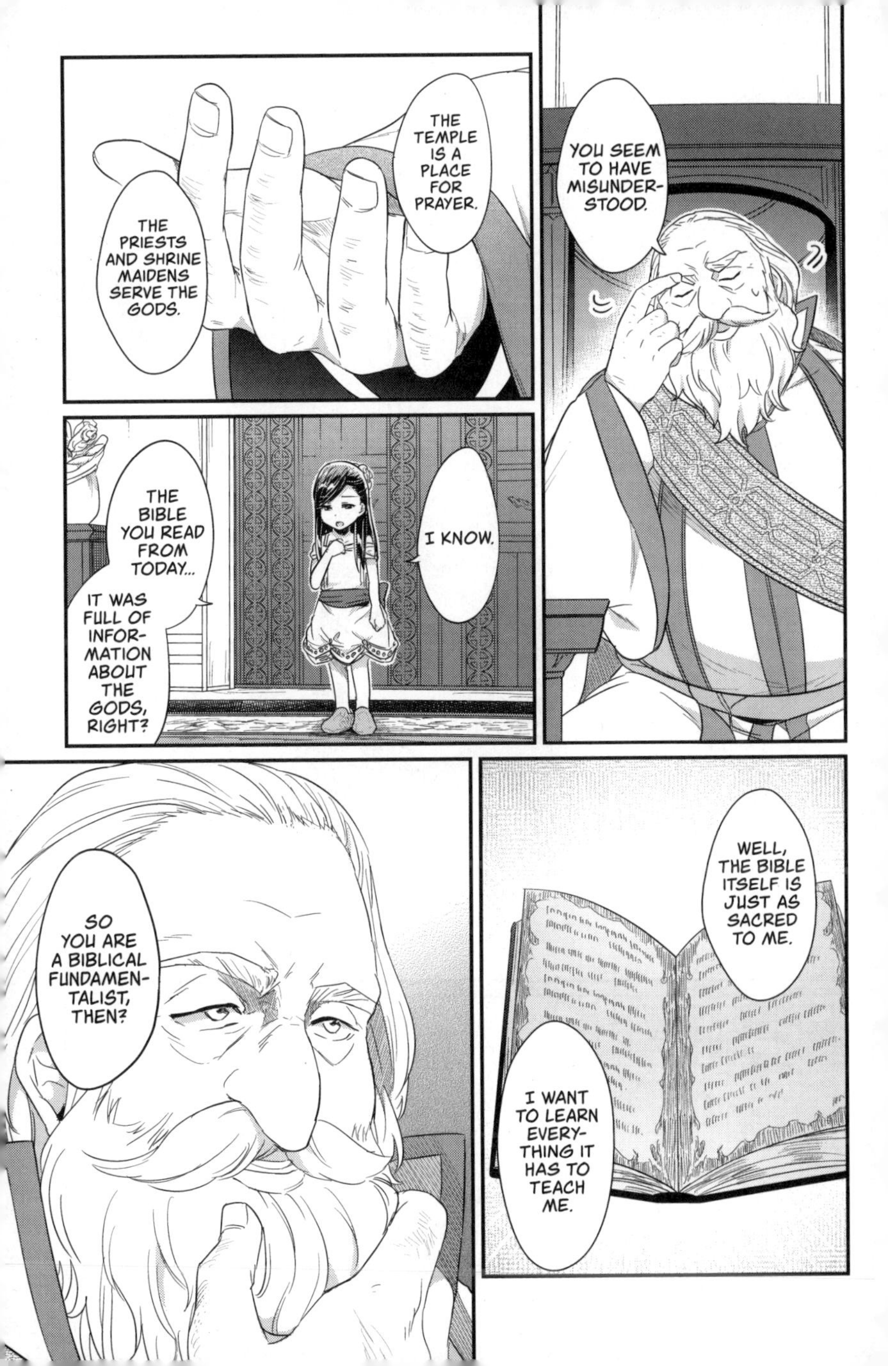
YOU SEEM TO HAVE MISUNDER-STOOD.
THE TEMPLE IS A PLACE FOR PRAYER.
THE PRIESTS AND SHRINE MAIDENS SERVE THE GODS.
I KNOW.
THE BIBLE YOU READ FROM TODAY...
IT WAS FULL OF INFOR-MATION ABOUT THE GODS, RIGHT?
WELL, THE BIBLE ITSELF IS JUST AS SACRED TO ME.
I WANT TO LEARN EVERY-THING IT HAS TO TEACH ME.
SO YOU ARE A BIBLICAL FUNDAMEN-TALIST, THEN?

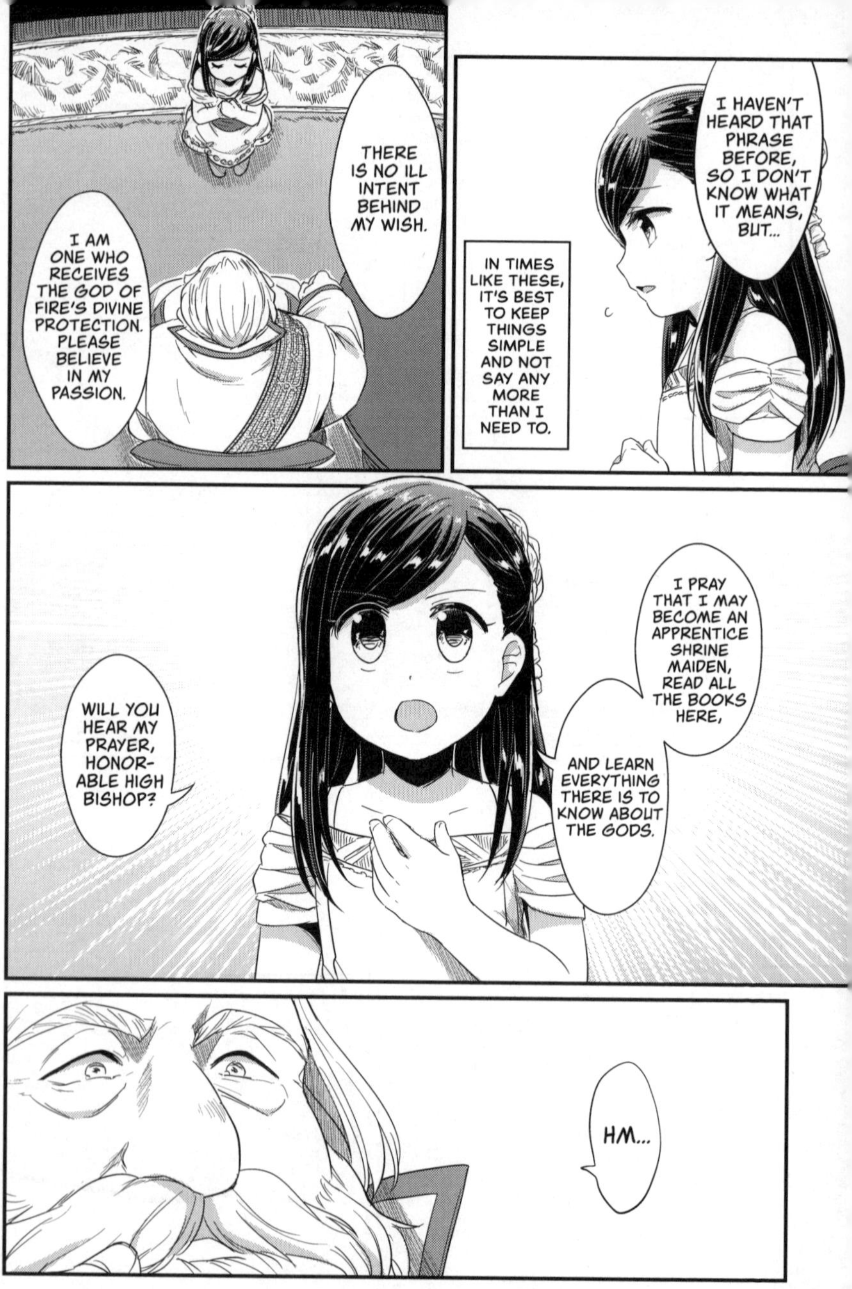
I HAVEN'T HEARD THAT PHRASE BEFORE, SO I DON'T KNOW WHAT IT MEANS, BUT...
IN TIMES LIKE THESE, IT'S BEST TO KEEP THINGS SIMPLE AND NOT SAY ANY MORE THAN I NEED TO.
THERE IS NO ILL INTENT BEHIND MY WISH.
I AM ONE WHO RECEIVES THE GOD OF FIRE'S DIVINE PROTECTION. PLEASE BELIEVE IN MY PASSION.
I PRAY THAT I MAY BECOME AN APPRENTICE SHRINE MAIDEN, READ ALL THE BOOKS HERE,
AND LEARN EVERYTHING THERE IS TO KNOW ABOUT THE GODS.
WILL YOU HEAR MY PRAYER, HONORABLE HIGH BISHOP?
HM...

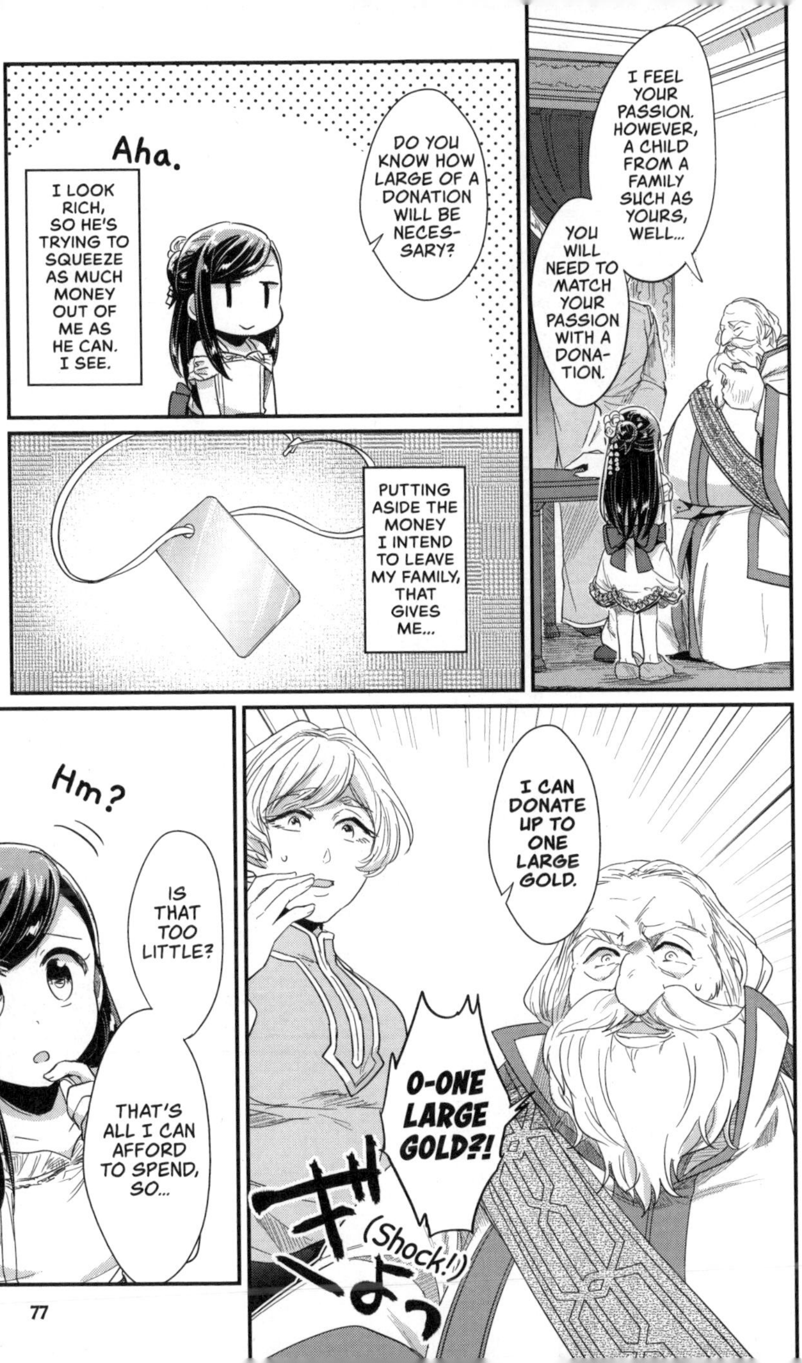
I FEEL YOUR PASSION. HOWEVER, A CHILD FROM A FAMILY SUCH AS YOURS, WELL...
YOU WILL NEED TO MATCH YOUR PASSION WITH A DONATION.
DO YOU KNOW HOW LARGE OF A DONATION WILL BE NECESSARY?
Aha.
I LOOK RICH, SO HE'S TRYING TO SQUEEZE AS MUCH MONEY OUT OF ME AS HE CAN. I SEE.
PUTTING ASIDE THE MONEY I INTEND TO LEAVE MY FAMILY, THAT GIVES ME...
I CAN DONATE UP TO ONE LARGE GOLD.
O-ONE LARGE GOLD?!
(Shock!)
Hm?
IS THAT TOO LITTLE?
THAT'S ALL I CAN AFFORD TO SPEND, SO...

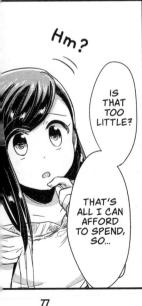

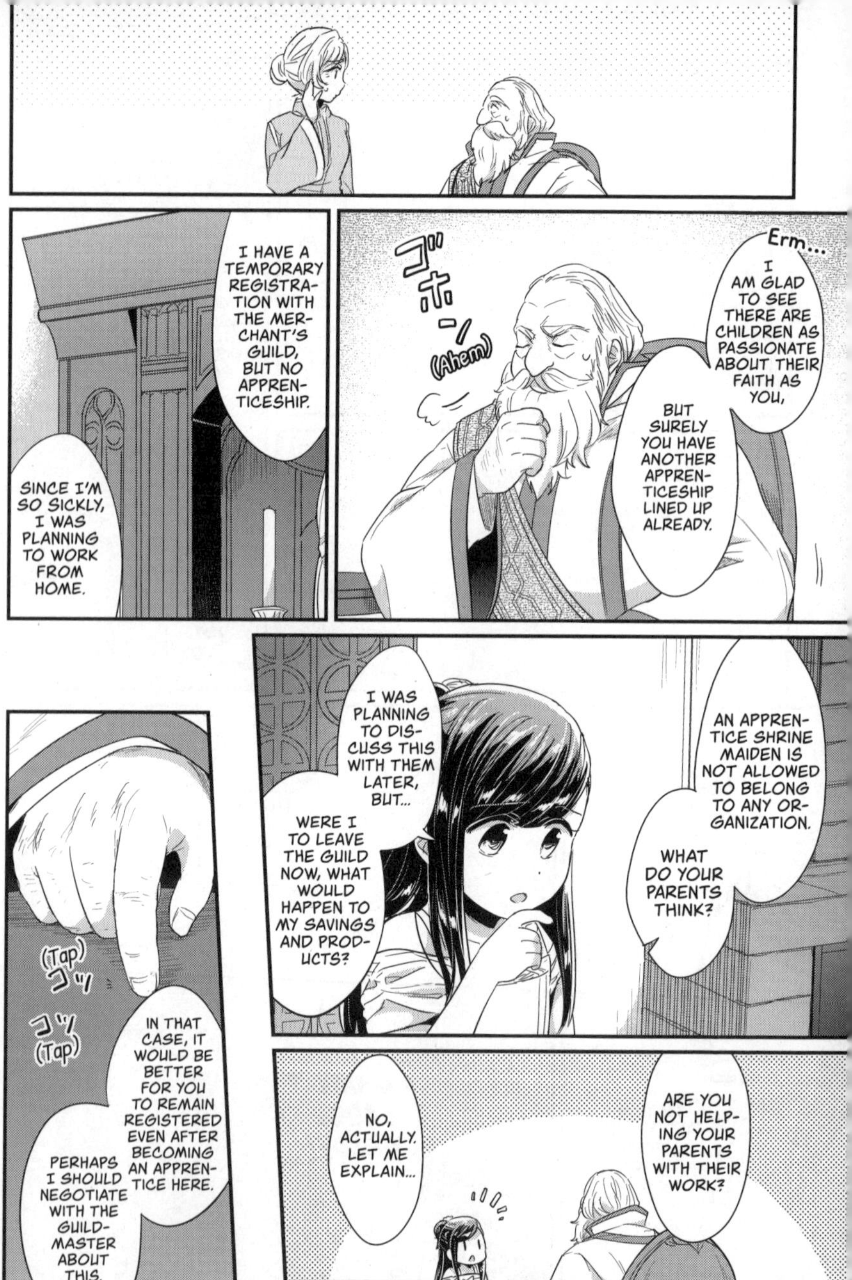
Erm... I AM GLAD TO SEE THERE ARE CHILDREN AS PASSIONATE ABOUT THEIR FAITH AS YOU,
BUT SURELY YOU HAVE ANOTHER APPRENTICESHIP LINED UP ALREADY.
ゴホー
(Ahem)
I HAVE A TEMPORARY REGISTRATION WITH THE MERCHANT'S GUILD, BUT NO APPRENTICESHIP.
SINCE I'M SO SICKLY, I WAS PLANNING TO WORK FROM HOME.
AN APPRENTICE SHRINE MAIDEN IS NOT ALLOWED TO BELONG TO ANY ORGANIZATION.
WHAT DO YOUR PARENTS THINK?
I WAS PLANNING TO DISCUSS THIS WITH THEM LATER, BUT...
WERE I TO LEAVE THE GUILD NOW, WHAT WOULD HAPPEN TO MY SAVINGS AND PRODUCTS?
ARE YOU NOT HELPING YOUR PARENTS WITH THEIR WORK?
NO, ACTUALLY. LET ME EXPLAIN...
(Tap) コッ
コッ (Tap)
IN THAT CASE, IT WOULD BE BETTER FOR YOU TO REMAIN REGISTERED EVEN AFTER BECOMING AN APPRENTICE HERE.
PERHAPS I SHOULD NEGOTIATE WITH THE GUILDMASTER ABOUT THIS.

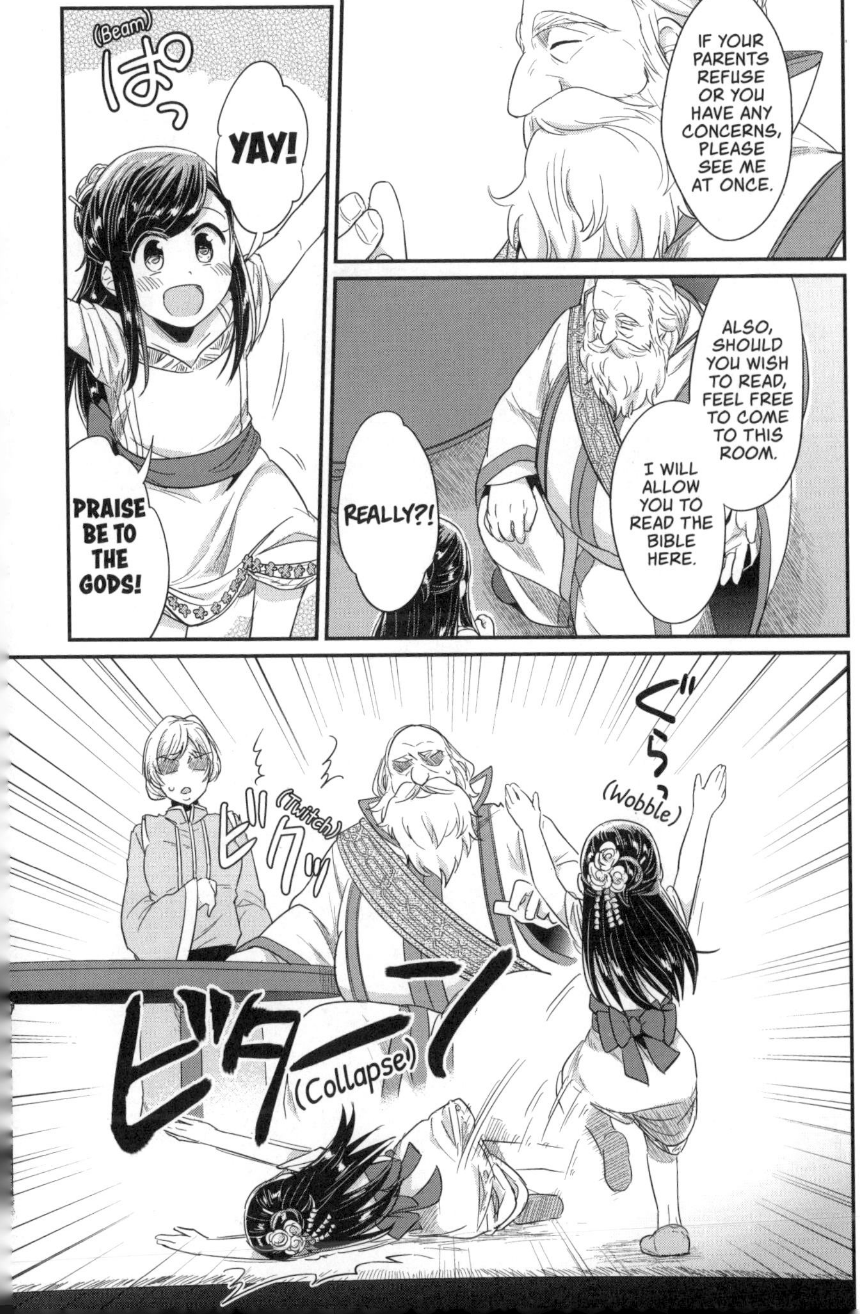
IF YOUR PARENTS REFUSE OR YOU HAVE ANY CONCERNS, PLEASE SEE ME AT ONCE.
ALSO, SHOULD YOU WISH TO READ, FEEL FREE TO COME TO THIS ROOM.
I WILL ALLOW YOU TO READ THE BIBLE HERE.
REALLY?!
(Beam)
ぱっ
YAY!
PRAISE BE TO THE GODS!
ぐらっ
(Wobble)
ビクッ
(Twitch)
ビターン
(Collapse)

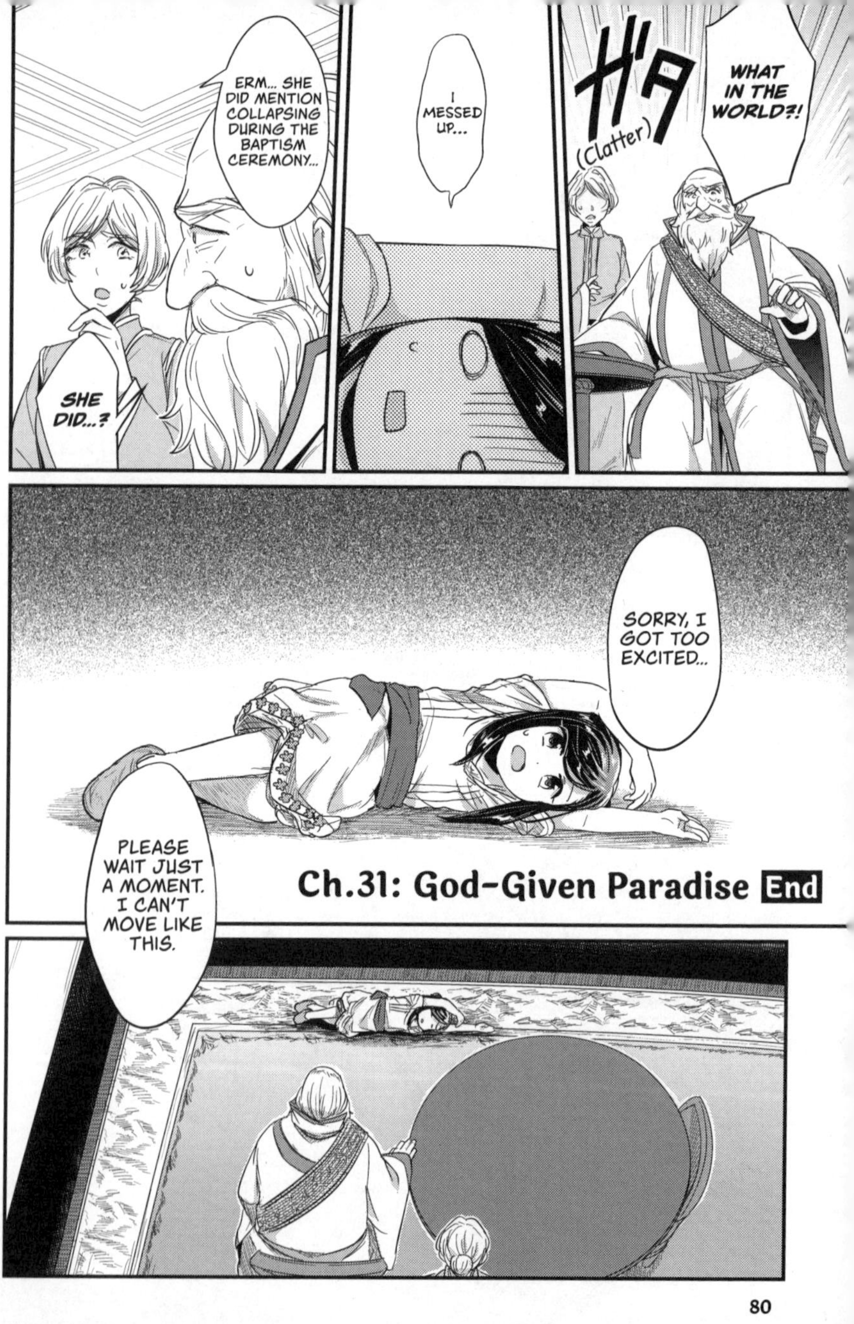

ガタ
(Clatter)
WHAT IN THE WORLD?!
I MESSED UP...
ERM... SHE DID MENTION COLLAPSING DURING THE BAPTISM CEREMONY...
SHE DID...?
SORRY, I GOT TOO EXCITED...
PLEASE WAIT JUST A MOMENT. I CAN'T MOVE LIKE THIS.
Ch.31: God-Given Paradise End

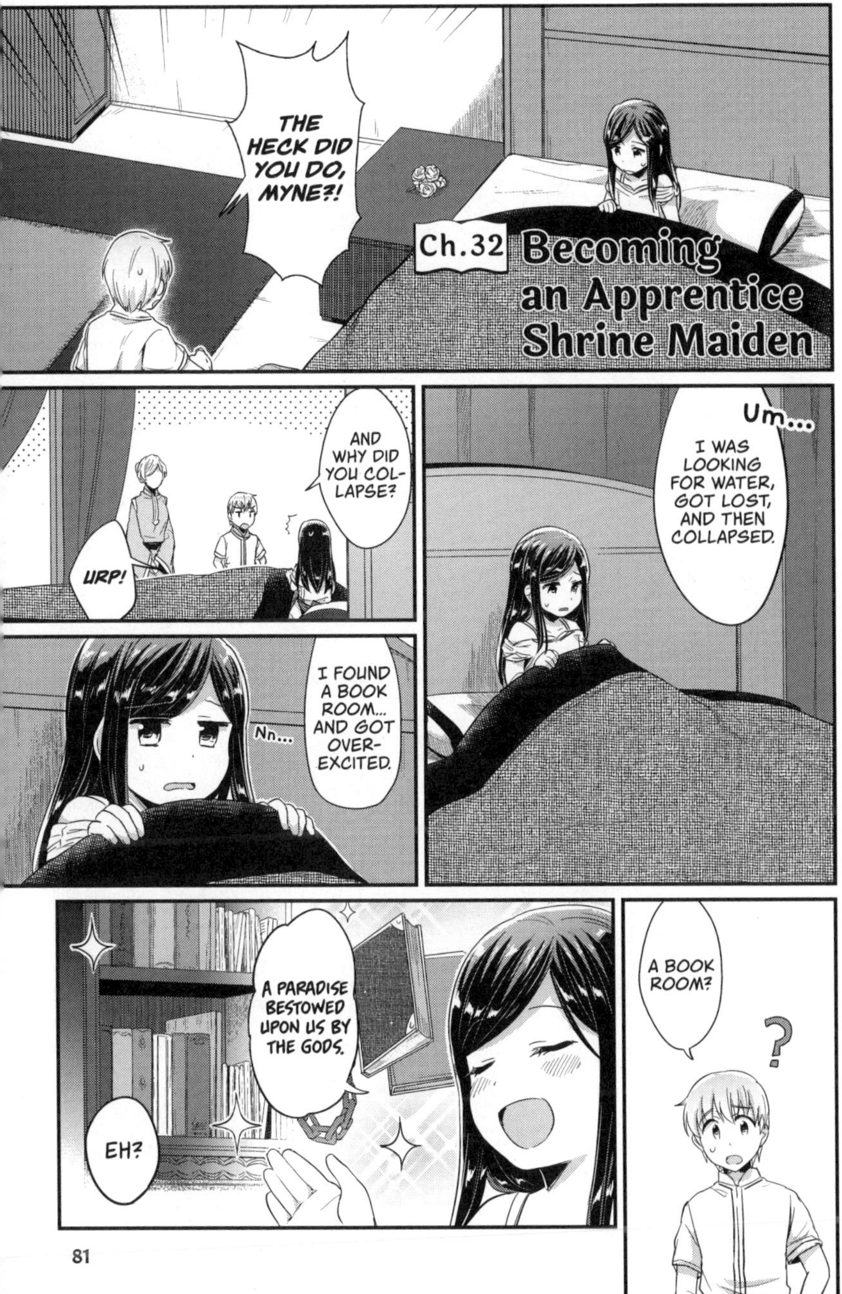
THE HECK DID YOU DO, MYNE?!
Ch.32 Becoming an Apprentice Shrine Maiden
Um...
I WAS LOOKING FOR WATER, GOT LOST, AND THEN COLLAPSED.
AND WHY DID YOU COL-LAPSE?
URP!
I FOUND A BOOK ROOM... AND GOT OVER-EXCITED.
Nn...
A BOOK ROOM?
?
A PARADISE BESTOWED UPON US BY THE GODS.
EH?

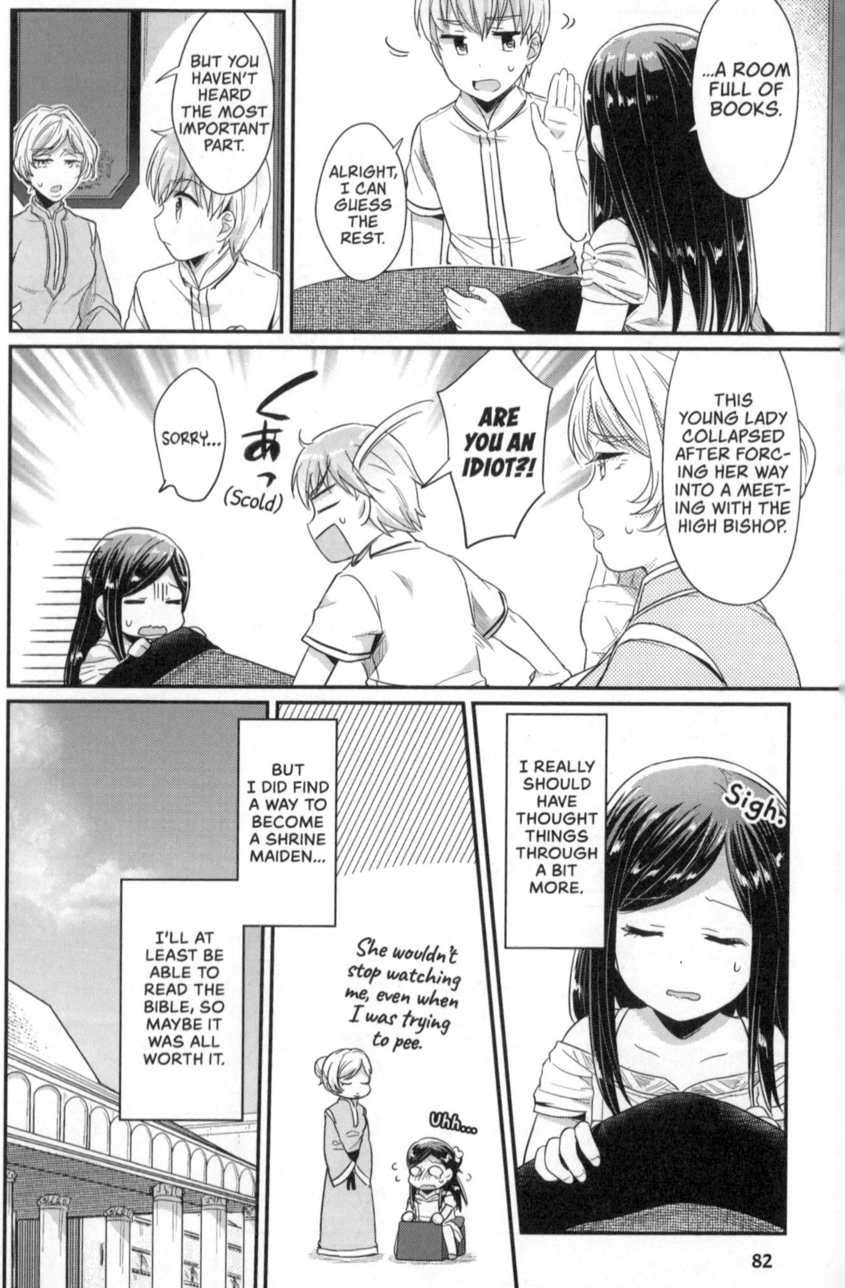
...A ROOM FULL OF BOOKS.
ALRIGHT, I CAN GUESS THE REST.
BUT YOU HAVEN'T HEARD THE MOST IMPORTANT PART.
THIS YOUNG LADY COLLAPSED AFTER FORCING HER WAY INTO A MEETING WITH THE HIGH BISHOP.
ARE YOU AN IDIOT?!
(Scold)
SORRY...
I REALLY SHOULD HAVE THOUGHT THINGS THROUGH A BIT MORE.
Sigh.
BUT I DID FIND A WAY TO BECOME A SHRINE MAIDEN...
She wouldn't stop watching me, even when I was trying to pee.
Uhh...
I'LL AT LEAST BE ABLE TO READ THE BIBLE, SO MAYBE IT WAS ALL WORTH IT.

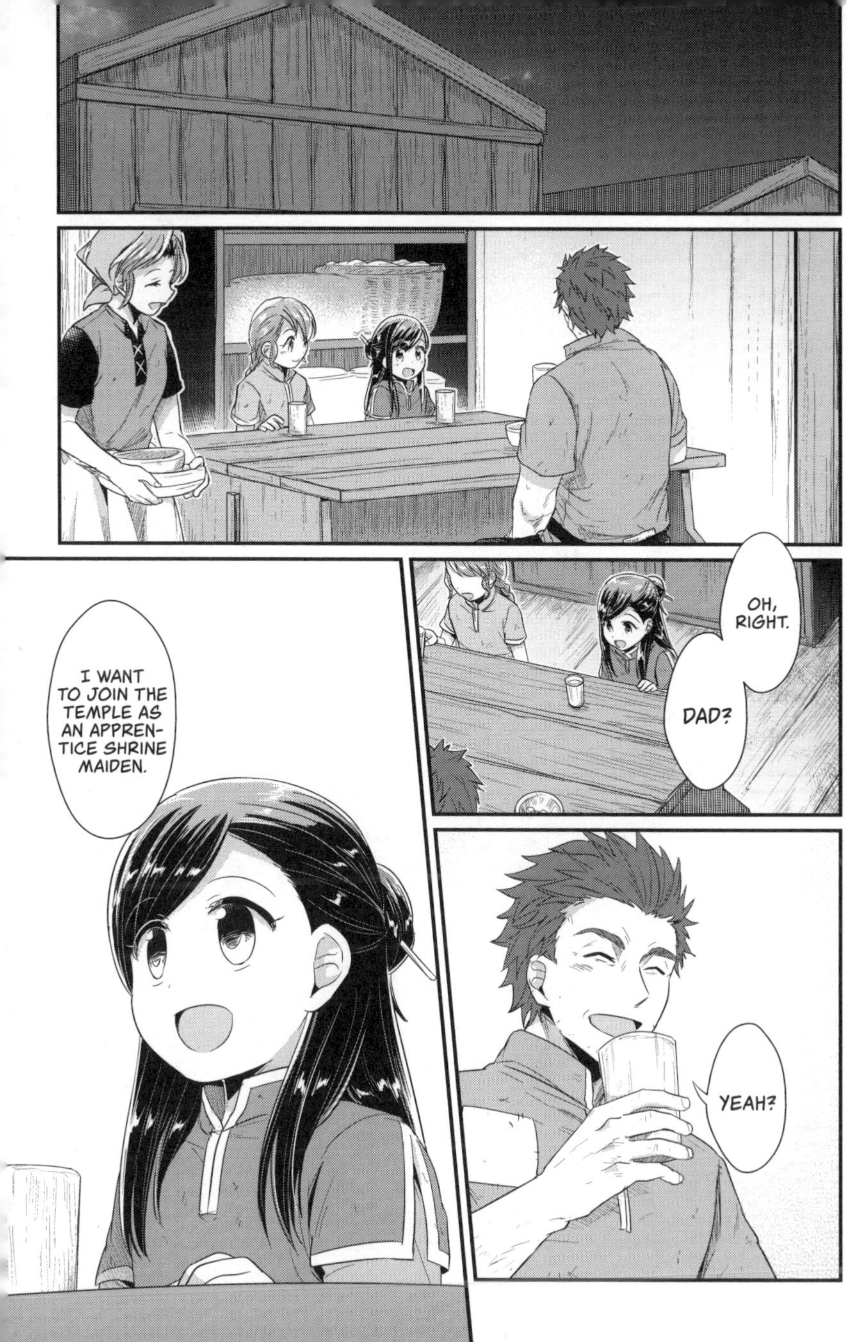
OH, RIGHT.
DAD?
YEAH?
I WANT TO JOIN THE TEMPLE AS AN APPRENTICE SHRINE MAIDEN.

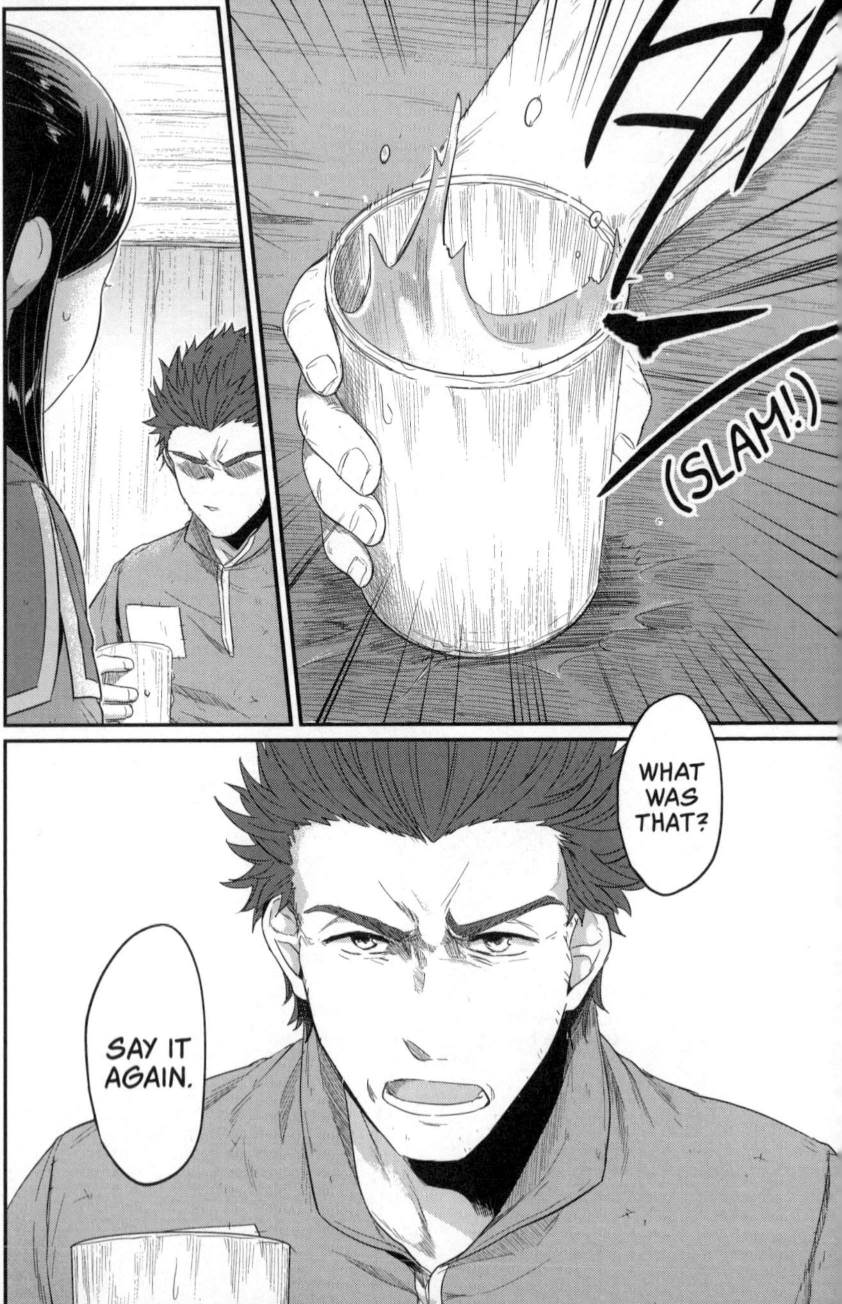
(SLAM!)
WHAT WAS THAT?
SAY IT AGAIN.

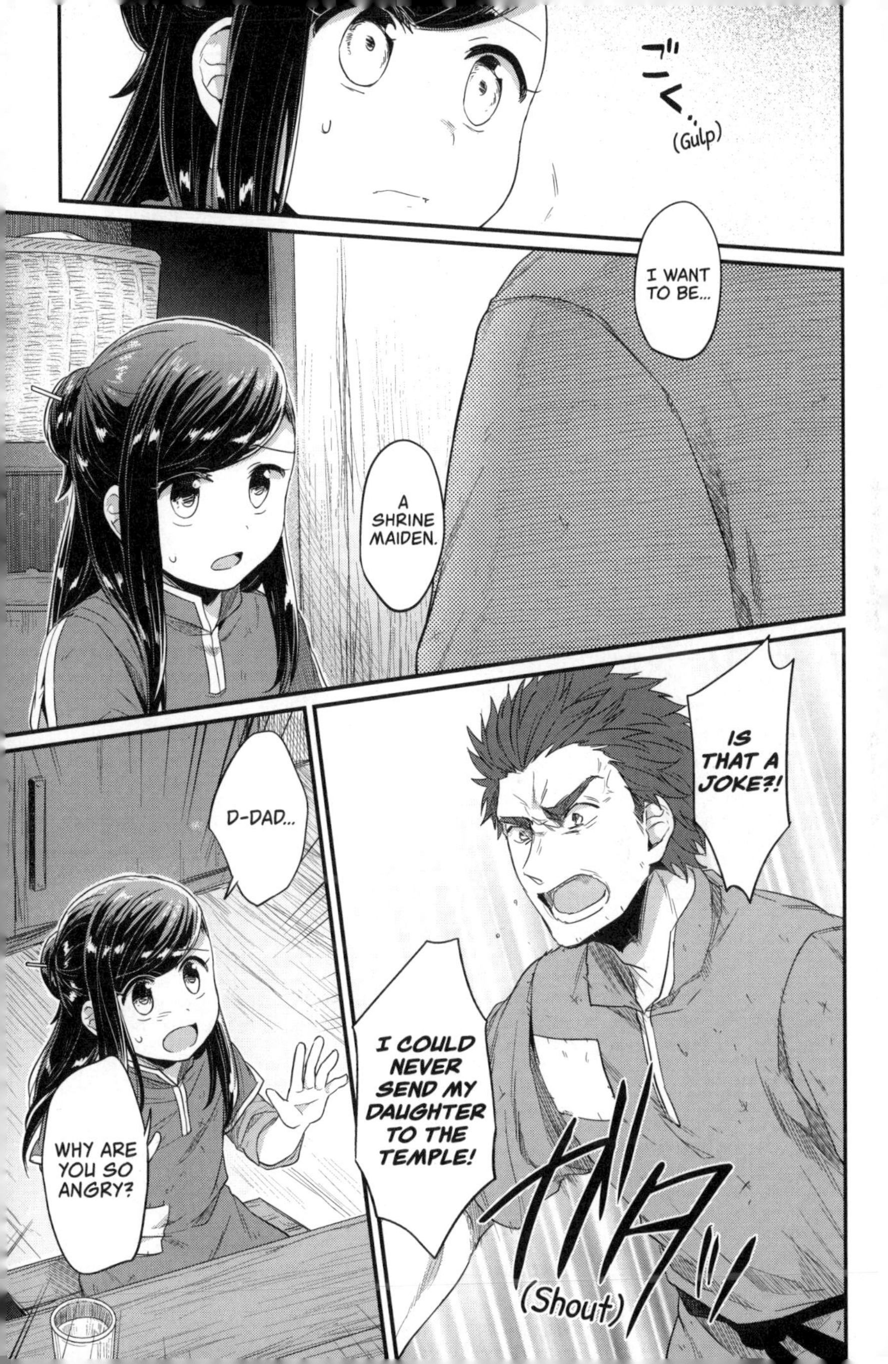
ゴく…
(Gulp)
I WANT TO BE...
A SHRINE MAIDEN.
IS THAT A JOKE?!
I COULD NEVER SEND MY DAUGHTER TO THE TEMPLE!
(Shout)
D-DAD...
WHY ARE YOU SO ANGRY?

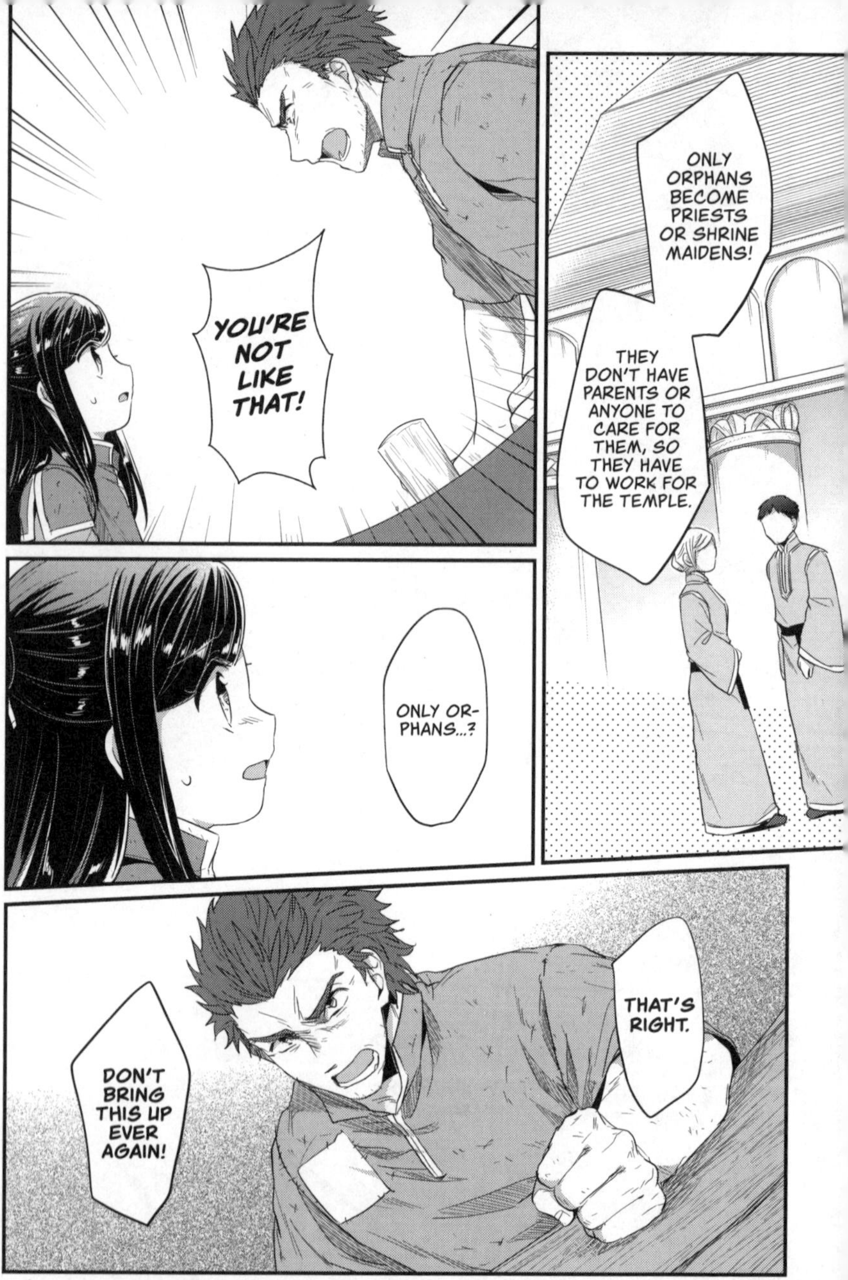
ONLY ORPHANS BECOME PRIESTS OR SHRINE MAIDENS!
THEY DON'T HAVE PARENTS OR ANYONE TO CARE FOR THEM, SO THEY HAVE TO WORK FOR THE TEMPLE.
YOU'RE NOT LIKE THAT!
ONLY OR-PHANS...?
THAT'S RIGHT.
DON'T BRING THIS UP EVER AGAIN!

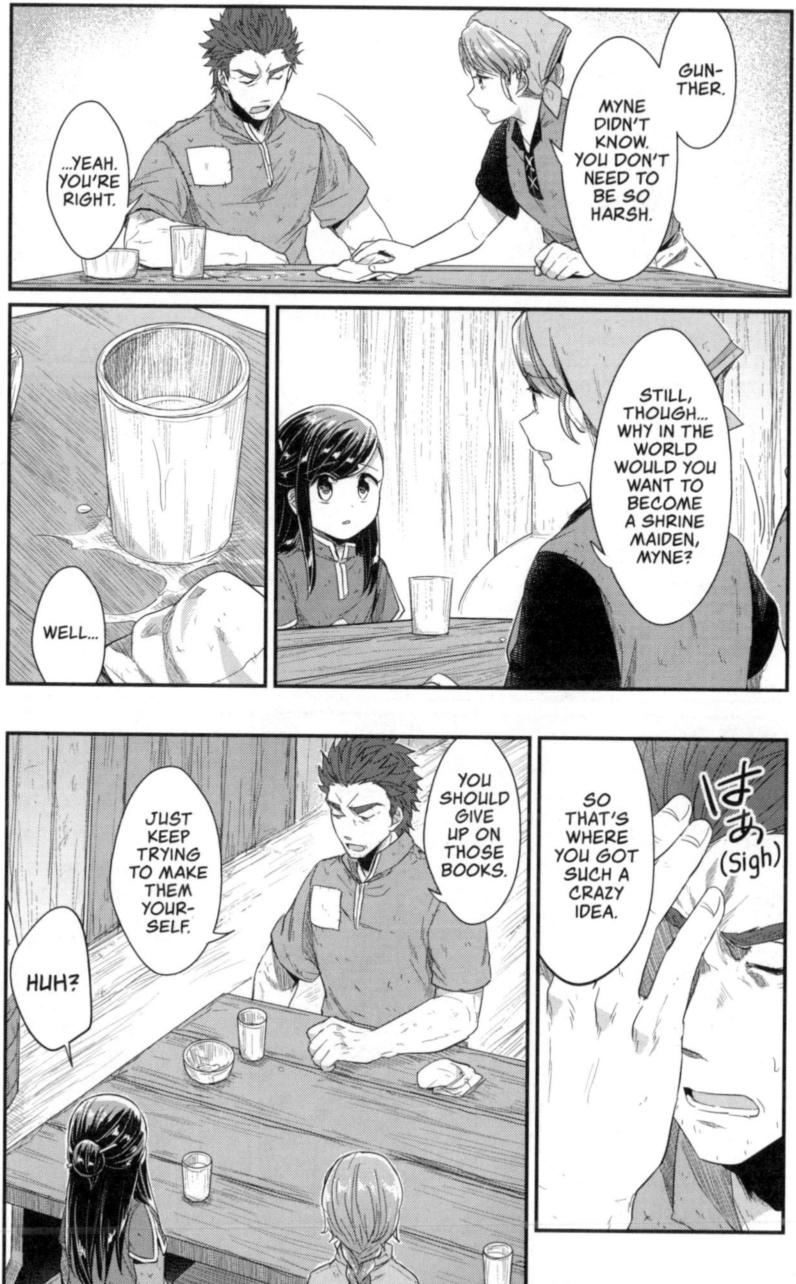
GUNTHER.
MYNE DIDN'T KNOW. YOU DON'T NEED TO BE SO HARSH.
...YEAH. YOU'RE RIGHT.
STILL, THOUGH... WHY IN THE WORLD WOULD YOU WANT TO BECOME A SHRINE MAIDEN, MYNE?
WELL...
はあ
(Sigh)
SO THAT'S WHERE YOU GOT SUCH A CRAZY IDEA.
YOU SHOULD GIVE UP ON THOSE BOOKS.
JUST KEEP TRYING TO MAKE THEM YOURSELF.
HUH?

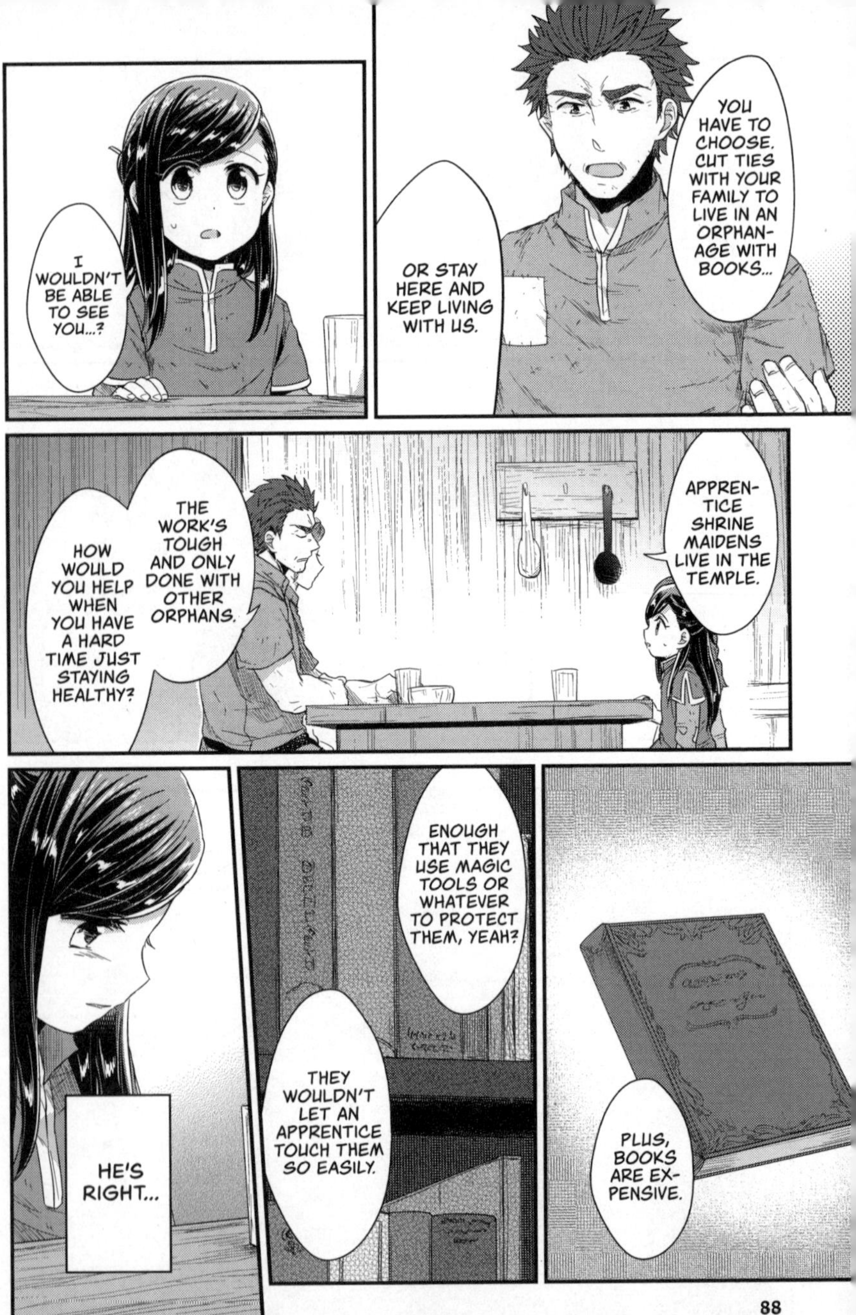
YOU HAVE TO CHOOSE. CUT TIES WITH YOUR FAMILY TO LIVE IN AN ORPHANAGE WITH BOOKS...
OR STAY HERE AND KEEP LIVING WITH US.
I WOULDN'T BE ABLE TO SEE YOU...?
APPRENTICE SHRINE MAIDENS LIVE IN THE TEMPLE.
THE WORK'S TOUGH AND ONLY DONE WITH OTHER ORPHANS.
HOW WOULD YOU HELP WHEN YOU HAVE A HARD TIME JUST STAYING HEALTHY?
PLUS, BOOKS ARE EXPENSIVE.
ENOUGH THAT THEY USE MAGIC TOOLS OR WHATEVER TO PROTECT THEM, YEAH?
THEY WOULDN'T LET AN APPRENTICE TOUCH THEM SO EASILY.
HE'S RIGHT...

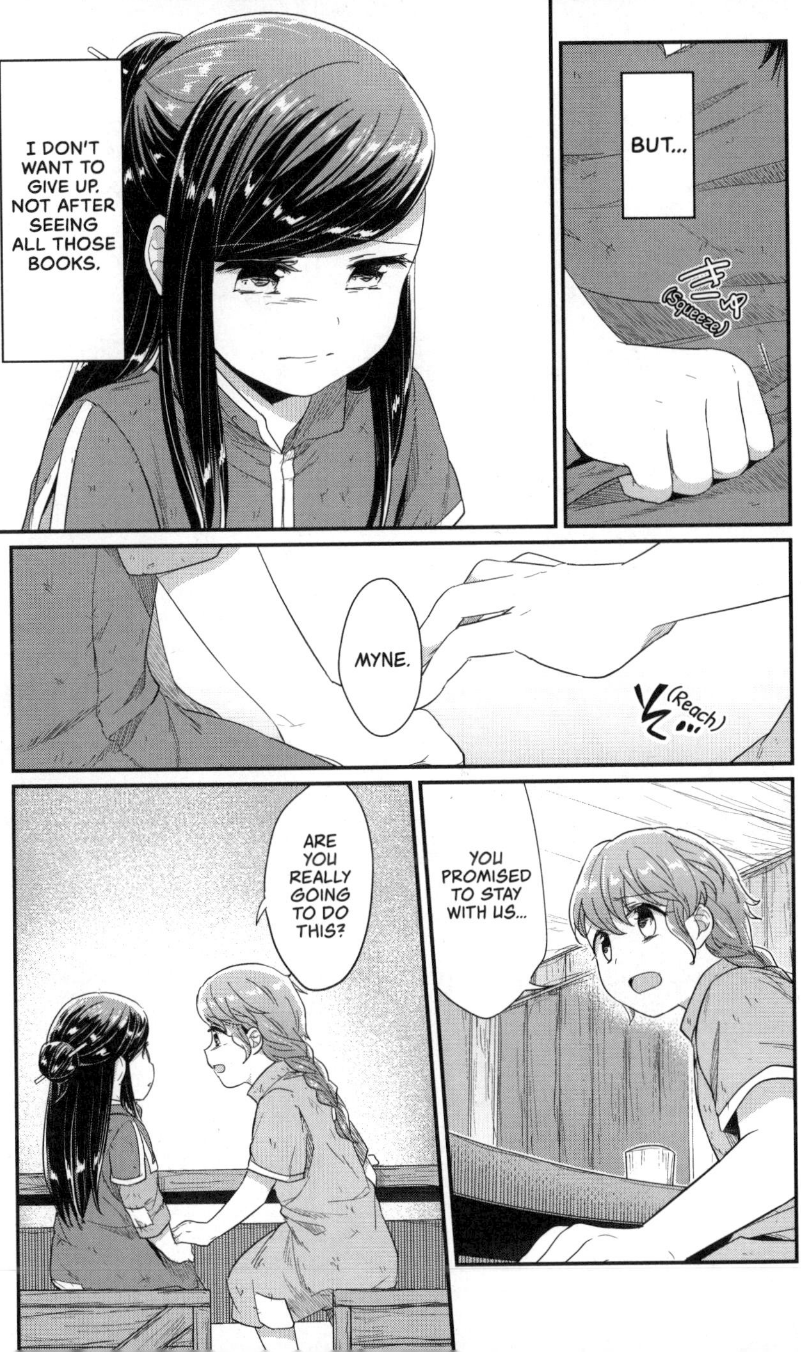
BUT...
(Squeeze)
I DON'T WANT TO GIVE UP. NOT AFTER SEEING ALL THOSE BOOKS.
MYNE.
(Reach)
YOU PROMISED TO STAY WITH US...
ARE YOU REALLY GOING TO DO THIS?

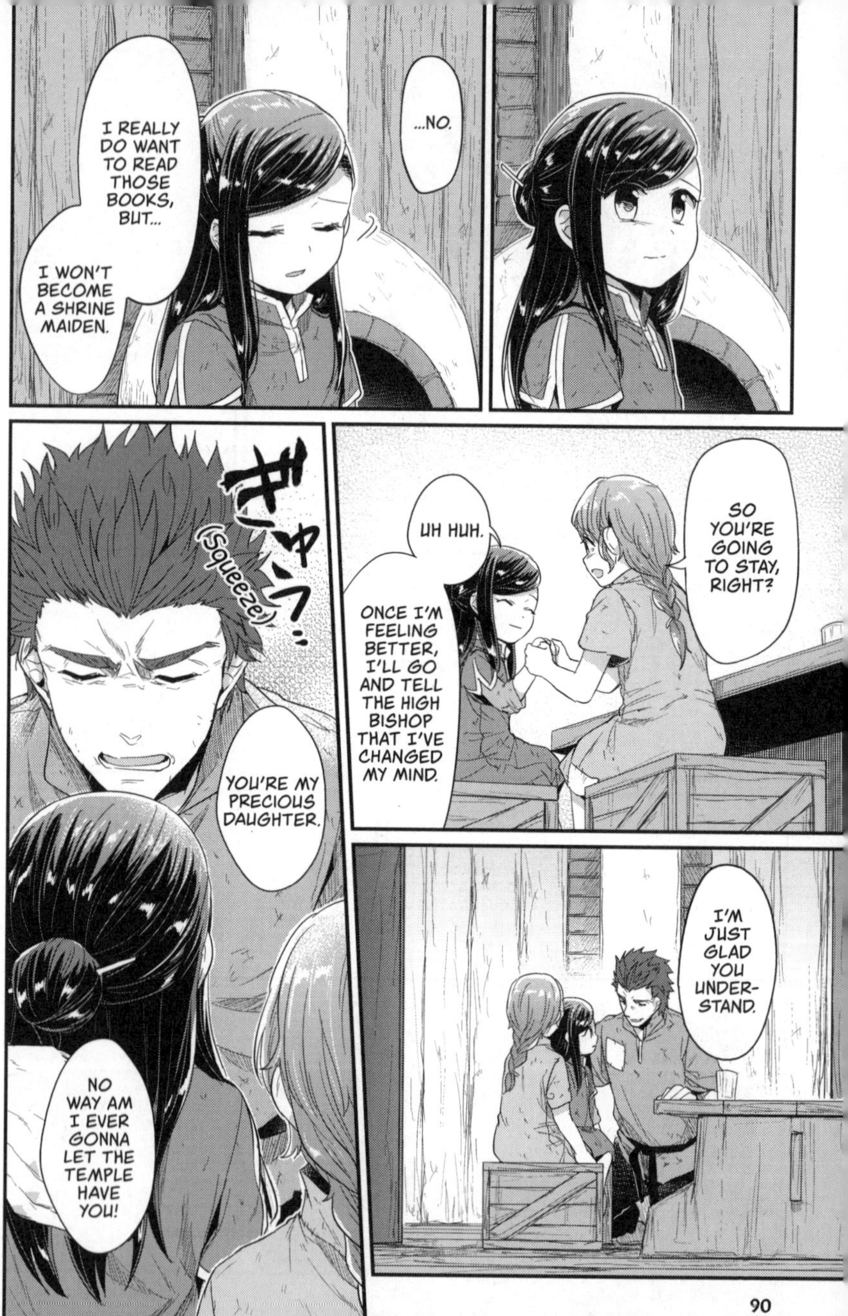
...NO.
I REALLY DO WANT TO READ THOSE BOOKS, BUT...
I WON'T BECOME A SHRINE MAIDEN.
SO YOU'RE GOING TO STAY, RIGHT?
UH HUH.
ONCE I'M FEELING BETTER, I'LL GO AND TELL THE HIGH BISHOP THAT I'VE CHANGED MY MIND.
I'M JUST GLAD YOU UNDERSTAND.
ぎゅっ
(squeeze)
YOU'RE MY PRECIOUS DAUGHTER.
NO WAY AM I EVER GONNA LET THE TEMPLE HAVE YOU!

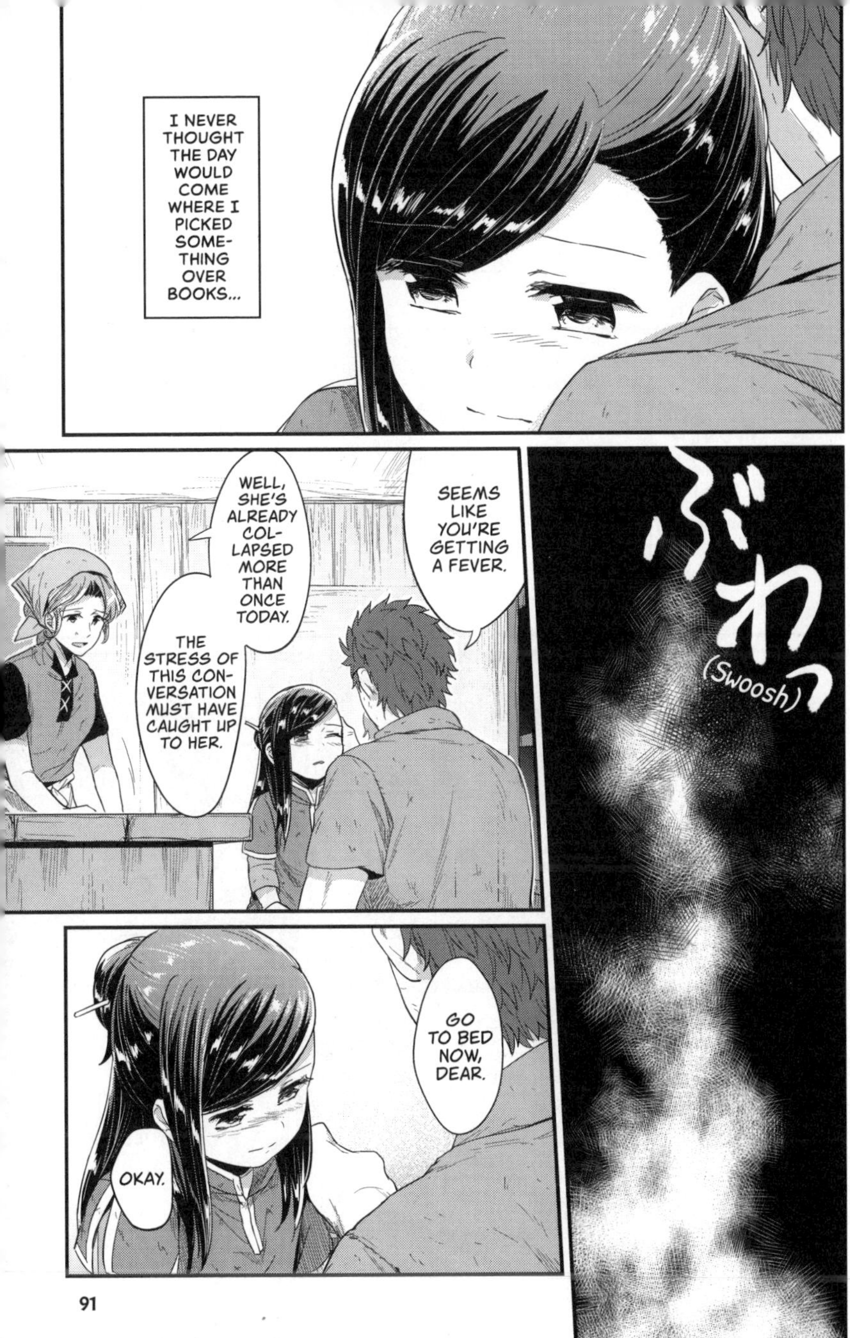
I NEVER THOUGHT THE DAY WOULD COME WHERE I PICKED SOMETHING OVER BOOKS...
ぶわっ
(Swoosh)
SEEMS LIKE YOU'RE GETTING A FEVER.
WELL, SHE'S ALREADY COLLAPSED MORE THAN ONCE TODAY.
THE STRESS OF THIS CONVERSATION MUST HAVE CAUGHT UP TO HER.
GO TO BED NOW, DEAR.
OKAY.

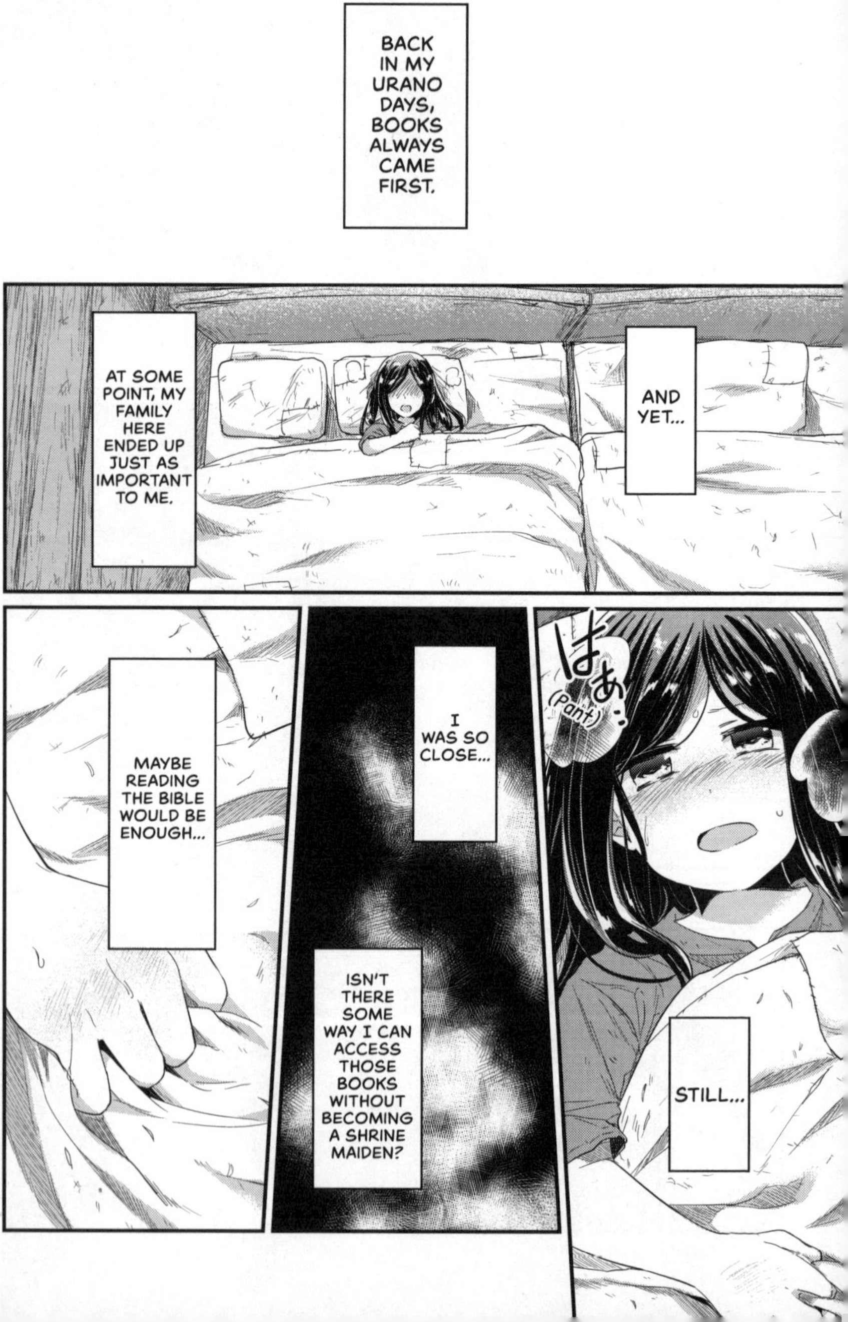
BACK IN MY URANO DAYS, BOOKS ALWAYS CAME FIRST.
AND YET...
AT SOME POINT, MY FAMILY HERE ENDED UP JUST AS IMPORTANT TO ME.
はぁ
(Pant)
STILL...
I WAS SO CLOSE...
ISN'T THERE SOME WAY I CAN ACCESS THOSE BOOKS WITHOUT BECOMING A SHRINE MAIDEN?
MAYBE READING THE BIBLE WOULD BE ENOUGH...

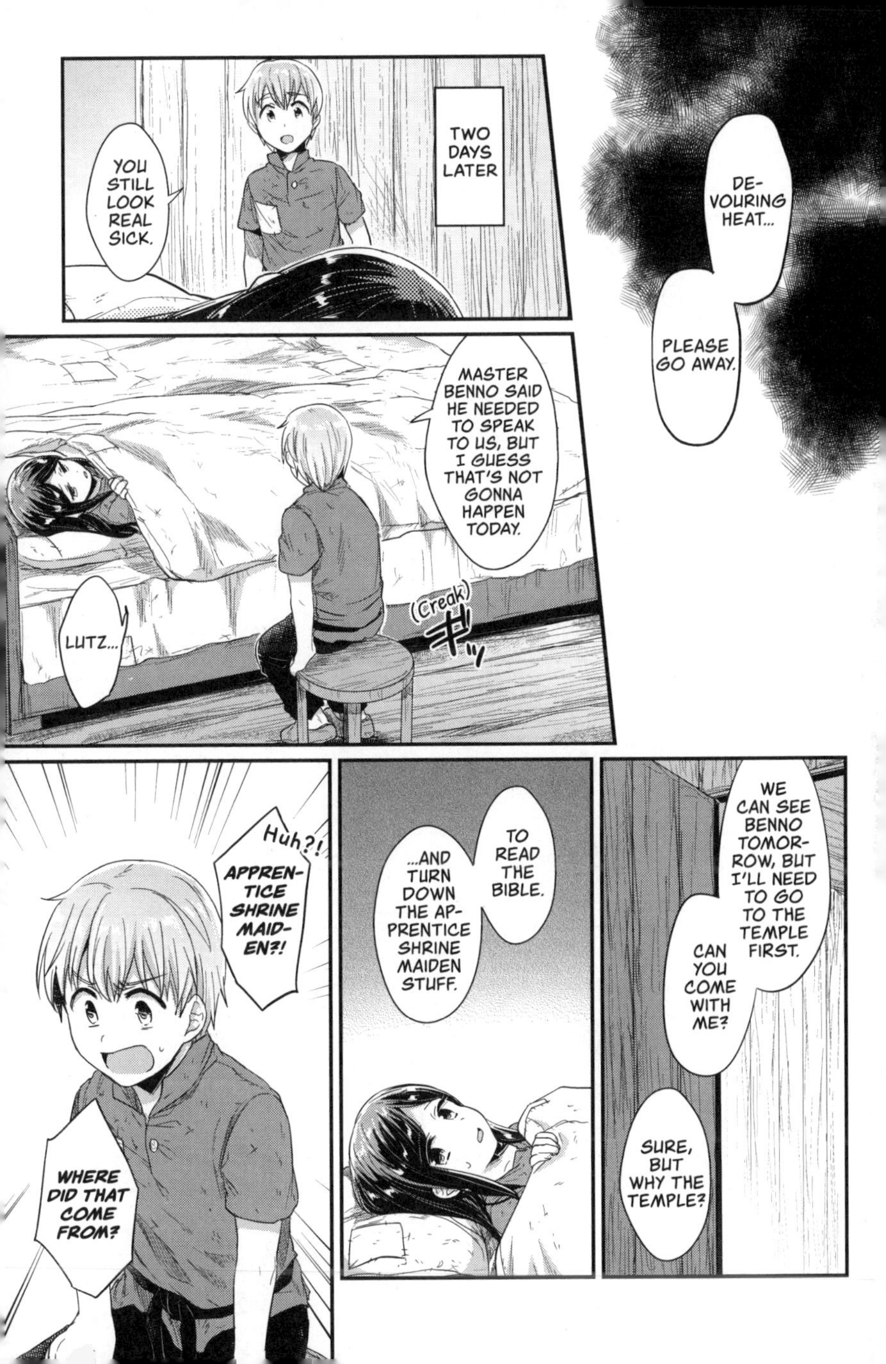

DEVOURING HEAT...
PLEASE GO AWAY.
TWO DAYS LATER
YOU STILL LOOK REAL SICK.
MASTER BENNO SAID HE NEEDED TO SPEAK TO US, BUT I GUESS THAT'S NOT GONNA HAPPEN TODAY.
(creak)
LUTZ...
WE CAN SEE BENNO TOMORROW, BUT I'LL NEED TO GO TO THE TEMPLE FIRST.
CAN YOU COME WITH ME?
SURE, BUT WHY THE TEMPLE?
TO READ THE BIBLE.
...AND TURN DOWN THE APPRENTICE SHRINE MAIDEN STUFF.
Huh?!
APPRENTICE SHRINE MAIDEN?!
WHERE DID THAT COME FROM?

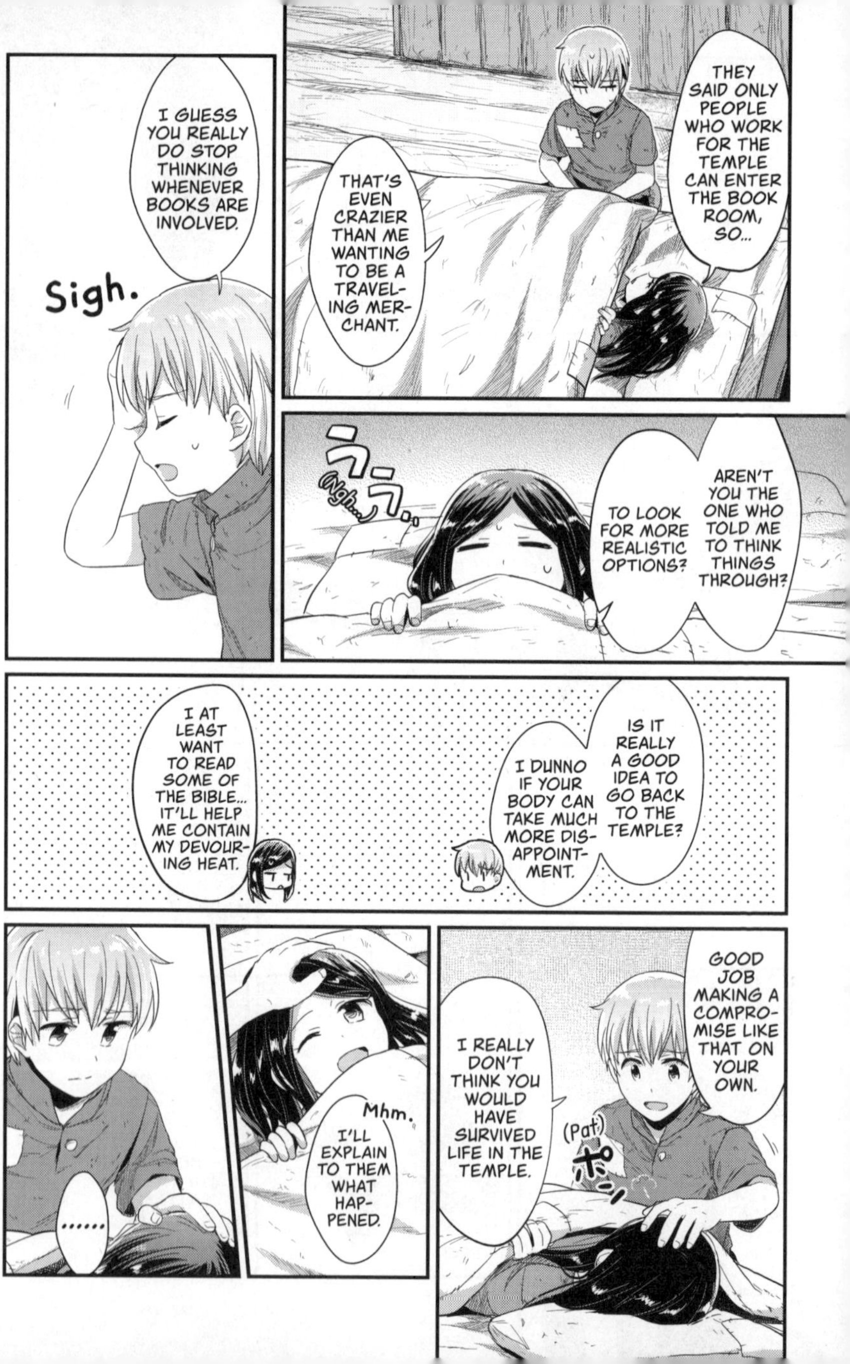

THEY SAID ONLY PEOPLE WHO WORK FOR THE TEMPLE CAN ENTER THE BOOK ROOM, SO...
THAT'S EVEN CRAZIER THAN ME WANTING TO BE A TRAVELING MERCHANT.
うう..
(Ngh...)
AREN'T YOU THE ONE WHO TOLD ME TO THINK THINGS THROUGH?
TO LOOK FOR MORE REALISTIC OPTIONS?
I GUESS YOU REALLY DO STOP THINKING WHENEVER BOOKS ARE INVOLVED.
Sigh.
IS IT REALLY A GOOD IDEA TO GO BACK TO THE TEMPLE?
I DUNNO IF YOUR BODY CAN TAKE MUCH MORE DISAPPOINTMENT.
I AT LEAST WANT TO READ SOME OF THE BIBLE... IT'LL HELP ME CONTAIN MY DEVOURING HEAT.
GOOD JOB MAKING A COMPROMISE LIKE THAT ON YOUR OWN.
(Pat)
ポー
I REALLY DON'T THINK YOU WOULD HAVE SURVIVED LIFE IN THE TEMPLE.
Mhm.
I'LL EXPLAIN TO THEM WHAT HAPPENED.
......

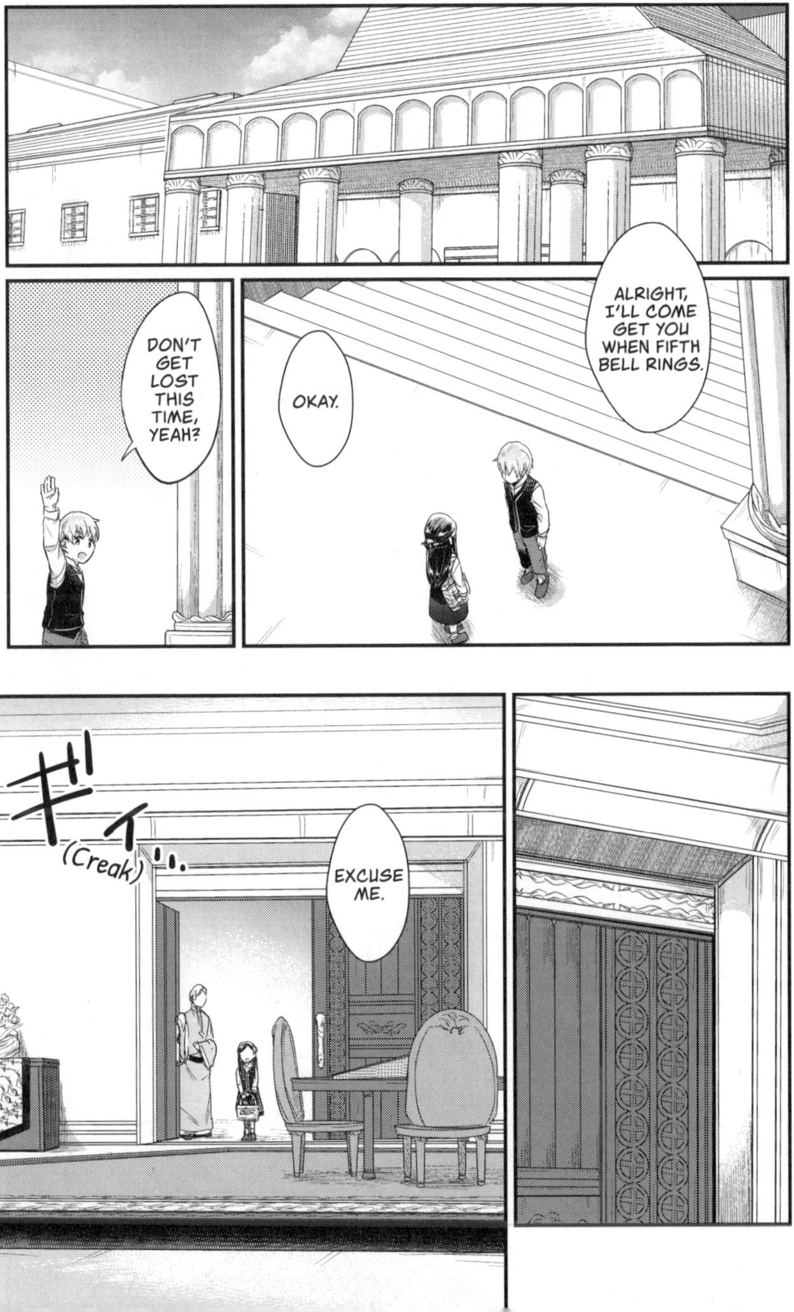
ALRIGHT, I'LL COME GET YOU WHEN FIFTH BELL RINGS.
OKAY.
DON'T GET LOST THIS TIME, YEAH?
EXCUSE ME.
ギイ
(Creak)

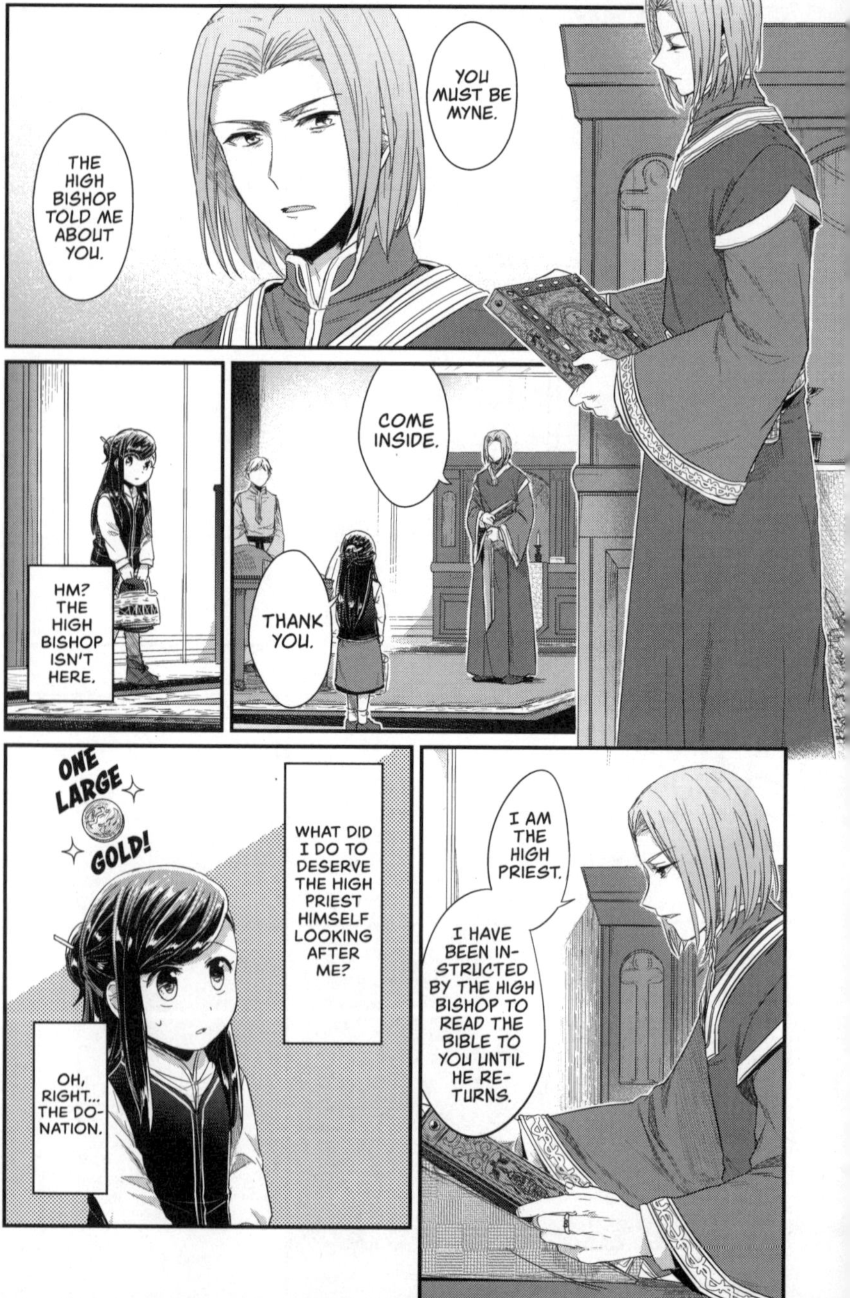
YOU MUST BE MYNE.
THE HIGH BISHOP TOLD ME ABOUT YOU.
COME INSIDE.
THANK YOU.
HM? THE HIGH BISHOP ISN'T HERE.
I AM THE HIGH PRIEST.
I HAVE BEEN IN-STRUCTED BY THE HIGH BISHOP TO READ THE BIBLE TO YOU UNTIL HE RE-TURNS.
WHAT DID I DO TO DESERVE THE HIGH PRIEST HIMSELF LOOKING AFTER ME?
ONE LARGE GOLD!
OH, RIGHT... THE DO-NATION.

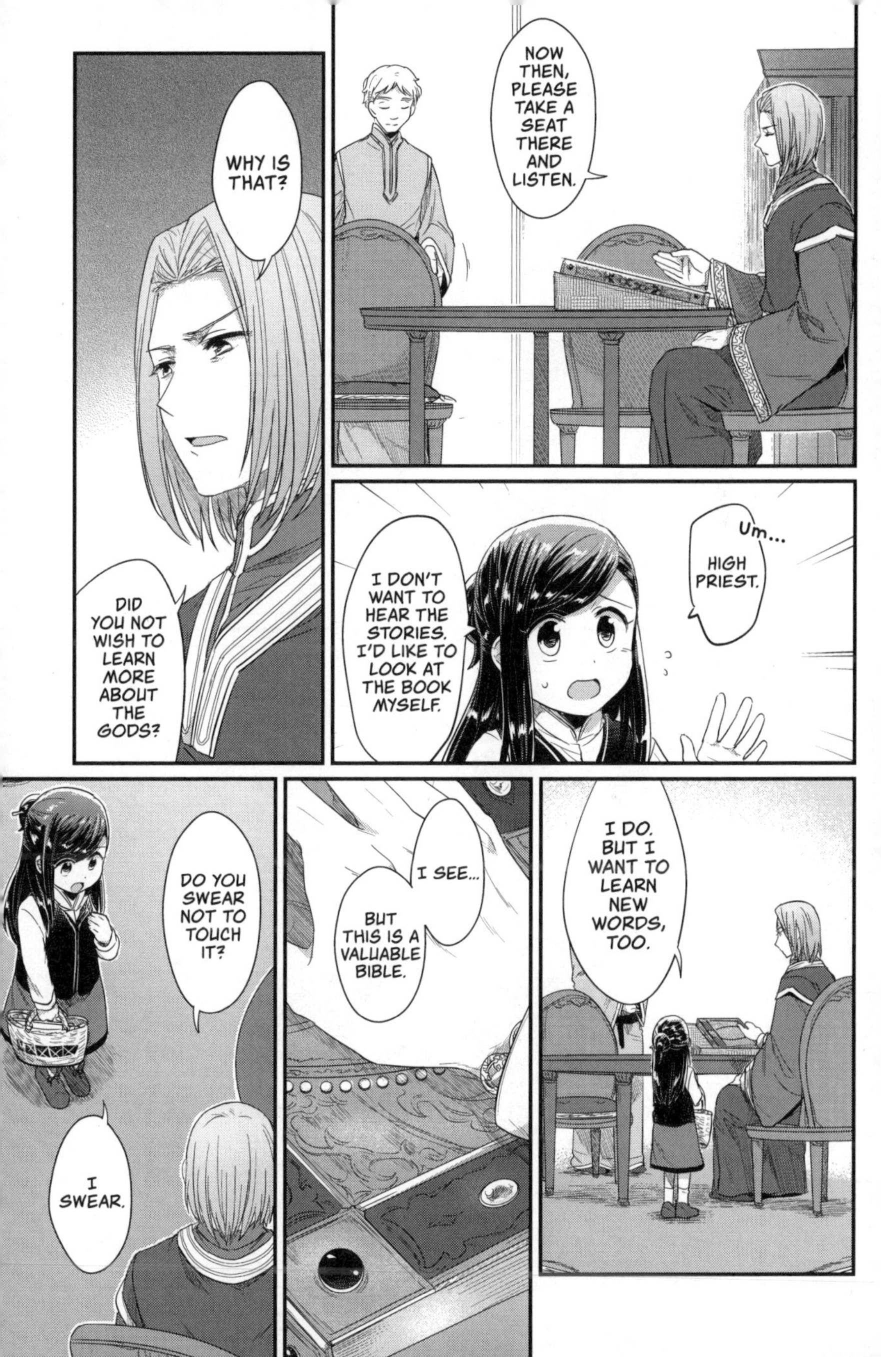
NOW THEN, PLEASE TAKE A SEAT THERE AND LISTEN.
Um...
HIGH PRIEST.
I DON'T WANT TO HEAR THE STORIES. I'D LIKE TO LOOK AT THE BOOK MYSELF.
WHY IS THAT?
DID YOU NOT WISH TO LEARN MORE ABOUT THE GODS?
I DO. BUT I WANT TO LEARN NEW WORDS, TOO.
I SEE...
BUT THIS IS A VALUABLE BIBLE.
DO YOU SWEAR NOT TO TOUCH IT?
I SWEAR.

THANK YOU.

(Plop)
ぽすっ

パラ…
(Turn)

AAH! I ACTUALLY GET TO READ UP CLOSE!

THE PARCH-MENT SMELLS SO NICE!

ぱぁぁ
(Beam)

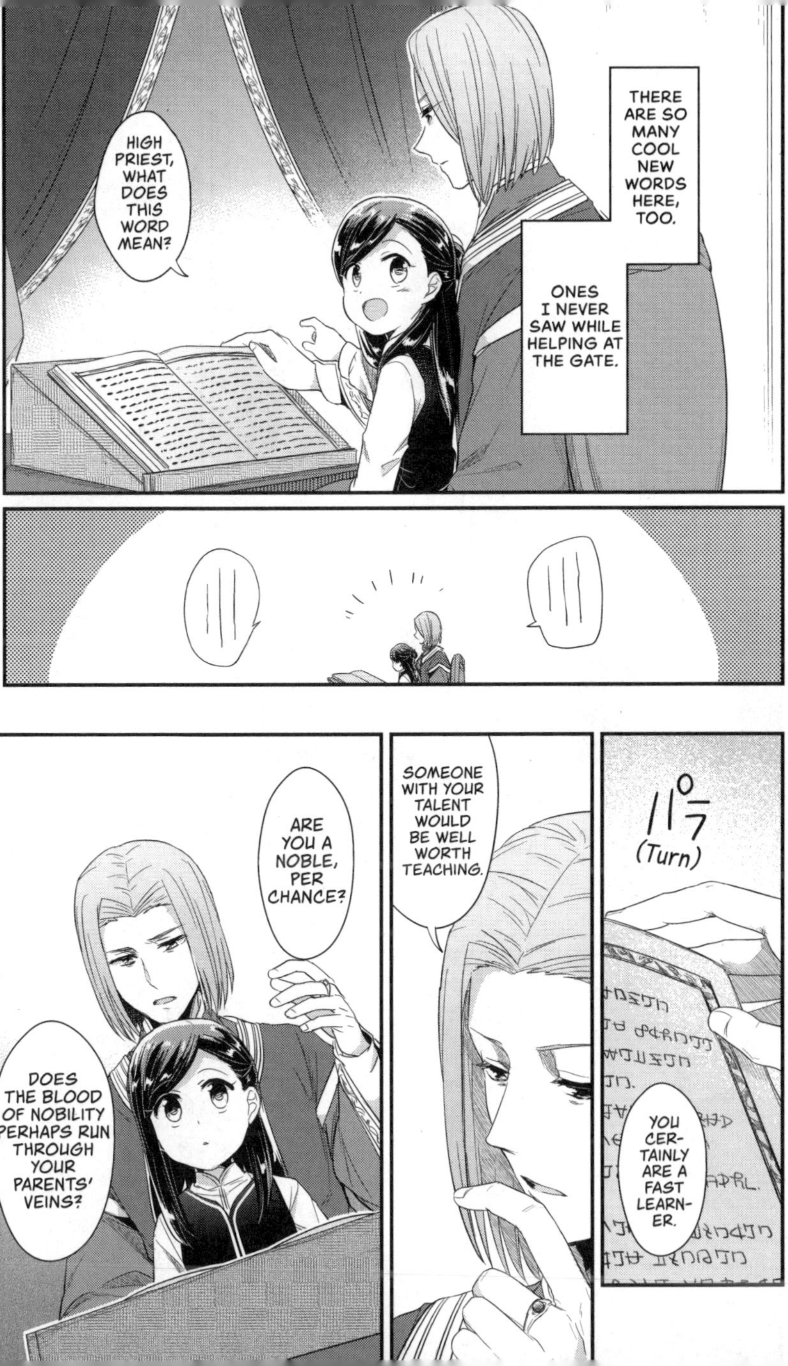
THERE ARE SO MANY COOL NEW WORDS HERE, TOO.
ONES I NEVER SAW WHILE HELPING AT THE GATE.
HIGH PRIEST, WHAT DOES THIS WORD MEAN?
(Turn)
YOU CER-TAINLY ARE A FAST LEARN-ER.
SOMEONE WITH YOUR TALENT WOULD BE WELL WORTH TEACHING.
ARE YOU A NOBLE, PER CHANCE?
DOES THE BLOOD OF NOBILITY PERHAPS RUN THROUGH YOUR PARENTS' VEINS?

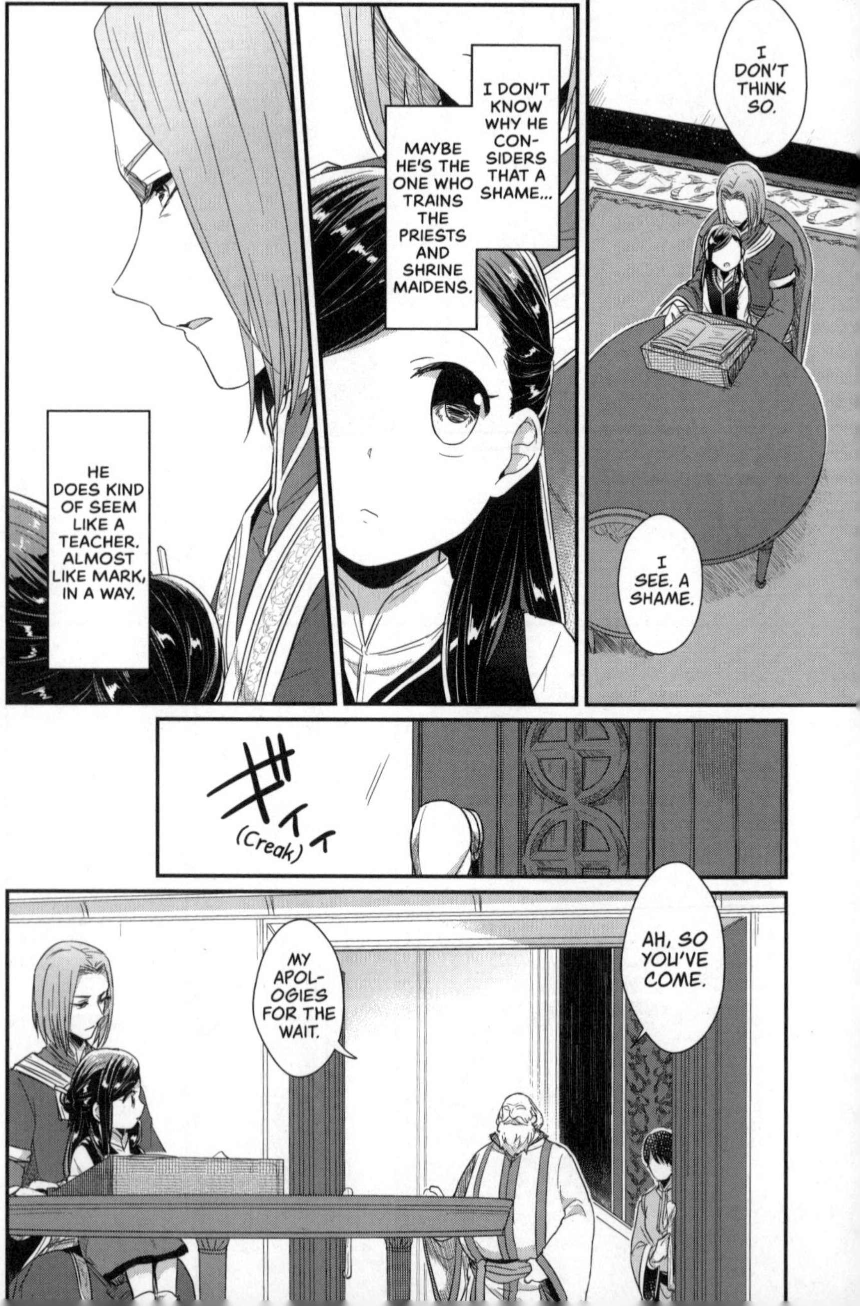
I DON'T THINK SO.
I SEE. A SHAME.
I DON'T KNOW WHY HE CONSIDERS THAT A SHAME...
MAYBE HE'S THE ONE WHO TRAINS THE PRIESTS AND SHRINE MAIDENS.
HE DOES KIND OF SEEM LIKE A TEACHER. ALMOST LIKE MARK, IN A WAY.
ギイイ (Creak)
AH, SO YOU'VE COME.
MY APOLOGIES FOR THE WAIT.

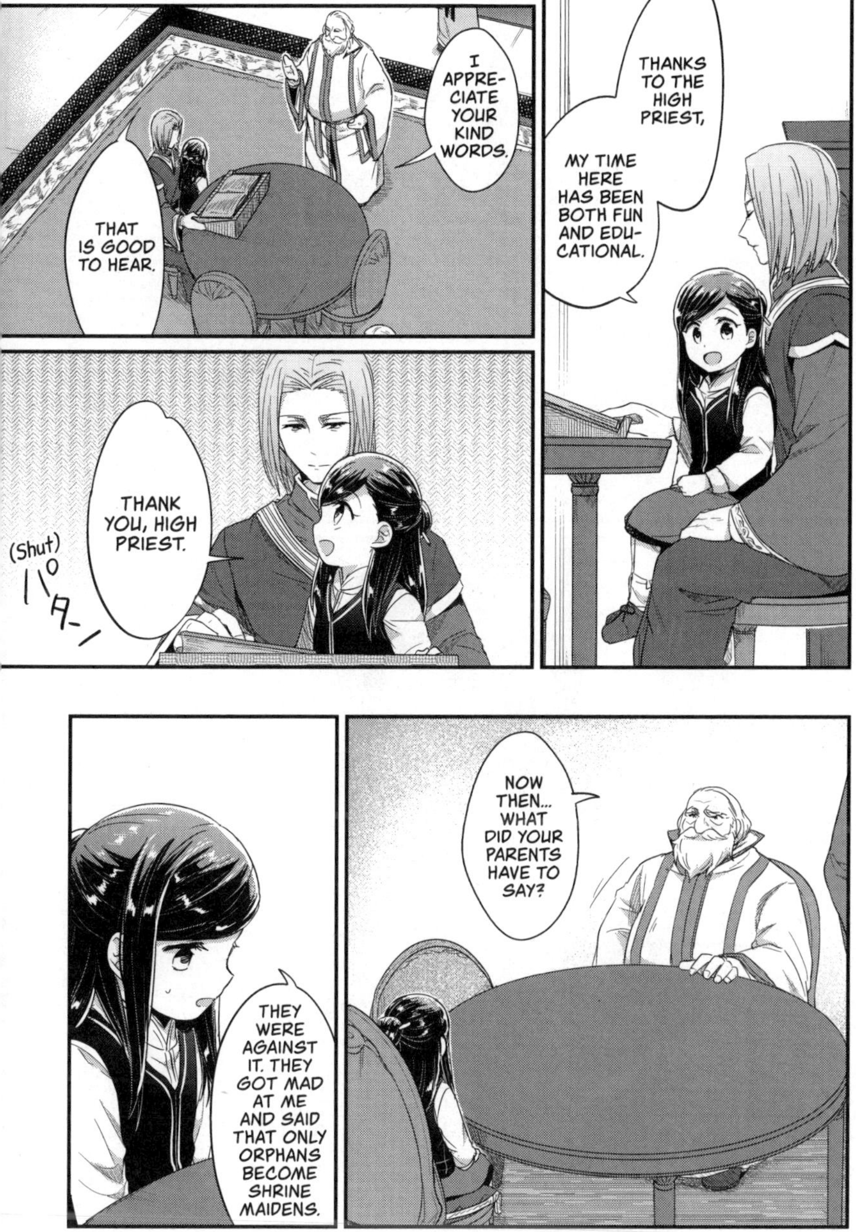
THANKS TO THE HIGH PRIEST,
MY TIME HERE HAS BEEN BOTH FUN AND EDU-CATIONAL.
I APPRE-CIATE YOUR KIND WORDS.
THAT IS GOOD TO HEAR.
THANK YOU, HIGH PRIEST.
(Shut)
NOW THEN... WHAT DID YOUR PARENTS HAVE TO SAY?
THEY WERE AGAINST IT. THEY GOT MAD AT ME AND SAID THAT ONLY ORPHANS BECOME SHRINE MAIDENS.

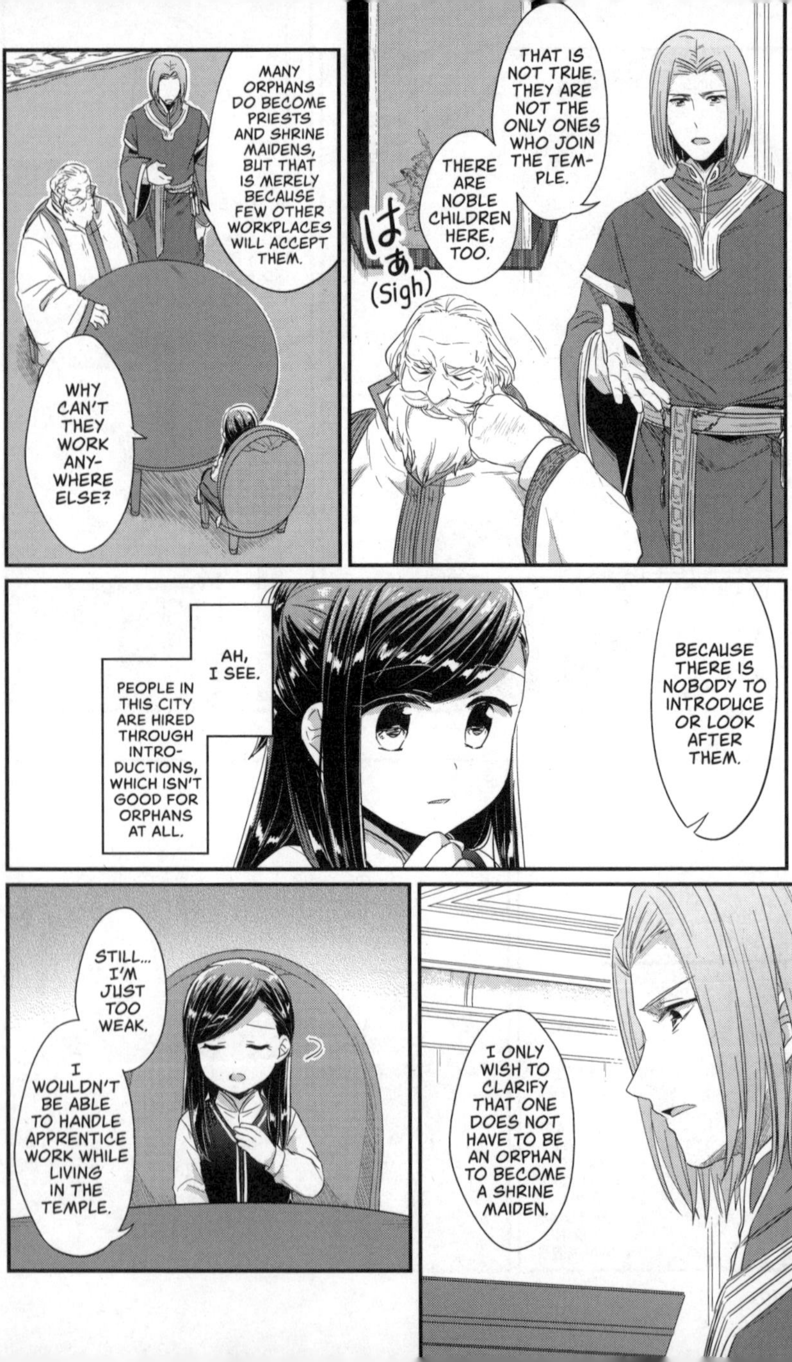
THAT IS NOT TRUE. THEY ARE NOT THE ONLY ONES WHO JOIN THE TEM-PLE.
THERE ARE NOBLE CHILDREN HERE, TOO.
はぁ
(Sigh)
MANY ORPHANS DO BECOME PRIESTS AND SHRINE MAIDENS, BUT THAT IS MERELY BECAUSE FEW OTHER WORKPLACES WILL ACCEPT THEM.
WHY CAN'T THEY WORK ANY-WHERE ELSE?
BECAUSE THERE IS NOBODY TO INTRODUCE OR LOOK AFTER THEM.
AH, I SEE.
PEOPLE IN THIS CITY ARE HIRED THROUGH INTRO-DUCTIONS, WHICH ISN'T GOOD FOR ORPHANS AT ALL.
I ONLY WISH TO CLARIFY THAT ONE DOES NOT HAVE TO BE AN ORPHAN TO BECOME A SHRINE MAIDEN.
STILL... I'M JUST TOO WEAK.
I WOULDN'T BE ABLE TO HANDLE APPRENTICE WORK WHILE LIVING IN THE TEMPLE.

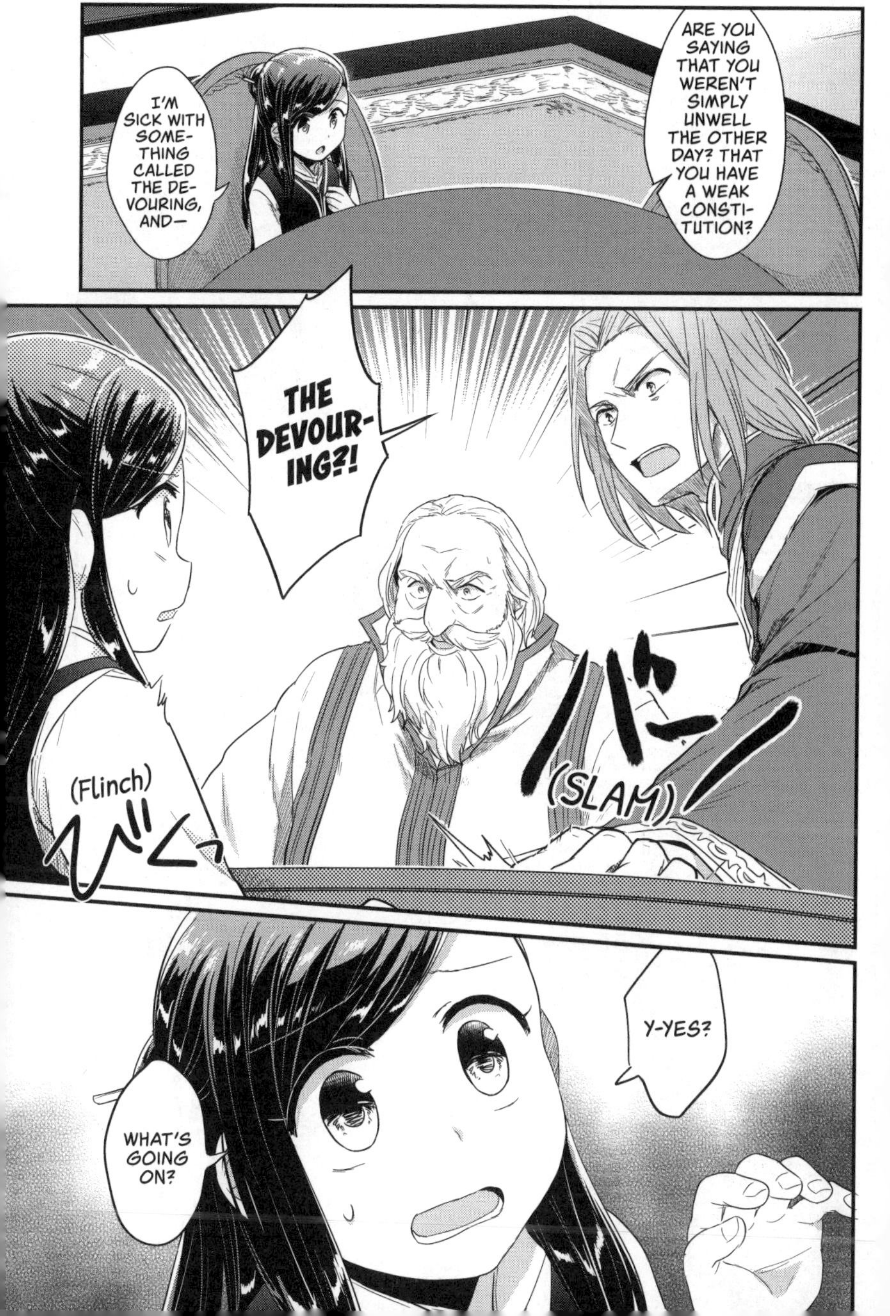
ARE YOU SAYING THAT YOU WEREN'T SIMPLY UNWELL THE OTHER DAY? THAT YOU HAVE A WEAK CONSTI-TUTION?
I'M SICK WITH SOME-THING CALLED THE DE-VOURING, AND—
THE DEVOUR-ING?!
(SLAM)
(Flinch)
Y-YES?
WHAT'S GOING ON?

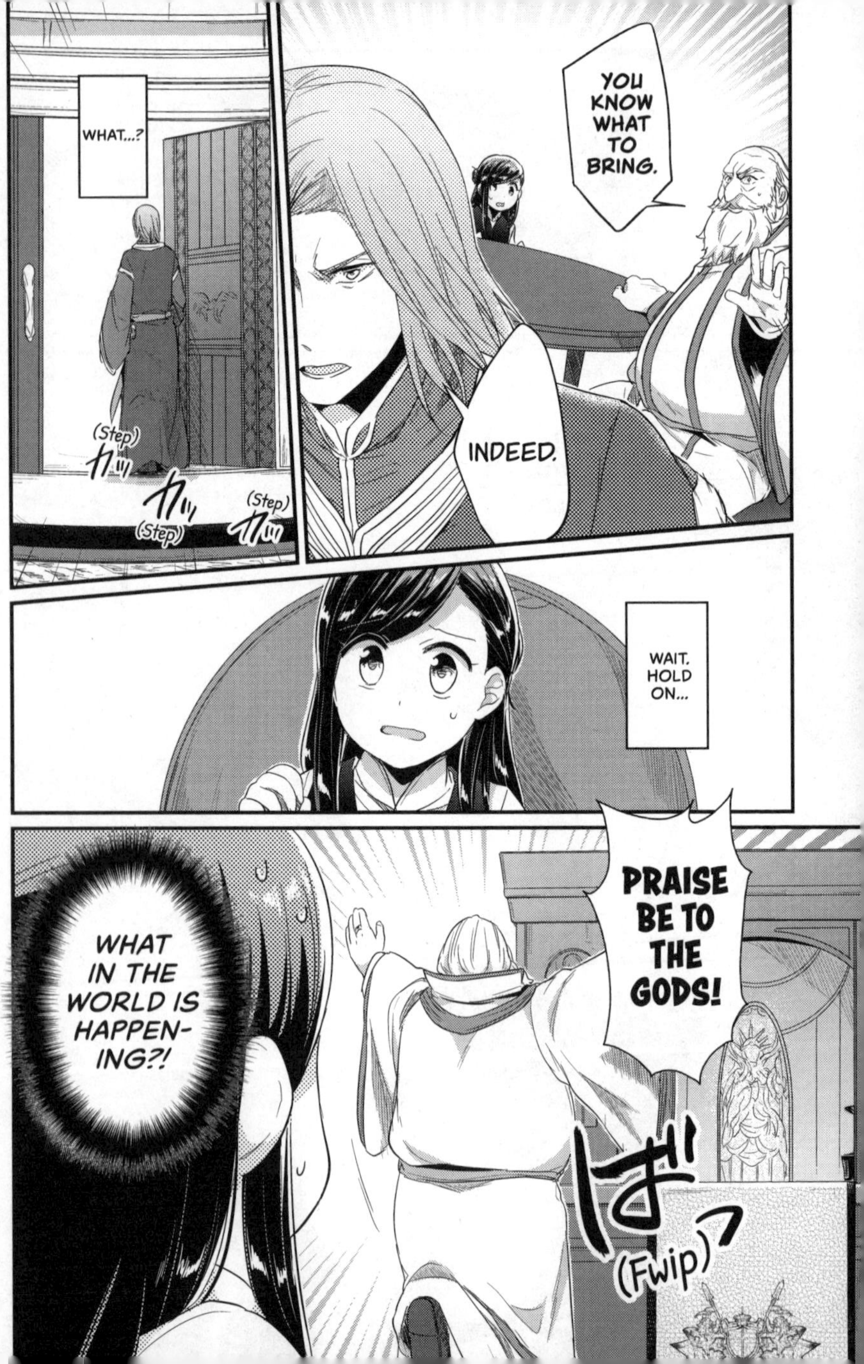

YOU KNOW WHAT TO BRING.
INDEED.
WHAT...?
(Step) カッ
(Step) カッ
(Step) カッ
WAIT. HOLD ON...
PRAISE BE TO THE GODS!
ばっ (Fwip)
WHAT IN THE WORLD IS HAPPEN-ING?!

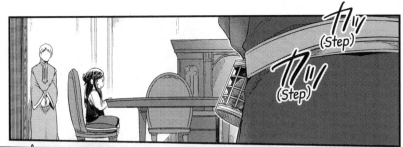

トッ
(Step)

トッ
(Step)

(Reveal)

PLEASE TOUCH THIS CHALICE.

YES. HURRY.

WHA...?

IS THAT REALLY OKAY?

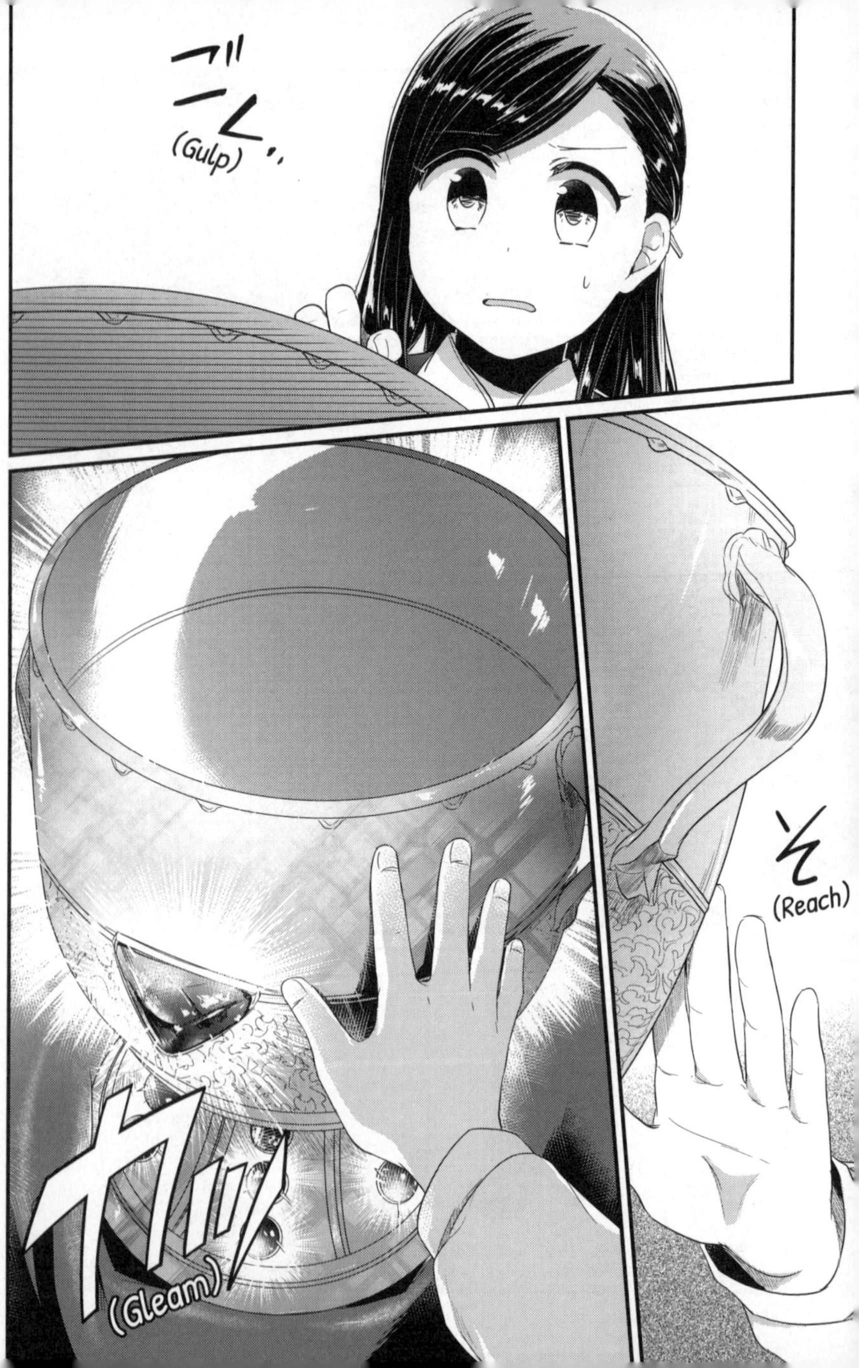
(Gulp)
(Reach)
(Gleam)

Eep!

WHAT WAS THAT?!

ニく
(Nod)

ぱっ
(Retract)

WE WISH TO SPEAK WITH YOUR PARENTS.

MYNE.

MOM, DAD...

I'M SORRY.

I THINK THINGS JUST TOOK A REALLY, REALLY BAD TURN.

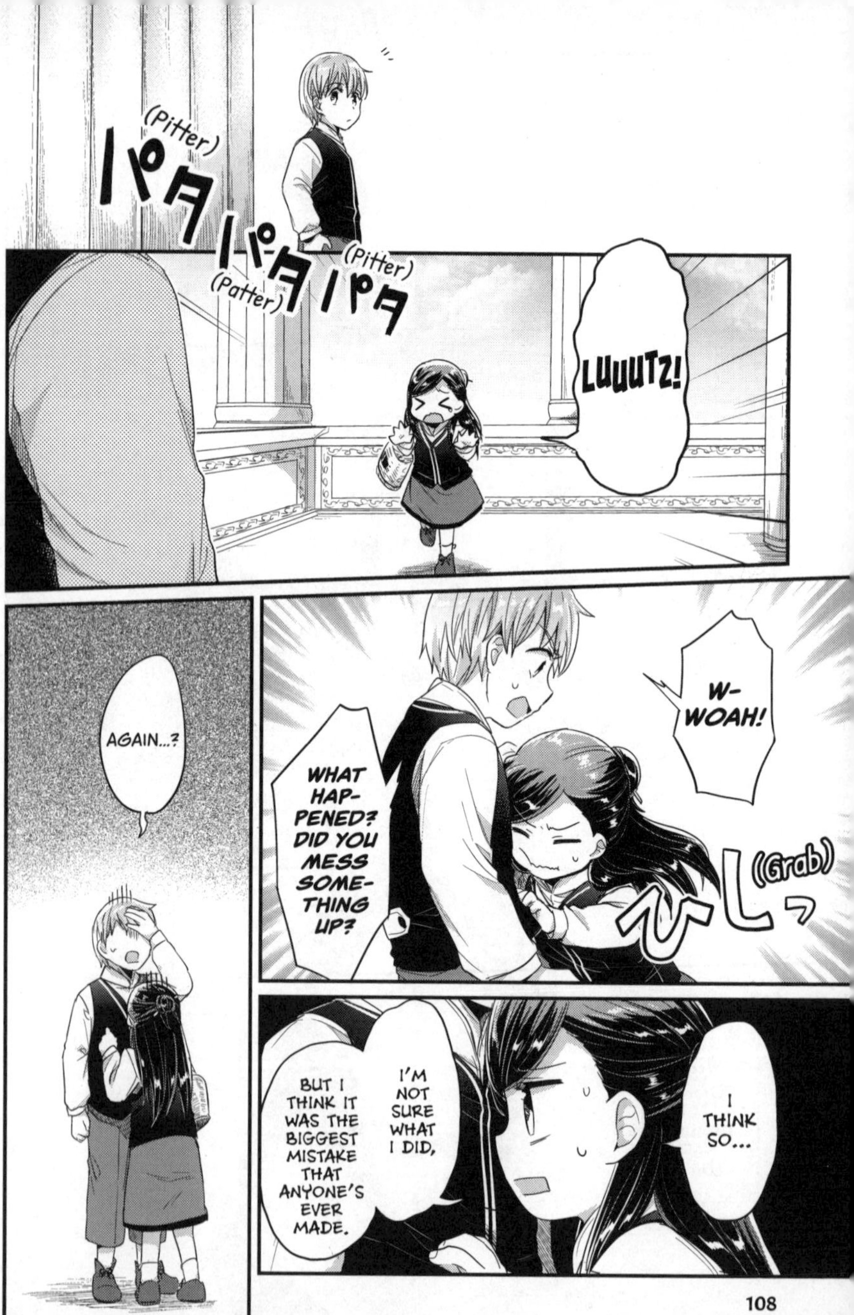
(Pitter)
パタ
(Patter)
パタ
(Pitter)
パタ
LUUUTZ!
W-WOAH!
WHAT HAPPENED? DID YOU MESS SOMETHING UP?
(Grab)
ひしっ
I THINK SO...
I'M NOT SURE WHAT I DID,
BUT I THINK IT WAS THE BIGGEST MISTAKE THAT ANYONE'S EVER MADE.
AGAIN...?

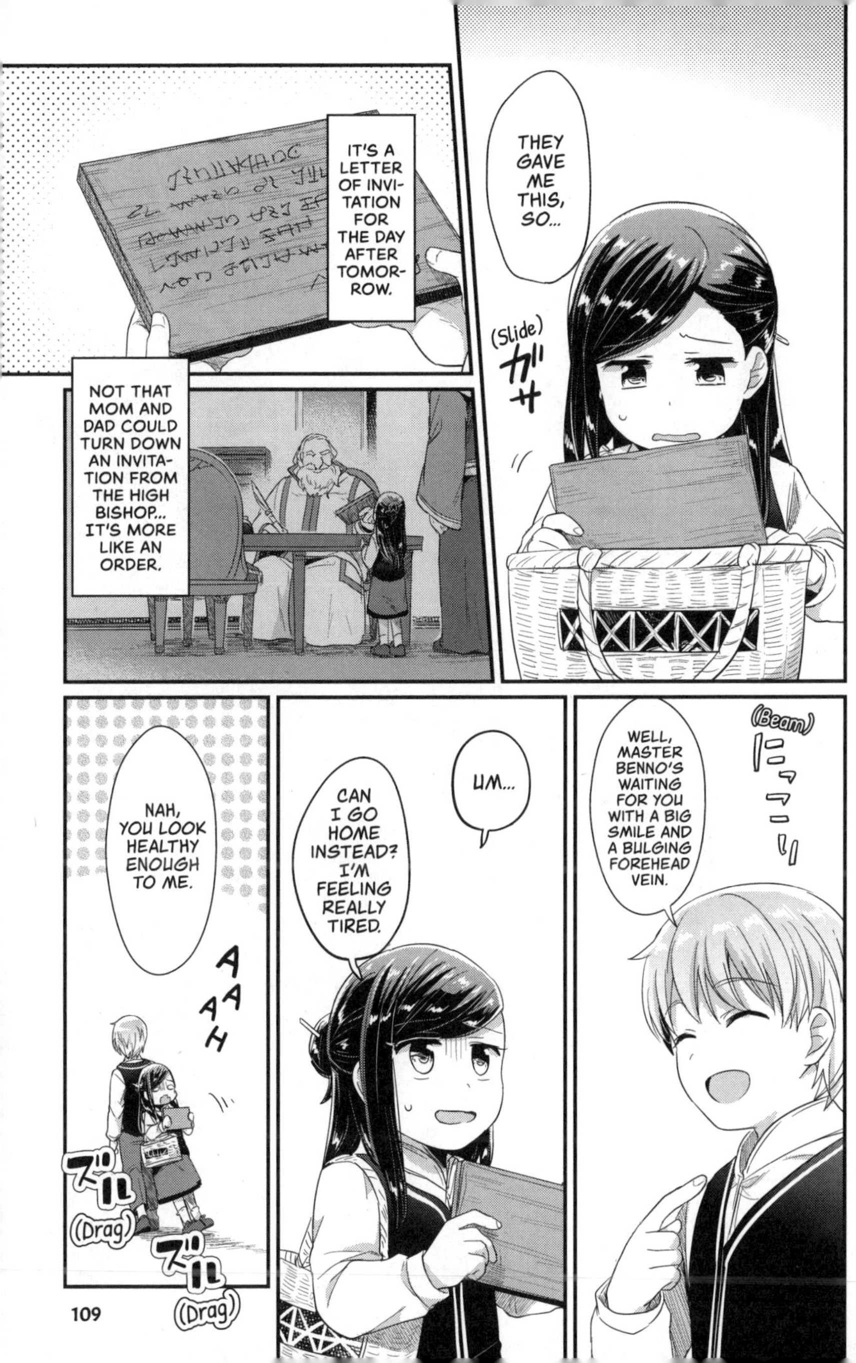

THEY GAVE ME THIS, SO...
(Slide)
IT'S A LETTER OF INVITATION FOR THE DAY AFTER TOMORROW.
NOT THAT MOM AND DAD COULD TURN DOWN AN INVITATION FROM THE HIGH BISHOP... IT'S MORE LIKE AN ORDER.
(Beam)
WELL, MASTER BENNO'S WAITING FOR YOU WITH A BIG SMILE AND A BULGING FOREHEAD VEIN.
UM...
CAN I GO HOME INSTEAD? I'M FEELING REALLY TIRED.
NAH, YOU LOOK HEALTHY ENOUGH TO ME.
AAAH
ズル
(Drag)
ズル
(Drag)

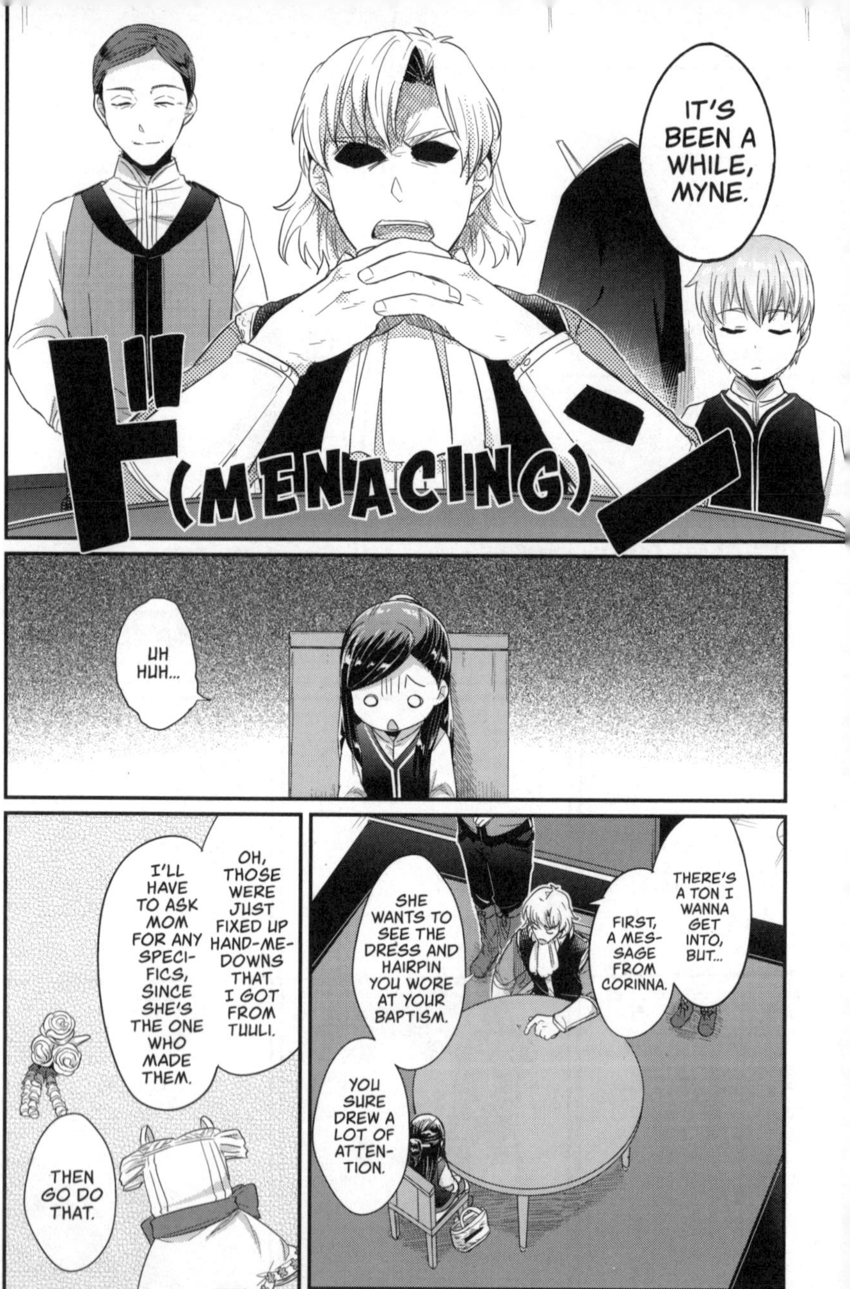
IT'S BEEN A WHILE, MYNE.
(MENACING)
UH HUH...
THERE'S A TON I WANNA GET INTO, BUT...
FIRST, A MESSAGE FROM CORINNA.
SHE WANTS TO SEE THE DRESS AND HAIRPIN YOU WORE AT YOUR BAPTISM.
YOU SURE DREW A LOT OF ATTENTION.
OH, THOSE WERE JUST FIXED UP HAND-ME-DOWNS THAT I GOT FROM TUULI.
I'LL HAVE TO ASK MOM FOR ANY SPECIFICS, SINCE SHE'S THE ONE WHO MADE THEM.
THEN GO DO THAT.

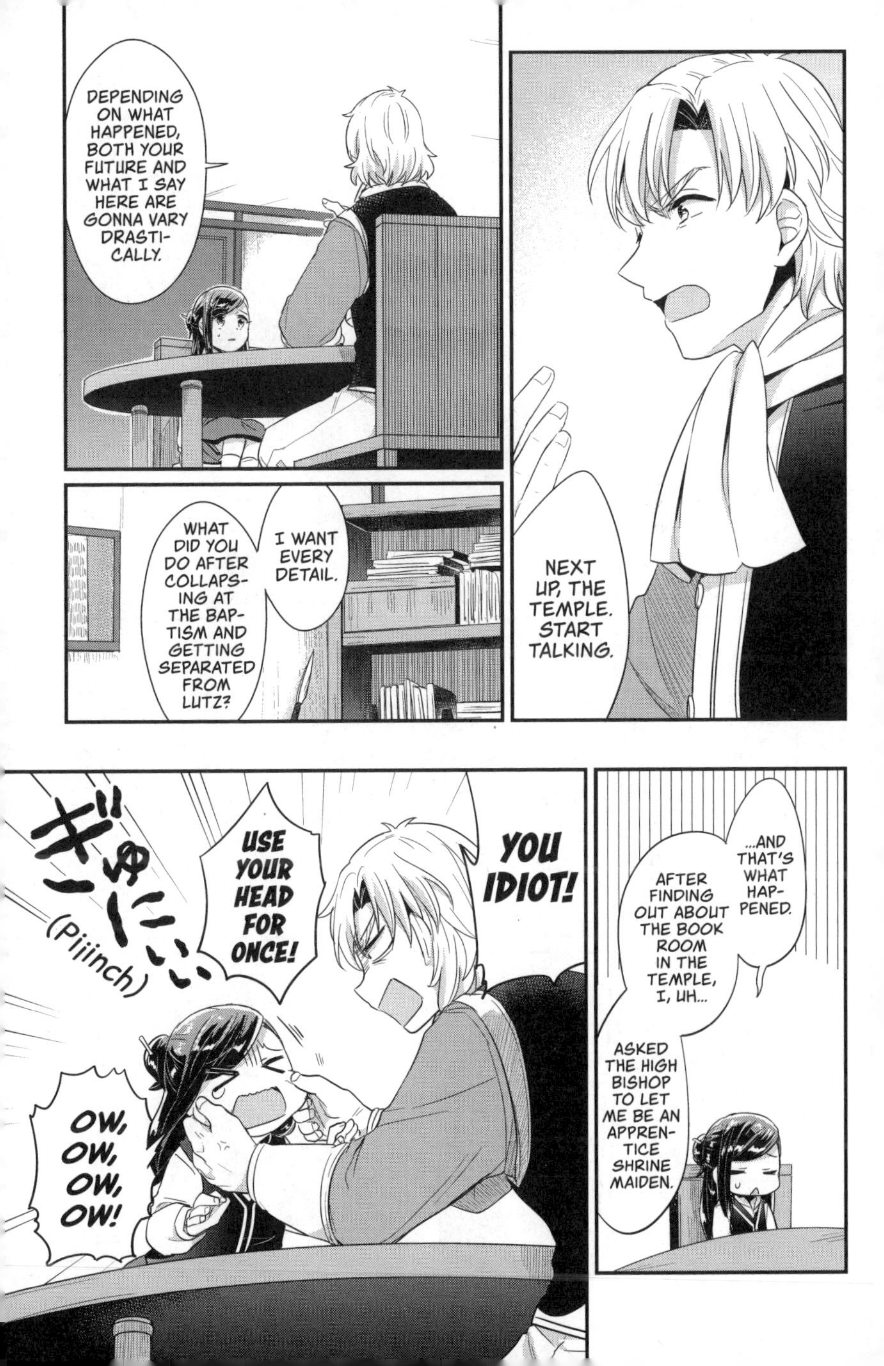
NEXT UP, THE TEMPLE. START TALKING.
DEPENDING ON WHAT HAPPENED, BOTH YOUR FUTURE AND WHAT I SAY HERE ARE GONNA VARY DRASTI-CALLY.
I WANT EVERY DETAIL.
WHAT DID YOU DO AFTER COLLAPS-ING AT THE BAP-TISM AND GETTING SEPARATED FROM LUTZ?
...AND THAT'S WHAT HAP-PENED.
AFTER FINDING OUT ABOUT THE BOOK ROOM IN THE TEMPLE, I, UH...
ASKED THE HIGH BISHOP TO LET ME BE AN APPREN-TICE SHRINE MAIDEN.
YOU IDIOT!
USE YOUR HEAD FOR ONCE!
ぎゅーにぃ
(Pijiinch)
OW, OW, OW, OW!

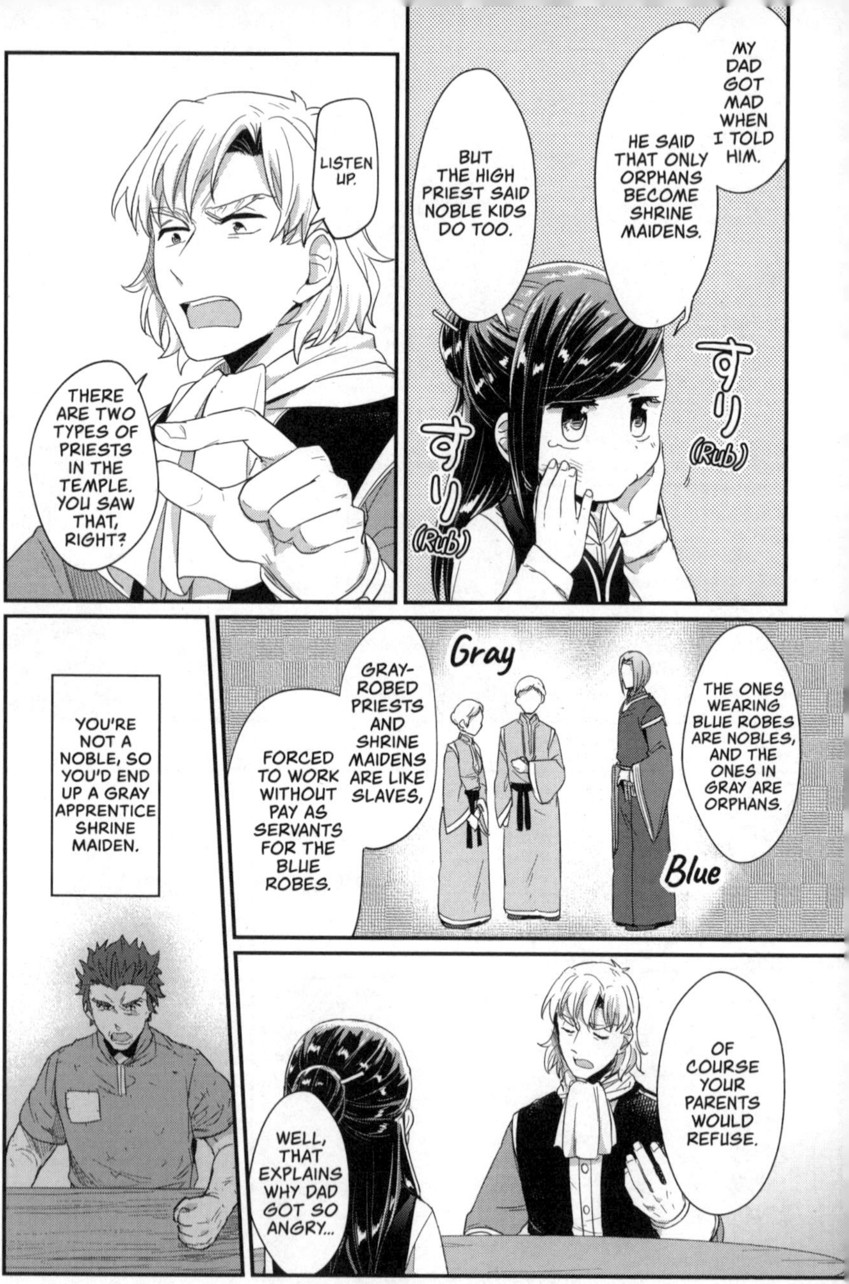
MY DAD GOT MAD WHEN I TOLD HIM.
HE SAID THAT ONLY ORPHANS BECOME SHRINE MAIDENS.
BUT THE HIGH PRIEST SAID NOBLE KIDS DO TOO.
すり
(Rub)
すり
(Rub)
LISTEN UP.
THERE ARE TWO TYPES OF PRIESTS IN THE TEMPLE. YOU SAW THAT, RIGHT?
THE ONES WEARING BLUE ROBES ARE NOBLES, AND THE ONES IN GRAY ARE ORPHANS.
Gray
Blue
GRAY-ROBED PRIESTS AND SHRINE MAIDENS ARE LIKE SLAVES,
FORCED TO WORK WITHOUT PAY AS SERVANTS FOR THE BLUE ROBES.
OF COURSE YOUR PARENTS WOULD REFUSE.
WELL, THAT EXPLAINS WHY DAD GOT SO ANGRY...
YOU'RE NOT A NOBLE, SO YOU'D END UP A GRAY APPRENTICE SHRINE MAIDEN.

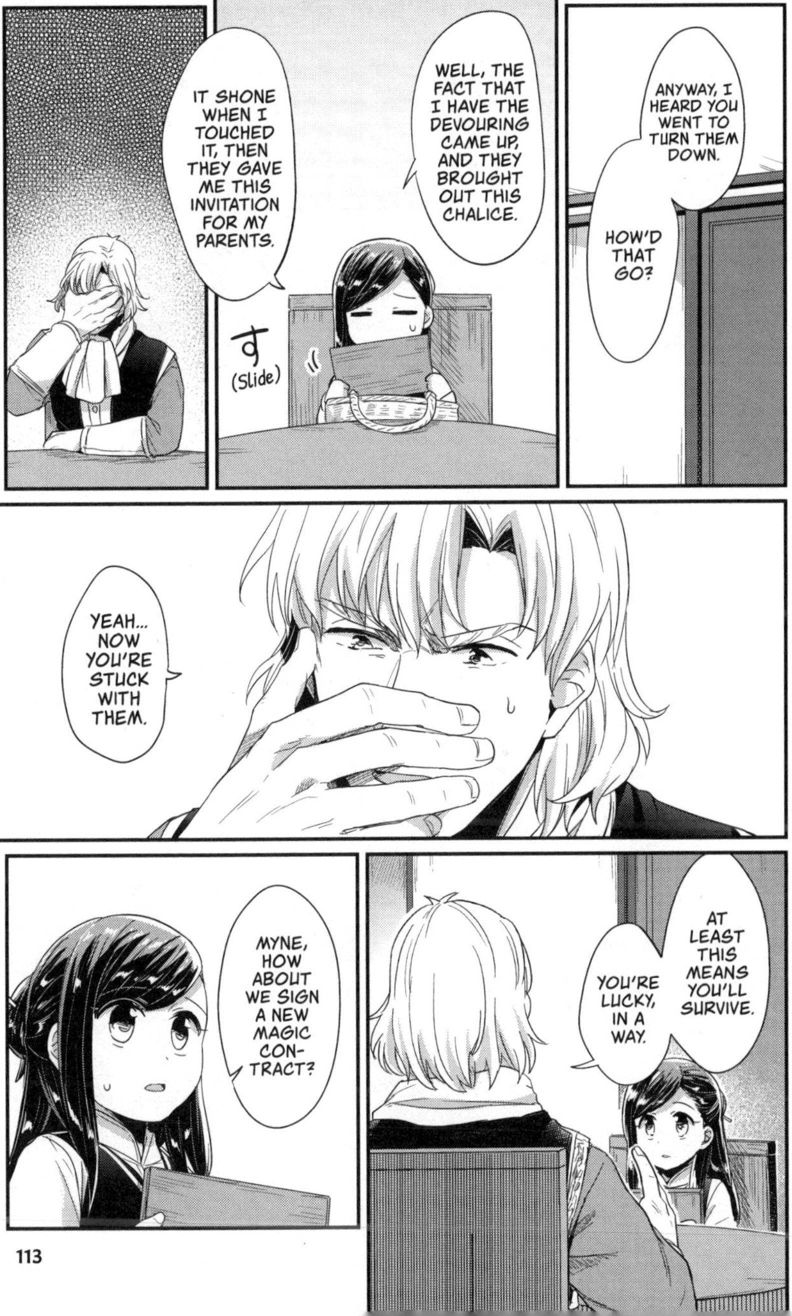
ANYWAY, I HEARD YOU WENT TO TURN THEM DOWN.
HOW'D THAT GO?
WELL, THE FACT THAT I HAVE THE DEVOURING CAME UP, AND THEY BROUGHT OUT THIS CHALICE.
す
(Slide)
IT SHONE WHEN I TOUCHED IT, THEN THEY GAVE ME THIS INVITATION FOR MY PARENTS.
YEAH... NOW YOU'RE STUCK WITH THEM.
AT LEAST THIS MEANS YOU'LL SURVIVE.
YOU'RE LUCKY, IN A WAY.
MYNE, HOW ABOUT WE SIGN A NEW MAGIC CON-TRACT?

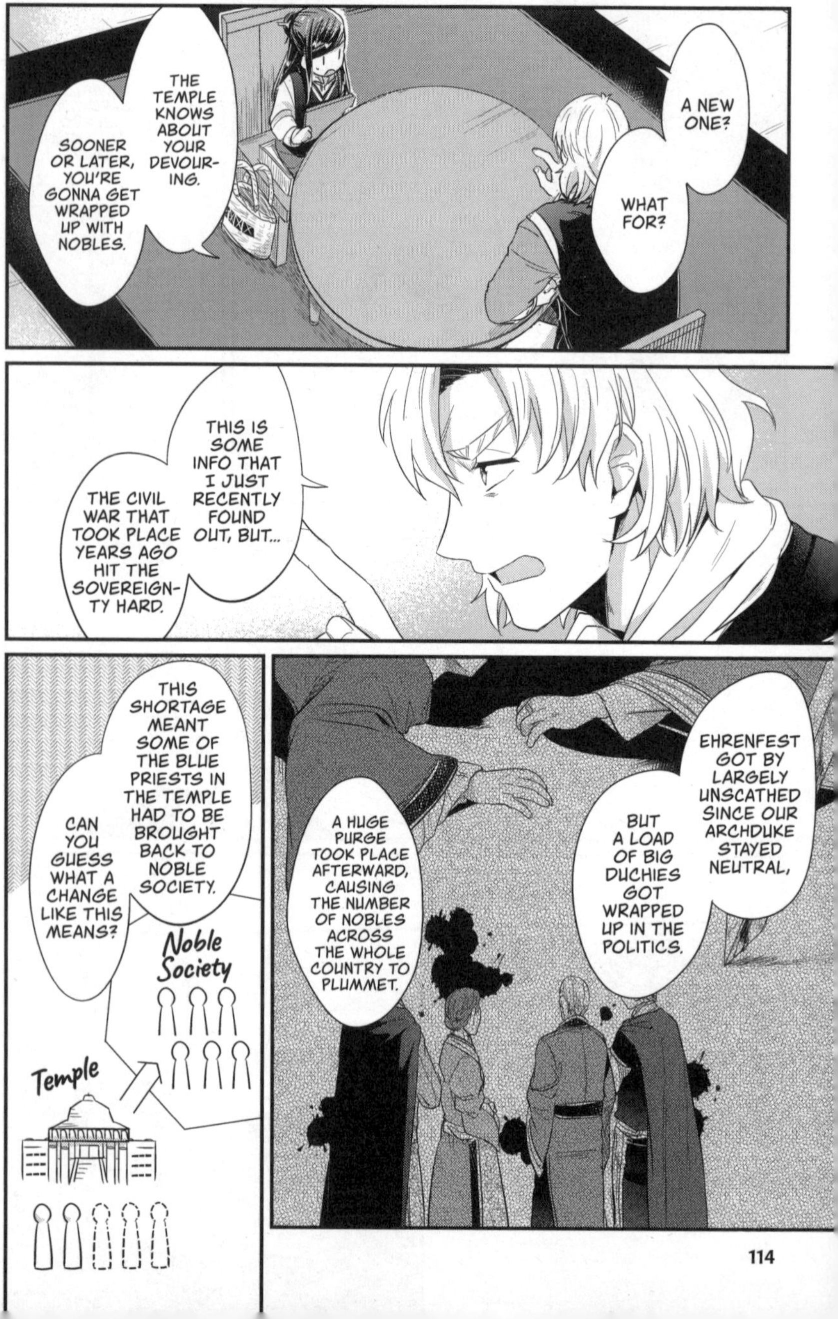
A NEW ONE?
WHAT FOR?
THE TEMPLE KNOWS ABOUT YOUR DEVOURING.
SOONER OR LATER, YOU'RE GONNA GET WRAPPED UP WITH NOBLES.
THIS IS SOME INFO THAT I JUST RECENTLY FOUND OUT, BUT...
THE CIVIL WAR THAT TOOK PLACE YEARS AGO HIT THE SOVEREIGNTY HARD.
EHRENFEST GOT BY LARGELY UNSCATHED SINCE OUR ARCHDUKE STAYED NEUTRAL,
BUT A LOAD OF BIG DUCHIES GOT WRAPPED UP IN THE POLITICS.
A HUGE PURGE TOOK PLACE AFTERWARD, CAUSING THE NUMBER OF NOBLES ACROSS THE WHOLE COUNTRY TO PLUMMET.
THIS SHORTAGE MEANT SOME OF THE BLUE PRIESTS IN THE TEMPLE HAD TO BE BROUGHT BACK TO NOBLE SOCIETY.
CAN YOU GUESS WHAT A CHANGE LIKE THIS MEANS?
Noble Society
Temple

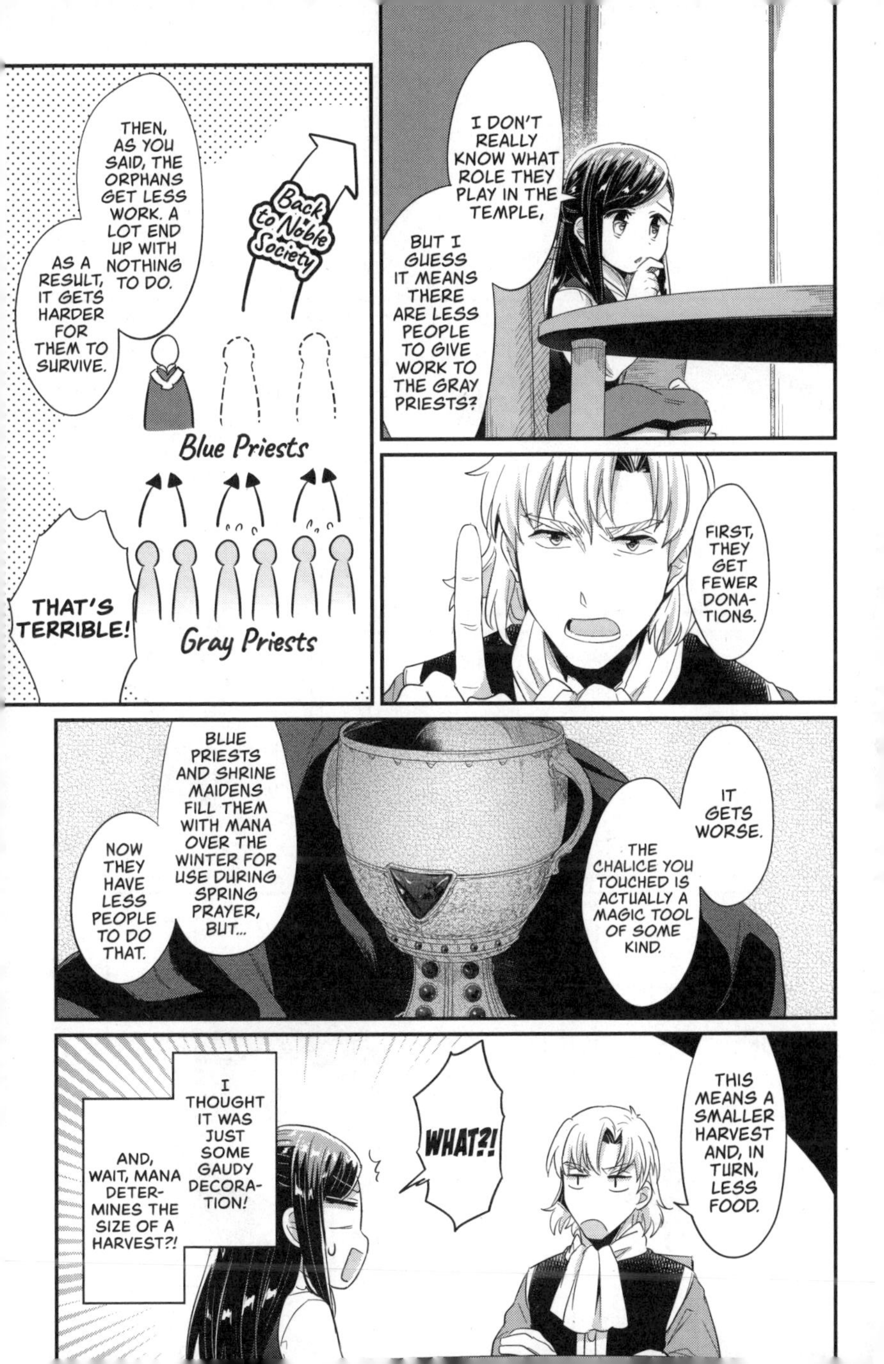
I DON'T REALLY KNOW WHAT ROLE THEY PLAY IN THE TEMPLE,
BUT I GUESS IT MEANS THERE ARE LESS PEOPLE TO GIVE WORK TO THE GRAY PRIESTS?
FIRST, THEY GET FEWER DONA-TIONS.
THEN, AS YOU SAID, THE ORPHANS GET LESS WORK. A LOT END UP WITH NOTHING TO DO.
AS A RESULT, IT GETS HARDER FOR THEM TO SURVIVE.
Back to Noble Society
Blue Priests
Gray Priests
THAT'S TERRIBLE!
IT GETS WORSE.
THE CHALICE YOU TOUCHED IS ACTUALLY A MAGIC TOOL OF SOME KIND.
BLUE PRIESTS AND SHRINE MAIDENS FILL THEM WITH MANA OVER THE WINTER FOR USE DURING SPRING PRAYER, BUT...
NOW THEY HAVE LESS PEOPLE TO DO THAT.
THIS MEANS A SMALLER HARVEST AND, IN TURN, LESS FOOD.
WHAT?!
I THOUGHT IT WAS JUST SOME GAUDY DECORA-TION!
AND, WAIT, MANA DETER-MINES THE SIZE OF A HARVEST?!

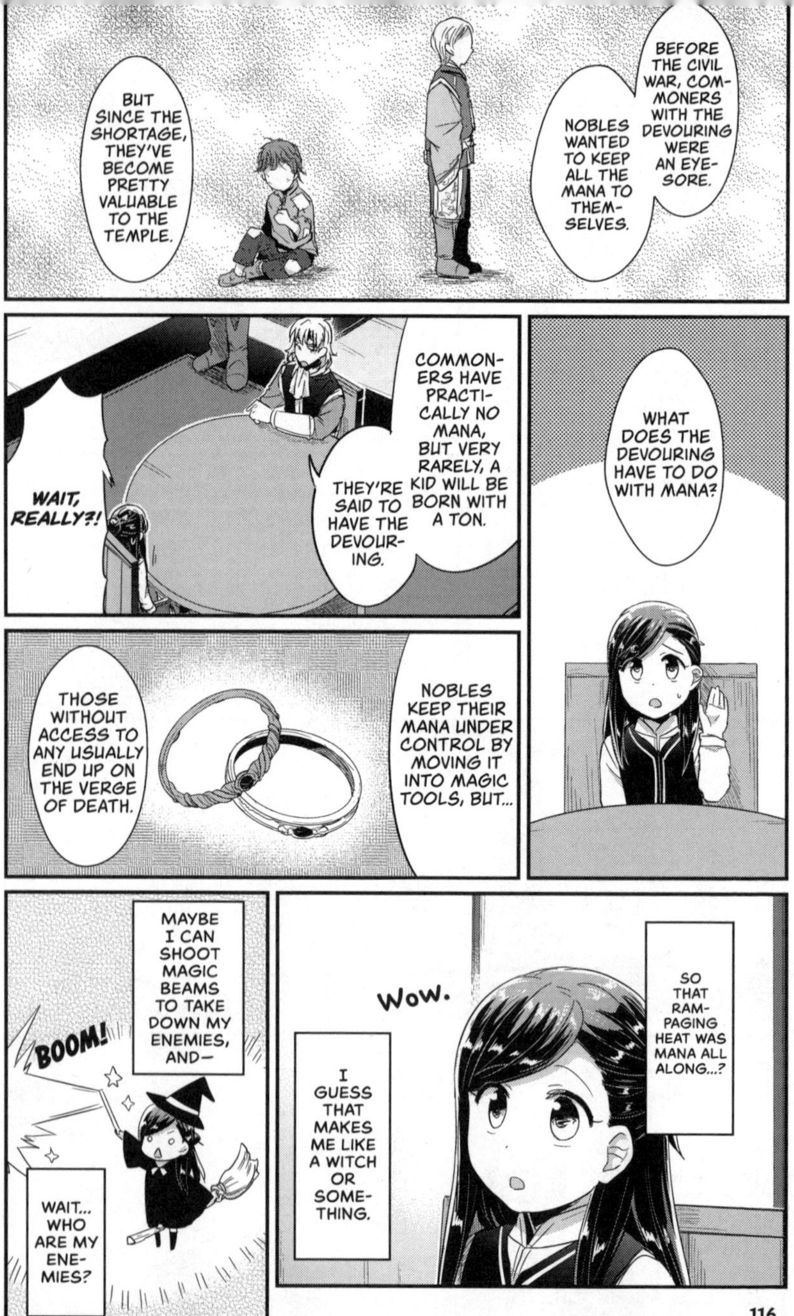
BEFORE THE CIVIL WAR, COMMONERS WITH THE DEVOURING WERE AN EYESORE.
NOBLES WANTED TO KEEP ALL THE MANA TO THEMSELVES.
BUT SINCE THE SHORTAGE, THEY'VE BECOME PRETTY VALUABLE TO THE TEMPLE.
WHAT DOES THE DEVOURING HAVE TO DO WITH MANA?
COMMONERS HAVE PRACTICALLY NO MANA, BUT VERY RARELY, A KID WILL BE BORN WITH A TON.
THEY'RE SAID TO HAVE THE DEVOURING.
WAIT, REALLY?!
NOBLES KEEP THEIR MANA UNDER CONTROL BY MOVING IT INTO MAGIC TOOLS, BUT...
THOSE WITHOUT ACCESS TO ANY USUALLY END UP ON THE VERGE OF DEATH.
SO THAT RAMPAGING HEAT WAS MANA ALL ALONG...?
Wow.
I GUESS THAT MAKES ME LIKE A WITCH OR SOMETHING.
MAYBE I CAN SHOOT MAGIC BEAMS TO TAKE DOWN MY ENEMIES, AND—
BOOM!
WAIT... WHO ARE MY ENEMIES?

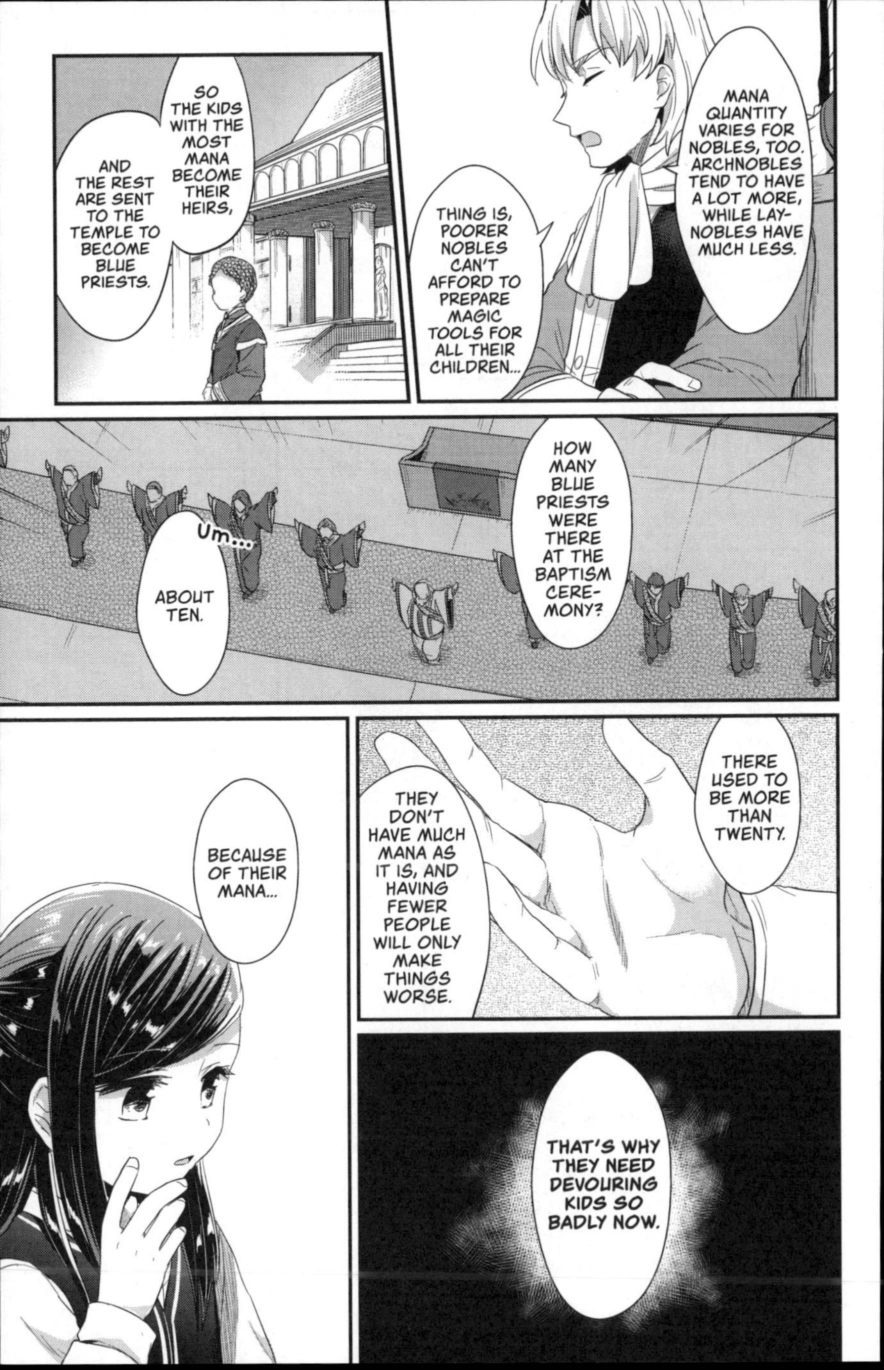
MANA QUANTITY VARIES FOR NOBLES, TOO. ARCHNOBLES TEND TO HAVE A LOT MORE, WHILE LAY-NOBLES HAVE MUCH LESS.
THING IS, POORER NOBLES CAN'T AFFORD TO PREPARE MAGIC TOOLS FOR ALL THEIR CHILDREN...
SO THE KIDS WITH THE MOST MANA BECOME THEIR HEIRS,
AND THE REST ARE SENT TO THE TEMPLE TO BECOME BLUE PRIESTS.
HOW MANY BLUE PRIESTS WERE THERE AT THE BAPTISM CEREMONY?
Um...
ABOUT TEN.
THERE USED TO BE MORE THAN TWENTY.
THEY DON'T HAVE MUCH MANA AS IT IS, AND HAVING FEWER PEOPLE WILL ONLY MAKE THINGS WORSE.
THAT'S WHY THEY NEED DEVOURING KIDS SO BADLY NOW.
BECAUSE OF THEIR MANA...

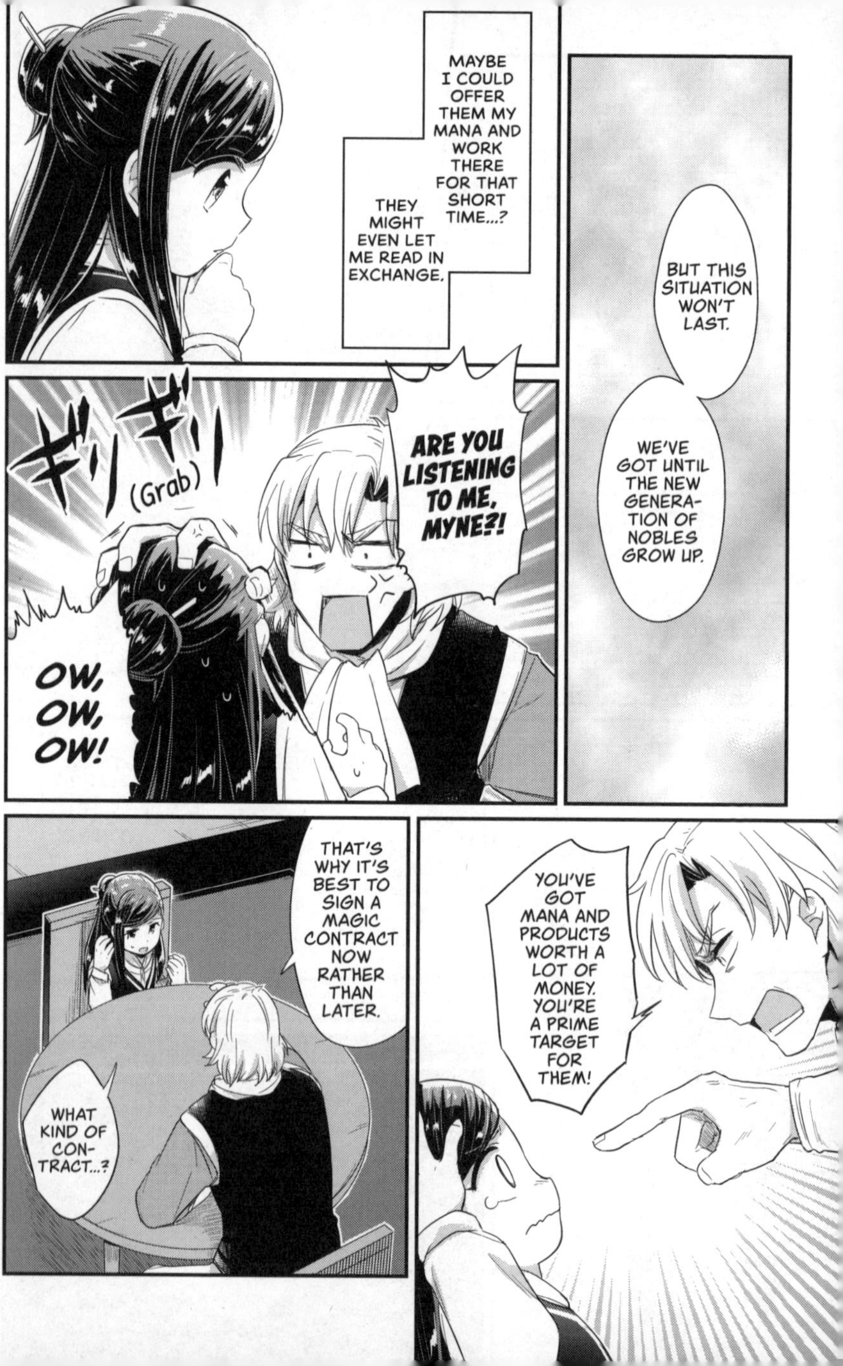
BUT THIS SITUATION WON'T LAST.
WE'VE GOT UNTIL THE NEW GENERATION OF NOBLES GROW UP.
MAYBE I COULD OFFER THEM MY MANA AND WORK THERE FOR THAT SHORT TIME...?
THEY MIGHT EVEN LET ME READ IN EXCHANGE.
ARE YOU LISTENING TO ME, MYNE?!
ギリ ギリ
(Grab)
OW, OW, OW!
YOU'VE GOT MANA AND PRODUCTS WORTH A LOT OF MONEY. YOU'RE A PRIME TARGET FOR THEM!
THAT'S WHY IT'S BEST TO SIGN A MAGIC CONTRACT NOW RATHER THAN LATER.
WHAT KIND OF CON-TRACT...?

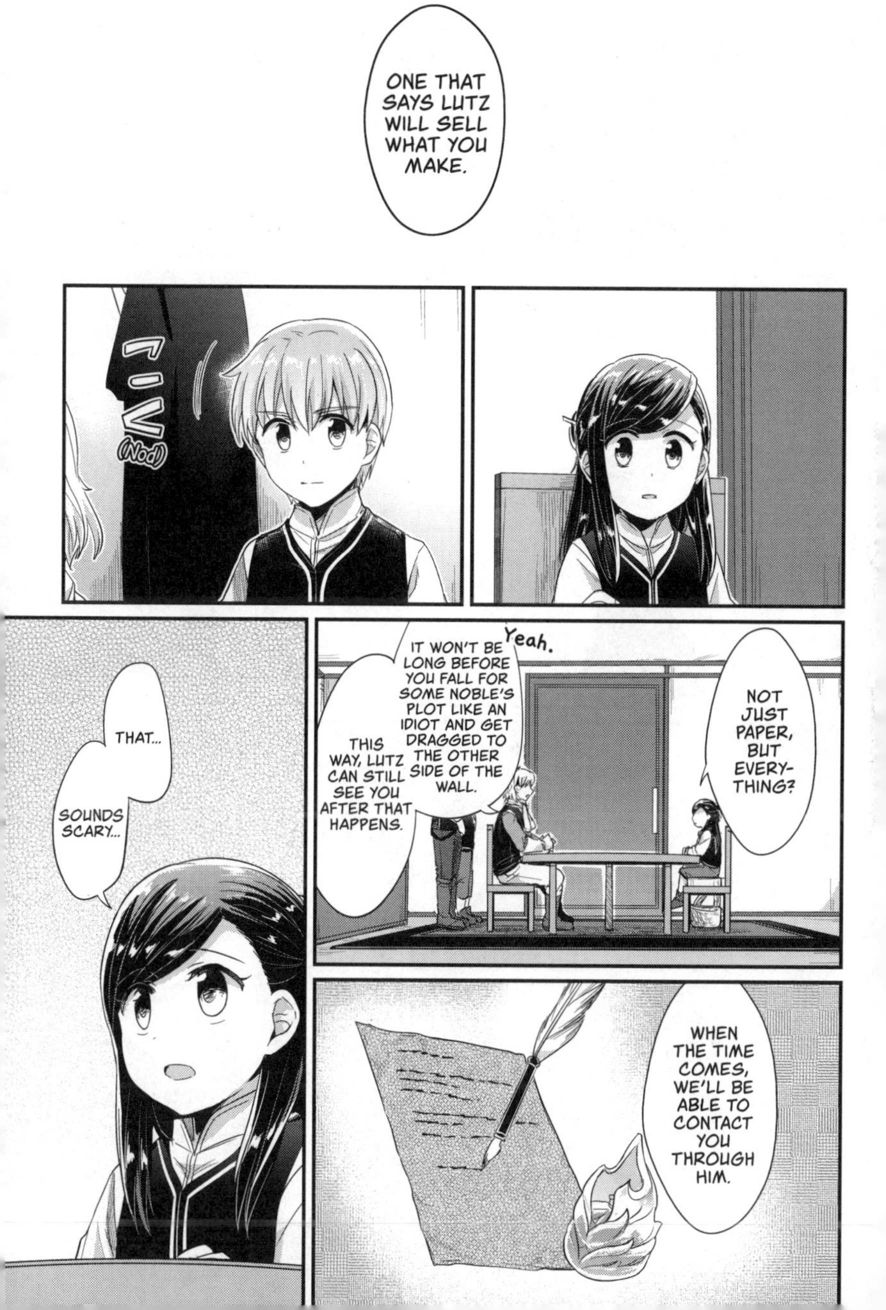
ONE THAT SAYS LUTZ WILL SELL WHAT YOU MAKE.
(Nod)
NOT JUST PAPER, BUT EVERY-THING?
Yeah.
IT WON'T BE LONG BEFORE YOU FALL FOR SOME NOBLE'S PLOT LIKE AN IDIOT AND GET DRAGGED TO THE OTHER SIDE OF THE WALL.
THIS WAY, LUTZ CAN STILL SEE YOU AFTER THAT HAPPENS.
WHEN THE TIME COMES, WE'LL BE ABLE TO CONTACT YOU THROUGH HIM.
THAT...
SOUNDS SCARY...

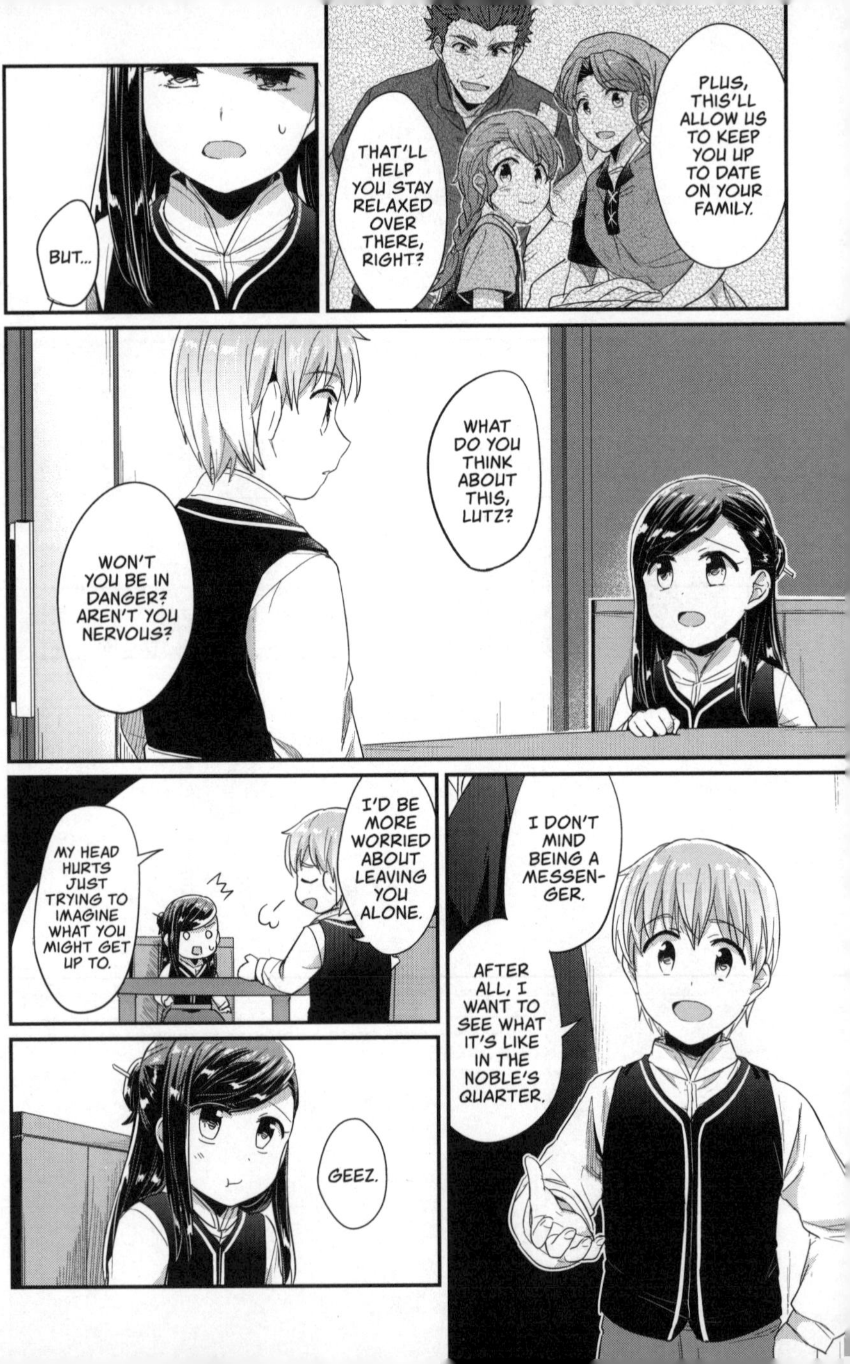
PLUS, THIS'LL ALLOW US TO KEEP YOU UP TO DATE ON YOUR FAMILY.
THAT'LL HELP YOU STAY RELAXED OVER THERE, RIGHT?
BUT...
WHAT DO YOU THINK ABOUT THIS, LUTZ?
WON'T YOU BE IN DANGER? AREN'T YOU NERVOUS?
I DON'T MIND BEING A MESSEN-GER.
AFTER ALL, I WANT TO SEE WHAT IT'S LIKE IN THE NOBLE'S QUARTER.
I'D BE MORE WORRIED ABOUT LEAVING YOU ALONE.
MY HEAD HURTS JUST TRYING TO IMAGINE WHAT YOU MIGHT GET UP TO.
GEEZ.

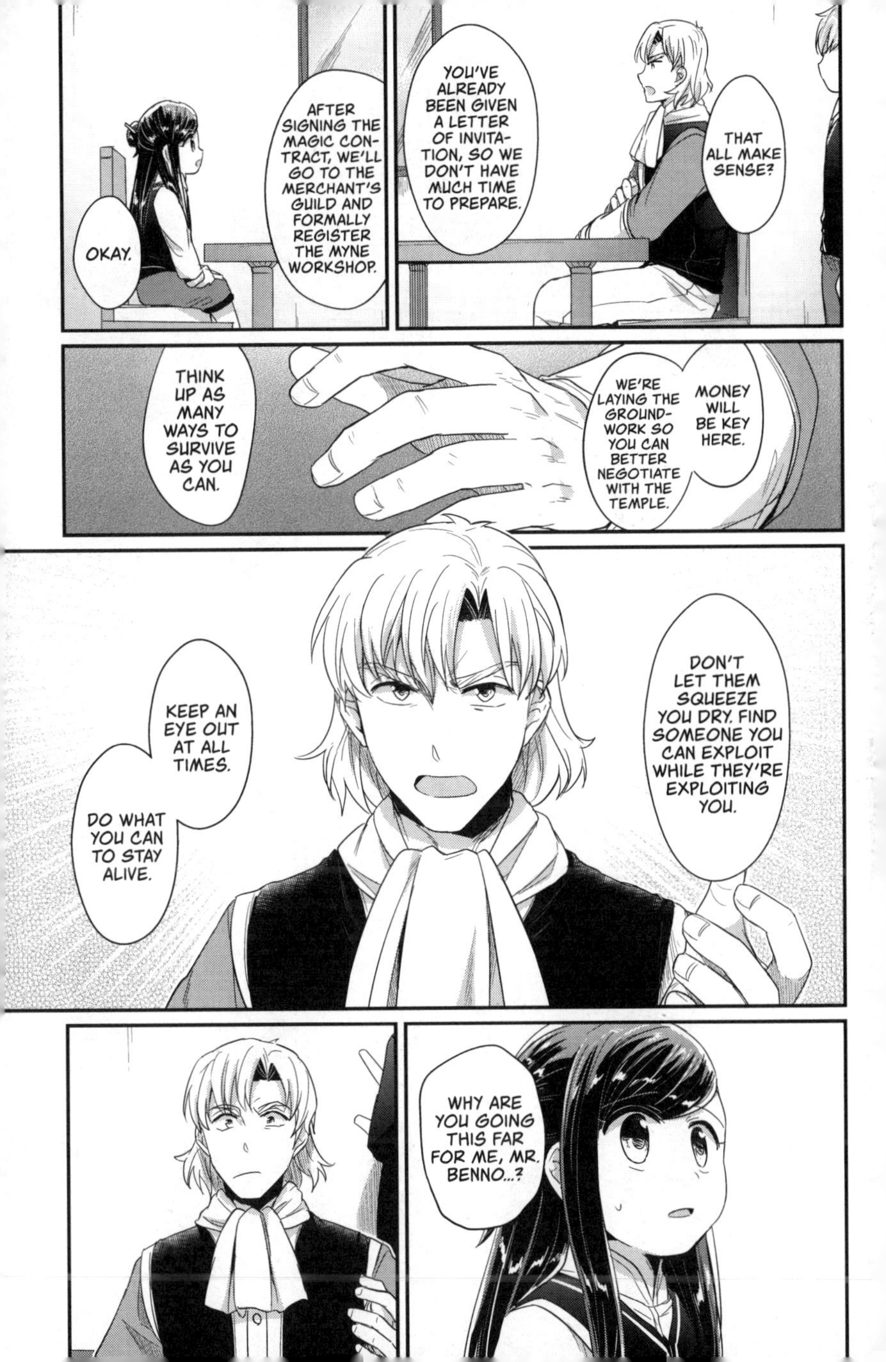
YOU'VE ALREADY BEEN GIVEN A LETTER OF INVITATION, SO WE DON'T HAVE MUCH TIME TO PREPARE.
THAT ALL MAKE SENSE?
AFTER SIGNING THE MAGIC CONTRACT, WE'LL GO TO THE MERCHANT'S GUILD AND FORMALLY REGISTER THE MYNE WORKSHOP.
OKAY.
MONEY WILL BE KEY HERE.
WE'RE LAYING THE GROUNDWORK SO YOU CAN BETTER NEGOTIATE WITH THE TEMPLE.
THINK UP AS MANY WAYS TO SURVIVE AS YOU CAN.
DON'T LET THEM SQUEEZE YOU DRY. FIND SOMEONE YOU CAN EXPLOIT WHILE THEY'RE EXPLOITING YOU.
KEEP AN EYE OUT AT ALL TIMES.
DO WHAT YOU CAN TO STAY ALIVE.
WHY ARE YOU GOING THIS FAR FOR ME, MR. BENNO...?

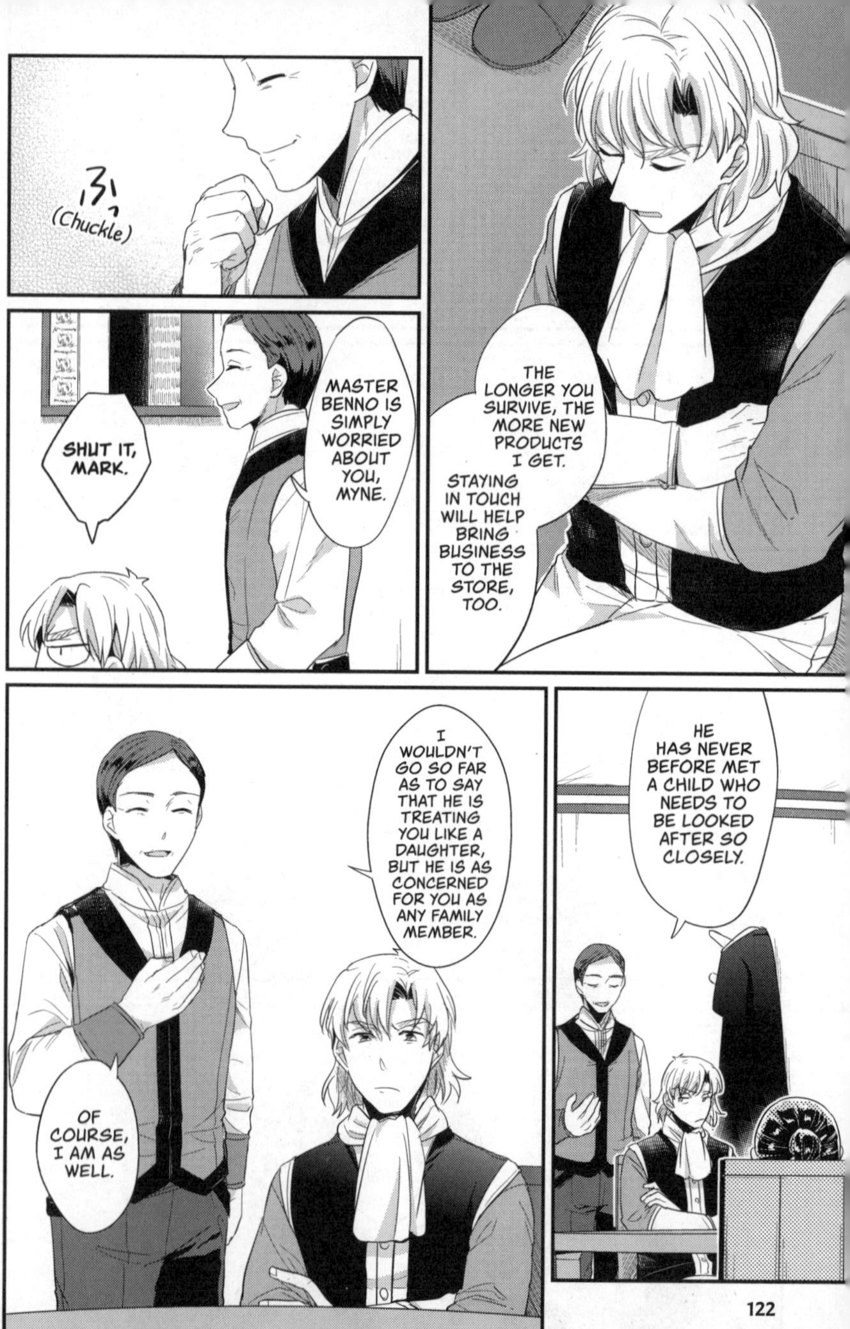
THE LONGER YOU SURVIVE, THE MORE NEW PRODUCTS I GET.
STAYING IN TOUCH WILL HELP BRING BUSINESS TO THE STORE, TOO.
ふっ
(Chuckle)
MASTER BENNO IS SIMPLY WORRIED ABOUT YOU, MYNE.
SHUT IT, MARK.
HE HAS NEVER BEFORE MET A CHILD WHO NEEDS TO BE LOOKED AFTER SO CLOSELY.
I WOULDN'T GO SO FAR AS TO SAY THAT HE IS TREATING YOU LIKE A DAUGHTER, BUT HE IS AS CONCERNED FOR YOU AS ANY FAMILY MEMBER.
OF COURSE, I AM AS WELL.

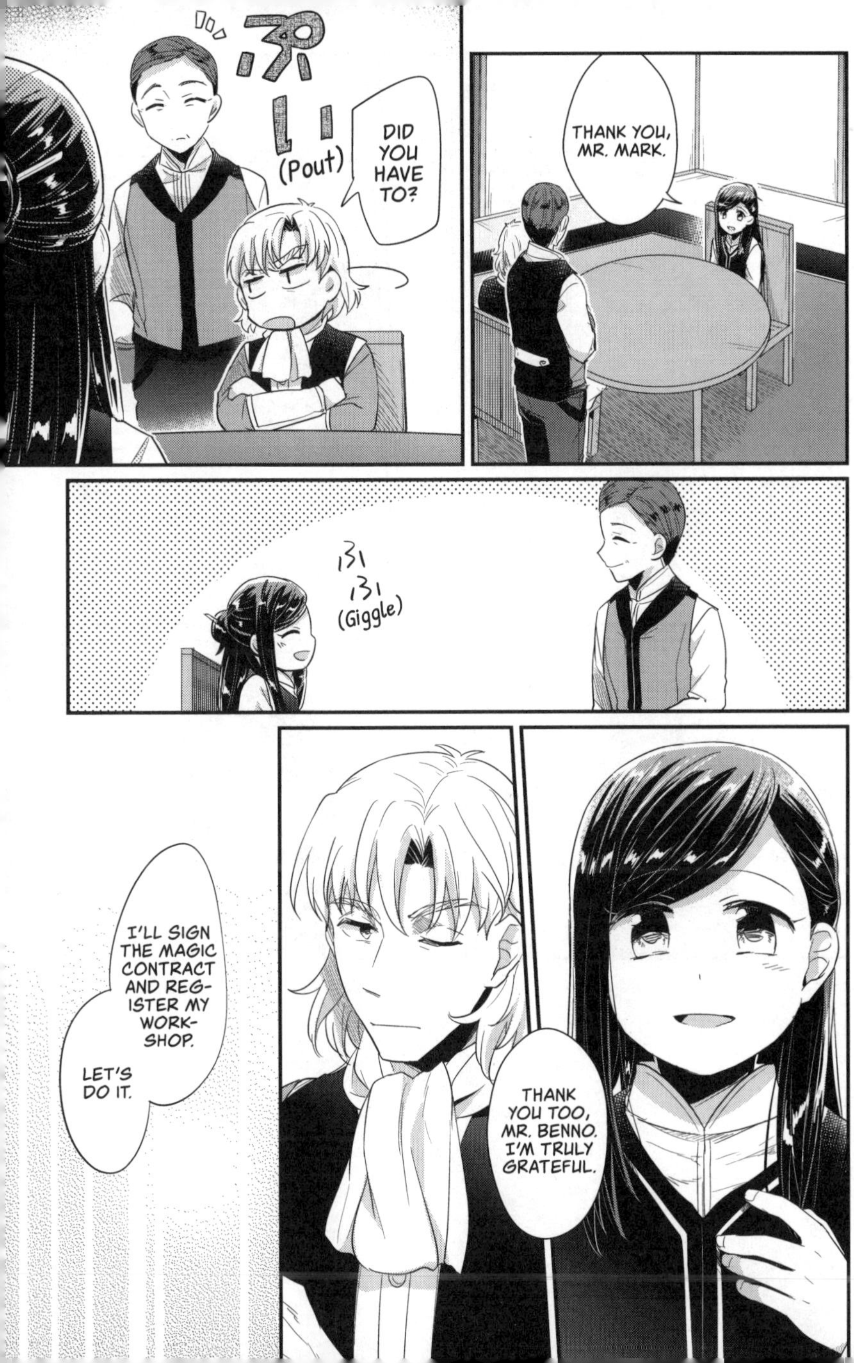
THANK YOU, MR. MARK.
(Pout)
DID YOU HAVE TO?
(Giggle)
THANK YOU TOO, MR. BENNO. I'M TRULY GRATEFUL.
I'LL SIGN THE MAGIC CONTRACT AND REGISTER MY WORKSHOP.
LET'S DO IT.

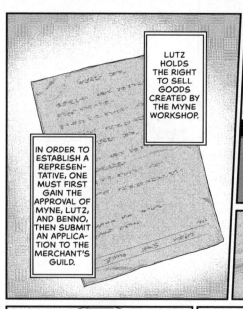

LUTZ HOLDS THE RIGHT TO SELL GOODS CREATED BY THE MYNE WORKSHOP.

IN ORDER TO ESTABLISH A REPRESENTATIVE, ONE MUST FIRST GAIN THE APPROVAL OF MYNE, LUTZ, AND BENNO, THEN SUBMIT AN APPLICATION TO THE MERCHANT'S GUILD.

YEAH.

HERE, LUTZ.

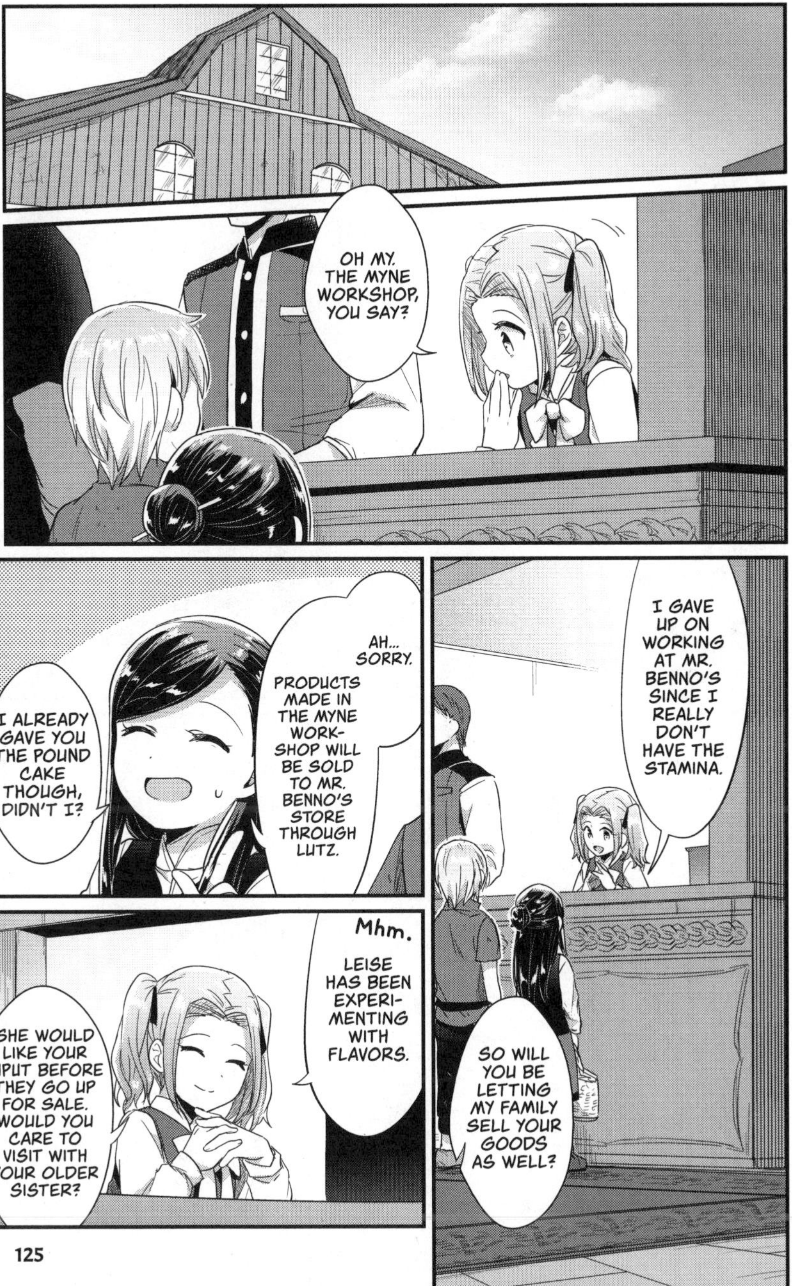
OH MY. THE MYNE WORKSHOP, YOU SAY?
I GAVE UP ON WORKING AT MR. BENNO'S SINCE I REALLY DON'T HAVE THE STAMINA.
SO WILL YOU BE LETTING MY FAMILY SELL YOUR GOODS AS WELL?
AH... SORRY.
PRODUCTS MADE IN THE MYNE WORK-SHOP WILL BE SOLD TO MR. BENNO'S STORE THROUGH LUTZ.
I ALREADY GAVE YOU THE POUND CAKE THOUGH, DIDN'T I?
Mhm.
LEISE HAS BEEN EXPERI-MENTING WITH FLAVORS.
SHE WOULD LIKE YOUR INPUT BEFORE THEY GO UP FOR SALE. WOULD YOU CARE TO VISIT WITH YOUR OLDER SISTER?

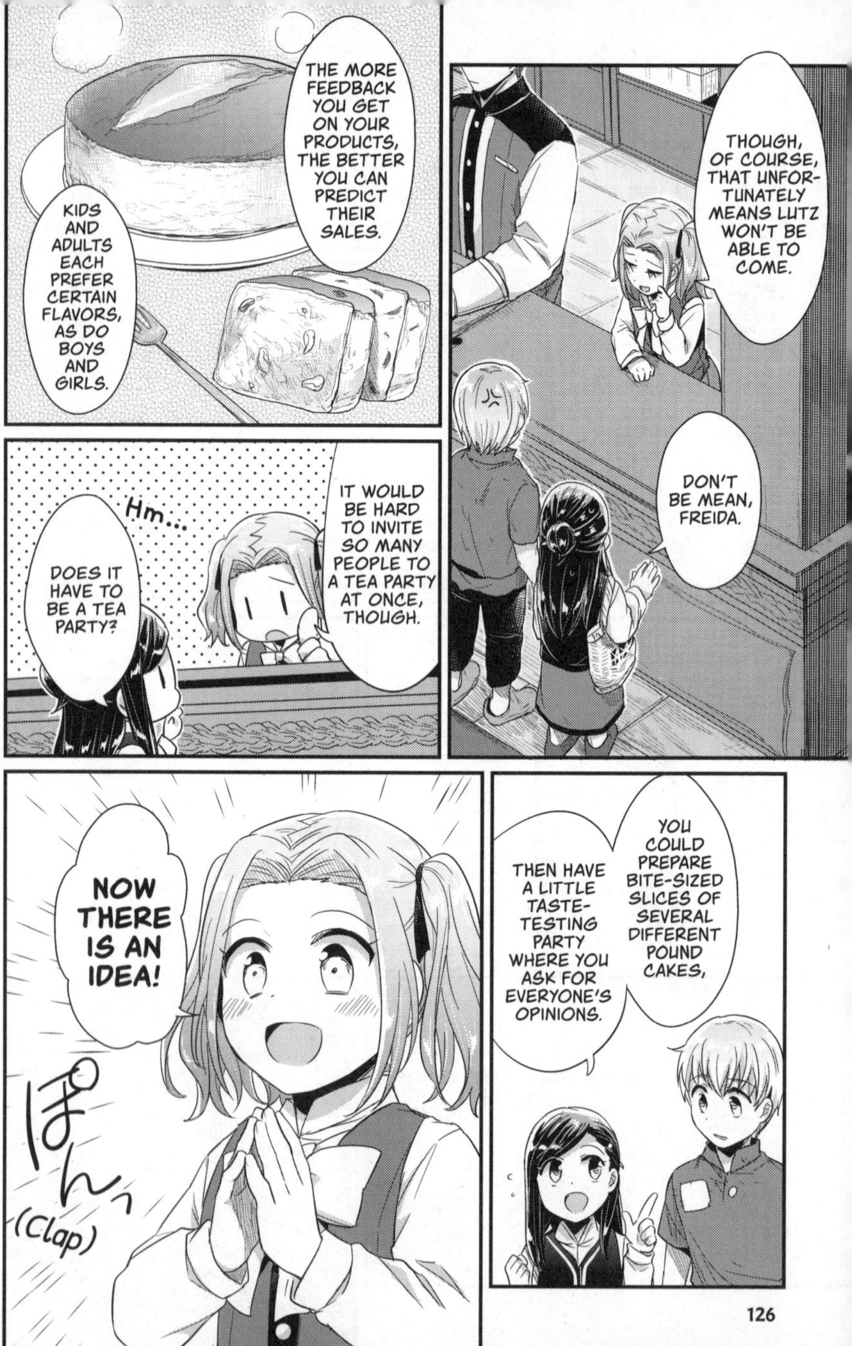
THOUGH, OF COURSE, THAT UNFORTUNATELY MEANS LUTZ WON'T BE ABLE TO COME.
DON'T BE MEAN, FREIDA.
THE MORE FEEDBACK YOU GET ON YOUR PRODUCTS, THE BETTER YOU CAN PREDICT THEIR SALES.
KIDS AND ADULTS EACH PREFER CERTAIN FLAVORS, AS DO BOYS AND GIRLS.
IT WOULD BE HARD TO INVITE SO MANY PEOPLE TO A TEA PARTY AT ONCE, THOUGH.
Hm...
DOES IT HAVE TO BE A TEA PARTY?
YOU COULD PREPARE BITE-SIZED SLICES OF SEVERAL DIFFERENT POUND CAKES,
THEN HAVE A LITTLE TASTE-TESTING PARTY WHERE YOU ASK FOR EVERYONE'S OPINIONS.
NOW THERE IS AN IDEA!
ぽん
(Clap)

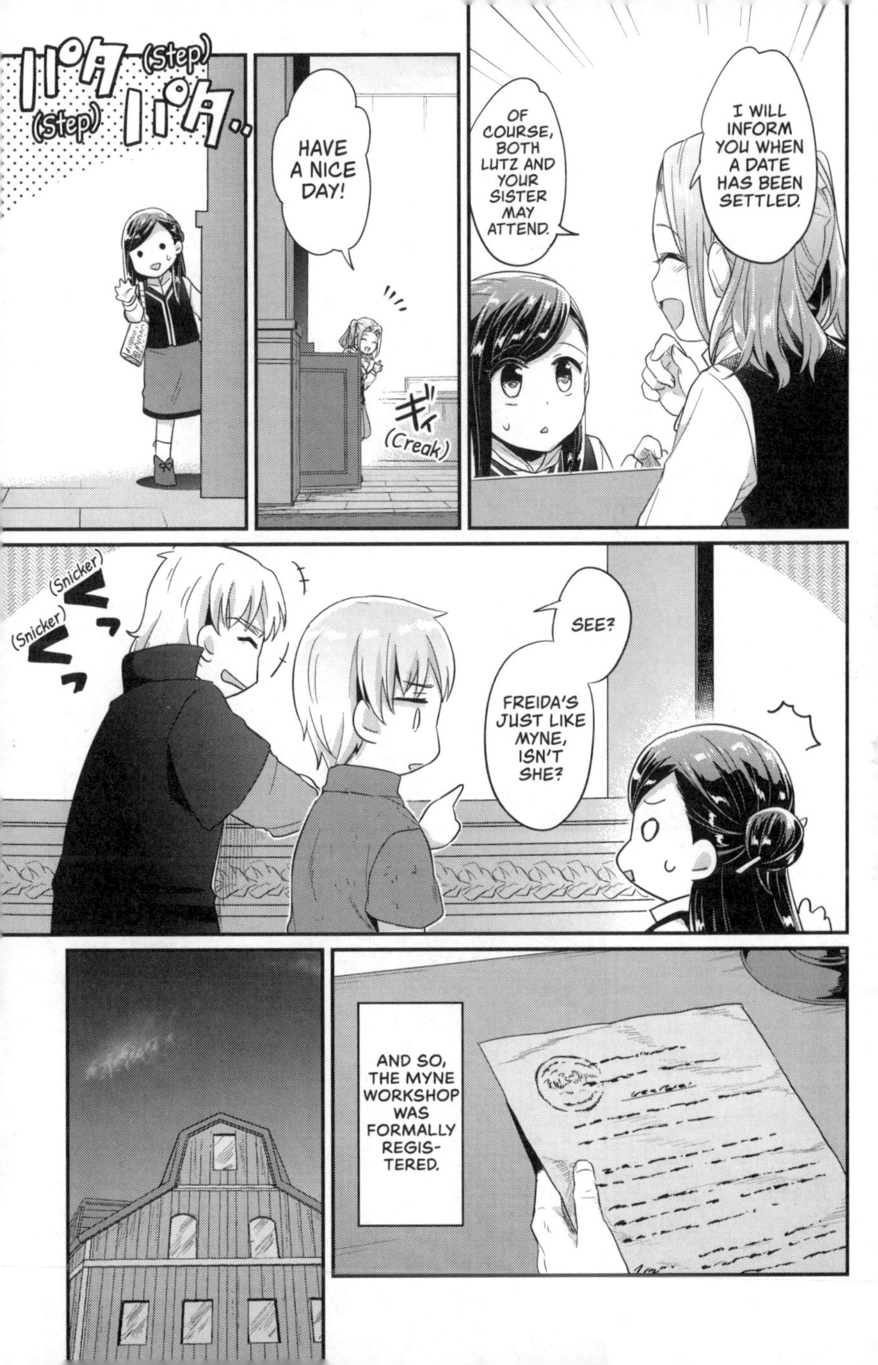
I WILL INFORM YOU WHEN A DATE HAS BEEN SETTLED.
OF COURSE, BOTH LUTZ AND YOUR SISTER MAY ATTEND.
HAVE A NICE DAY!
ギィ
(Creak)
パタ
(Step)
パタ..
(Step)
SEE?
FREIDA'S JUST LIKE MYNE, ISN'T SHE?
(Snicker)
(Snicker)
AND SO, THE MYNE WORKSHOP WAS FORMALLY REGIS-TERED.

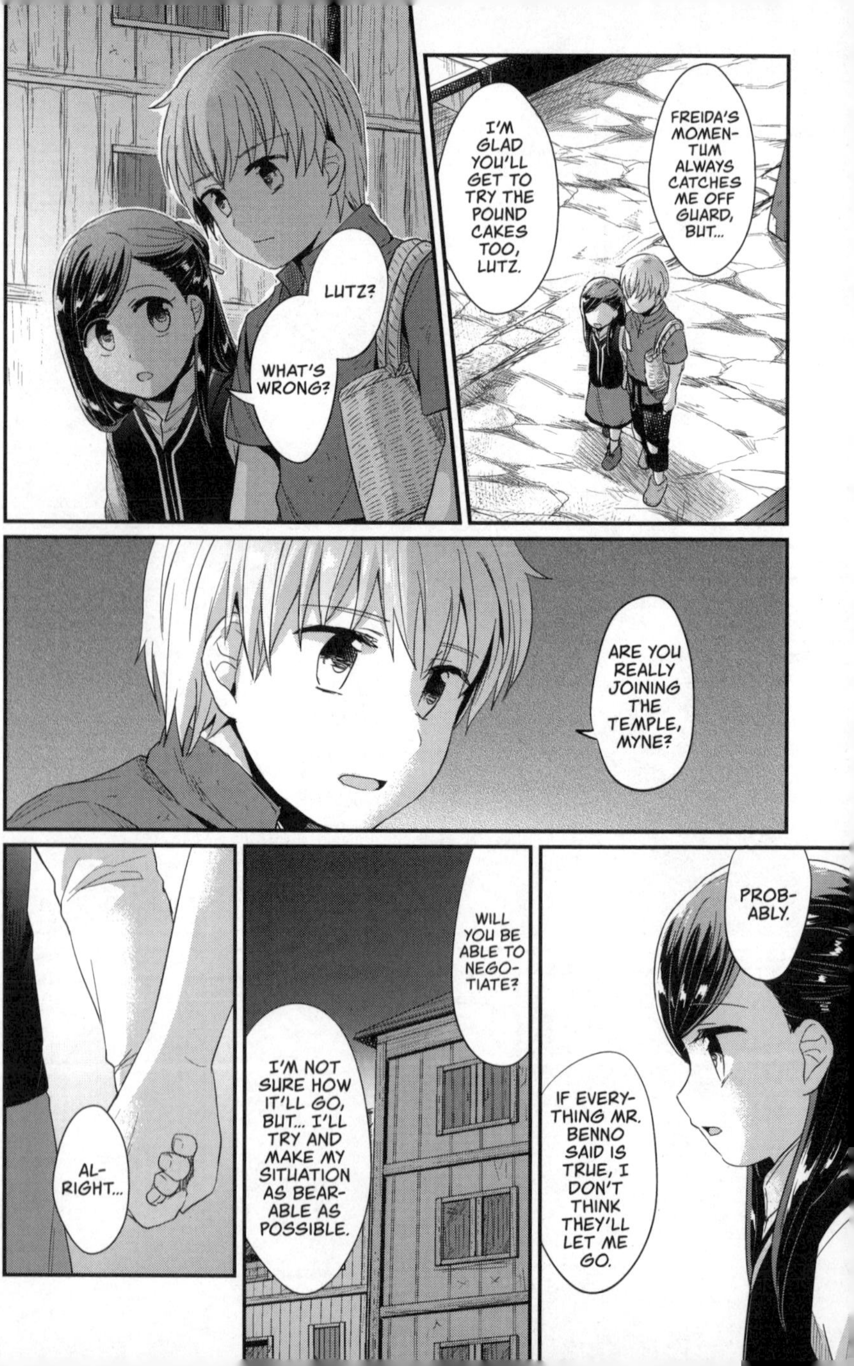
FREIDA'S MOMENTUM ALWAYS CATCHES ME OFF GUARD, BUT...
I'M GLAD YOU'LL GET TO TRY THE POUND CAKES TOO, LUTZ.
LUTZ?
WHAT'S WRONG?
ARE YOU REALLY JOINING THE TEMPLE, MYNE?
PROBABLY.
IF EVERYTHING MR. BENNO SAID IS TRUE, I DON'T THINK THEY'LL LET ME GO.
WILL YOU BE ABLE TO NEGOTIATE?
I'M NOT SURE HOW IT'LL GO, BUT... I'LL TRY AND MAKE MY SITUATION AS BEARABLE AS POSSIBLE.
ALRIGHT...

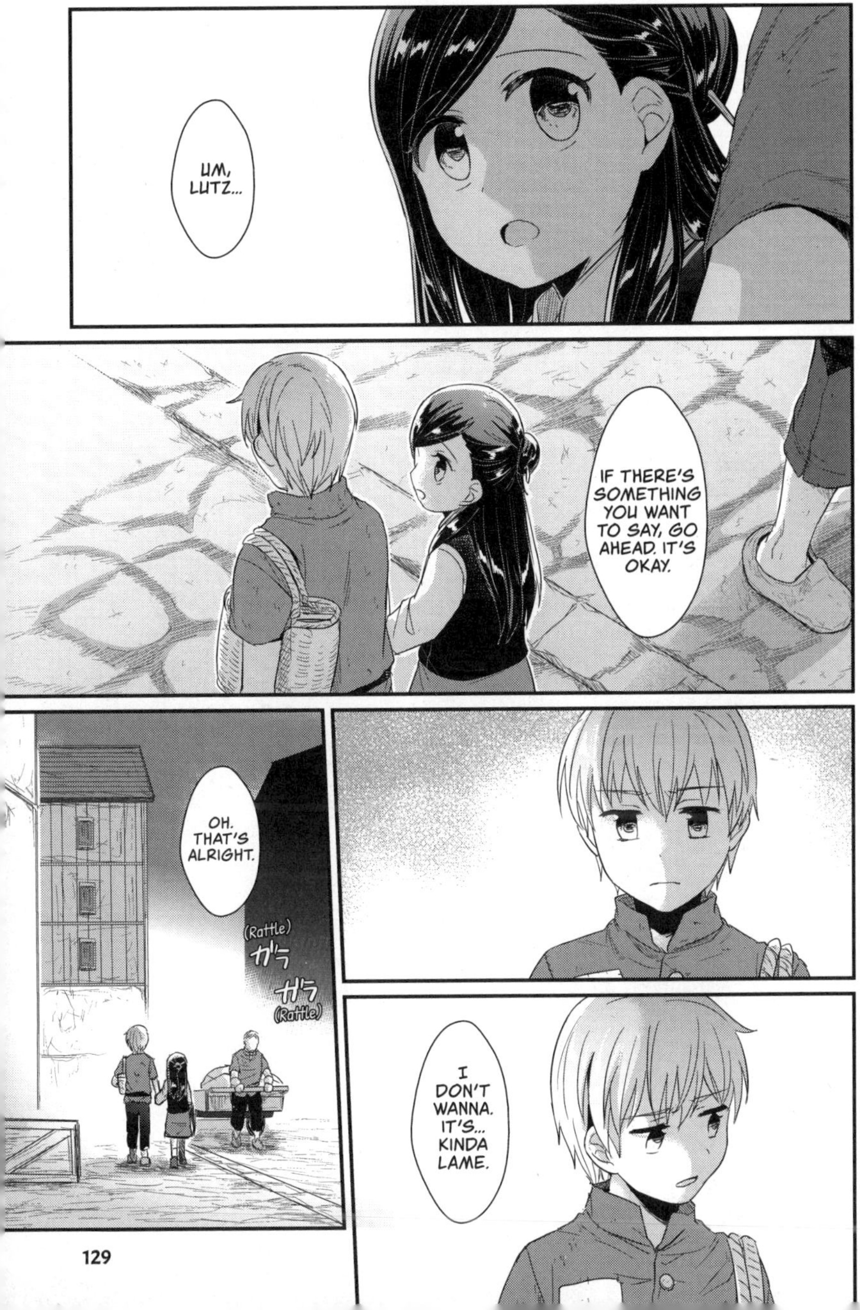

UM, LUTZ...
IF THERE'S SOMETHING YOU WANT TO SAY, GO AHEAD. IT'S OKAY.
I DON'T WANNA. IT'S... KINDA LAME.
OH. THAT'S ALRIGHT.
(Rattle) ガラ
ガラ (Rattle)

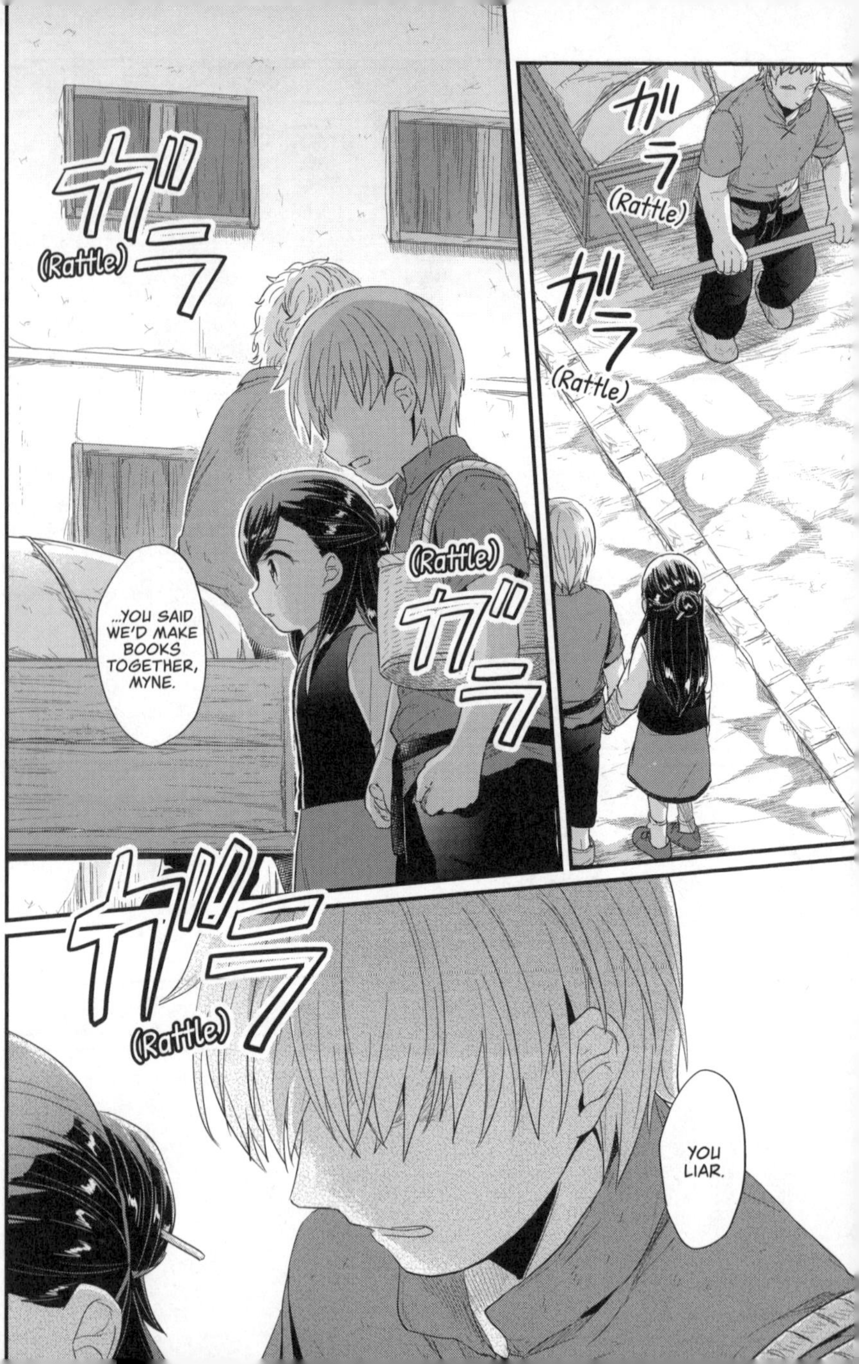
ガラ
(Rattle)
ガラ
(Rattle)
ガラ
(Rattle)
...YOU SAID WE'D MAKE BOOKS TOGETHER, MYNE.
(Rattle)
ガラ
ガラ
(Rattle)
YOU LIAR.

I'M SORRY, LUTZ...

YOU... DON'T NEED TO APOLO- GIZE.

THERE'S NOTHING I CAN DO ABOUT IT. I KNOW THAT.

BUT I WANT TO MAKE SURE YOU'RE SAFE THERE, HOWEVER I CAN.

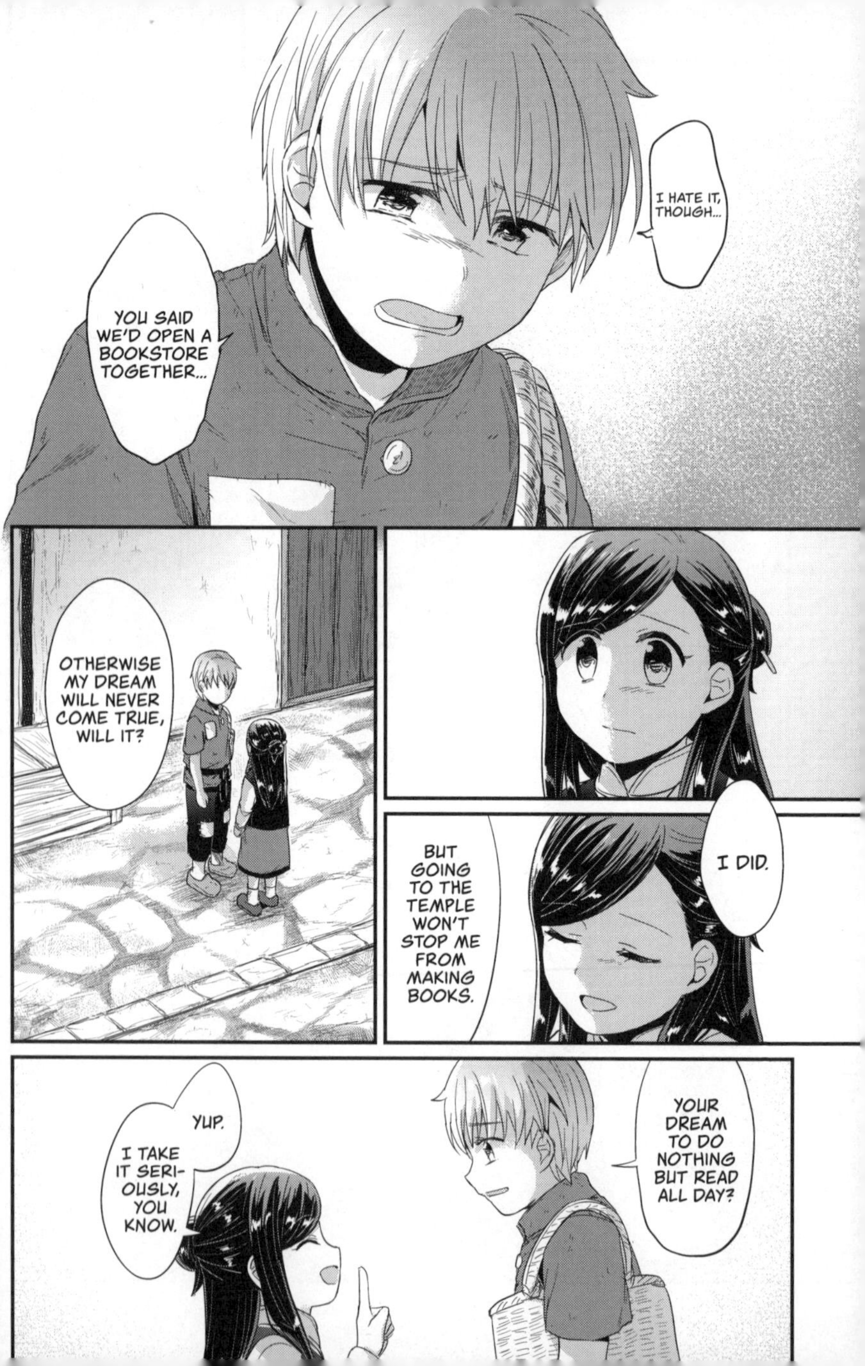
I HATE IT, THOUGH...
YOU SAID WE'D OPEN A BOOKSTORE TOGETHER...
I DID.
BUT GOING TO THE TEMPLE WON'T STOP ME FROM MAKING BOOKS.
OTHERWISE MY DREAM WILL NEVER COME TRUE, WILL IT?
YOUR DREAM TO DO NOTHING BUT READ ALL DAY?
YUP.
I TAKE IT SERI-OUSLY, YOU KNOW.

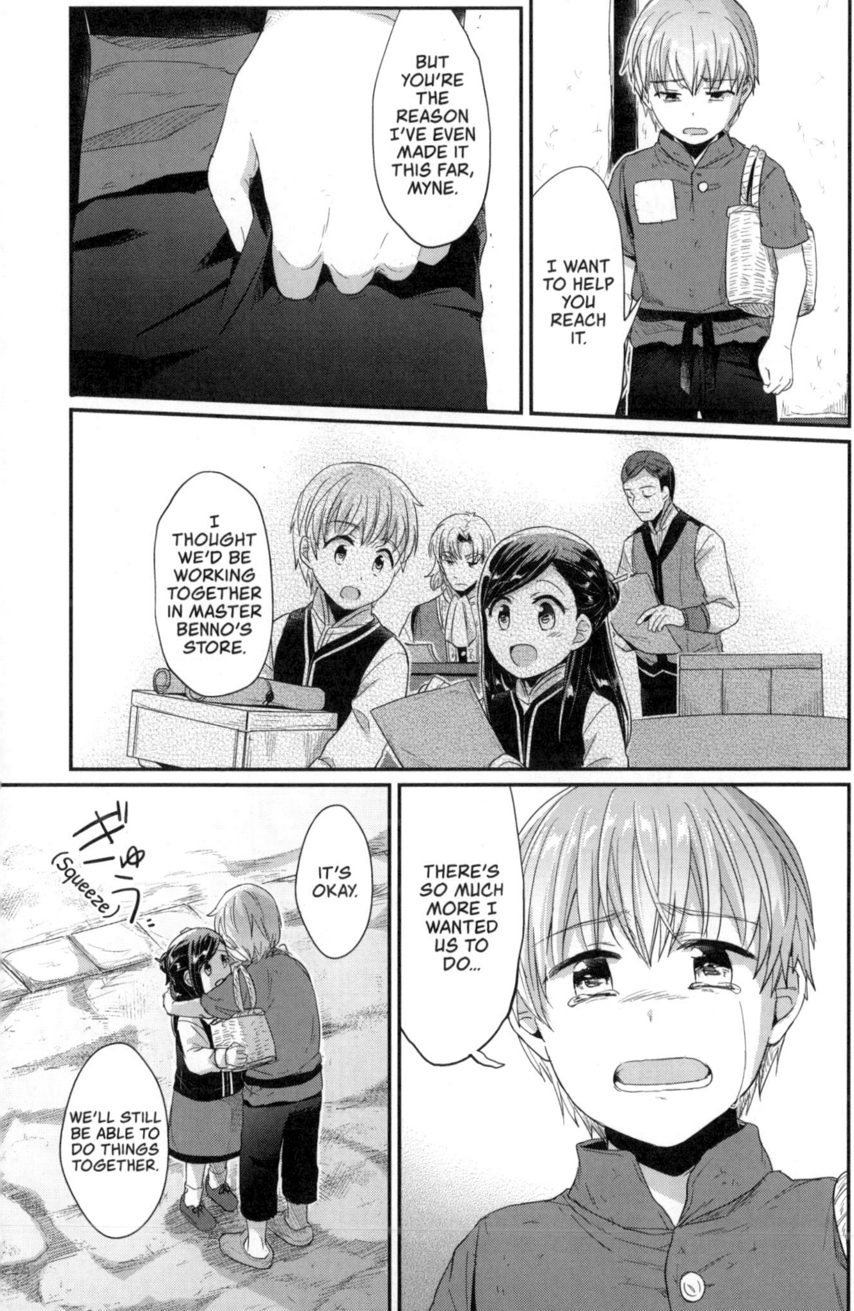
I WANT TO HELP YOU REACH IT.
BUT YOU'RE THE REASON I'VE EVEN MADE IT THIS FAR, MYNE.
I THOUGHT WE'D BE WORKING TOGETHER IN MASTER BENNO'S STORE.
THERE'S SO MUCH MORE I WANTED US TO DO...
IT'S OKAY.
(Squeeze)
WE'LL STILL BE ABLE TO DO THINGS TOGETHER.

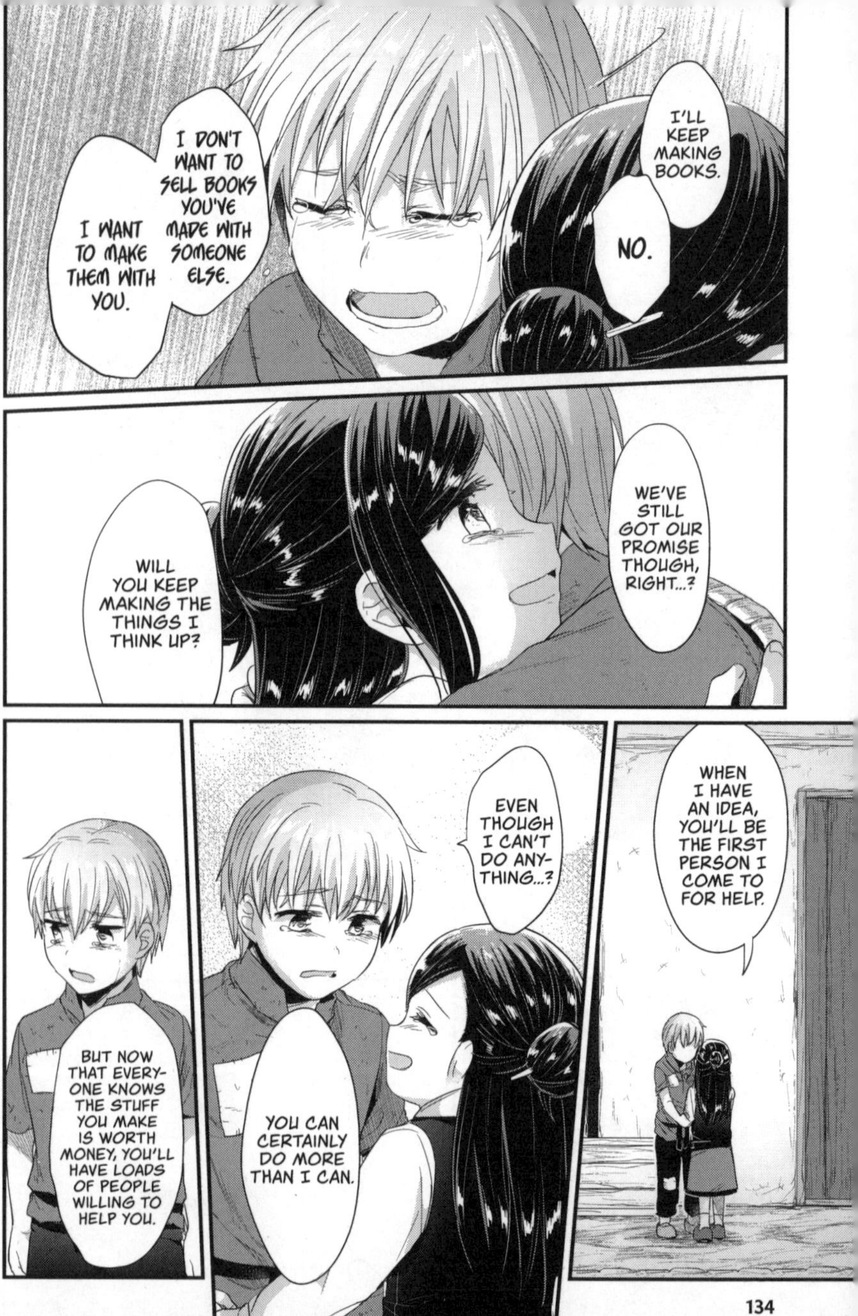
I'LL KEEP MAKING BOOKS.
NO.
I DON'T WANT TO SELL BOOKS YOU'VE MADE WITH SOMEONE ELSE.
I WANT TO MAKE THEM WITH YOU.
WE'VE STILL GOT OUR PROMISE THOUGH, RIGHT...?
WILL YOU KEEP MAKING THE THINGS I THINK UP?
WHEN I HAVE AN IDEA, YOU'LL BE THE FIRST PERSON I COME TO FOR HELP.
EVEN THOUGH I CAN'T DO ANYTHING...?
YOU CAN CERTAINLY DO MORE THAN I CAN.
BUT NOW THAT EVERYONE KNOWS THE STUFF YOU MAKE IS WORTH MONEY, YOU'LL HAVE LOADS OF PEOPLE WILLING TO HELP YOU.

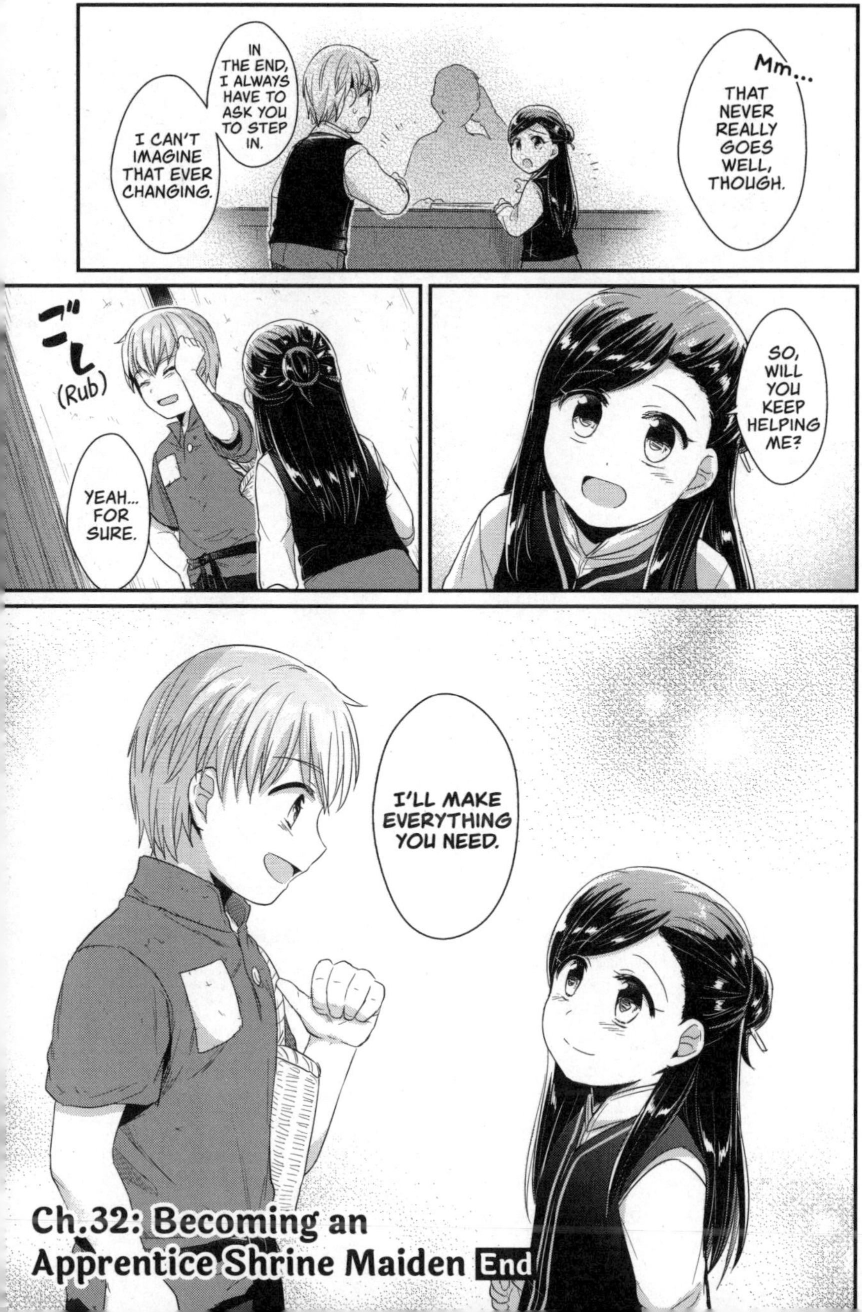
Mm...
THAT NEVER REALLY GOES WELL, THOUGH.
IN THE END, I ALWAYS HAVE TO ASK YOU TO STEP IN.
I CAN'T IMAGINE THAT EVER CHANGING.
SO, WILL YOU KEEP HELPING ME?
ゴし
(Rub)
YEAH... FOR SURE.
I'LL MAKE EVERYTHING YOU NEED.

Ch.32: Becoming an Apprentice Shrine Maiden End

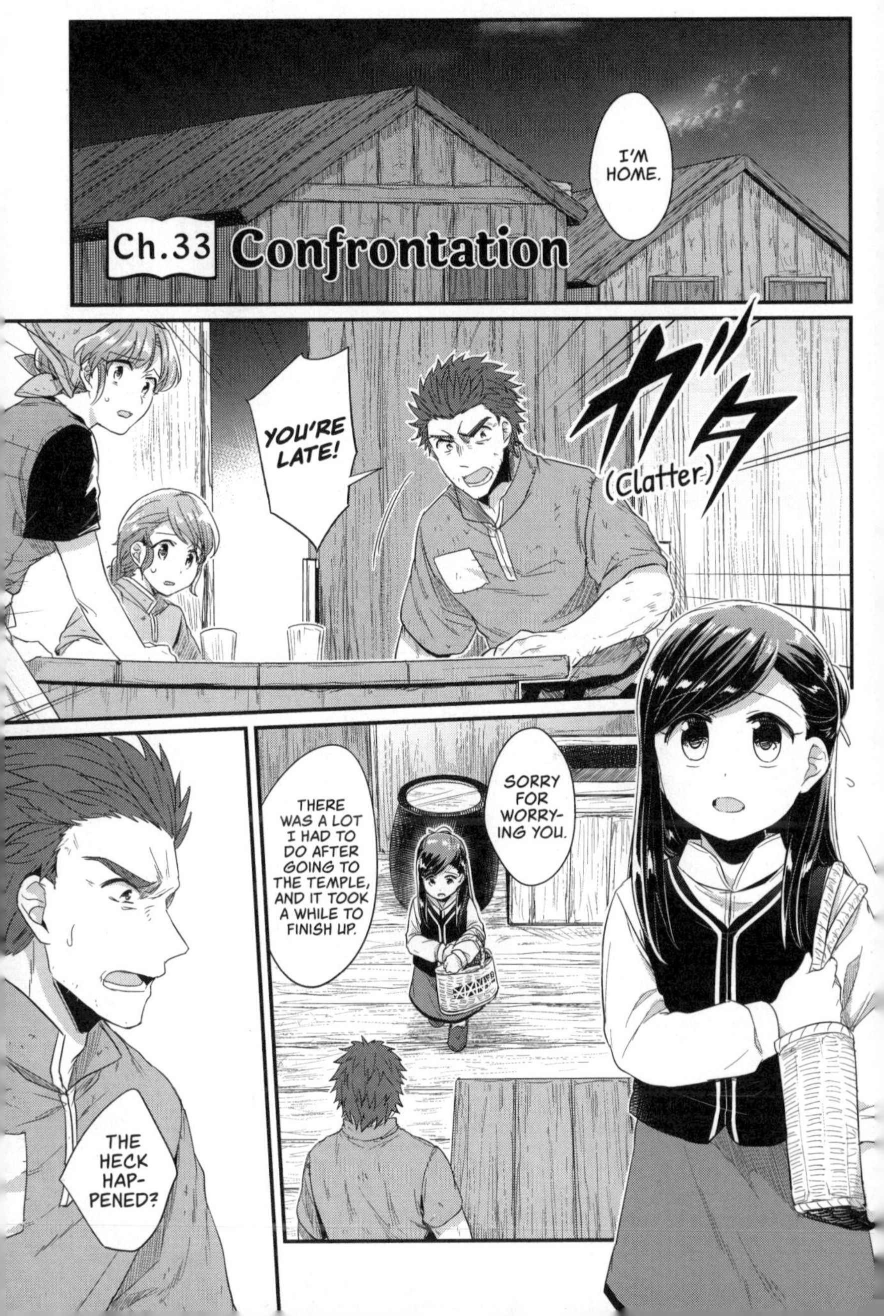
Ch.33 Confrontation
I'M HOME.
ガタ
(Clatter)
YOU'RE LATE!
SORRY FOR WORRYING YOU.
THERE WAS A LOT I HAD TO DO AFTER GOING TO THE TEMPLE, AND IT TOOK A WHILE TO FINISH UP.
THE HECK HAPPENED?

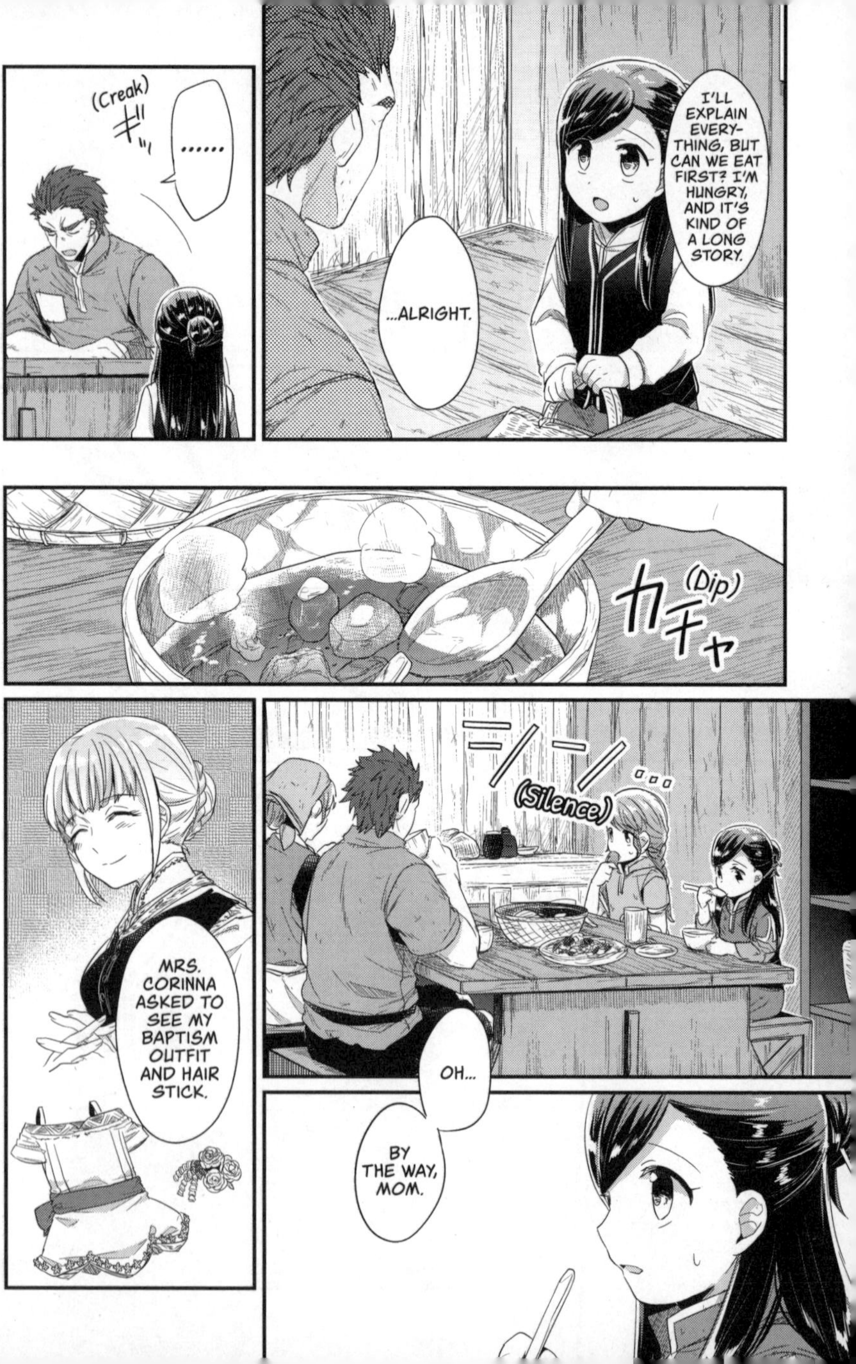
I'LL EXPLAIN EVERYTHING, BUT CAN WE EAT FIRST? I'M HUNGRY, AND IT'S KIND OF A LONG STORY.
...ALRIGHT.
(Creak)
ギ
......
カチャ
(Dip)
シーン
(Silence)
OH...
BY THE WAY, MOM.
MRS. CORINNA ASKED TO SEE MY BAPTISM OUTFIT AND HAIR STICK.

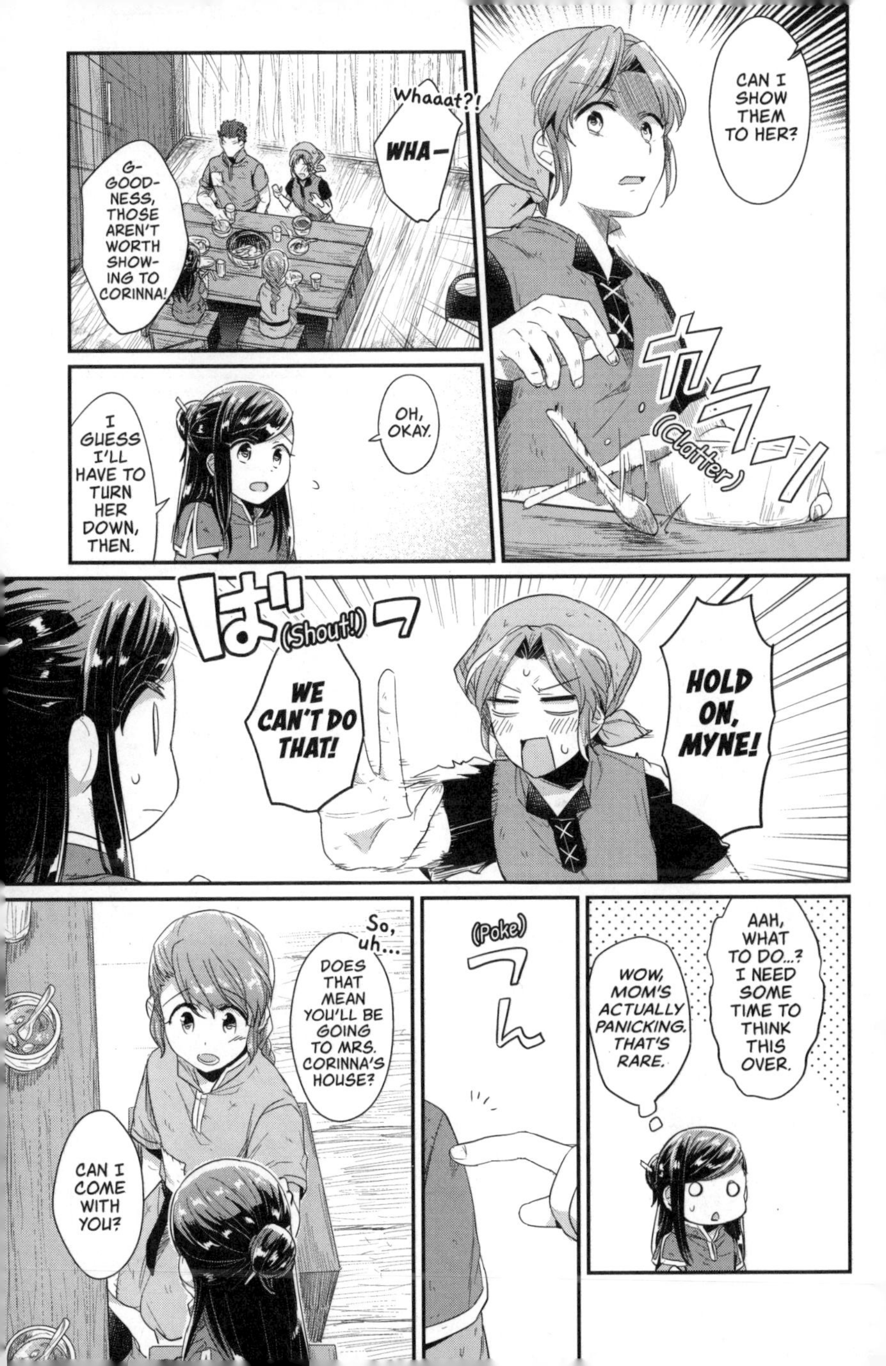
CAN I SHOW THEM TO HER?
カラーン
(Clatter)
Whaaat?!
WHA—
G-GOODNESS, THOSE AREN'T WORTH SHOWING TO CORINNA!
OH, OKAY.
I GUESS I'LL HAVE TO TURN HER DOWN, THEN.
HOLD ON, MYNE!
ばっ
(Shout!)
WE CAN'T DO THAT!
AAH, WHAT TO DO...? I NEED SOME TIME TO THINK THIS OVER.
WOW, MOM'S ACTUALLY PANICKING. THAT'S RARE.
(Poke)
つん
So, uh...
DOES THAT MEAN YOU'LL BE GOING TO MRS. CORINNA'S HOUSE?
CAN I COME WITH YOU?

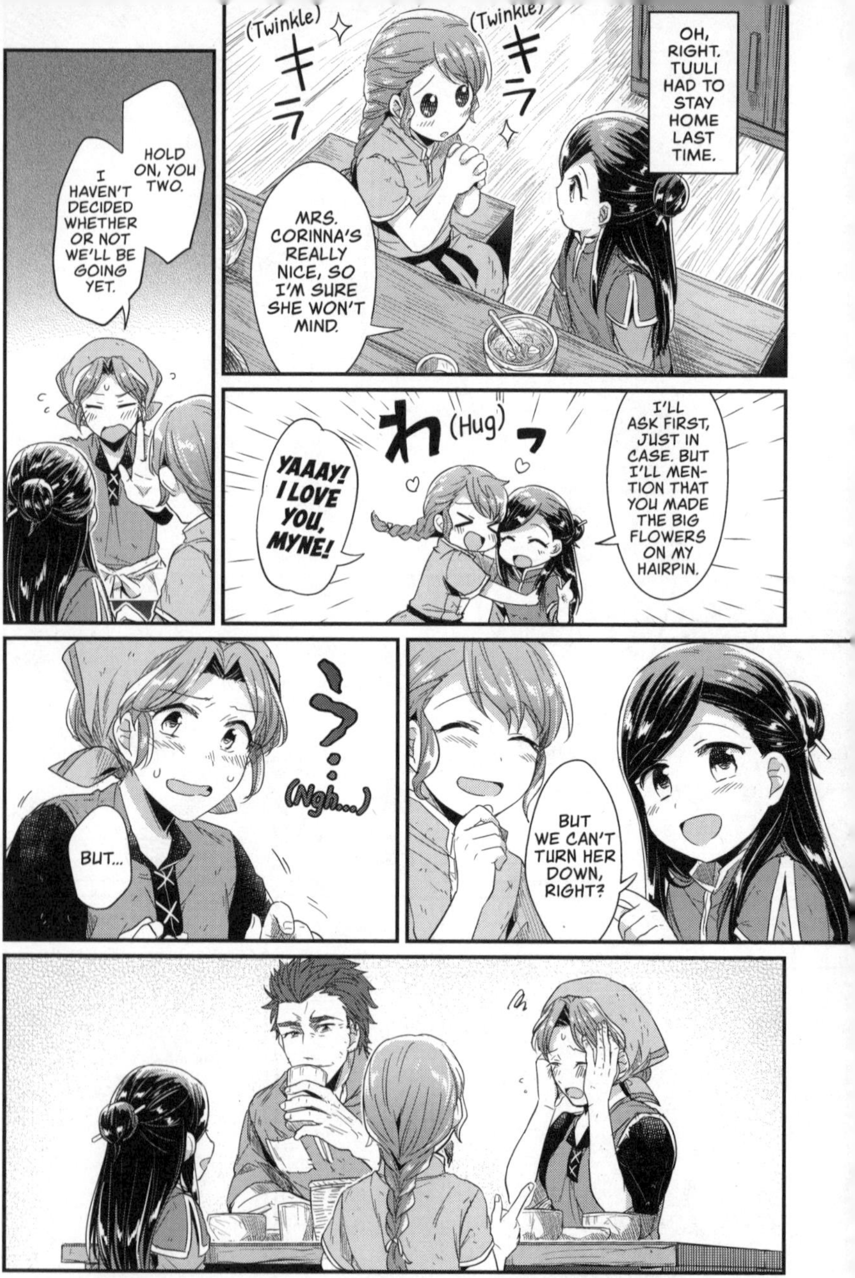
OH, RIGHT. TUULI HAD TO STAY HOME LAST TIME.
キラ (Twinkle)
キラ (Twinkle)
MRS. CORINNA'S REALLY NICE, SO I'M SURE SHE WON'T MIND.
I'LL ASK FIRST, JUST IN CASE. BUT I'LL MENTION THAT YOU MADE THE BIG FLOWERS ON MY HAIRPIN.
わっ (Hug)
YAAAY! I LOVE YOU, MYNE!
HOLD ON, YOU TWO.
I HAVEN'T DECIDED WHETHER OR NOT WE'LL BE GOING YET.
BUT WE CAN'T TURN HER DOWN, RIGHT?
う… (Ngh...)
BUT...

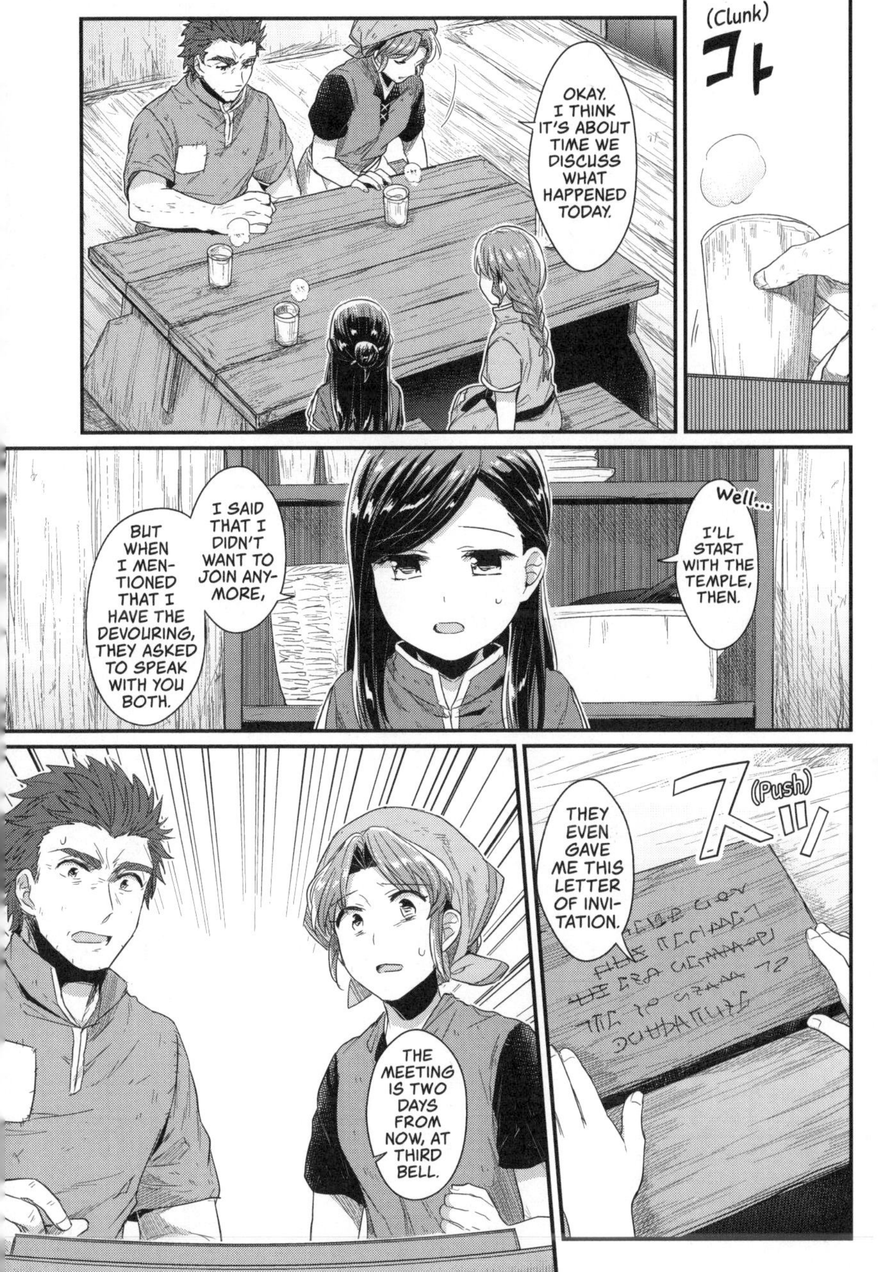
(Clunk)
コト
OKAY. I THINK IT'S ABOUT TIME WE DISCUSS WHAT HAPPENED TODAY.
Well...
I'LL START WITH THE TEMPLE, THEN.
I SAID THAT I DIDN'T WANT TO JOIN ANYMORE,
BUT WHEN I MENTIONED THAT I HAVE THE DEVOURING, THEY ASKED TO SPEAK WITH YOU BOTH.
(Push)
スッ
THEY EVEN GAVE ME THIS LETTER OF INVITATION.
THE MEETING IS TWO DAYS FROM NOW, AT THIRD BELL.

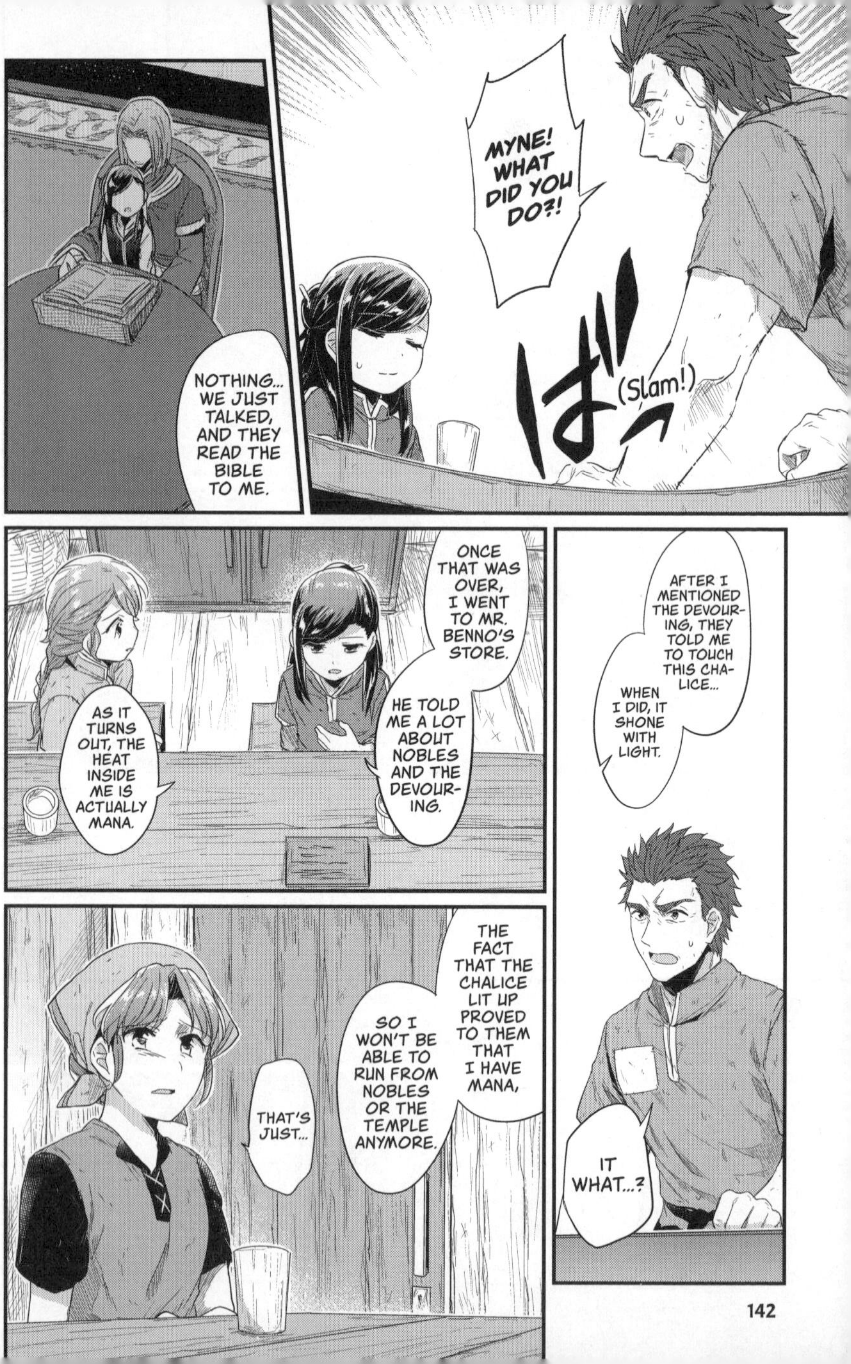
MYNE! WHAT DID YOU DO?!
ばっ
(Slam!)
NOTHING... WE JUST TALKED, AND THEY READ THE BIBLE TO ME.
AFTER I MENTIONED THE DEVOURING, THEY TOLD ME TO TOUCH THIS CHALICE...
WHEN I DID, IT SHONE WITH LIGHT.
ONCE THAT WAS OVER, I WENT TO MR. BENNO'S STORE.
HE TOLD ME A LOT ABOUT NOBLES AND THE DEVOURING.
AS IT TURNS OUT, THE HEAT INSIDE ME IS ACTUALLY MANA.
IT WHAT...?
THE FACT THAT THE CHALICE LIT UP PROVED TO THEM THAT I HAVE MANA,
SO I WON'T BE ABLE TO RUN FROM NOBLES OR THE TEMPLE ANYMORE.
THAT'S JUST...

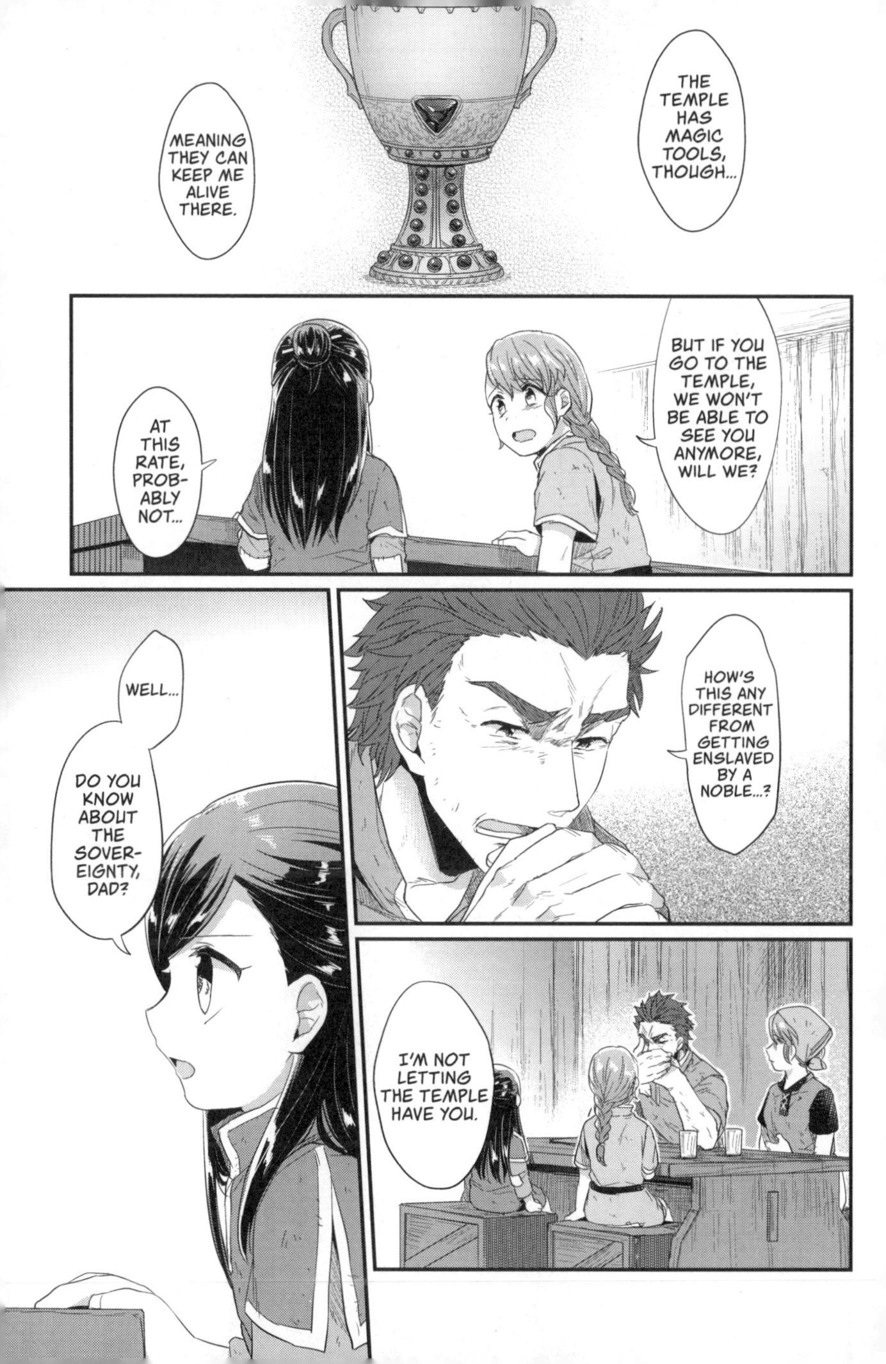
THE TEMPLE HAS MAGIC TOOLS, THOUGH...
MEANING THEY CAN KEEP ME ALIVE THERE.
BUT IF YOU GO TO THE TEMPLE, WE WON'T BE ABLE TO SEE YOU ANYMORE, WILL WE?
AT THIS RATE, PROB-ABLY NOT...
HOW'S THIS ANY DIFFERENT FROM GETTING ENSLAVED BY A NOBLE...?
I'M NOT LETTING THE TEMPLE HAVE YOU.
WELL...
DO YOU KNOW ABOUT THE SOVER-EIGNTY, DAD?

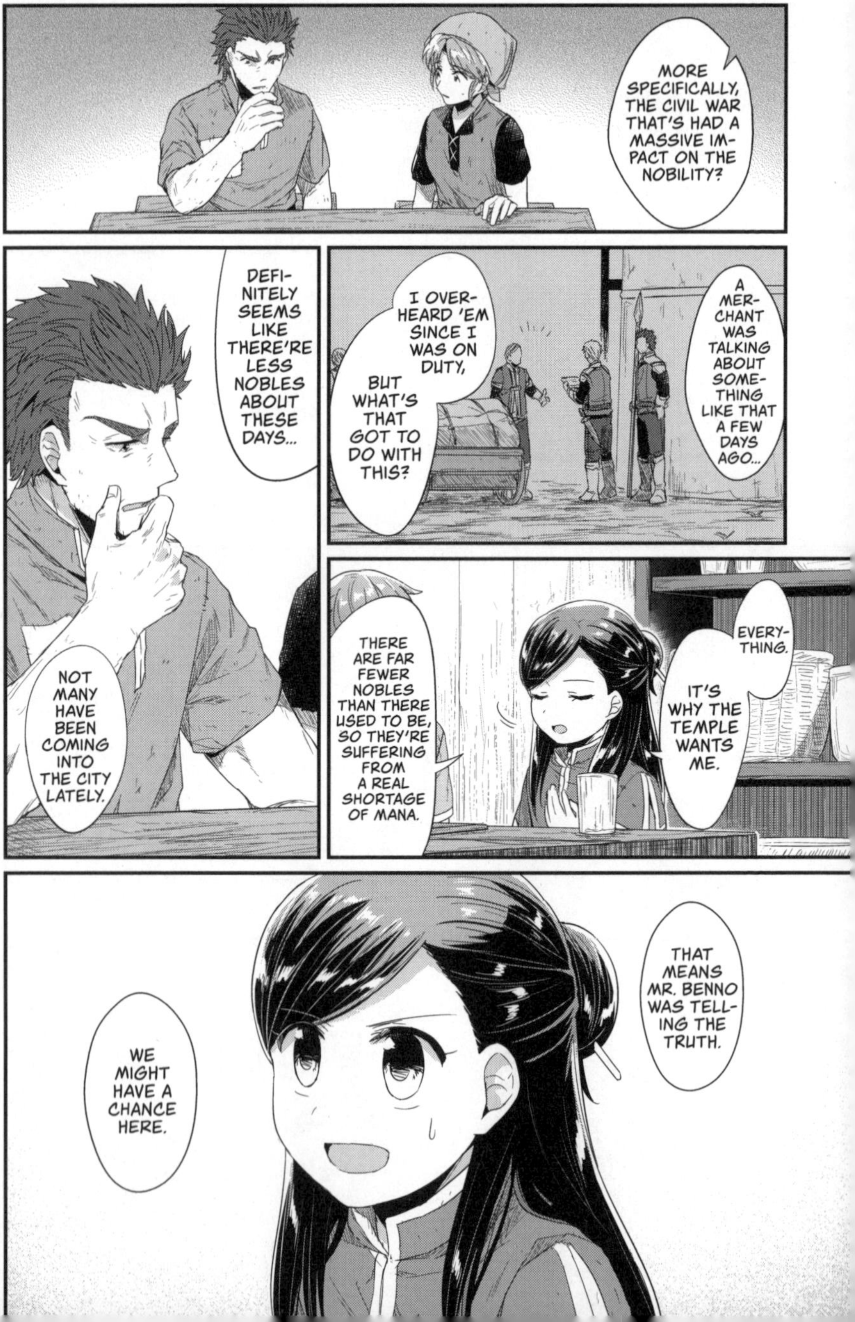
MORE SPECIFICALLY, THE CIVIL WAR THAT'S HAD A MASSIVE IMPACT ON THE NOBILITY?
A MERCHANT WAS TALKING ABOUT SOMETHING LIKE THAT A FEW DAYS AGO...
I OVERHEARD 'EM SINCE I WAS ON DUTY,
BUT WHAT'S THAT GOT TO DO WITH THIS?
EVERYTHING.
IT'S WHY THE TEMPLE WANTS ME.
THERE ARE FAR FEWER NOBLES THAN THERE USED TO BE, SO THEY'RE SUFFERING FROM A REAL SHORTAGE OF MANA.
DEFINITELY SEEMS LIKE THERE'RE LESS NOBLES ABOUT THESE DAYS...
NOT MANY HAVE BEEN COMING INTO THE CITY LATELY.
THAT MEANS MR. BENNO WAS TELLING THE TRUTH.
WE MIGHT HAVE A CHANCE HERE.

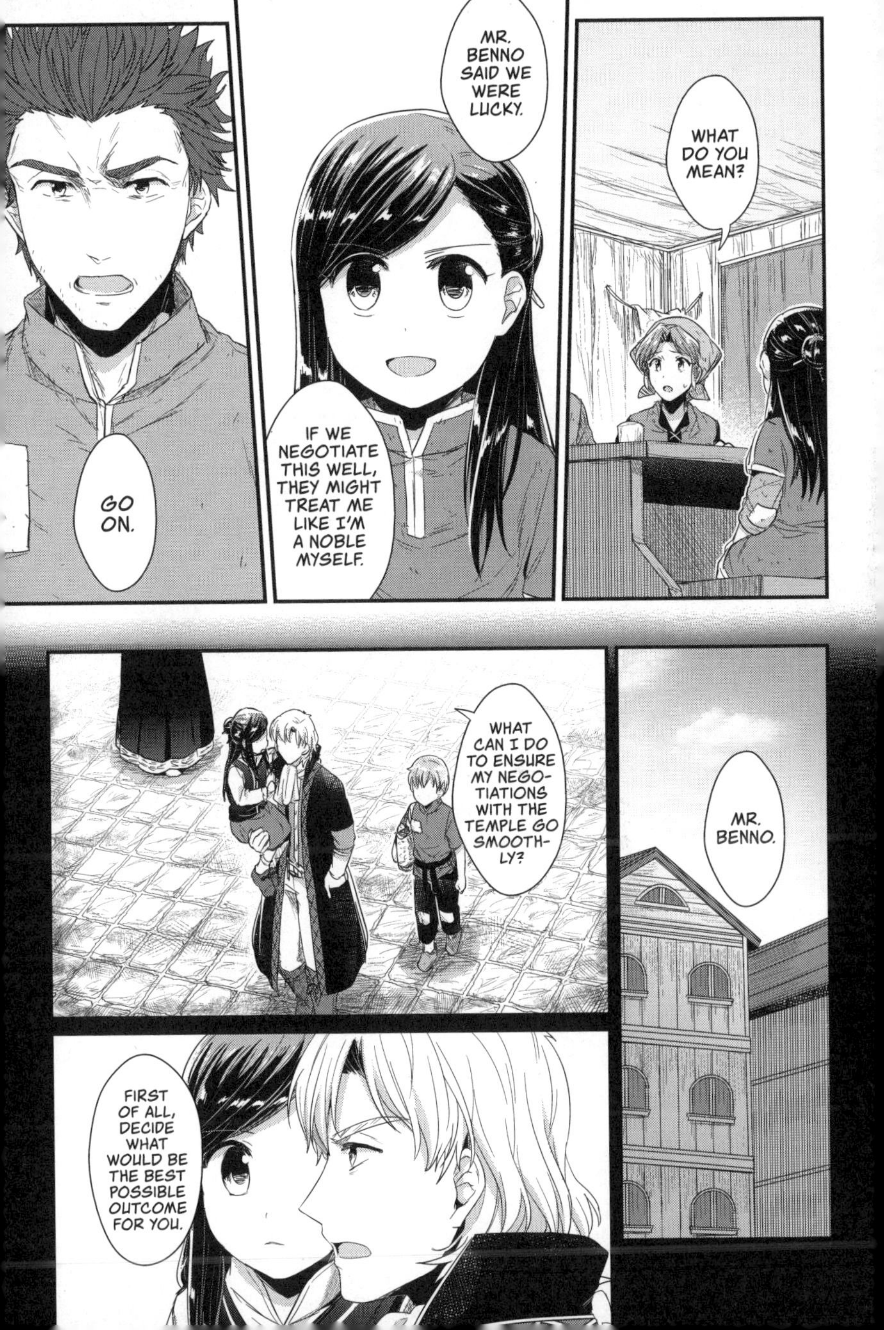
WHAT DO YOU MEAN?
MR. BENNO SAID WE WERE LUCKY.
IF WE NEGOTIATE THIS WELL, THEY MIGHT TREAT ME LIKE I'M A NOBLE MYSELF.
GO ON.
MR. BENNO.
WHAT CAN I DO TO ENSURE MY NEGO-TIATIONS WITH THE TEMPLE GO SMOOTH-LY?
FIRST OF ALL, DECIDE WHAT WOULD BE THE BEST POSSIBLE OUTCOME FOR YOU.

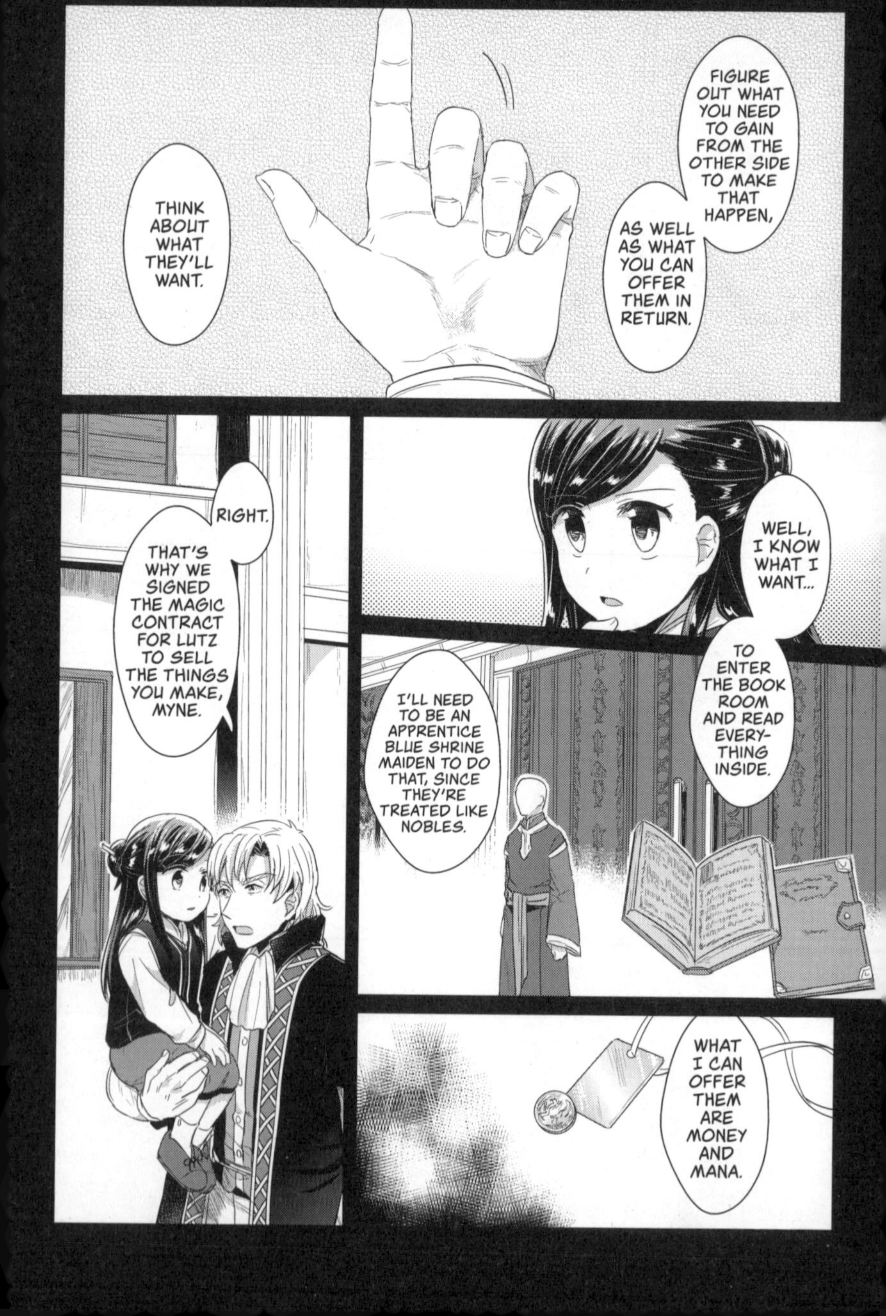
FIGURE OUT WHAT YOU NEED TO GAIN FROM THE OTHER SIDE TO MAKE THAT HAPPEN,
AS WELL AS WHAT YOU CAN OFFER THEM IN RETURN.
THINK ABOUT WHAT THEY'LL WANT.
WELL, I KNOW WHAT I WANT...
TO ENTER THE BOOK ROOM AND READ EVERY-THING INSIDE.
I'LL NEED TO BE AN APPRENTICE BLUE SHRINE MAIDEN TO DO THAT, SINCE THEY'RE TREATED LIKE NOBLES.
WHAT I CAN OFFER THEM ARE MONEY AND MANA.
RIGHT.
THAT'S WHY WE SIGNED THE MAGIC CONTRACT FOR LUTZ TO SELL THE THINGS YOU MAKE, MYNE.

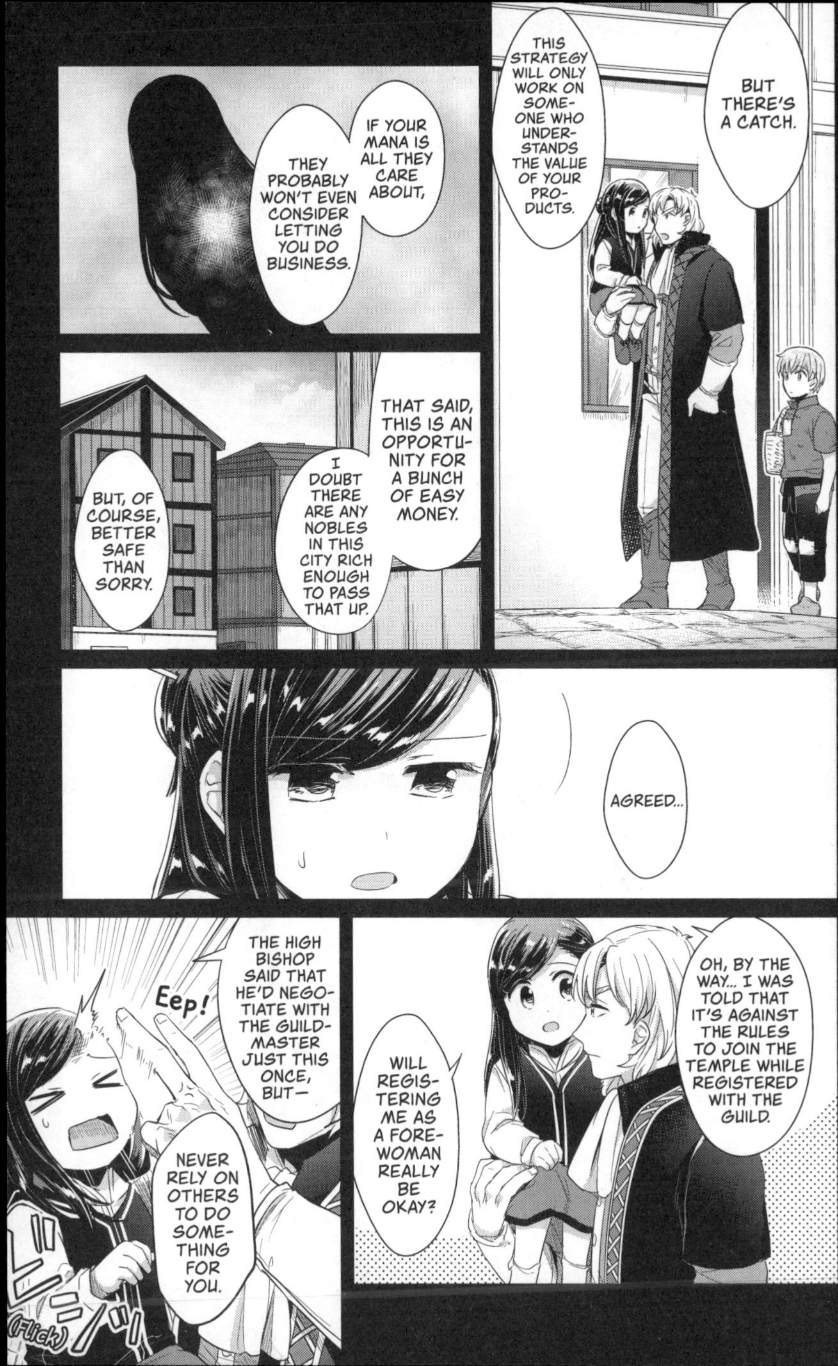

BUT THERE'S A CATCH.
THIS STRATEGY WILL ONLY WORK ON SOMEONE WHO UNDERSTANDS THE VALUE OF YOUR PRODUCTS.
IF YOUR MANA IS ALL THEY CARE ABOUT,
THEY PROBABLY WON'T EVEN CONSIDER LETTING YOU DO BUSINESS.
THAT SAID, THIS IS AN OPPORTUNITY FOR A BUNCH OF EASY MONEY.
I DOUBT THERE ARE ANY NOBLES IN THIS CITY RICH ENOUGH TO PASS THAT UP.
BUT, OF COURSE, BETTER SAFE THAN SORRY.
AGREED...
OH, BY THE WAY... I WAS TOLD THAT IT'S AGAINST THE RULES TO JOIN THE TEMPLE WHILE REGISTERED WITH THE GUILD.
WILL REGISTERING ME AS A FOREWOMAN REALLY BE OKAY?
THE HIGH BISHOP SAID THAT HE'D NEGOTIATE WITH THE GUILDMASTER JUST THIS ONCE, BUT—
Eep!
NEVER RELY ON OTHERS TO DO SOMETHING FOR YOU.
(Flick)

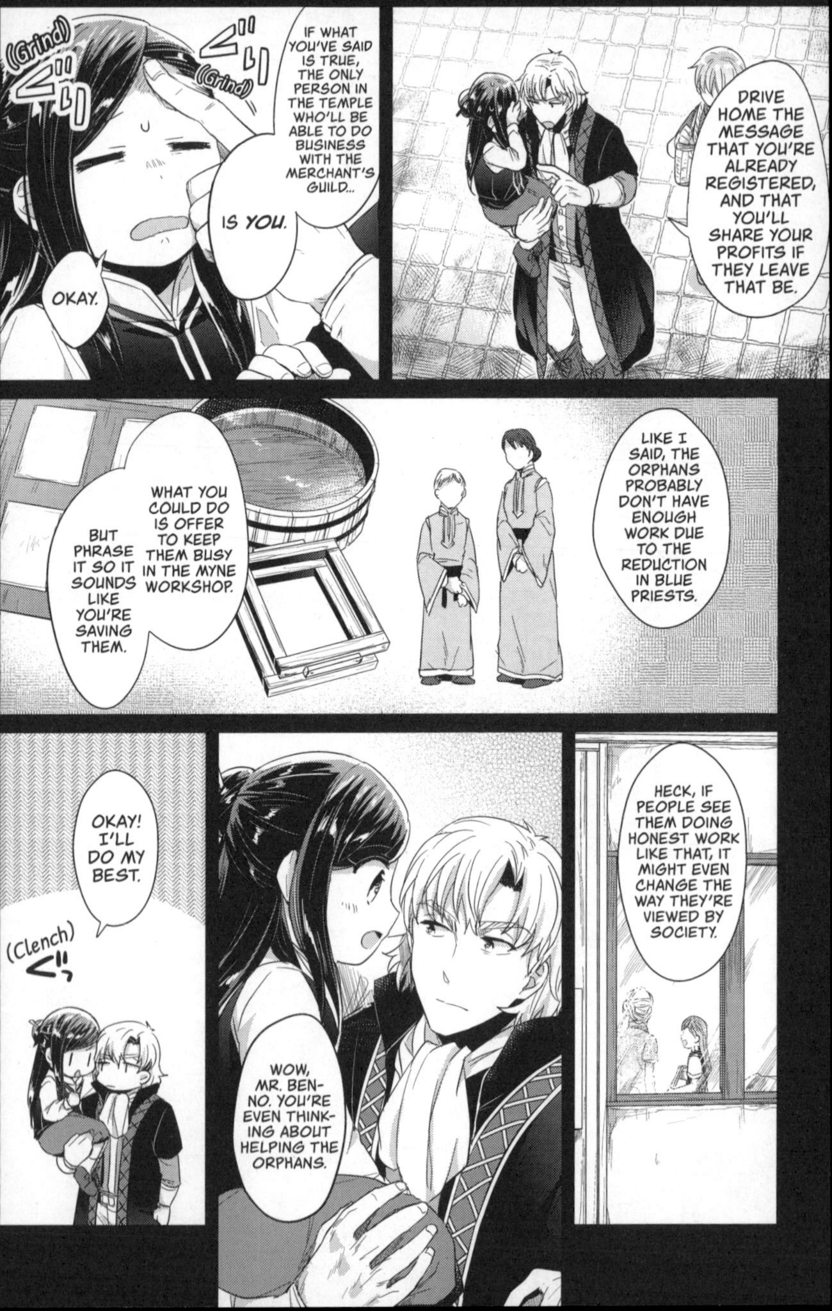
DRIVE HOME THE MESSAGE THAT YOU'RE ALREADY REGISTERED, AND THAT YOU'LL SHARE YOUR PROFITS IF THEY LEAVE THAT BE.
IF WHAT YOU'VE SAID IS TRUE, THE ONLY PERSON IN THE TEMPLE WHO'LL BE ABLE TO DO BUSINESS WITH THE MERCHANT'S GUILD...
IS *YOU.*
(Grind)
(Grind)
OKAY.
LIKE I SAID, THE ORPHANS PROBABLY DON'T HAVE ENOUGH WORK DUE TO THE REDUCTION IN BLUE PRIESTS.
WHAT YOU COULD DO IS OFFER TO KEEP THEM BUSY IN THE MYNE WORKSHOP.
BUT PHRASE IT SO IT SOUNDS LIKE YOU'RE SAVING THEM.
HECK, IF PEOPLE SEE THEM DOING HONEST WORK LIKE THAT, IT MIGHT EVEN CHANGE THE WAY THEY'RE VIEWED BY SOCIETY.
WOW, MR. BEN-NO. YOU'RE EVEN THINK-ING ABOUT HELPING THE ORPHANS.
OKAY! I'LL DO MY BEST.
(Clench)

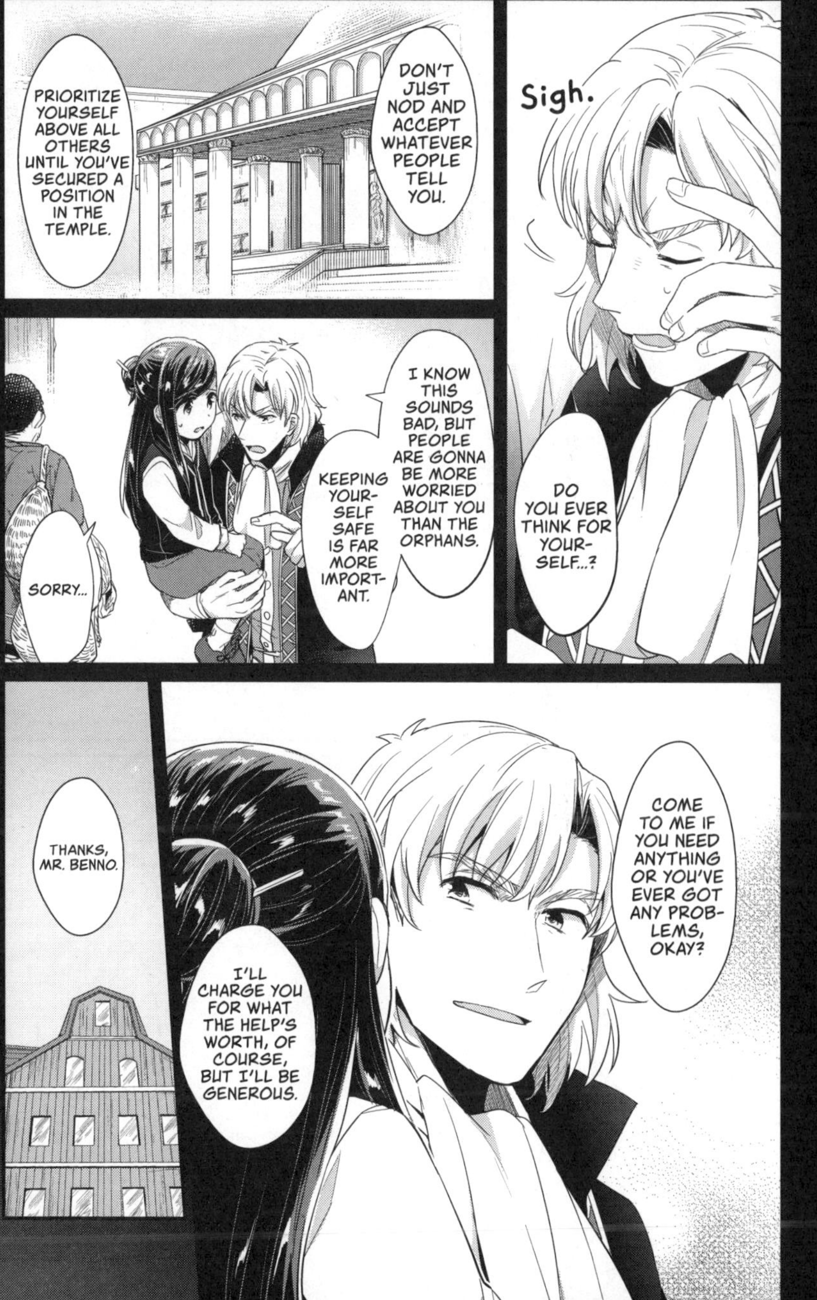

Sigh.
DO YOU EVER THINK FOR YOUR-SELF...?
DON'T JUST NOD AND ACCEPT WHATEVER PEOPLE TELL YOU.
PRIORITIZE YOURSELF ABOVE ALL OTHERS UNTIL YOU'VE SECURED A POSITION IN THE TEMPLE.
I KNOW THIS SOUNDS BAD, BUT PEOPLE ARE GONNA BE MORE WORRIED ABOUT YOU THAN THE ORPHANS.
KEEPING YOUR-SELF SAFE IS FAR MORE IMPORT-ANT.
SORRY...
COME TO ME IF YOU NEED ANYTHING OR YOU'VE EVER GOT ANY PROB-LEMS, OKAY?
I'LL CHARGE YOU FOR WHAT THE HELP'S WORTH, OF COURSE, BUT I'LL BE GENEROUS.
THANKS, MR. BENNO.

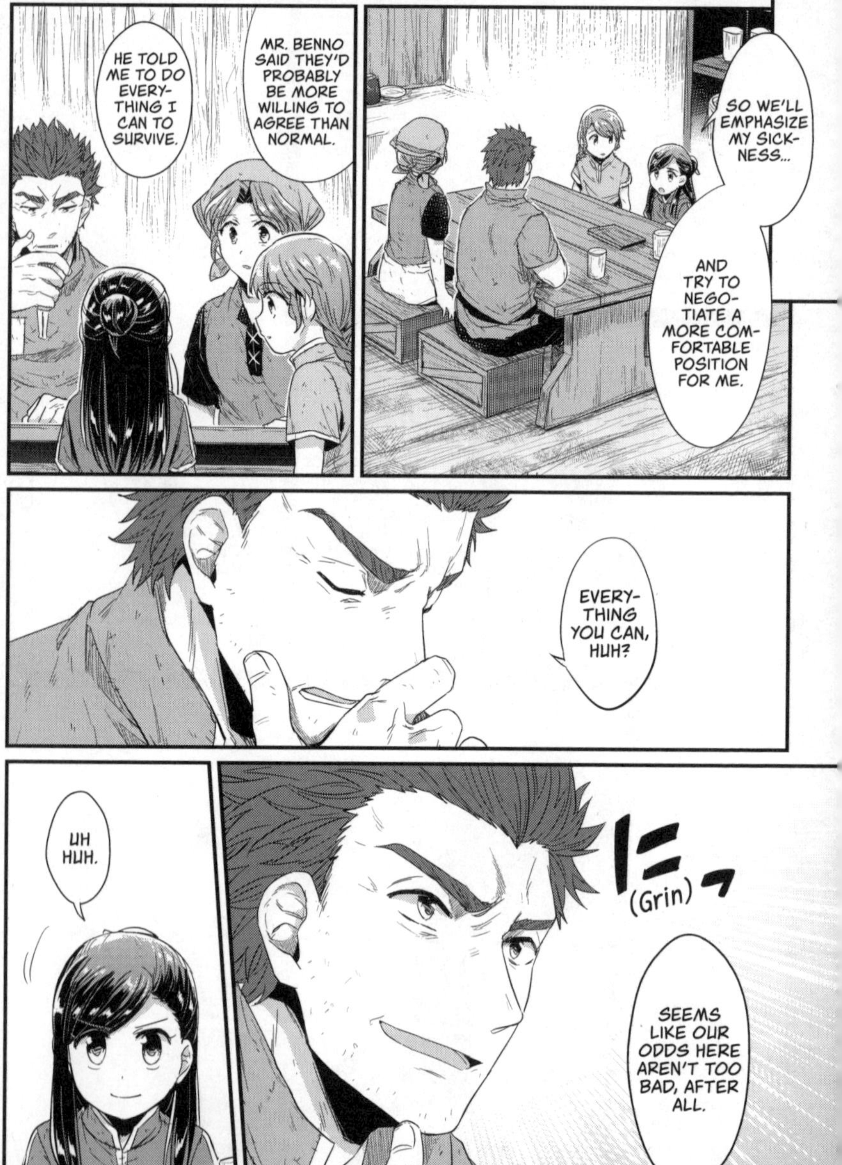
SO WE'LL EMPHASIZE MY SICK-NESS...
AND TRY TO NEGO-TIATE A MORE COM-FORTABLE POSITION FOR ME.
MR. BENNO SAID THEY'D PROBABLY BE MORE WILLING TO AGREE THAN NORMAL.
HE TOLD ME TO DO EVERY-THING I CAN TO SURVIVE.
EVERY-THING YOU CAN, HUH?
にっ
(Grin)
SEEMS LIKE OUR ODDS HERE AREN'T TOO BAD, AFTER ALL.
UH HUH.

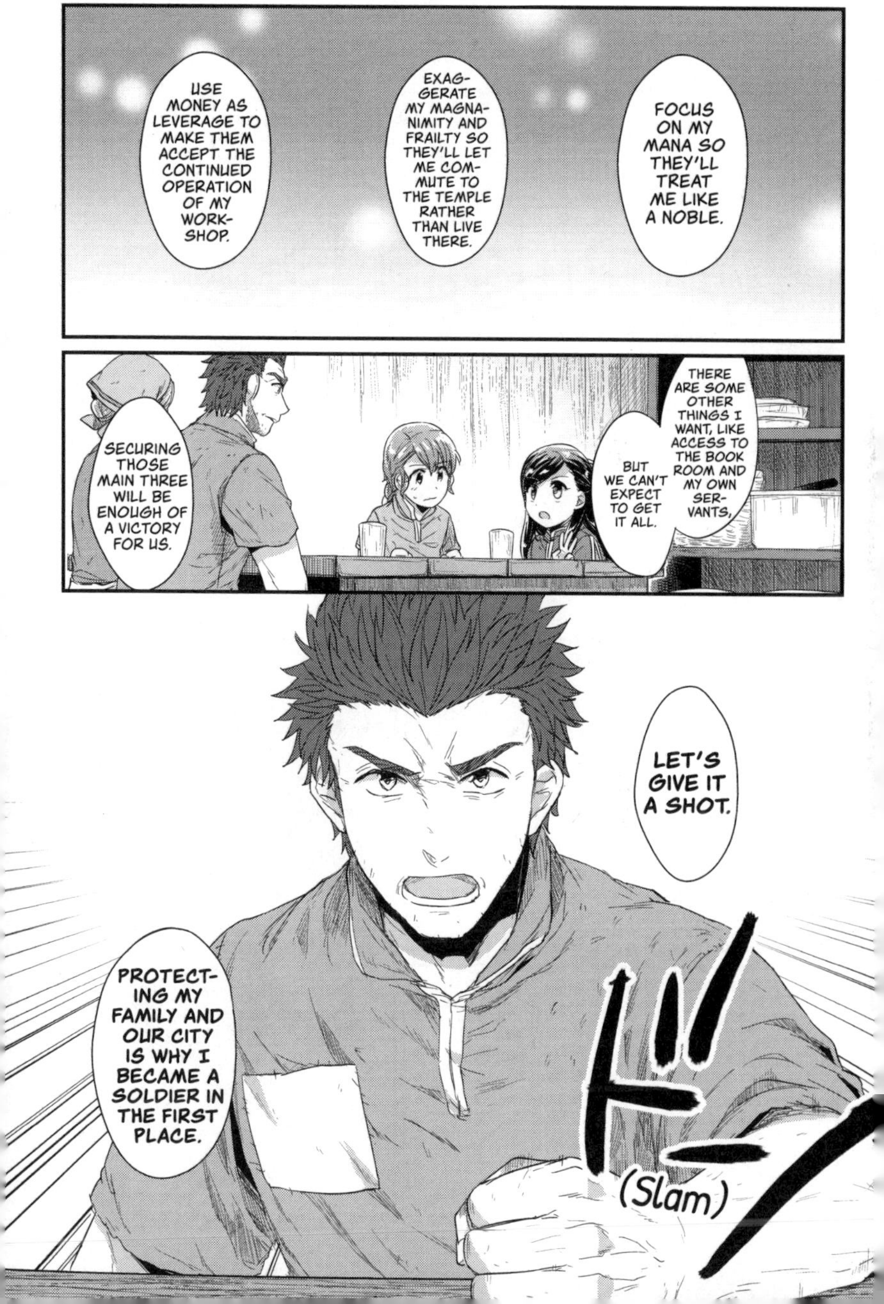
FOCUS ON MY MANA SO THEY'LL TREAT ME LIKE A NOBLE.
EXAGGERATE MY MAGNANIMITY AND FRAILTY SO THEY'LL LET ME COMMUTE TO THE TEMPLE RATHER THAN LIVE THERE.
USE MONEY AS LEVERAGE TO MAKE THEM ACCEPT THE CONTINUED OPERATION OF MY WORKSHOP.
THERE ARE SOME OTHER THINGS I WANT, LIKE ACCESS TO THE BOOK ROOM AND MY OWN SERVANTS,
BUT WE CAN'T EXPECT TO GET IT ALL.
SECURING THOSE MAIN THREE WILL BE ENOUGH OF A VICTORY FOR US.
LET'S GIVE IT A SHOT.
(Slam)
PROTECTING MY FAMILY AND OUR CITY IS WHY I BECAME A SOLDIER IN THE FIRST PLACE.

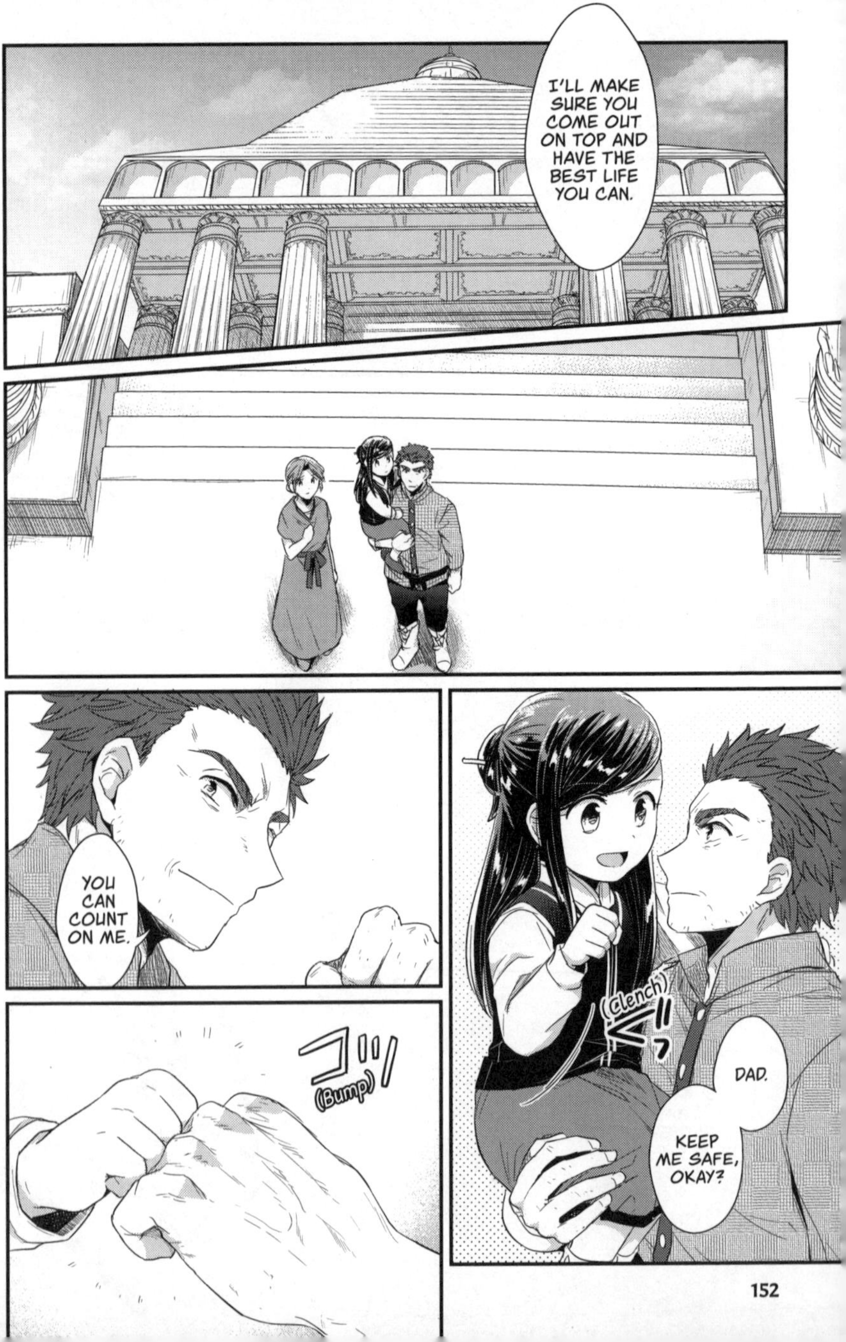
I'LL MAKE SURE YOU COME OUT ON TOP AND HAVE THE BEST LIFE YOU CAN.
(Clench)
DAD.
KEEP ME SAFE, OKAY?
YOU CAN COUNT ON ME.
(Bump)

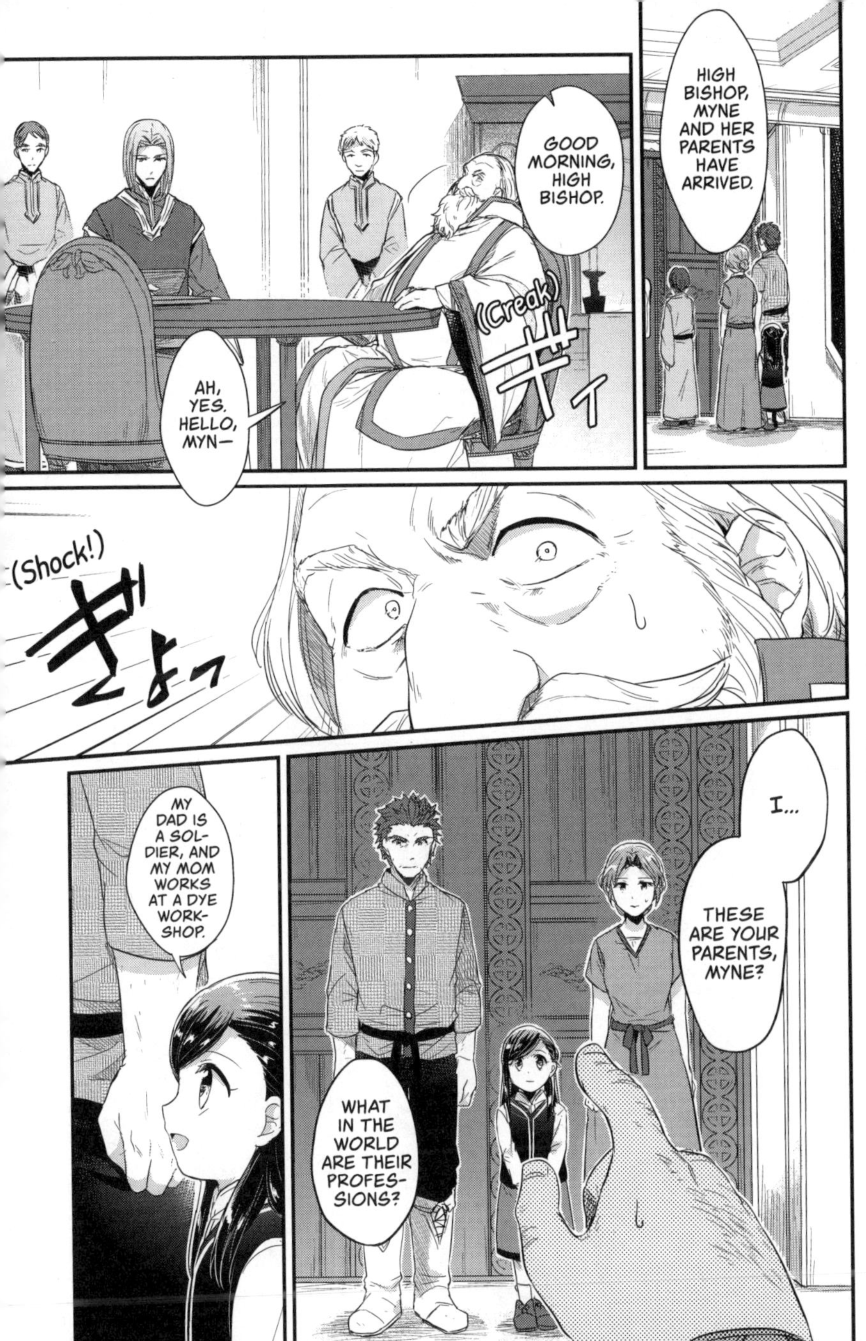
HIGH BISHOP, MYNE AND HER PARENTS HAVE ARRIVED.
GOOD MORNING, HIGH BISHOP.
(Creak)
ギィ
AH, YES. HELLO, MYN—
(Shock!)
ぎょっ
I...
THESE ARE YOUR PARENTS, MYNE?
WHAT IN THE WORLD ARE THEIR PROFESSIONS?
MY DAD IS A SOLDIER, AND MY MOM WORKS AT A DYE WORKSHOP.

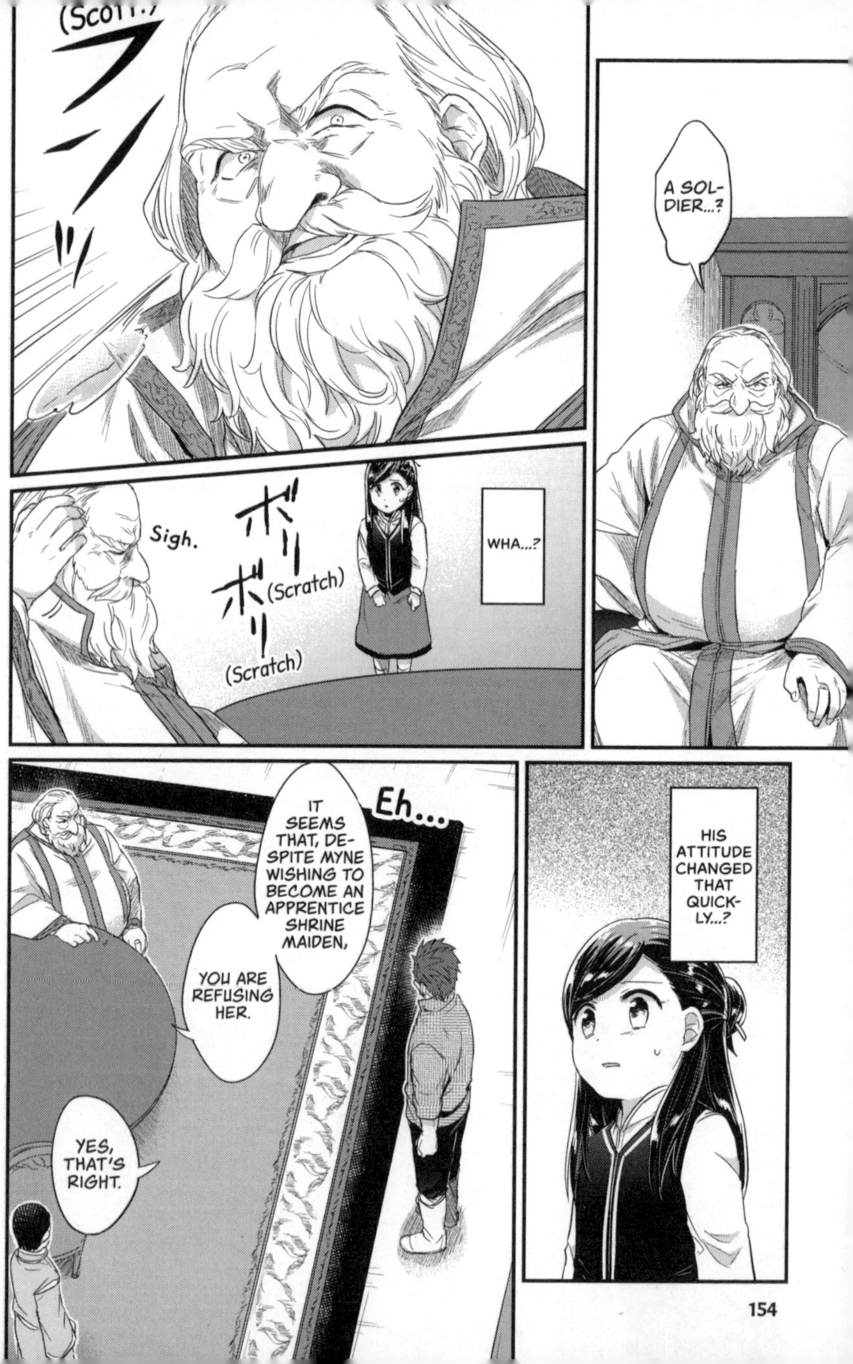
A SOL-
DIER...?
(Scoff.)
WHA...?
(Scratch)
(Scratch)
Sigh.
HIS ATTITUDE CHANGED THAT QUICK-LY...?
Eh...
IT SEEMS THAT, DE-SPITE MYNE WISHING TO BECOME AN APPRENTICE SHRINE MAIDEN,
YOU ARE REFUSING HER.
YES, THAT'S RIGHT.

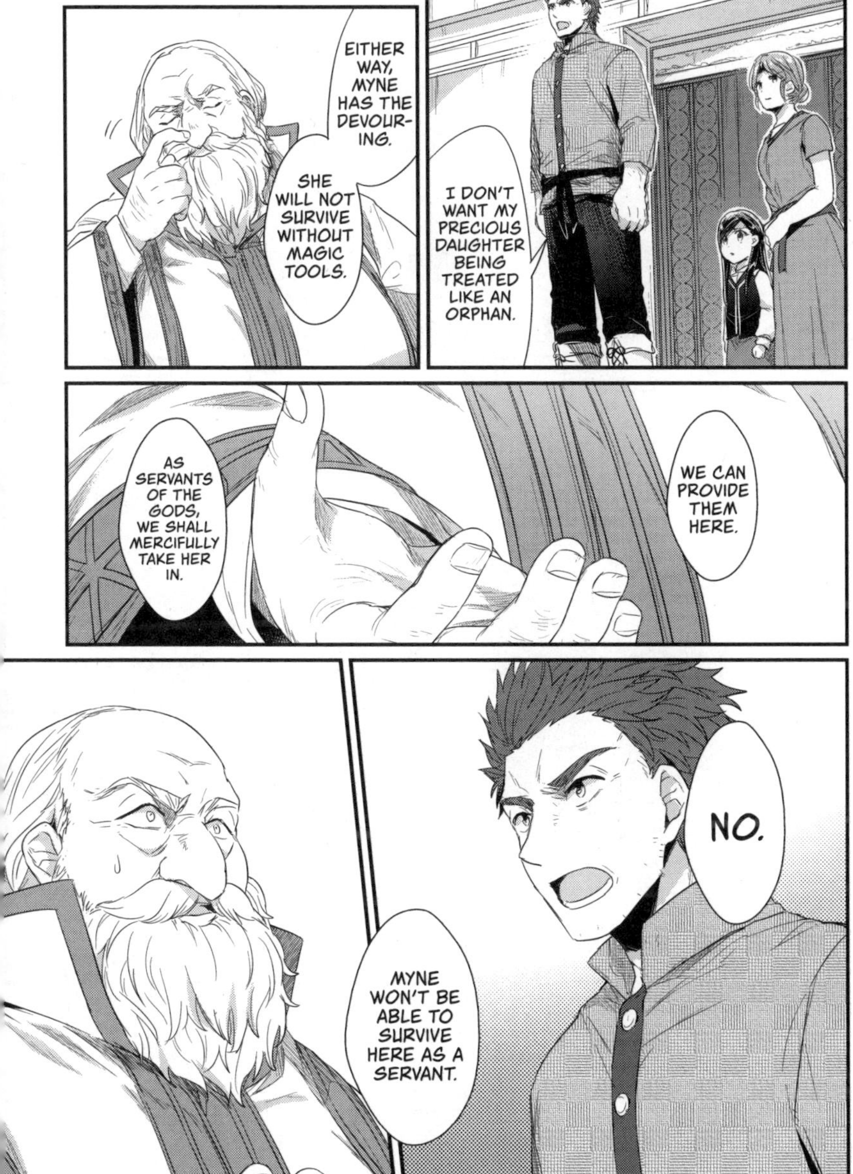
I DON'T WANT MY PRECIOUS DAUGHTER BEING TREATED LIKE AN ORPHAN.
EITHER WAY, MYNE HAS THE DEVOURING.
SHE WILL NOT SURVIVE WITHOUT MAGIC TOOLS.
WE CAN PROVIDE THEM HERE.
AS SERVANTS OF THE GODS, WE SHALL MERCIFULLY TAKE HER IN.
NO.
MYNE WON'T BE ABLE TO SURVIVE HERE AS A SERVANT.

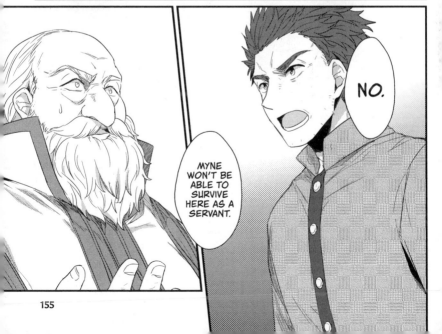

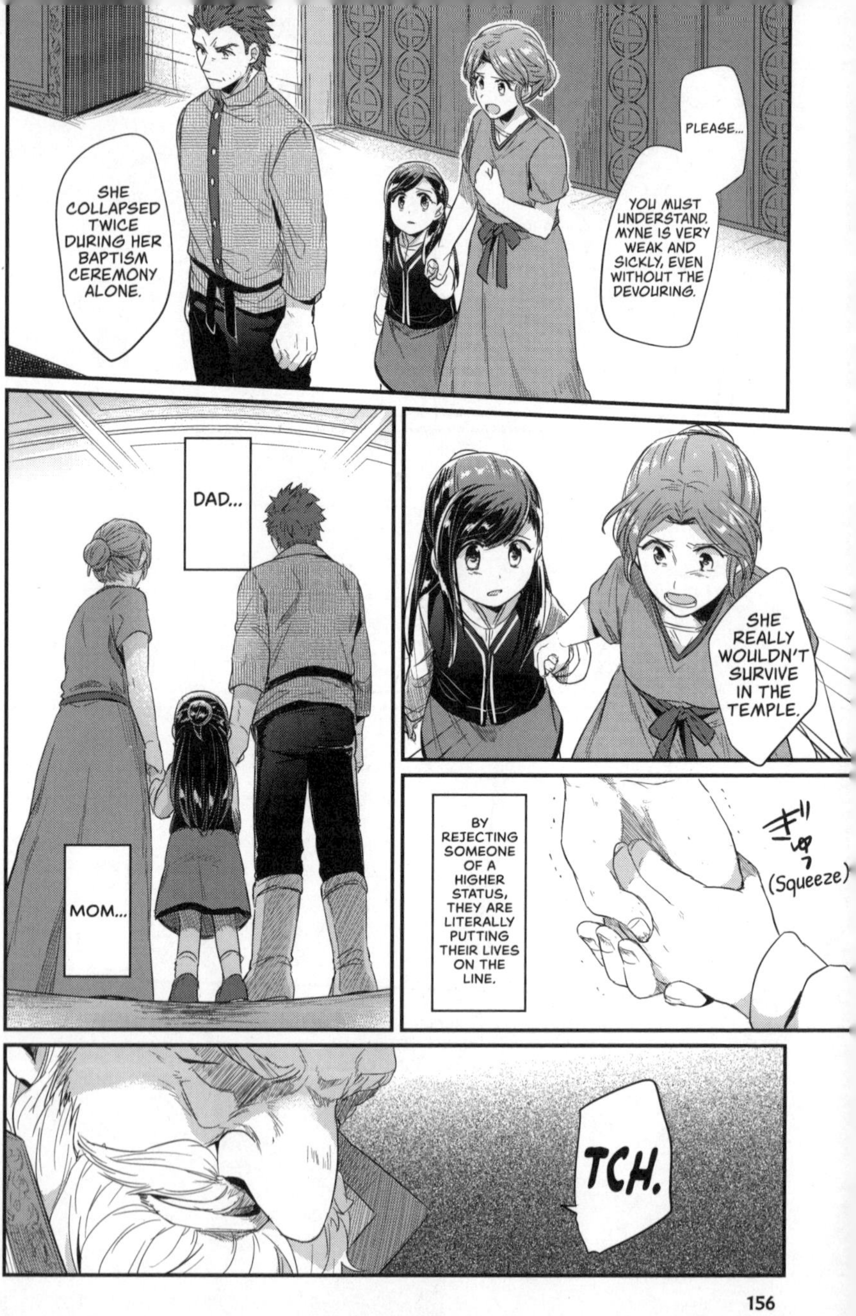

PLEASE...
YOU MUST UNDERSTAND. MYNE IS VERY WEAK AND SICKLY, EVEN WITHOUT THE DEVOURING.
SHE COLLAPSED TWICE DURING HER BAPTISM CEREMONY ALONE.
SHE REALLY WOULDN'T SURVIVE IN THE TEMPLE.
(Squeeze)
BY REJECTING SOMEONE OF A HIGHER STATUS, THEY ARE LITERALLY PUTTING THEIR LIVES ON THE LINE.
DAD...
MOM...
TCH.

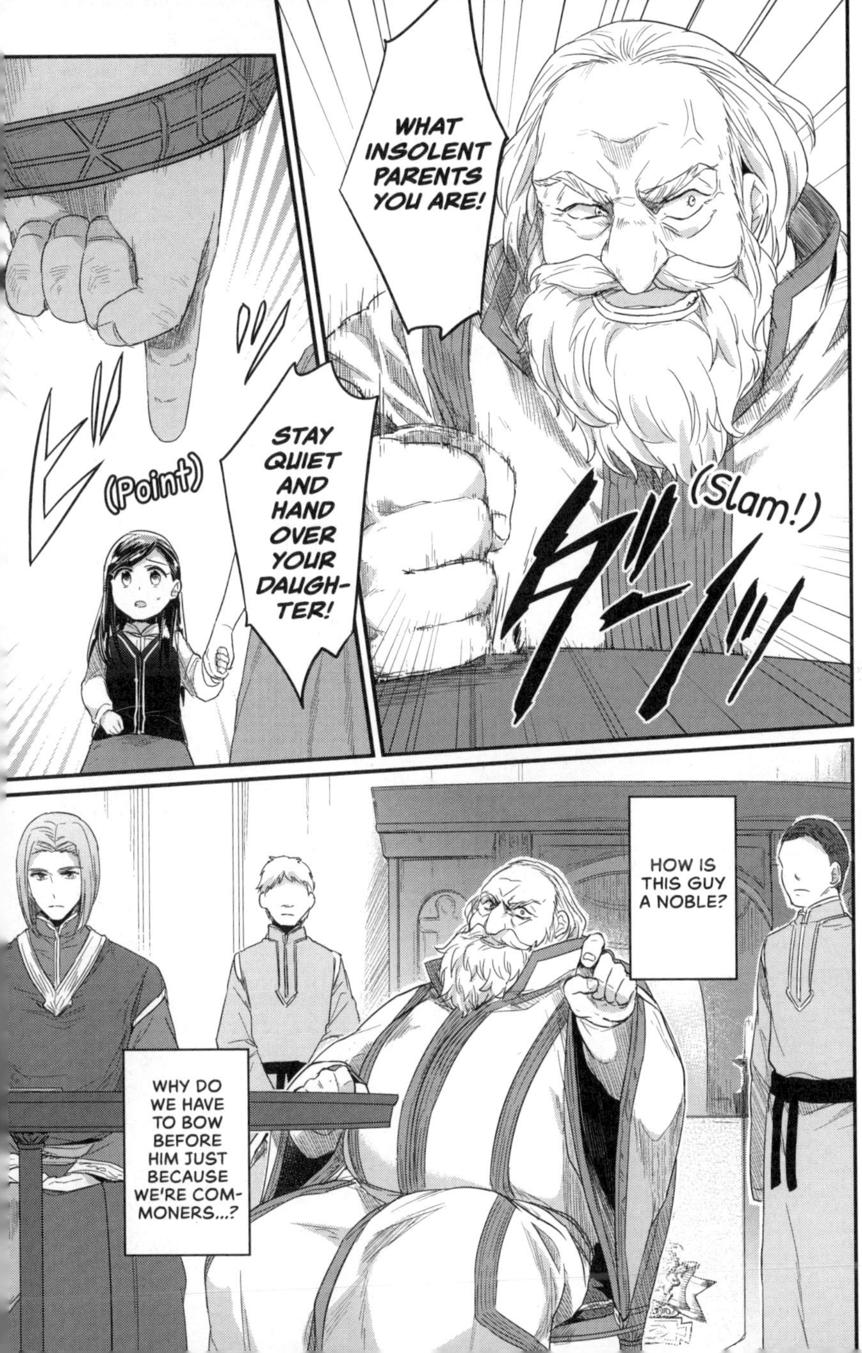
WHAT INSOLENT PARENTS YOU ARE!
(Slam!)
(Point)
STAY QUIET AND HAND OVER YOUR DAUGH-TER!
HOW IS THIS GUY A NOBLE?
WHY DO WE HAVE TO BOW BEFORE HIM JUST BECAUSE WE'RE COM-MONERS...?

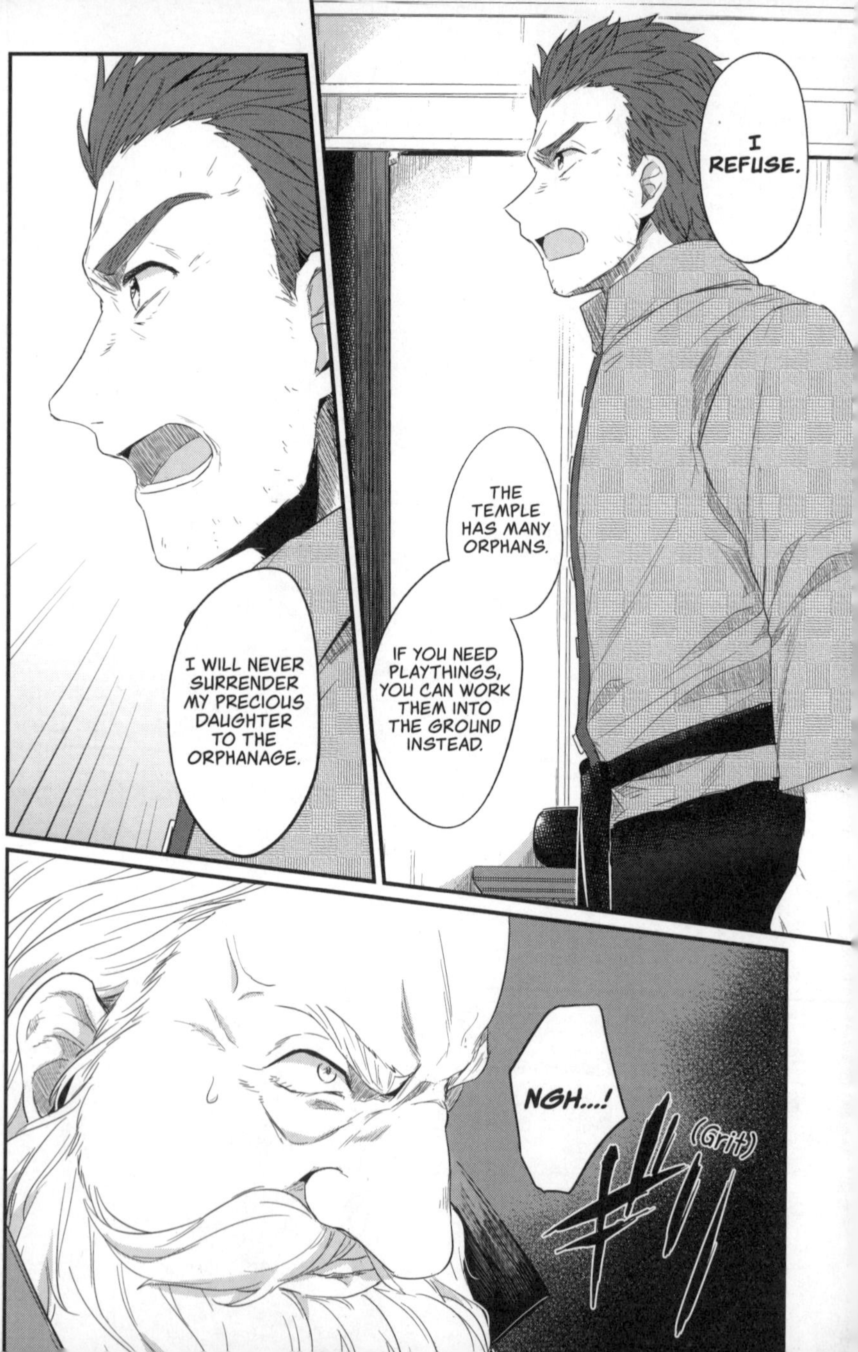
I REFUSE.
THE TEMPLE HAS MANY ORPHANS.
IF YOU NEED PLAYTHINGS, YOU CAN WORK THEM INTO THE GROUND INSTEAD.
I WILL NEVER SURRENDER MY PRECIOUS DAUGHTER TO THE ORPHANAGE.
NGH...!
(Grit)

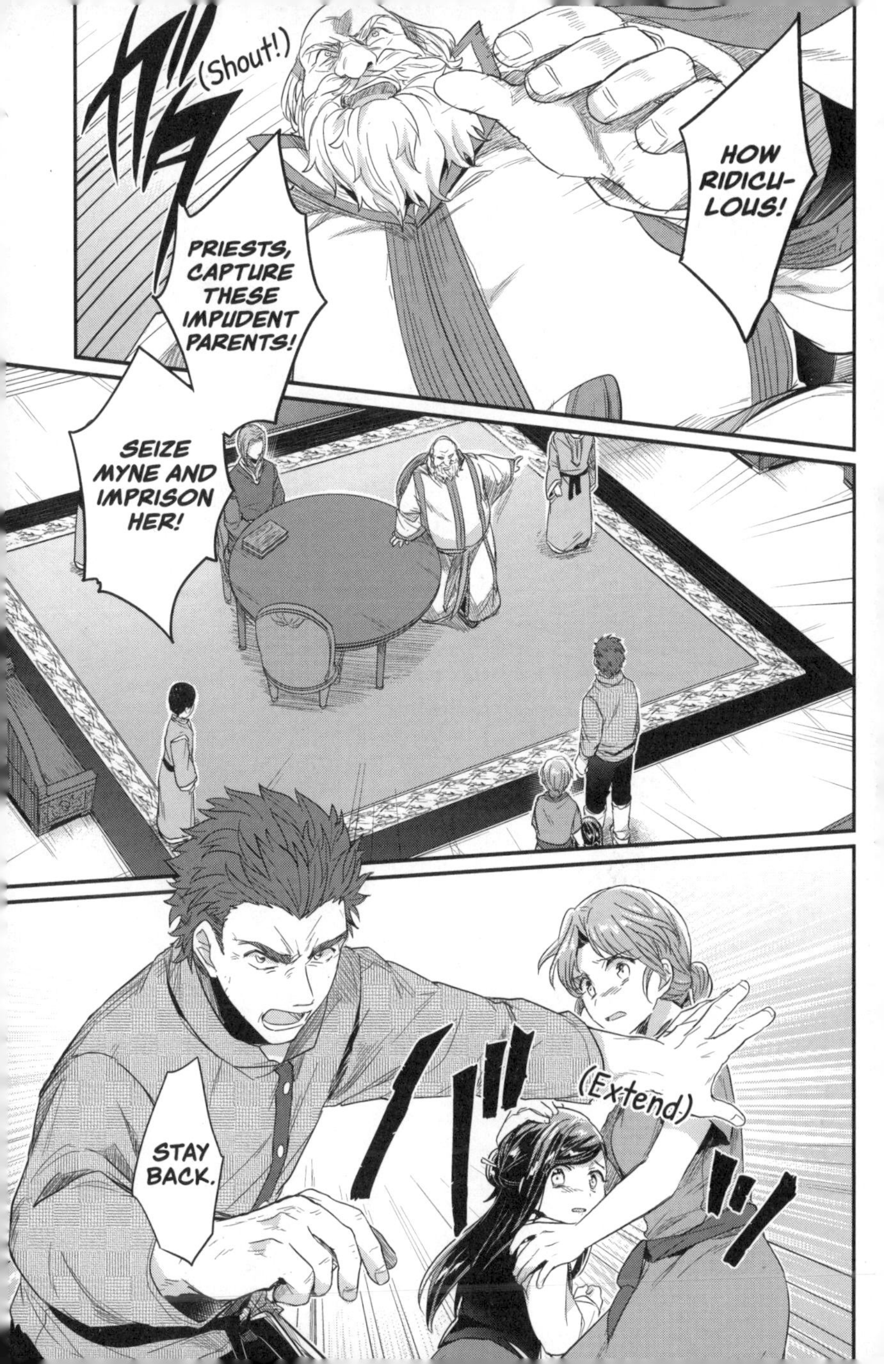
HOW RIDICULOUS!
(Shout!)
PRIESTS, CAPTURE THESE IMPUDENT PARENTS!
SEIZE MYNE AND IMPRISON HER!
(Extend)
STAY BACK.

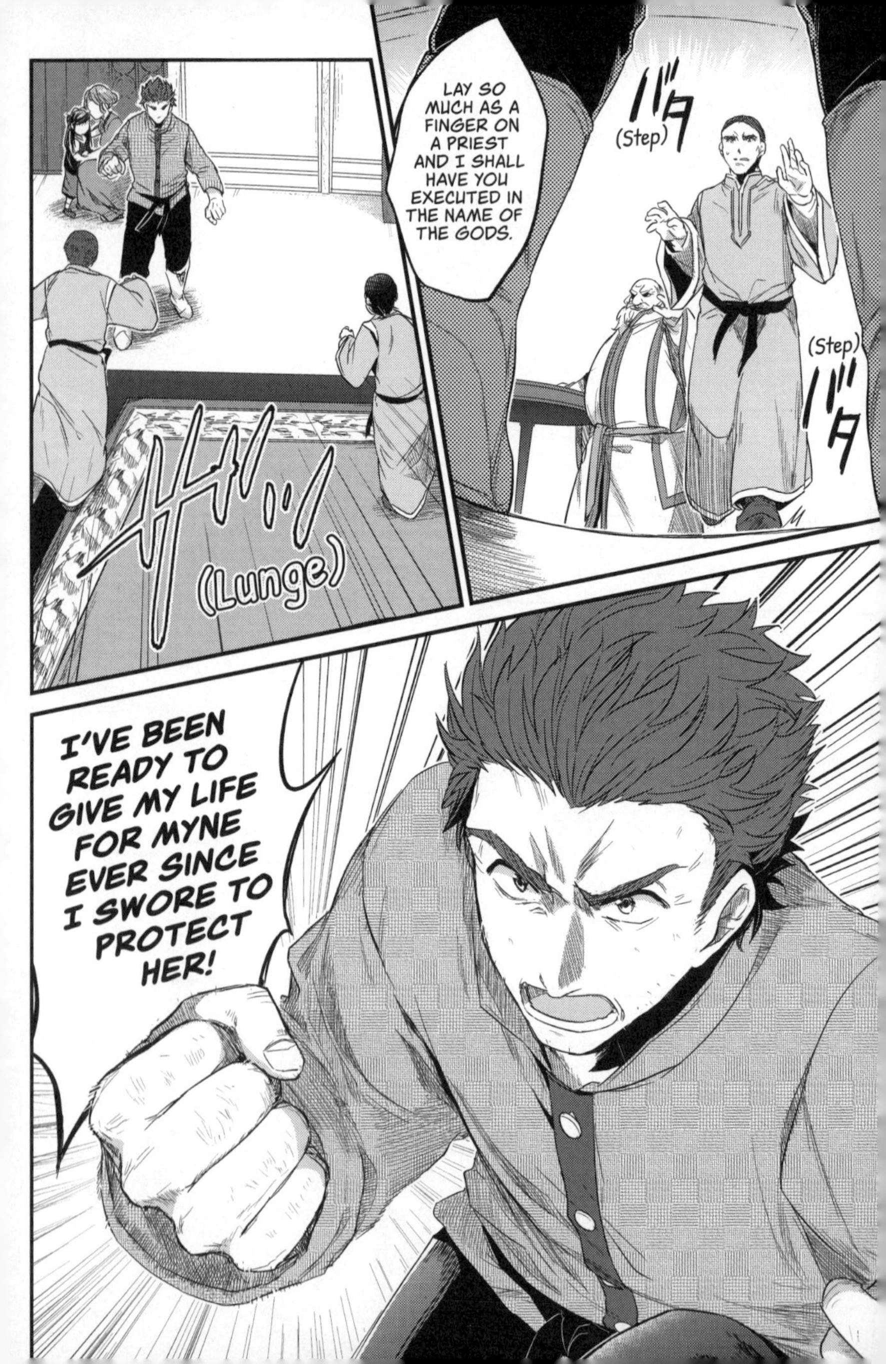
LAY SO MUCH AS A FINGER ON A PRIEST AND I SHALL HAVE YOU EXECUTED IN THE NAME OF THE GODS.
バタ
(Step)
(Step)
バタ
(Lunge)
I'VE BEEN READY TO GIVE MY LIFE FOR MYNE EVER SINCE I SWORE TO PROTECT HER!

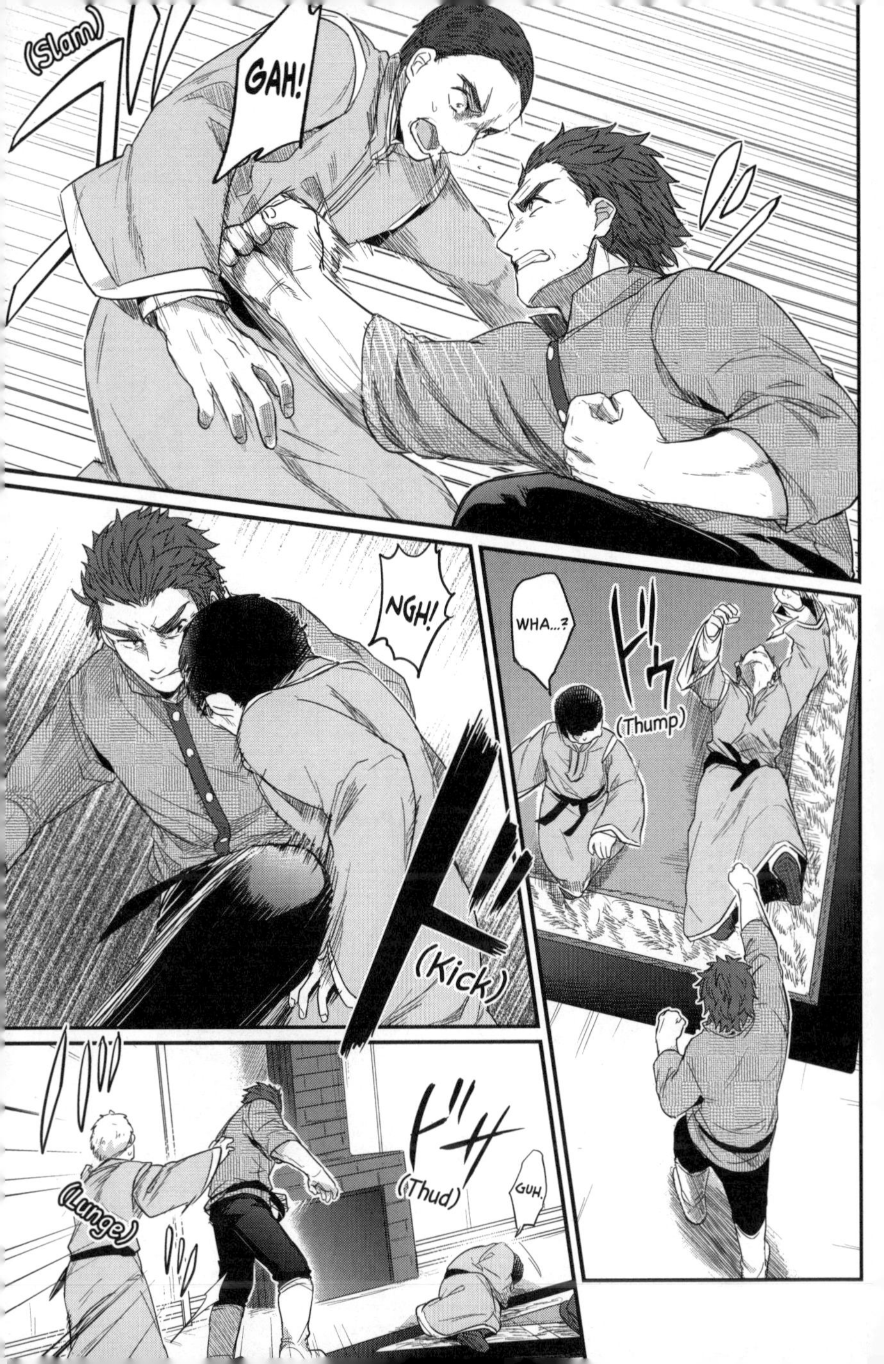
(Slam)
GAH!
WHA...?
ドゥ
(Thump)
NGH!
ド
(Kick)
ドサ
(Thud)
GUH.
(Lunge)

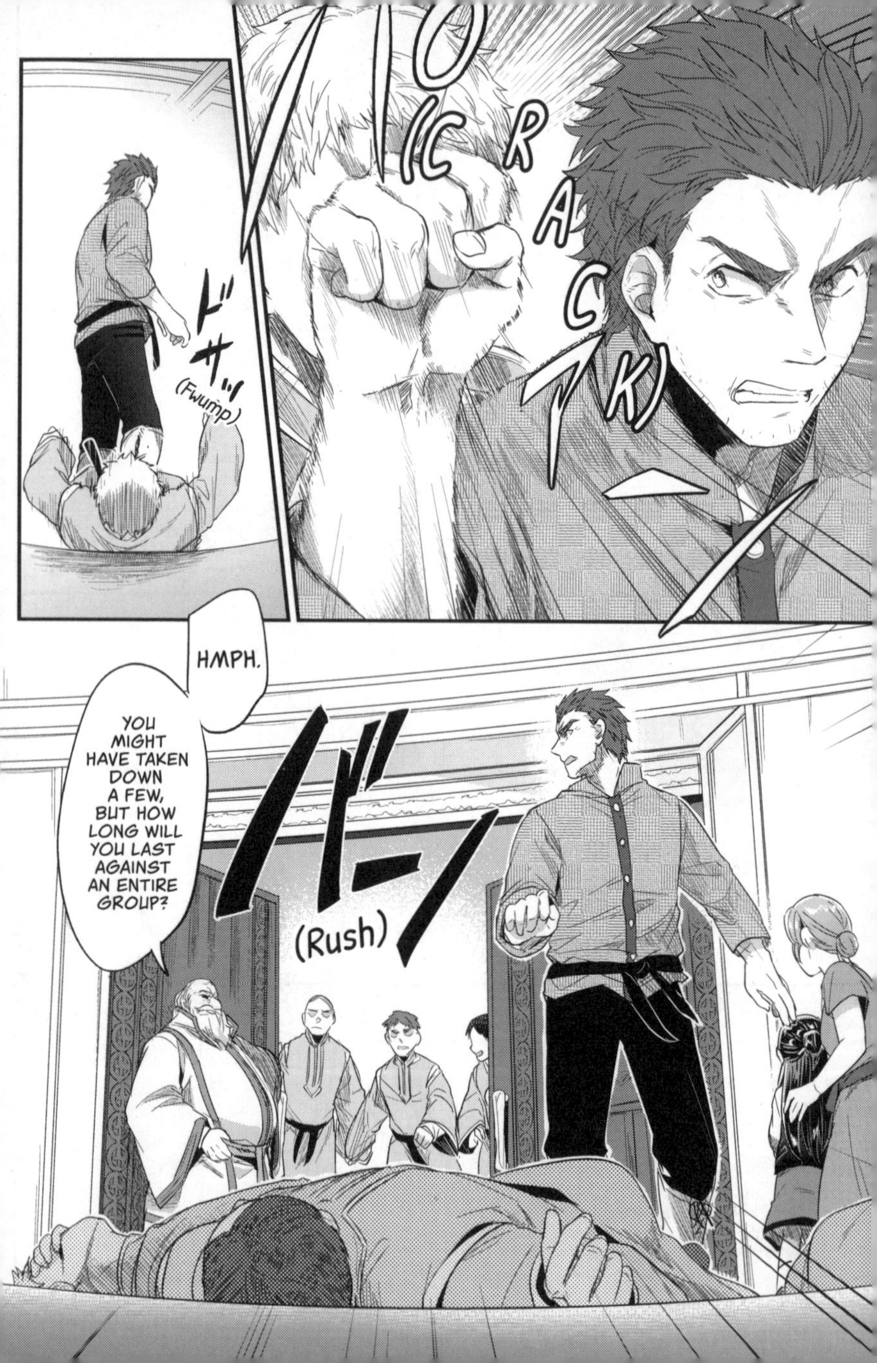

(CRACK)
ドサッ
(Fwump)
HMPH.
YOU MIGHT HAVE TAKEN DOWN A FEW, BUT HOW LONG WILL YOU LAST AGAINST AN ENTIRE GROUP?
(Rush)

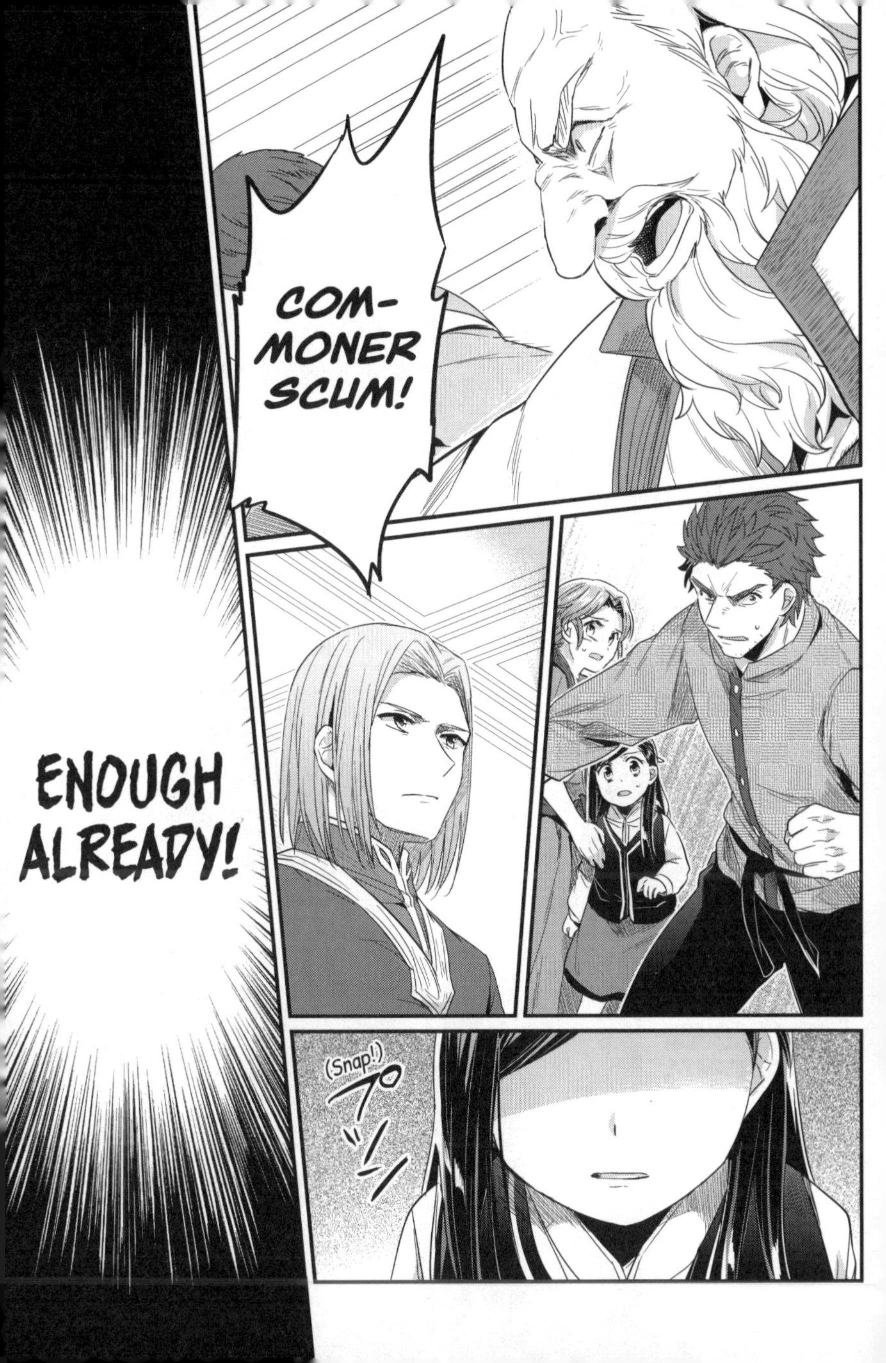
COM-MONER SCUM!
(Snap!)
ENOUGH ALREADY!

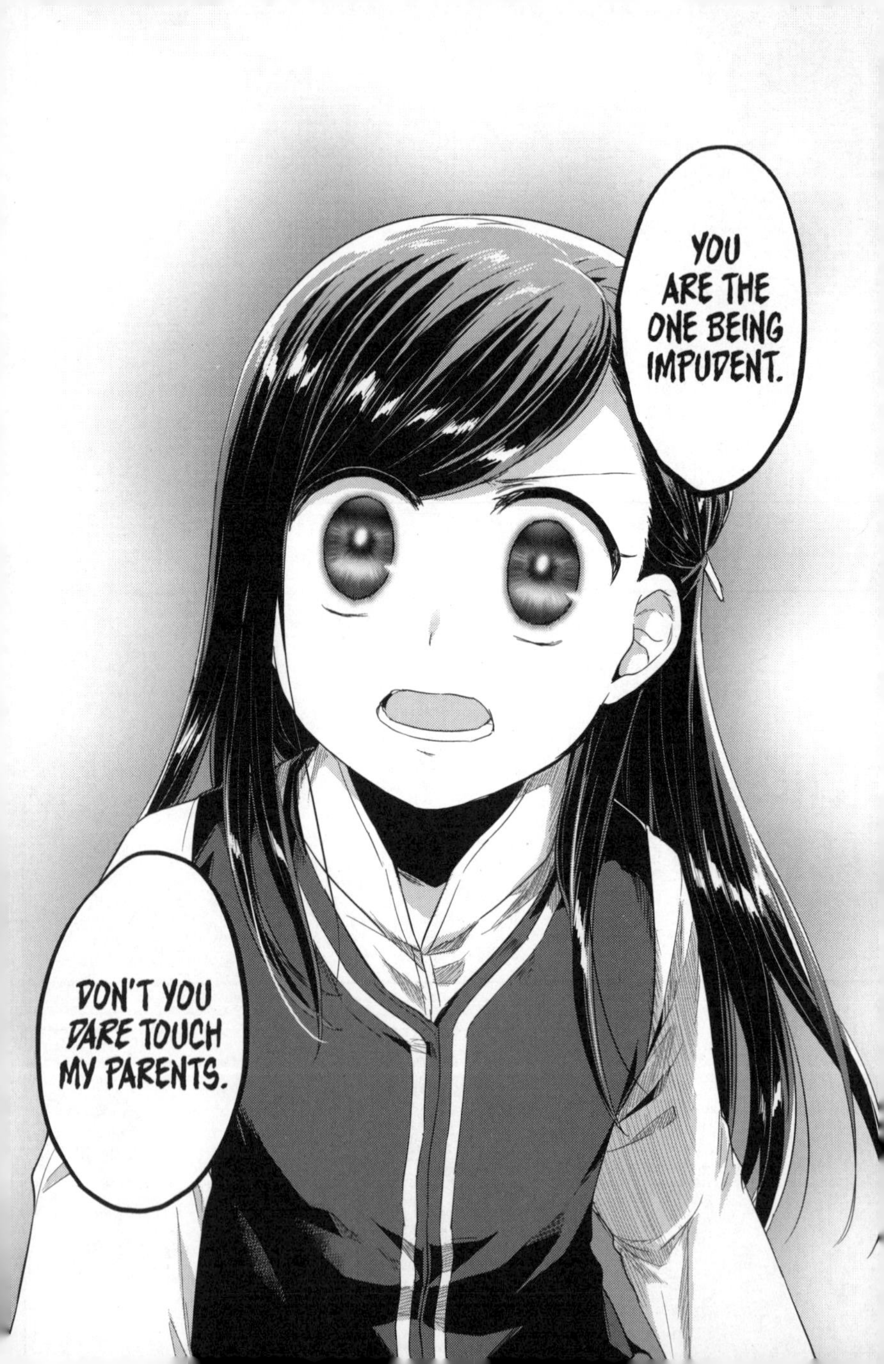
YOU ARE THE ONE BEING IMPUDENT.
DON'T YOU *DARE* TOUCH MY PARENTS.

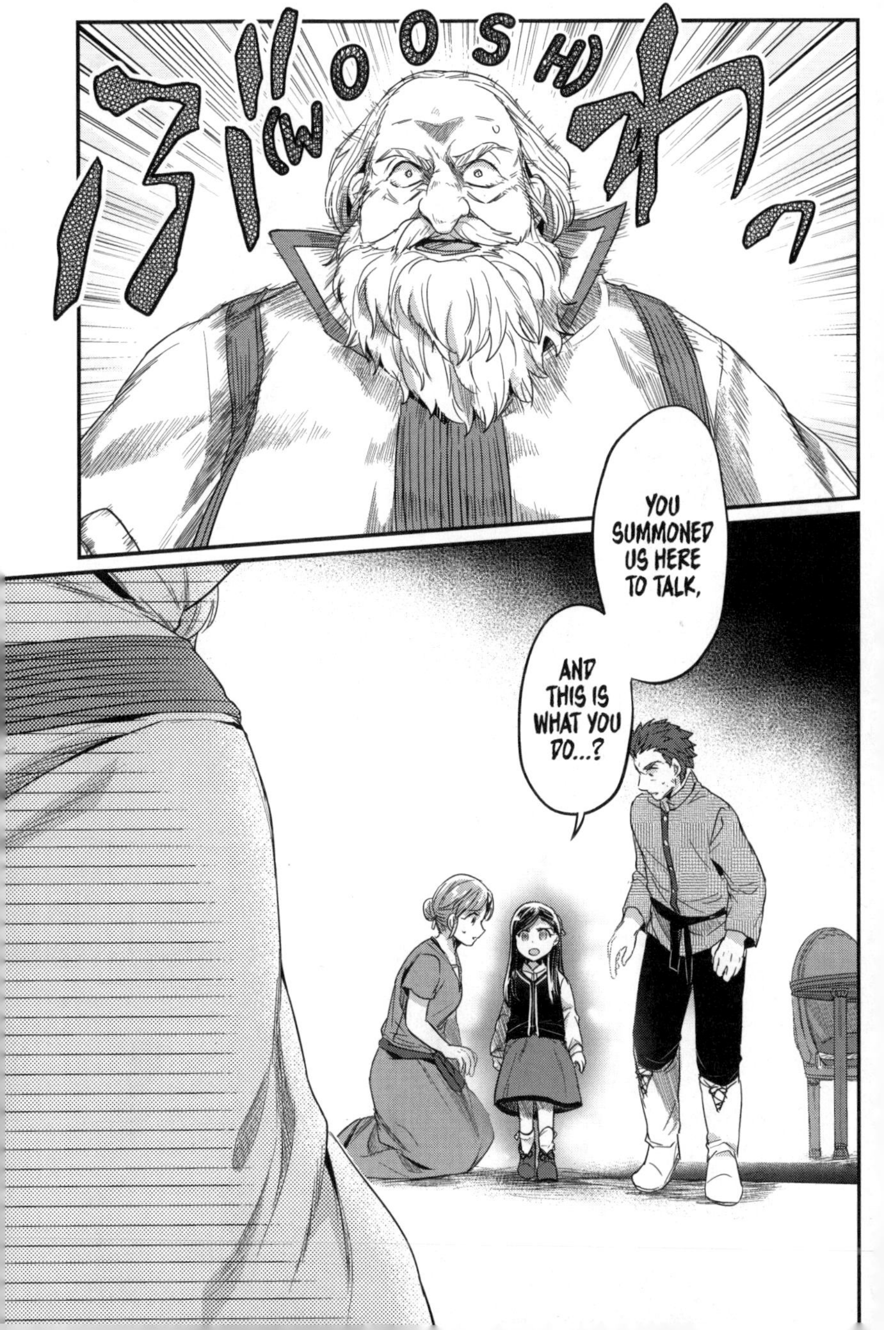
(WOOSH)
YOU SUMMONED US HERE TO TALK,
AND THIS IS WHAT YOU DO...?

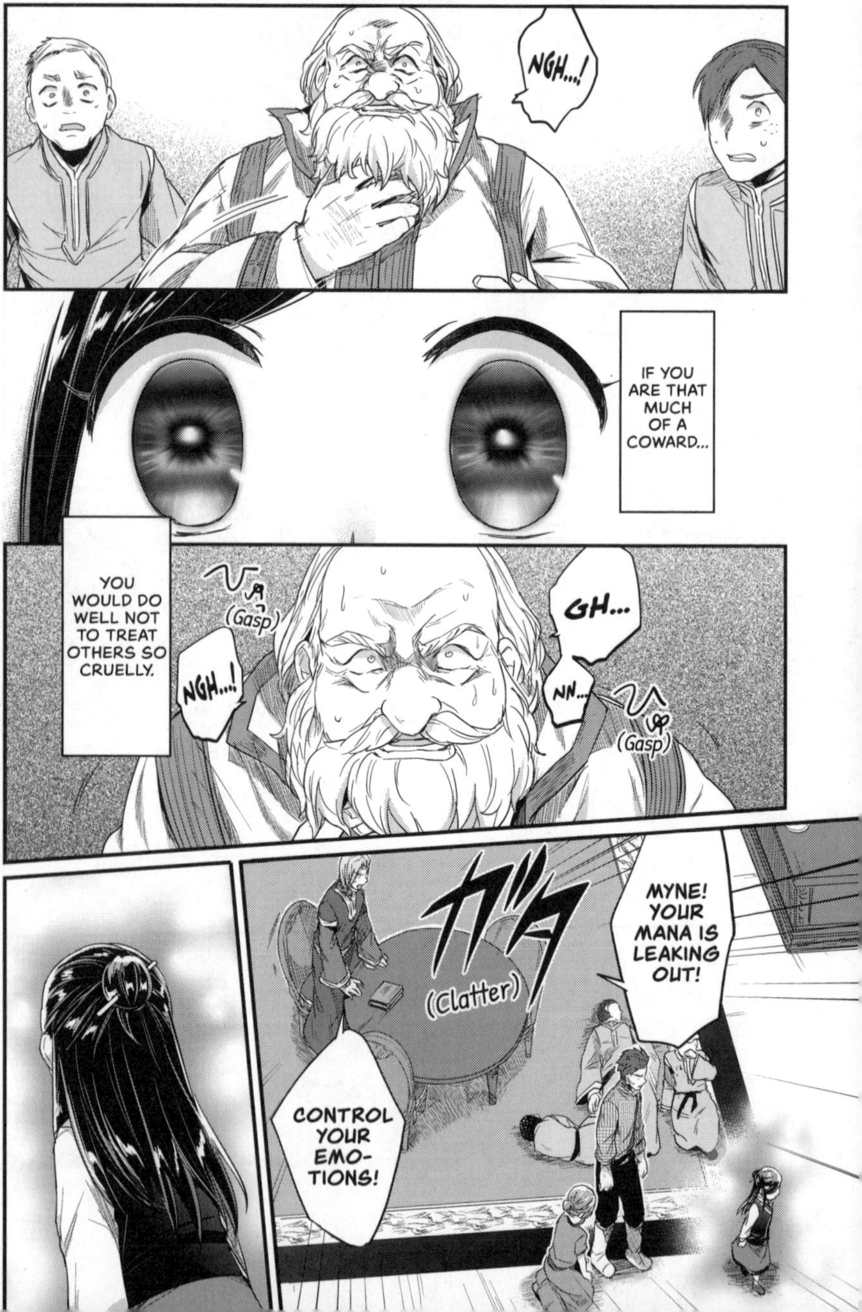
NGH...!
IF YOU ARE THAT MUCH OF A COWARD...
GH...
(Gasp)
NN...
YOU WOULD DO WELL NOT TO TREAT OTHERS SO CRUELLY.
(Gasp)
NGH...!
MYNE! YOUR MANA IS LEAKING OUT!
(Clatter)
CONTROL YOUR EMO-TIONS!

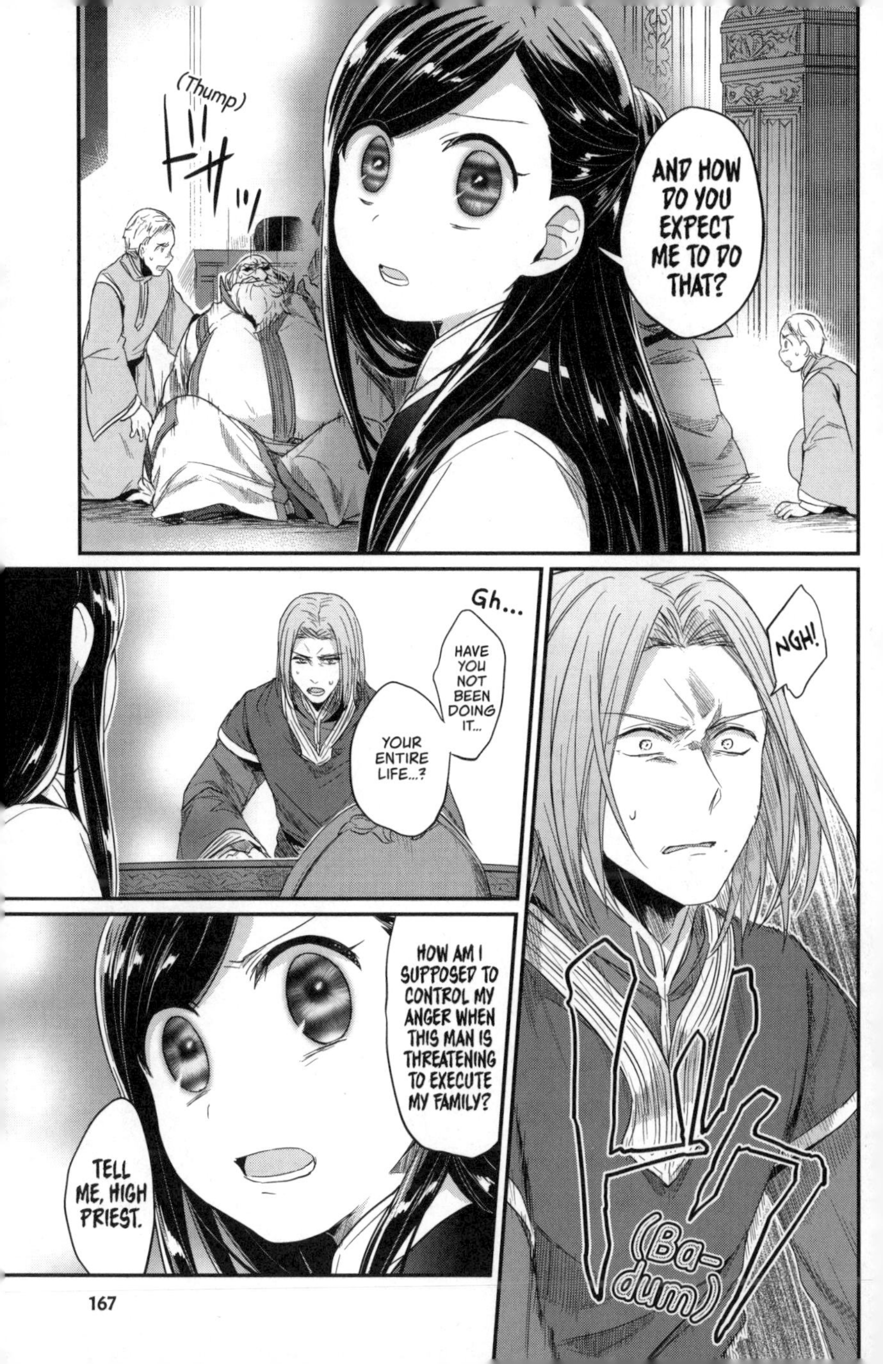
(Thump)
AND HOW DO YOU EXPECT ME TO DO THAT?
NGH!
(Ba-dum)
Gh...
HAVE YOU NOT BEEN DOING IT...
YOUR ENTIRE LIFE...?
HOW AM I SUPPOSED TO CONTROL MY ANGER WHEN THIS MAN IS THREATENING TO EXECUTE MY FAMILY?
TELL ME, HIGH PRIEST.

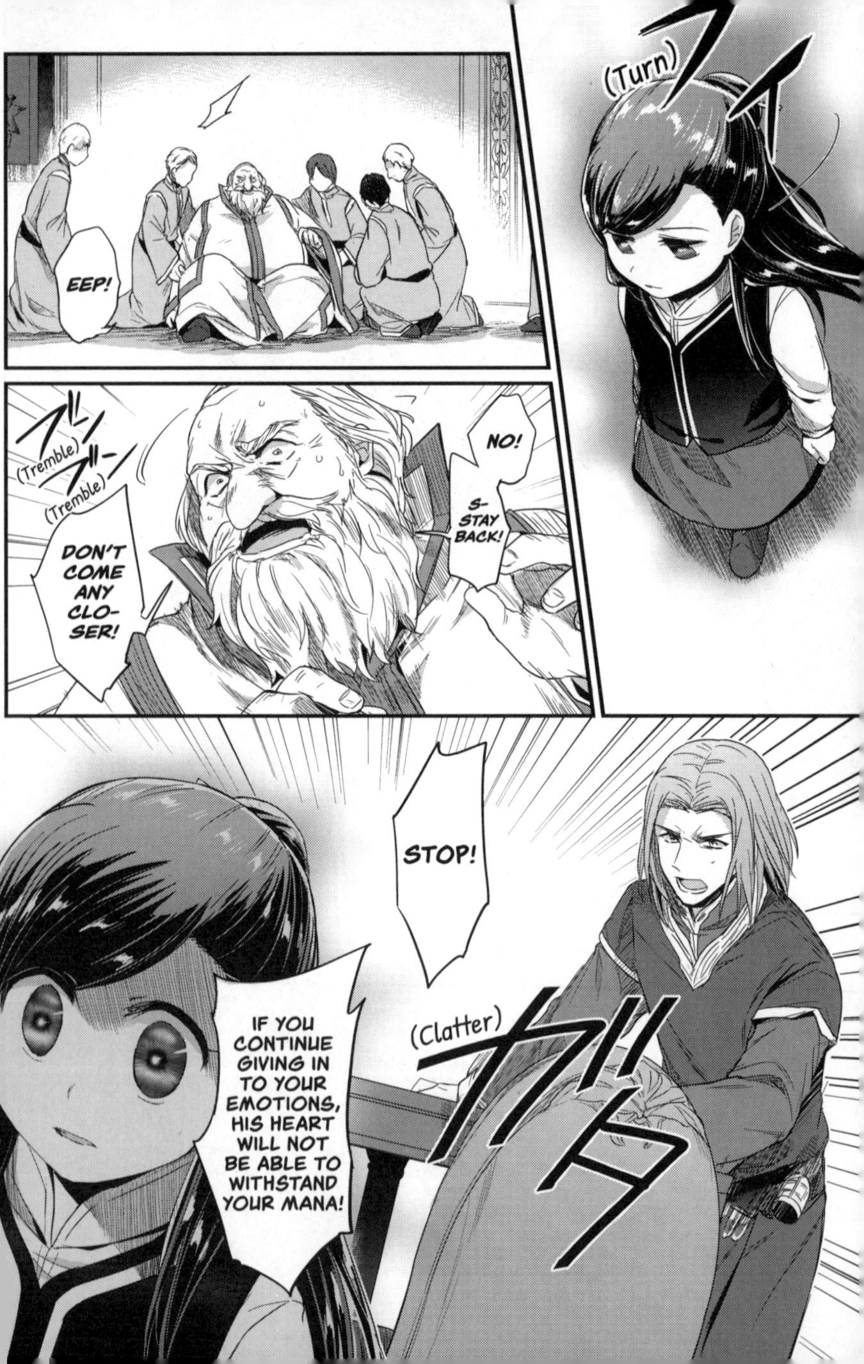
(Turn)
EEP!
NO!
S-STAY BACK!
(Tremble) (Tremble)
DON'T COME ANY CLO-SER!
STOP!
(Clatter)
IF YOU CONTINUE GIVING IN TO YOUR EMOTIONS, HIS HEART WILL NOT BE ABLE TO WITHSTAND YOUR MANA!

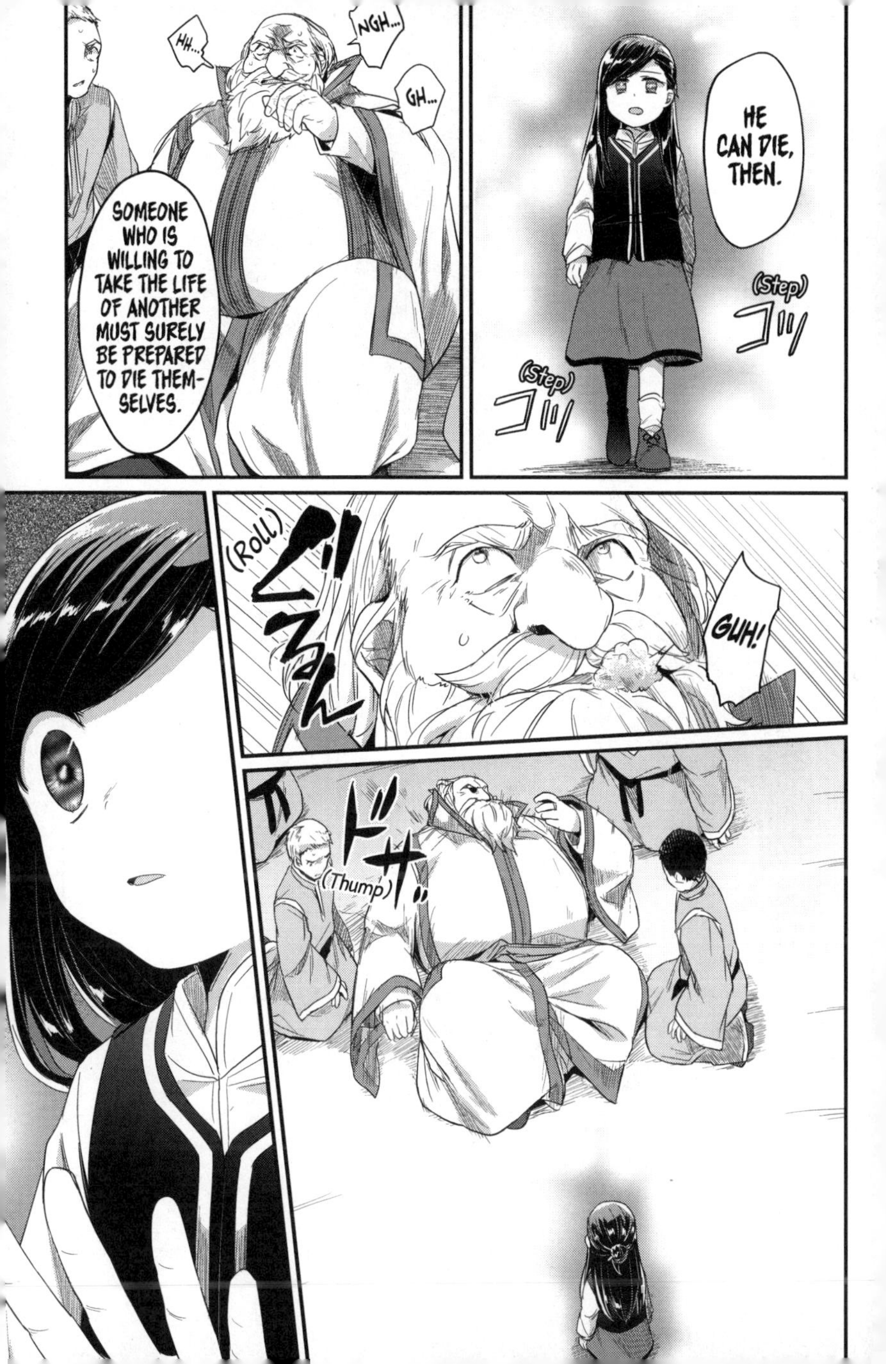
HE CAN DIE, THEN.
(Step)
(Step)
NGH...
GH...
HH...
SOMEONE WHO IS WILLING TO TAKE THE LIFE OF ANOTHER MUST SURELY BE PREPARED TO DIE THEMSELVES.
GUH!
(Roll)
(Thump)

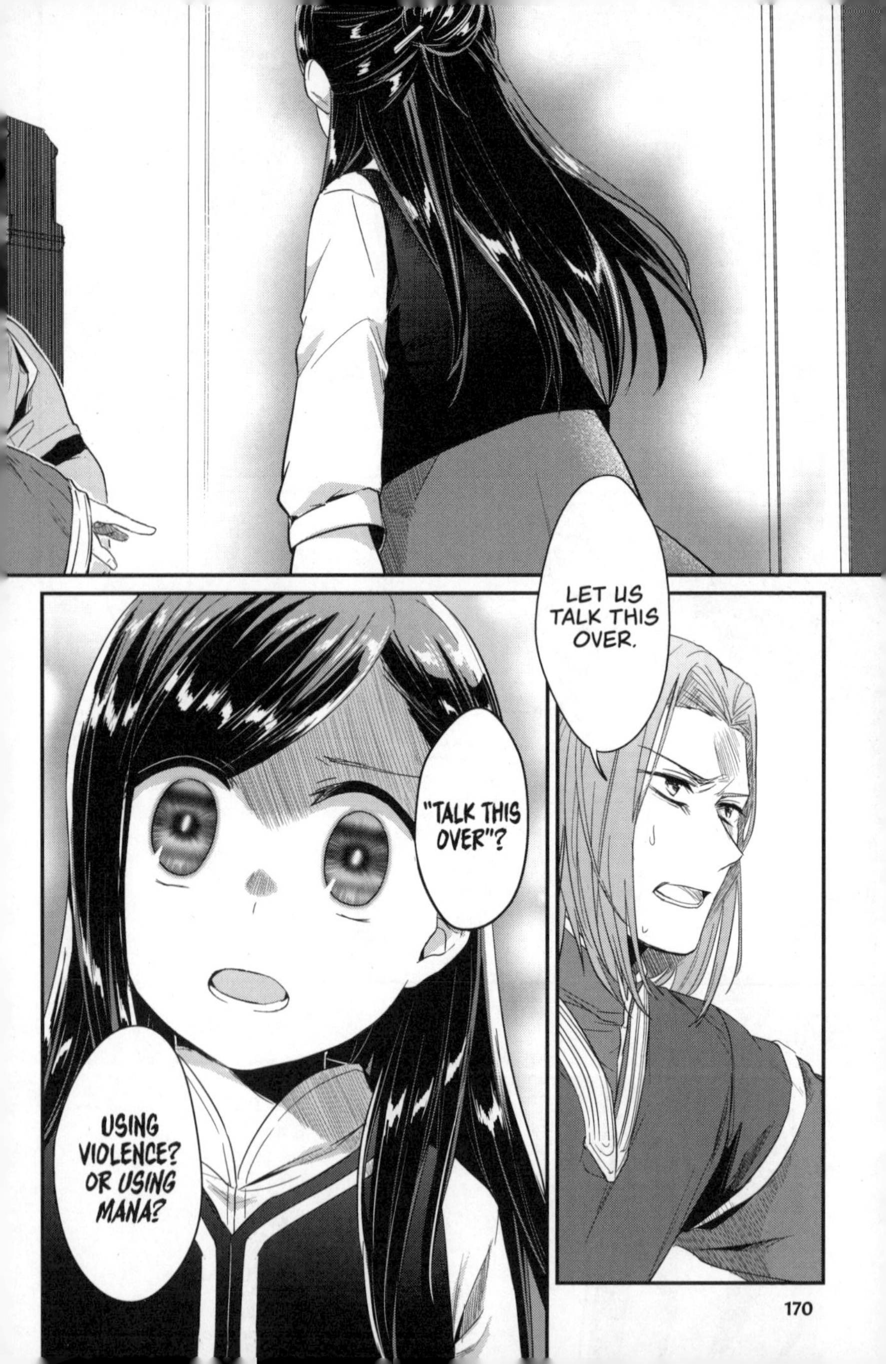
LET US TALK THIS OVER.
"TALK THIS OVER"?
USING VIOLENCE? OR USING MANA?

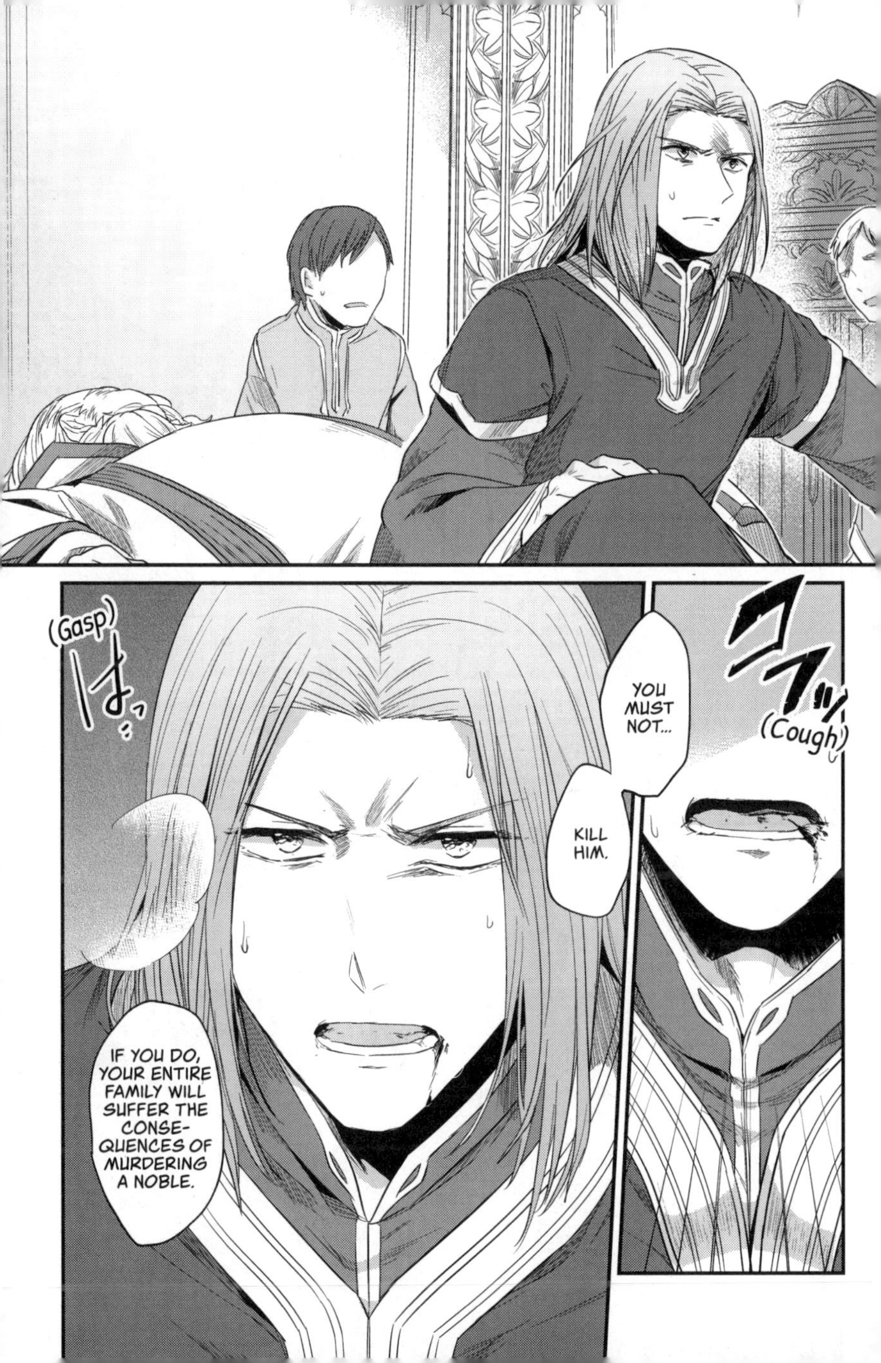
(Cough)
YOU MUST NOT...
KILL HIM.
(Gasp)
IF YOU DO, YOUR ENTIRE FAMILY WILL SUFFER THE CONSE-QUENCES OF MURDERING A NOBLE.

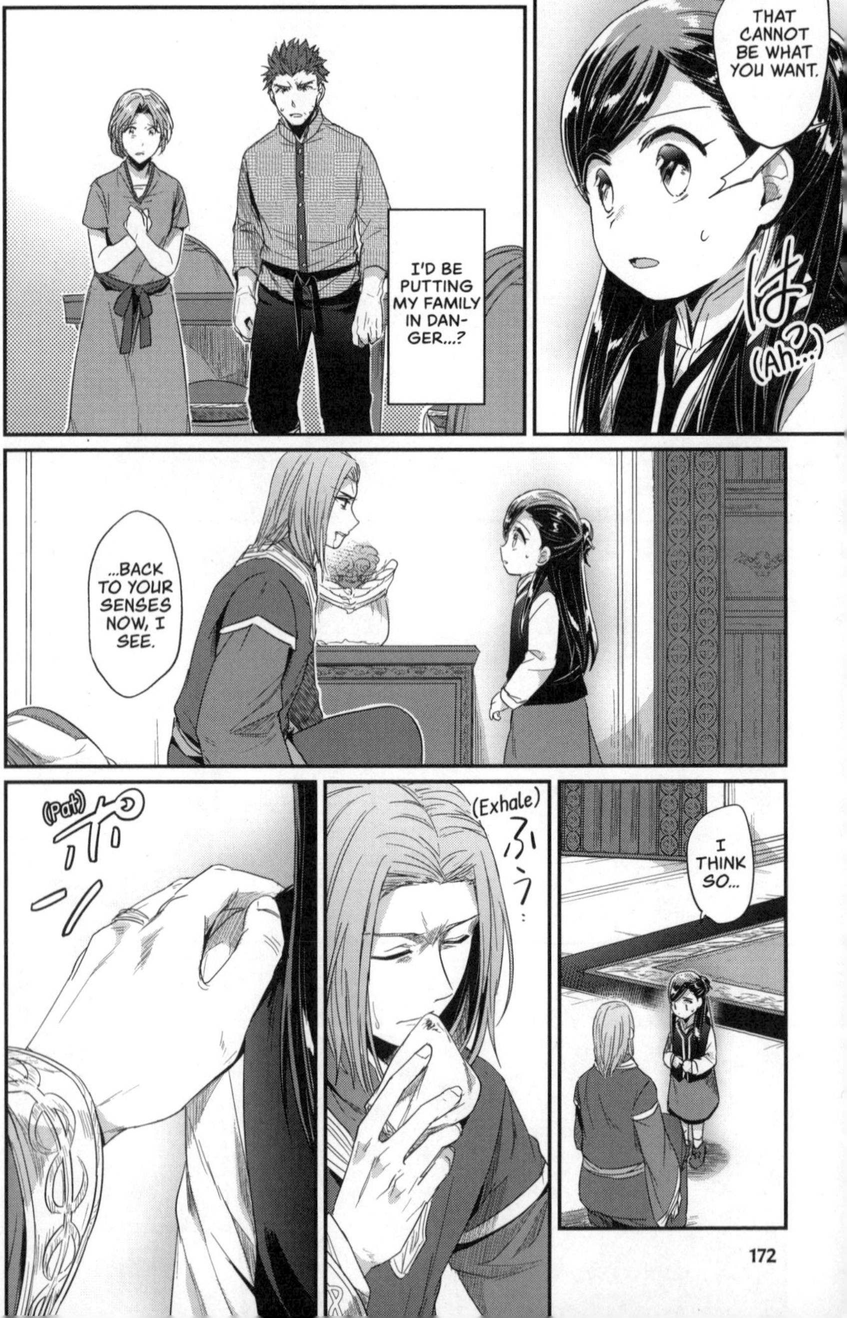
THAT CANNOT BE WHAT YOU WANT.
は (Ah...)
I'D BE PUTTING MY FAMILY IN DANGER...?
...BACK TO YOUR SENSES NOW, I SEE.
I THINK SO...
(Exhale) ふぅ
(Pat) ポン

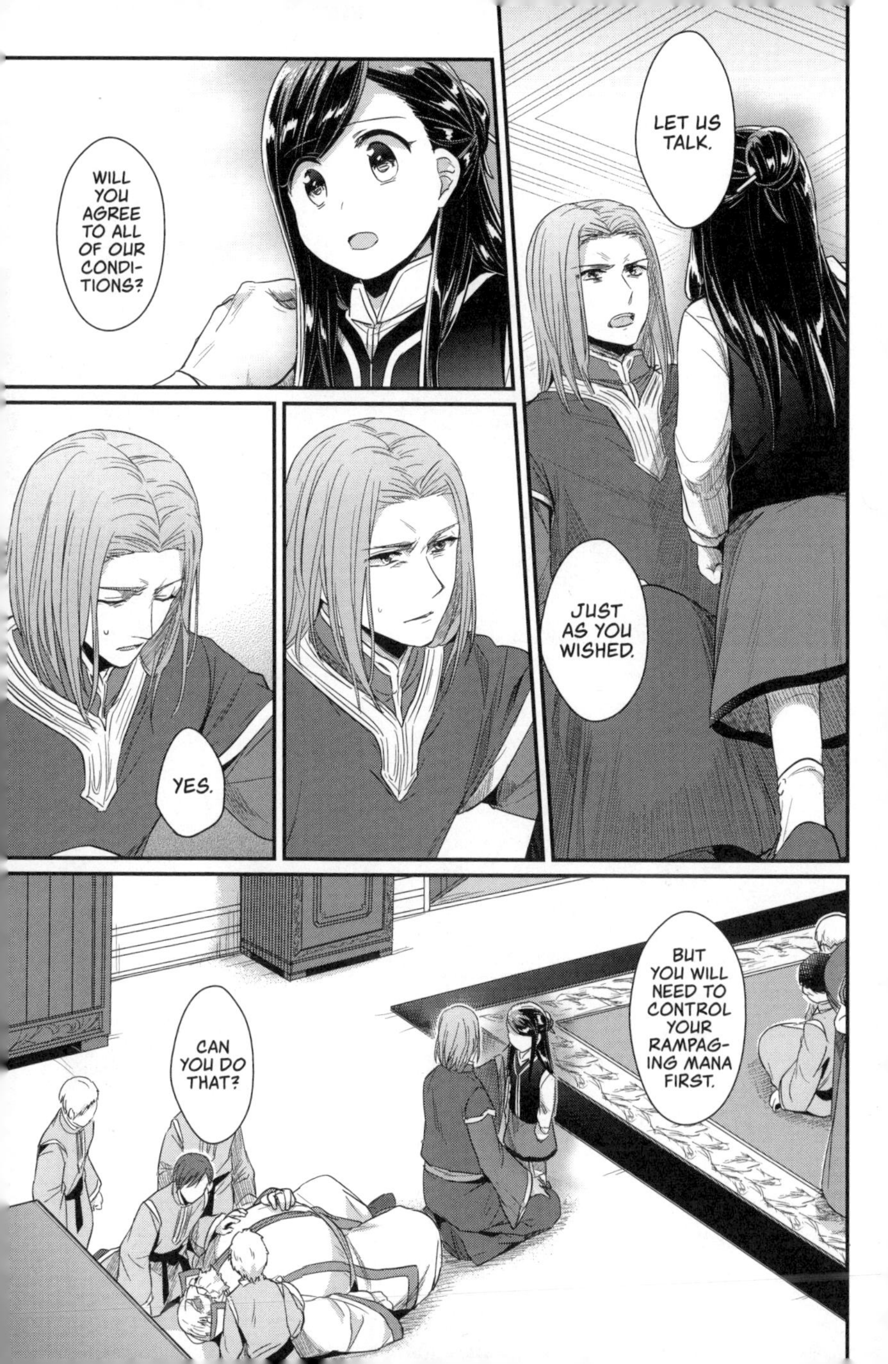
LET US TALK.
JUST AS YOU WISHED.
WILL YOU AGREE TO ALL OF OUR CONDITIONS?
YES.
BUT YOU WILL NEED TO CONTROL YOUR RAMPAGING MANA FIRST.
CAN YOU DO THAT?

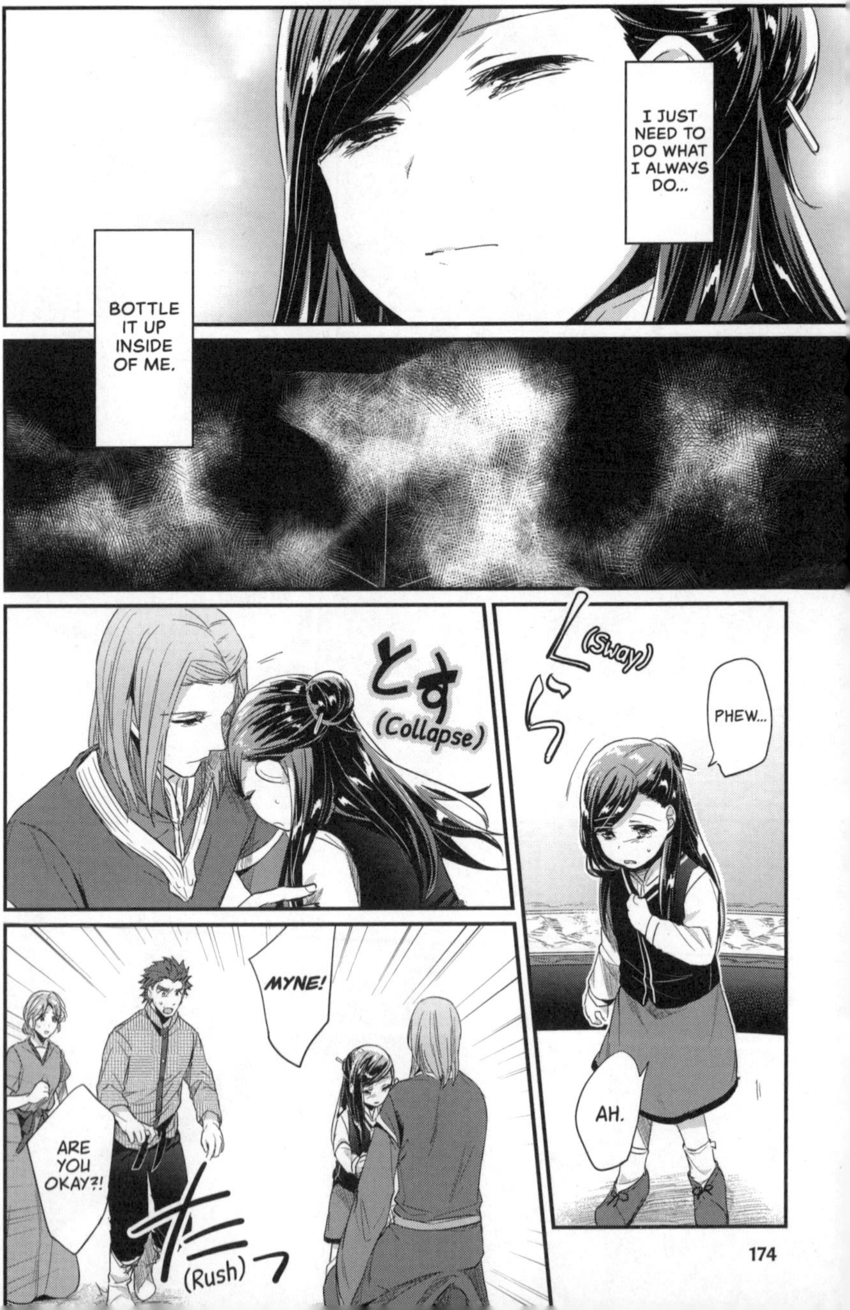
I JUST NEED TO DO WHAT I ALWAYS DO...
BOTTLE IT UP INSIDE OF ME.
(Sway)
PHEW...
AH.
とす
(Collapse)
MYNE!
ARE YOU OKAY?!
(Rush)

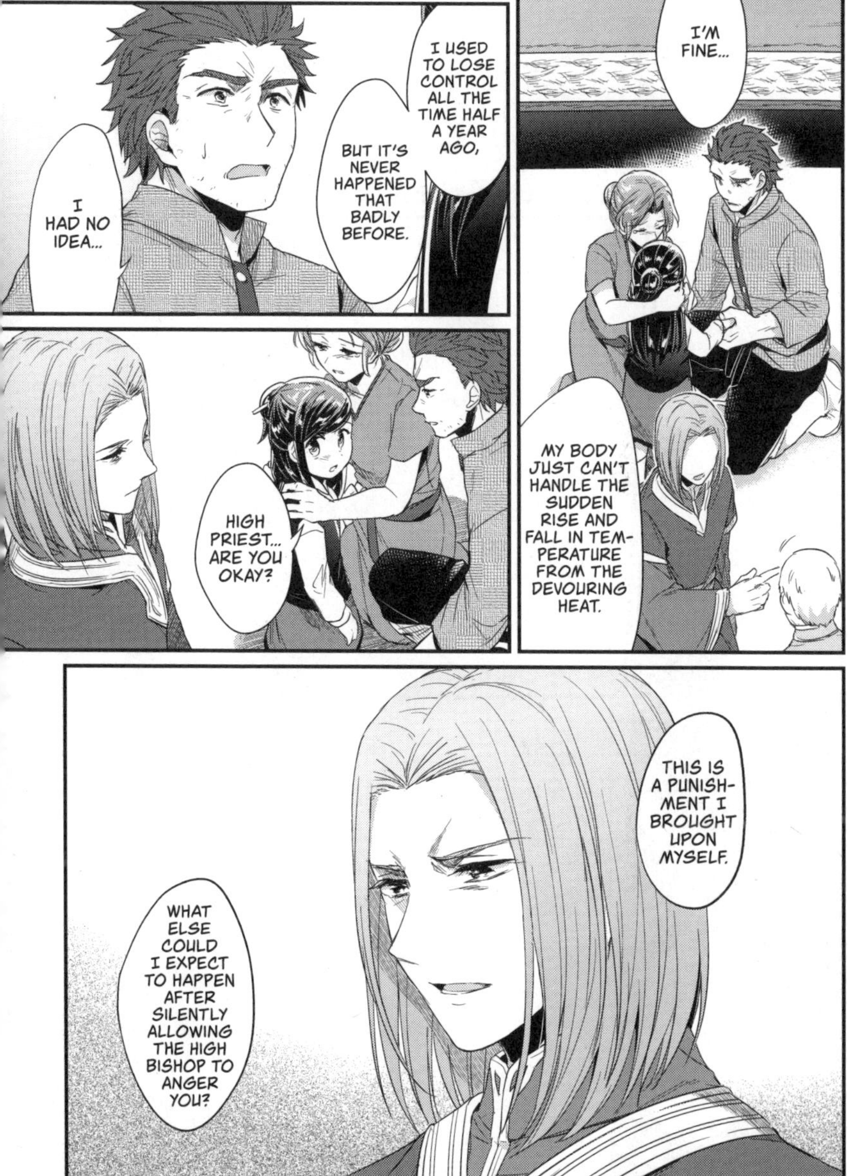
I'M FINE...
MY BODY JUST CAN'T HANDLE THE SUDDEN RISE AND FALL IN TEM-PERATURE FROM THE DEVOURING HEAT.
I USED TO LOSE CONTROL ALL THE TIME HALF A YEAR AGO,
BUT IT'S NEVER HAPPENED THAT BADLY BEFORE.
I HAD NO IDEA...
HIGH PRIEST... ARE YOU OKAY?
THIS IS A PUNISH-MENT I BROUGHT UPON MYSELF.
WHAT ELSE COULD I EXPECT TO HAPPEN AFTER SILENTLY ALLOWING THE HIGH BISHOP TO ANGER YOU?

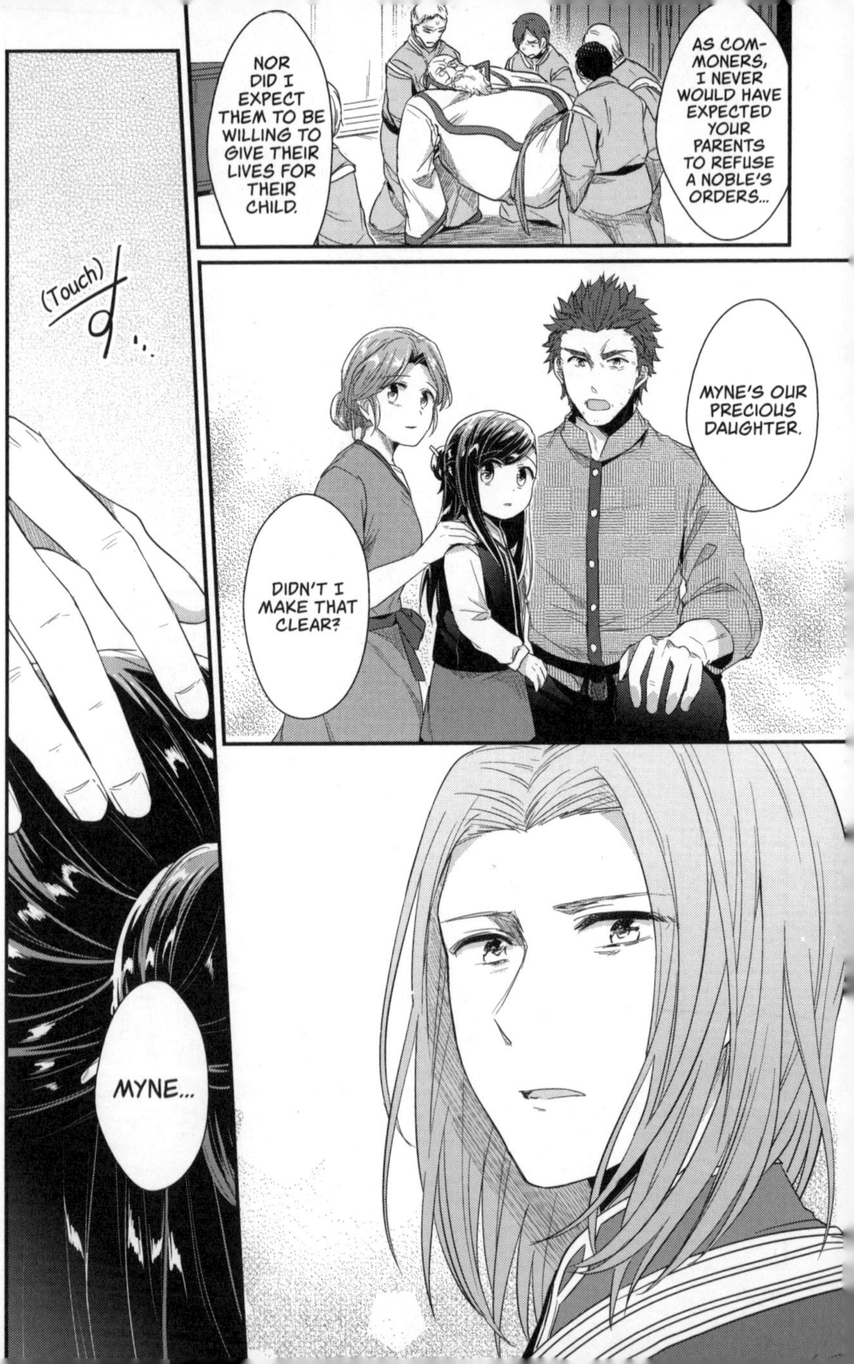
AS COMMONERS, I NEVER WOULD HAVE EXPECTED YOUR PARENTS TO REFUSE A NOBLE'S ORDERS...
NOR DID I EXPECT THEM TO BE WILLING TO GIVE THEIR LIVES FOR THEIR CHILD.
MYNE'S OUR PRECIOUS DAUGHTER.
DIDN'T I MAKE THAT CLEAR?
(Touch)
MYNE...

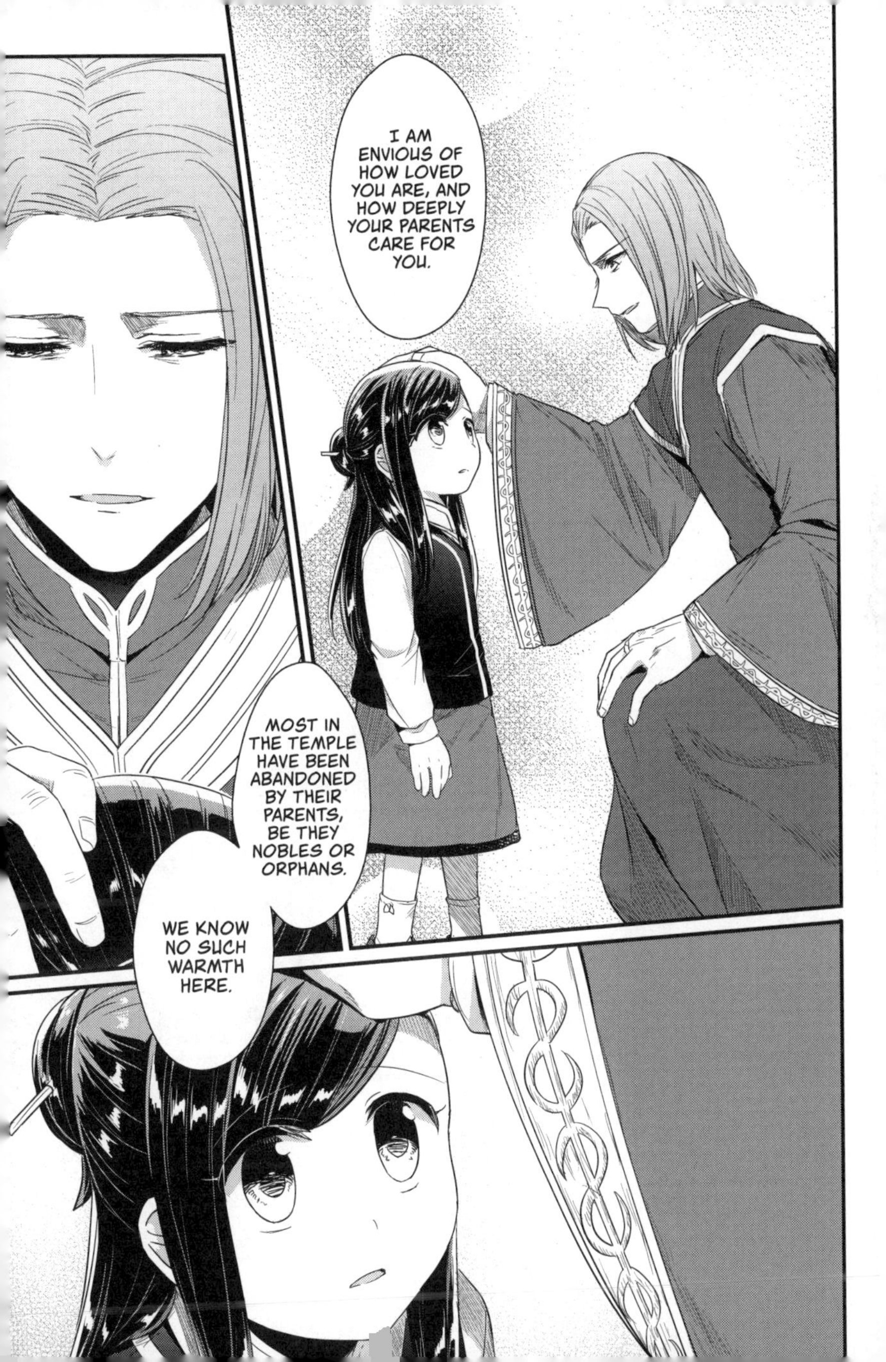
I AM ENVIOUS OF HOW LOVED YOU ARE, AND HOW DEEPLY YOUR PARENTS CARE FOR YOU.
MOST IN THE TEMPLE HAVE BEEN ABANDONED BY THEIR PARENTS, BE THEY NOBLES OR ORPHANS.
WE KNOW NO SUCH WARMTH HERE.

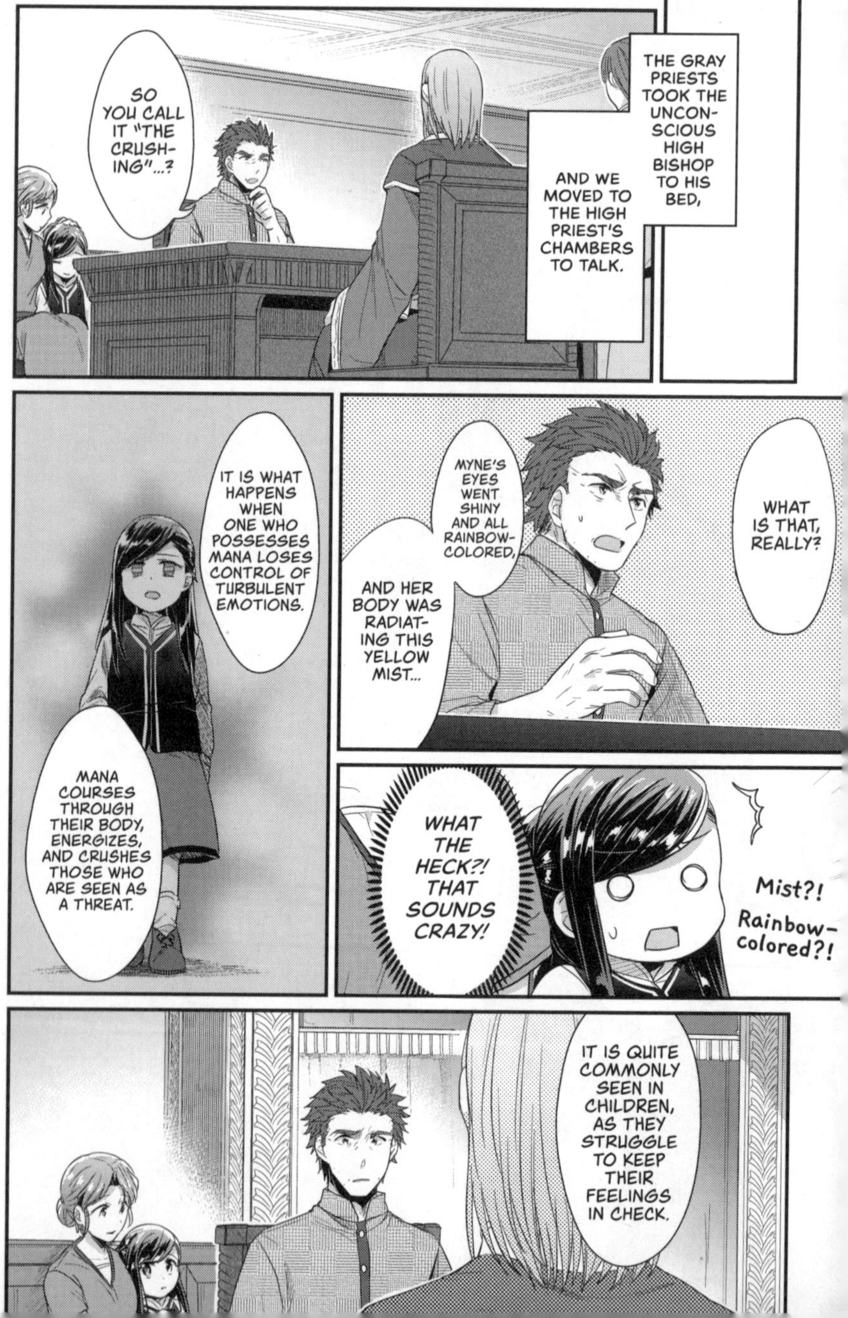
THE GRAY PRIESTS TOOK THE UNCONSCIOUS HIGH BISHOP TO HIS BED,
AND WE MOVED TO THE HIGH PRIEST'S CHAMBERS TO TALK.
SO YOU CALL IT "THE CRUSHING"...?
WHAT IS THAT, REALLY?
MYNE'S EYES WENT SHINY AND ALL RAINBOW-COLORED,
AND HER BODY WAS RADIATING THIS YELLOW MIST...
Mist?! Rainbow-colored?!
WHAT THE HECK?! THAT SOUNDS CRAZY!
IT IS WHAT HAPPENS WHEN ONE WHO POSSESSES MANA LOSES CONTROL OF TURBULENT EMOTIONS.
MANA COURSES THROUGH THEIR BODY, ENERGIZES, AND CRUSHES THOSE WHO ARE SEEN AS A THREAT.
IT IS QUITE COMMONLY SEEN IN CHILDREN, AS THEY STRUGGLE TO KEEP THEIR FEELINGS IN CHECK.

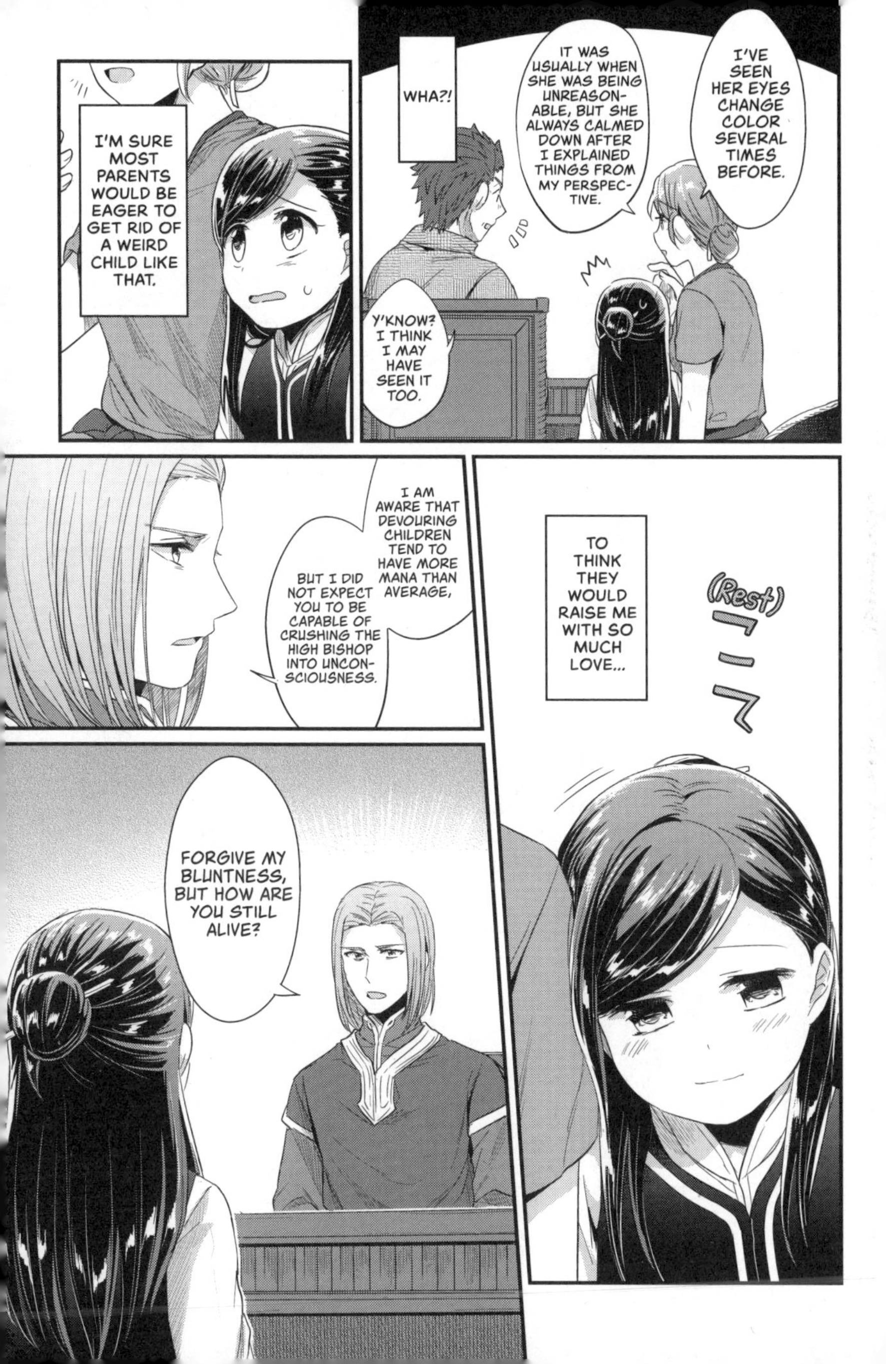
I'VE SEEN HER EYES CHANGE COLOR SEVERAL TIMES BEFORE.
IT WAS USUALLY WHEN SHE WAS BEING UNREASON-ABLE, BUT SHE ALWAYS CALMED DOWN AFTER I EXPLAINED THINGS FROM MY PERSPEC-TIVE.
WHA?!
Y'KNOW? I THINK I MAY HAVE SEEN IT TOO.
I'M SURE MOST PARENTS WOULD BE EAGER TO GET RID OF A WEIRD CHILD LIKE THAT.
TO THINK THEY WOULD RAISE ME WITH SO MUCH LOVE...
(Rest)
I AM AWARE THAT DEVOURING CHILDREN TEND TO HAVE MORE MANA THAN AVERAGE,
BUT I DID NOT EXPECT YOU TO BE CAPABLE OF CRUSHING THE HIGH BISHOP INTO UNCON-SCIOUSNESS.
FORGIVE MY BLUNTNESS, BUT HOW ARE YOU STILL ALIVE?

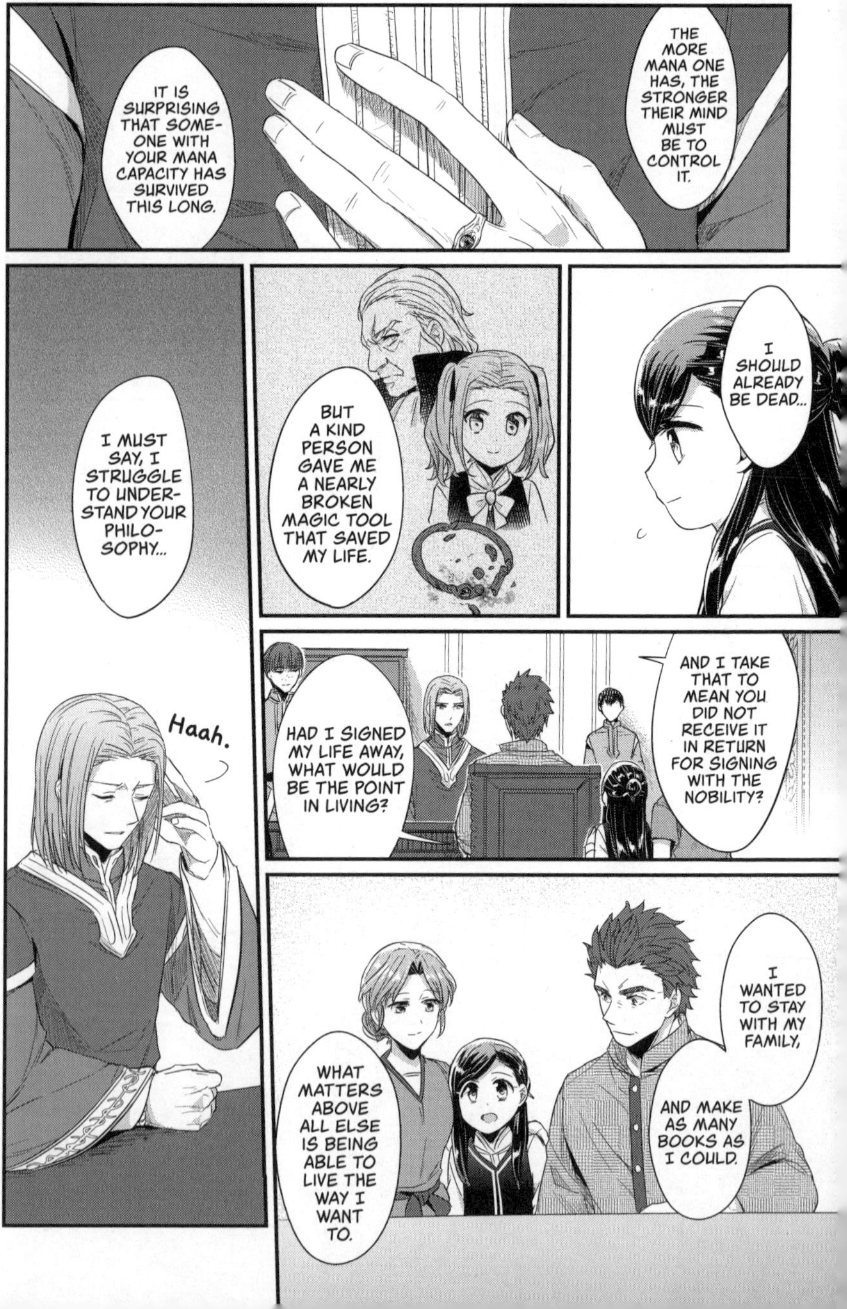
THE MORE MANA ONE HAS, THE STRONGER THEIR MIND MUST BE TO CONTROL IT.
IT IS SURPRISING THAT SOME-ONE WITH YOUR MANA CAPACITY HAS SURVIVED THIS LONG.
I SHOULD ALREADY BE DEAD...
BUT A KIND PERSON GAVE ME A NEARLY BROKEN MAGIC TOOL THAT SAVED MY LIFE.
AND I TAKE THAT TO MEAN YOU DID NOT RECEIVE IT IN RETURN FOR SIGNING WITH THE NOBILITY?
HAD I SIGNED MY LIFE AWAY, WHAT WOULD BE THE POINT IN LIVING?
I WANTED TO STAY WITH MY FAMILY,
AND MAKE AS MANY BOOKS AS I COULD.
WHAT MATTERS ABOVE ALL ELSE IS BEING ABLE TO LIVE THE WAY I WANT TO.
I MUST SAY, I STRUGGLE TO UNDER-STAND YOUR PHILO-SOPHY...
Haah.

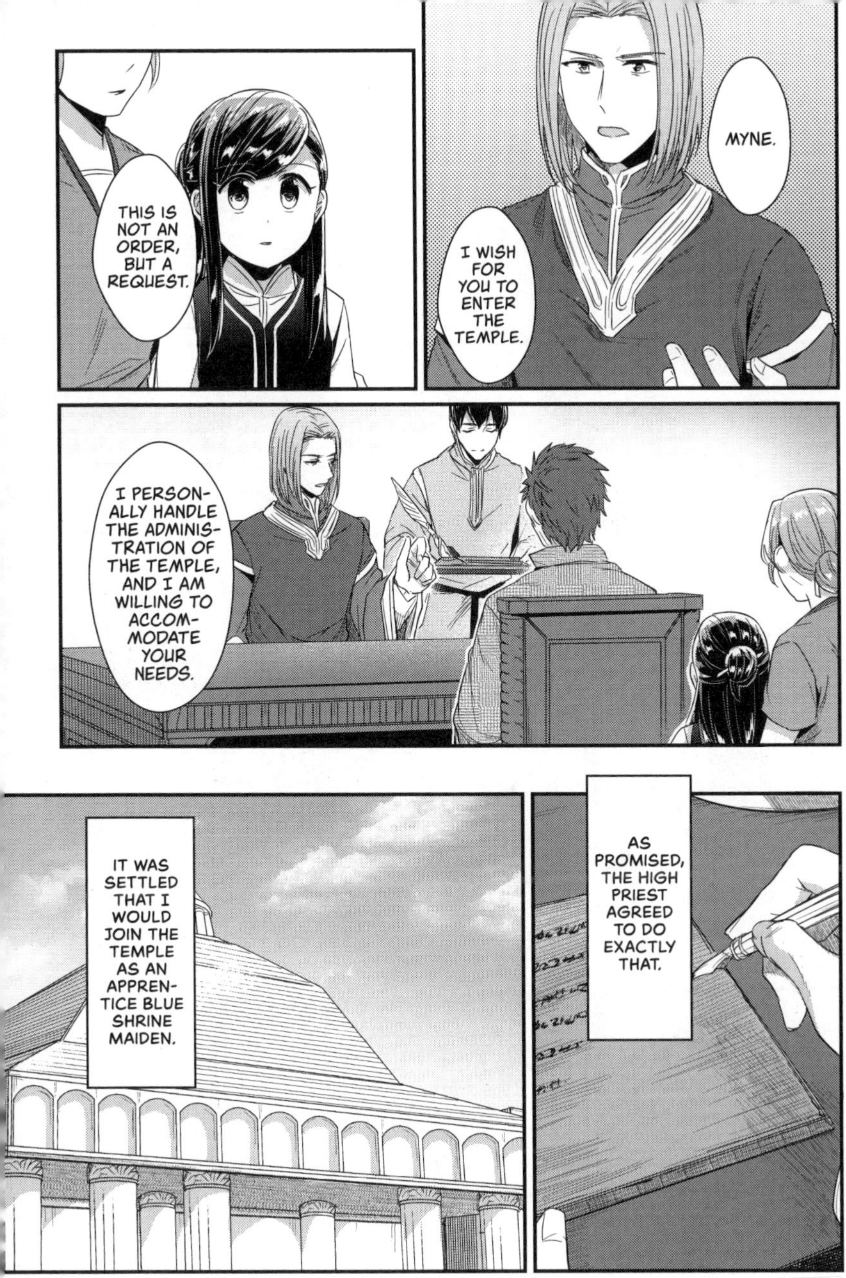
MYNE.
I WISH FOR YOU TO ENTER THE TEMPLE.
THIS IS NOT AN ORDER, BUT A REQUEST.
I PERSONALLY HANDLE THE ADMINISTRATION OF THE TEMPLE, AND I AM WILLING TO ACCOMMODATE YOUR NEEDS.
AS PROMISED, THE HIGH PRIEST AGREED TO DO EXACTLY THAT.
IT WAS SETTLED THAT I WOULD JOIN THE TEMPLE AS AN APPRENTICE BLUE SHRINE MAIDEN.

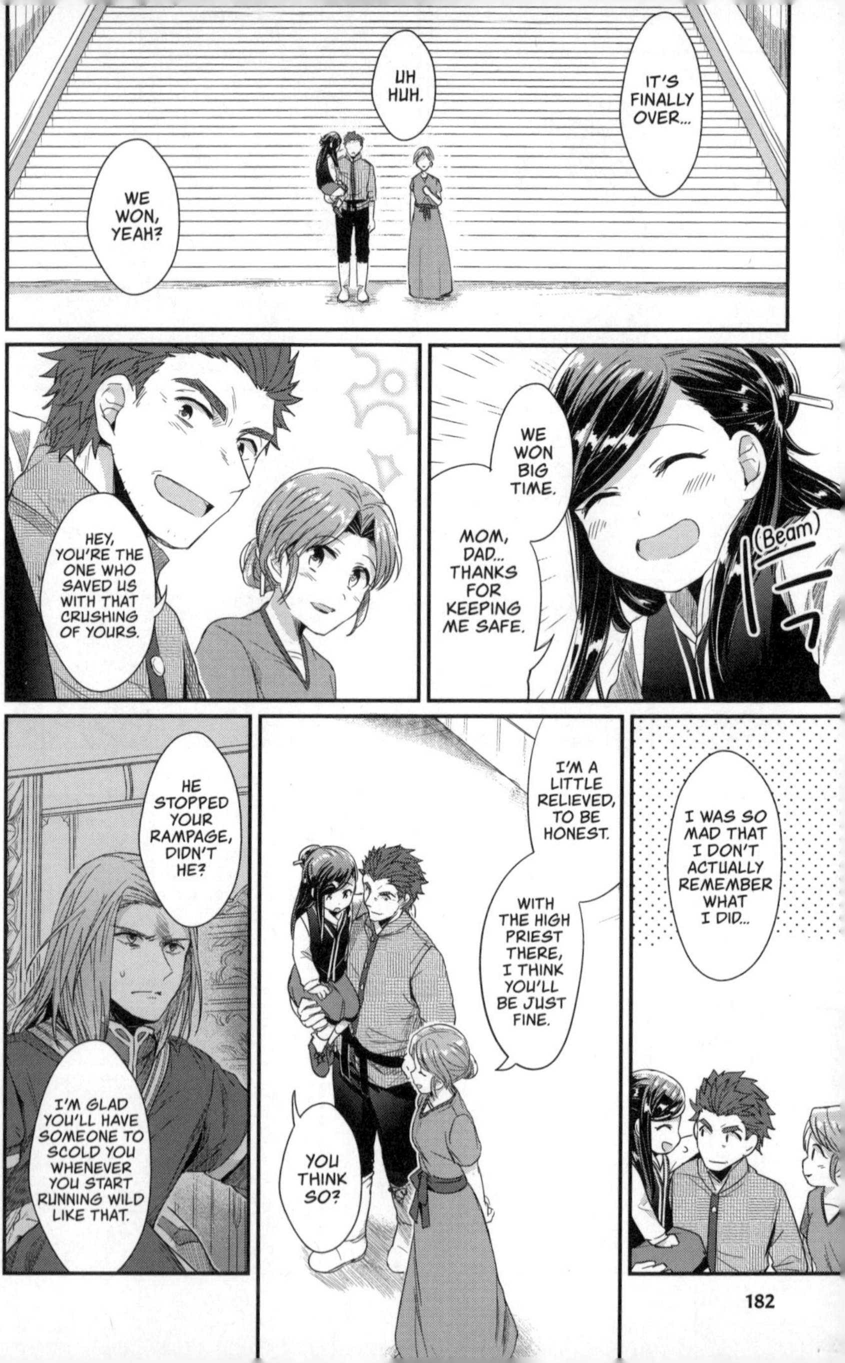
IT'S FINALLY OVER...
UH HUH.
WE WON, YEAH?
WE WON BIG TIME.
MOM, DAD... THANKS FOR KEEPING ME SAFE.
(Beam)
HEY, YOU'RE THE ONE WHO SAVED US WITH THAT CRUSHING OF YOURS.
I WAS SO MAD THAT I DON'T ACTUALLY REMEMBER WHAT I DID...
I'M A LITTLE RELIEVED, TO BE HONEST.
WITH THE HIGH PRIEST THERE, I THINK YOU'LL BE JUST FINE.
YOU THINK SO?
HE STOPPED YOUR RAMPAGE, DIDN'T HE?
I'M GLAD YOU'LL HAVE SOMEONE TO SCOLD YOU WHENEVER YOU START RUNNING WILD LIKE THAT.

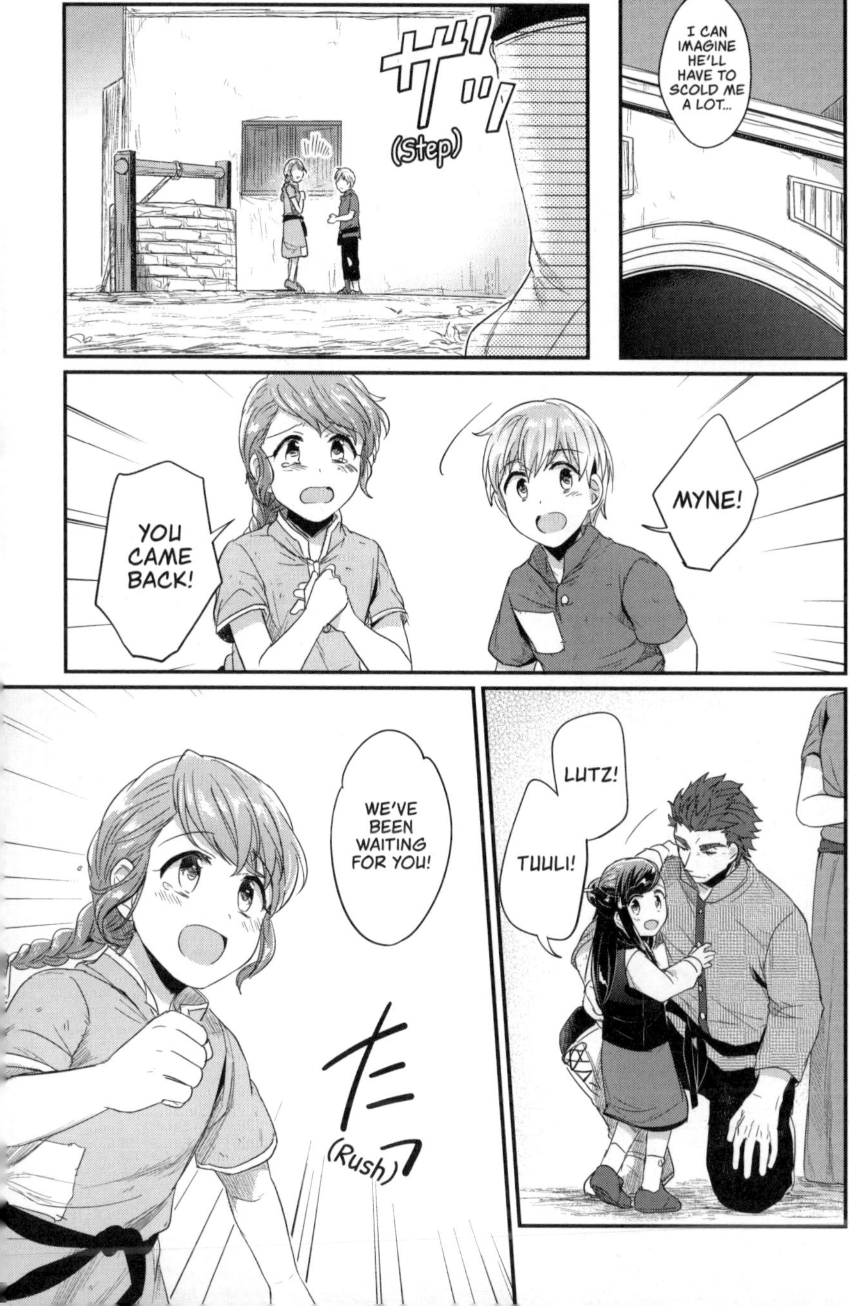
I CAN IMAGINE HE'LL HAVE TO SCOLD ME A LOT...
(Step)
MYNE!
YOU CAME BACK!
LUTZ!
TUULI!
WE'VE BEEN WAITING FOR YOU!
(Rush)

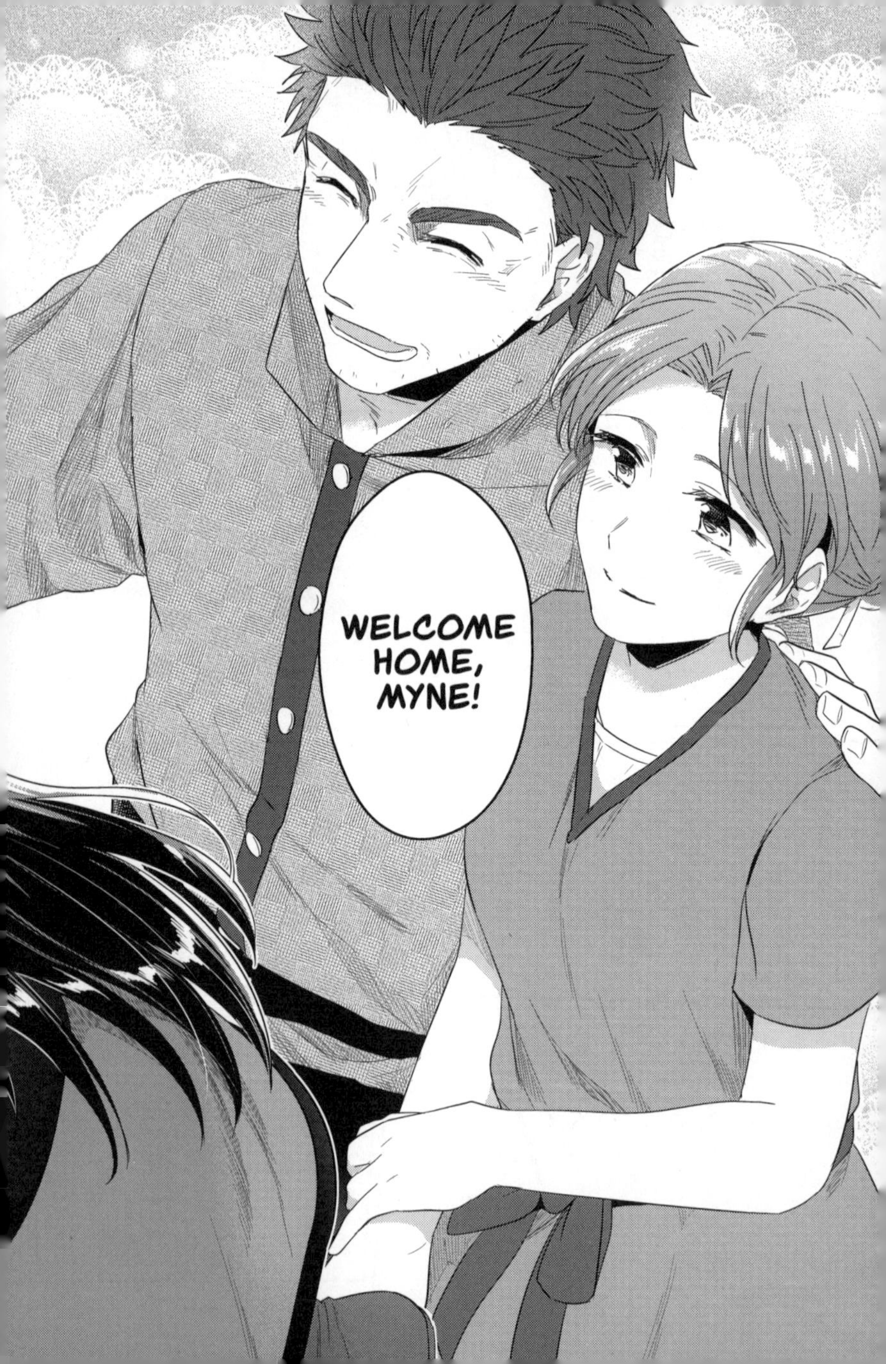
WELCOME HOME, MYNE!

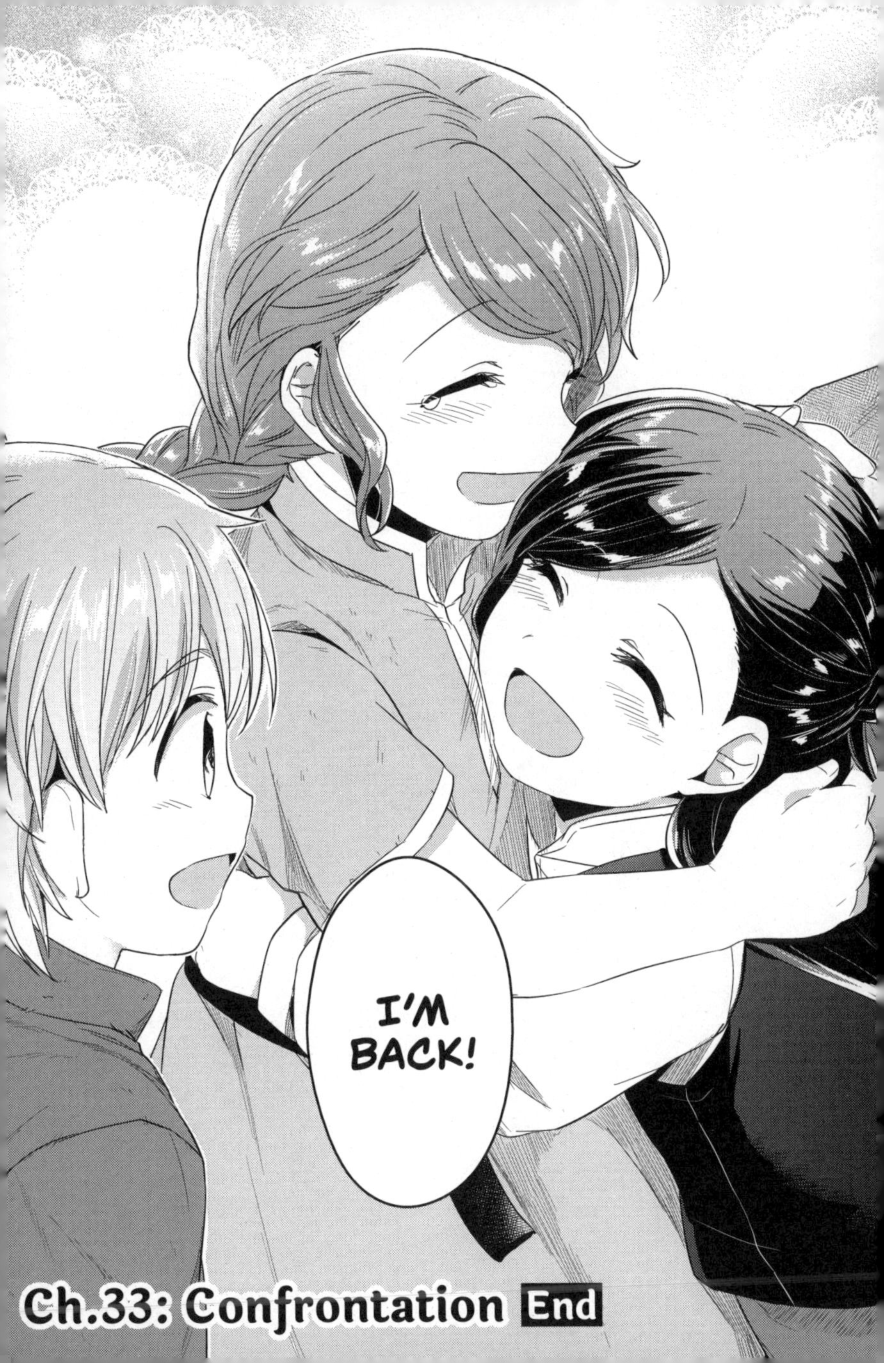
I'M BACK!
Ch.33: Confrontation End

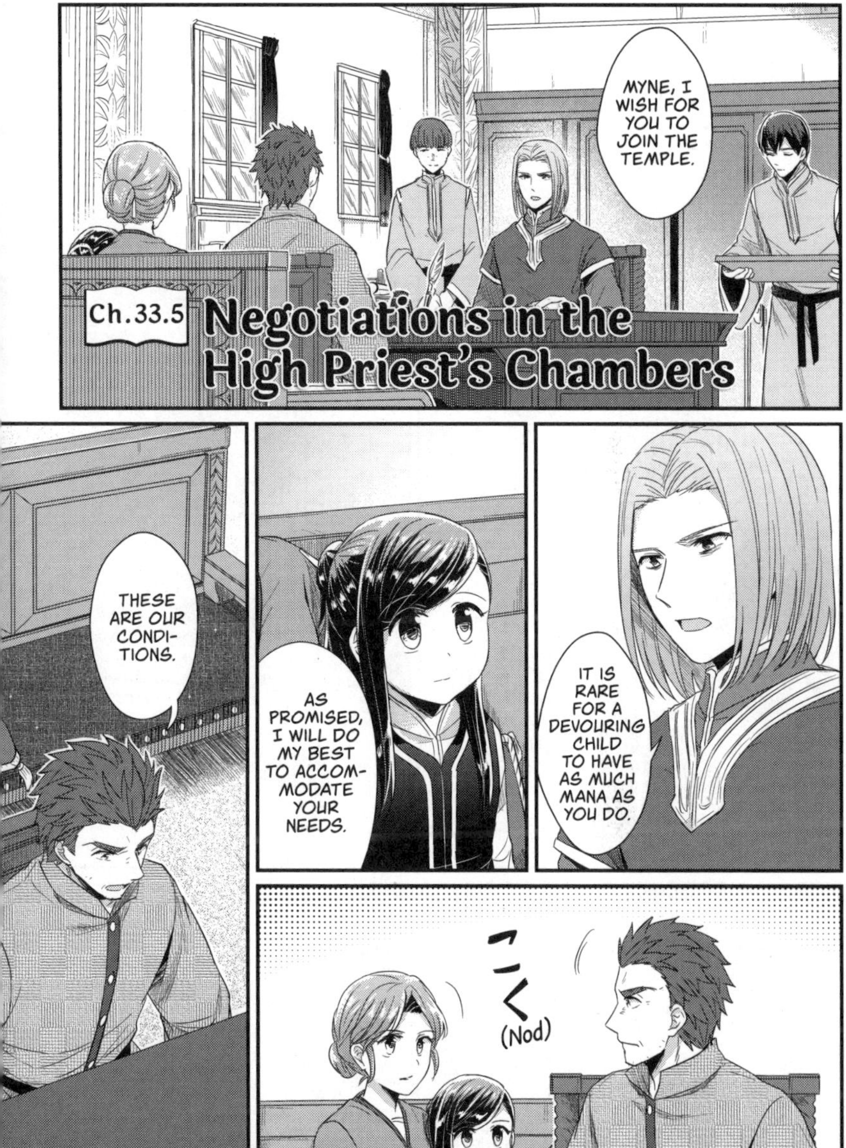
Ch.33.5
Negotiations in the High Priest's Chambers
MYNE, I WISH FOR YOU TO JOIN THE TEMPLE.
IT IS RARE FOR A DEVOURING CHILD TO HAVE AS MUCH MANA AS YOU DO.
AS PROMISED, I WILL DO MY BEST TO ACCOMMODATE YOUR NEEDS.
こく
(Nod)
THESE ARE OUR CONDITIONS.

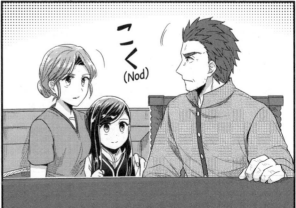

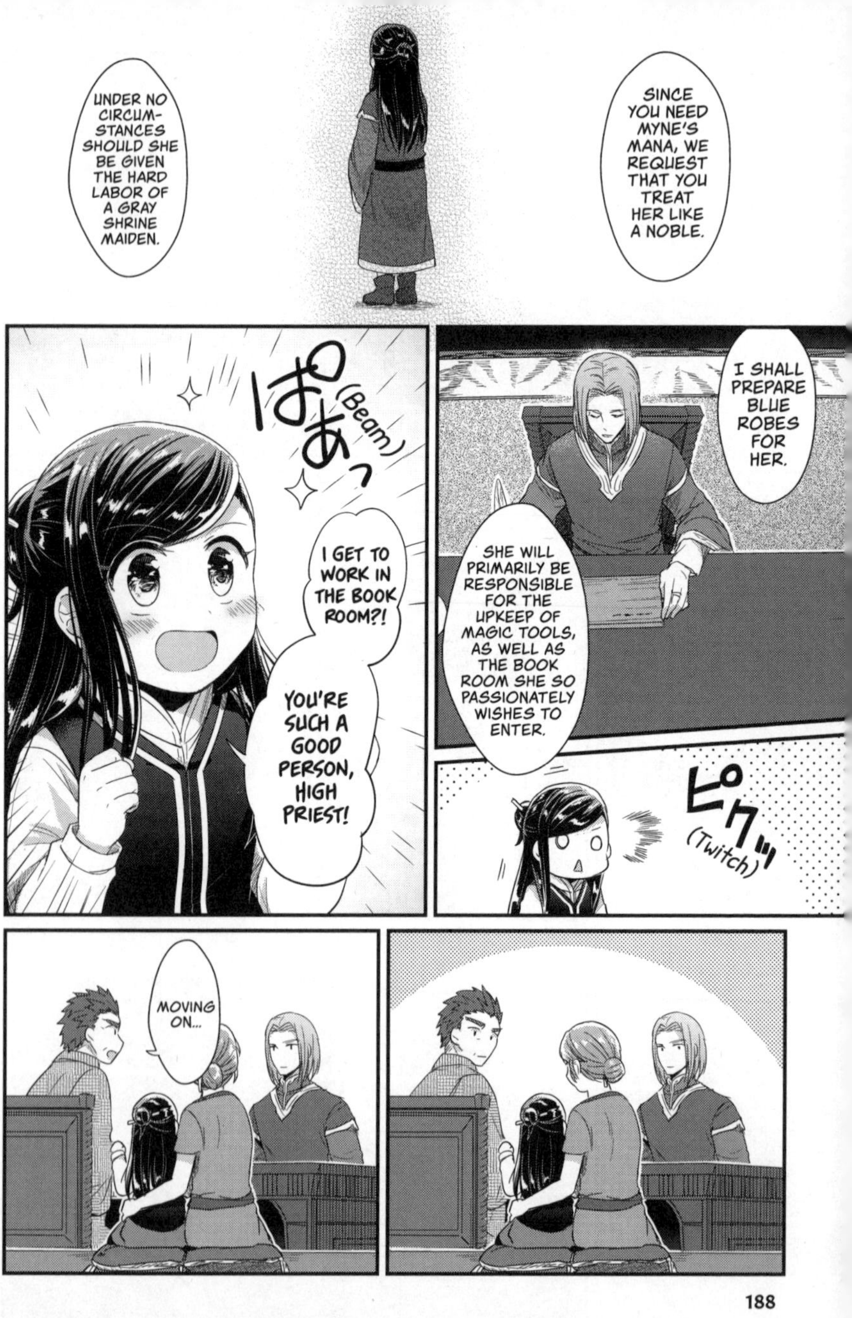
SINCE YOU NEED MYNE'S MANA, WE REQUEST THAT YOU TREAT HER LIKE A NOBLE.
UNDER NO CIRCUM-STANCES SHOULD SHE BE GIVEN THE HARD LABOR OF A GRAY SHRINE MAIDEN.
I SHALL PREPARE BLUE ROBES FOR HER.
SHE WILL PRIMARILY BE RESPONSIBLE FOR THE UPKEEP OF MAGIC TOOLS, AS WELL AS THE BOOK ROOM SHE SO PASSIONATELY WISHES TO ENTER.
ピクッ
(Twitch)
ぱあっ
(Beam)
I GET TO WORK IN THE BOOK ROOM?!
YOU'RE SUCH A GOOD PERSON, HIGH PRIEST!
MOVING ON...

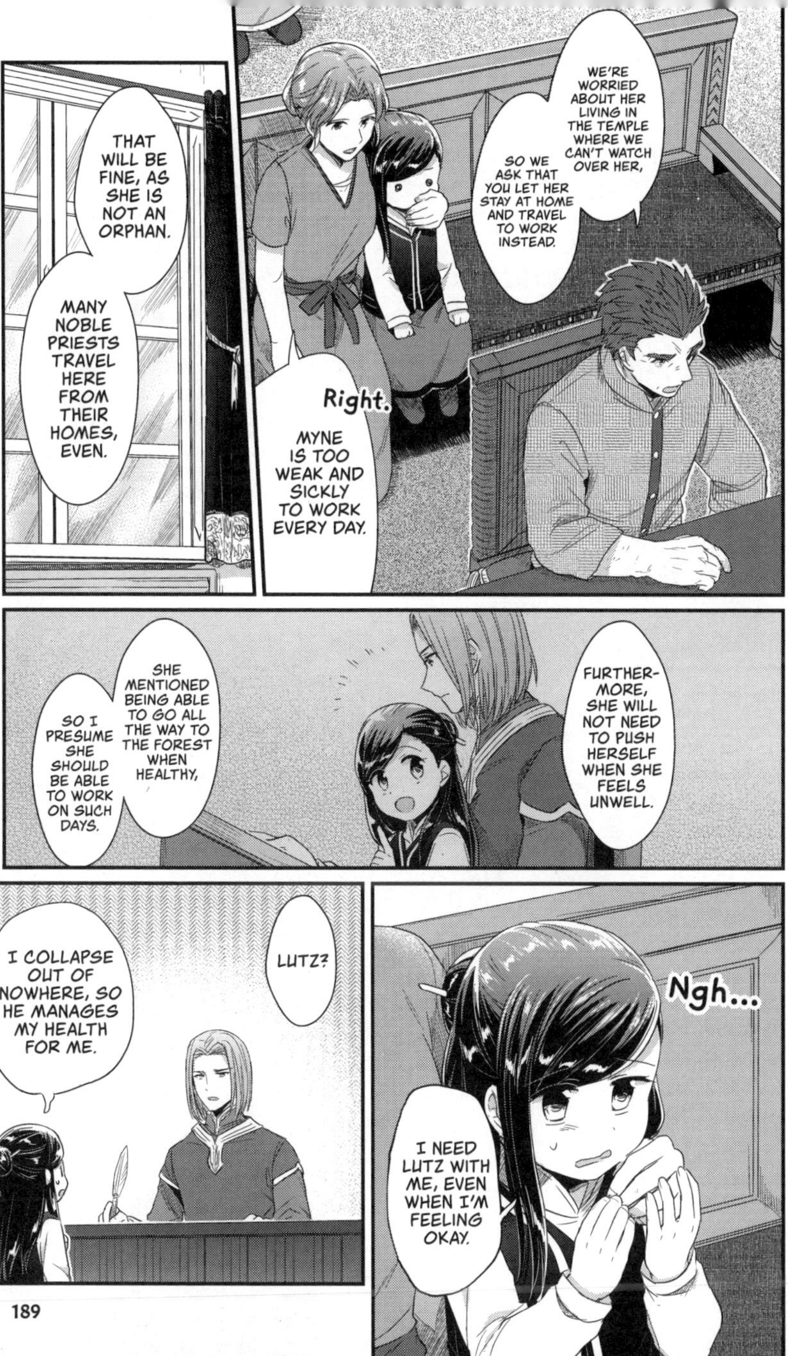
WE'RE WORRIED ABOUT HER LIVING IN THE TEMPLE WHERE WE CAN'T WATCH OVER HER,
SO WE ASK THAT YOU LET HER STAY AT HOME AND TRAVEL TO WORK INSTEAD.
Right.
MYNE IS TOO WEAK AND SICKLY TO WORK EVERY DAY.
THAT WILL BE FINE, AS SHE IS NOT AN ORPHAN.
MANY NOBLE PRIESTS TRAVEL HERE FROM THEIR HOMES, EVEN.
FURTHERMORE, SHE WILL NOT NEED TO PUSH HERSELF WHEN SHE FEELS UNWELL.
SHE MENTIONED BEING ABLE TO GO ALL THE WAY TO THE FOREST WHEN HEALTHY,
SO I PRESUME SHE SHOULD BE ABLE TO WORK ON SUCH DAYS.
Ngh...
I NEED LUTZ WITH ME, EVEN WHEN I'M FEELING OKAY.
LUTZ?
I COLLAPSE OUT OF NOWHERE, SO HE MANAGES MY HEALTH FOR ME.

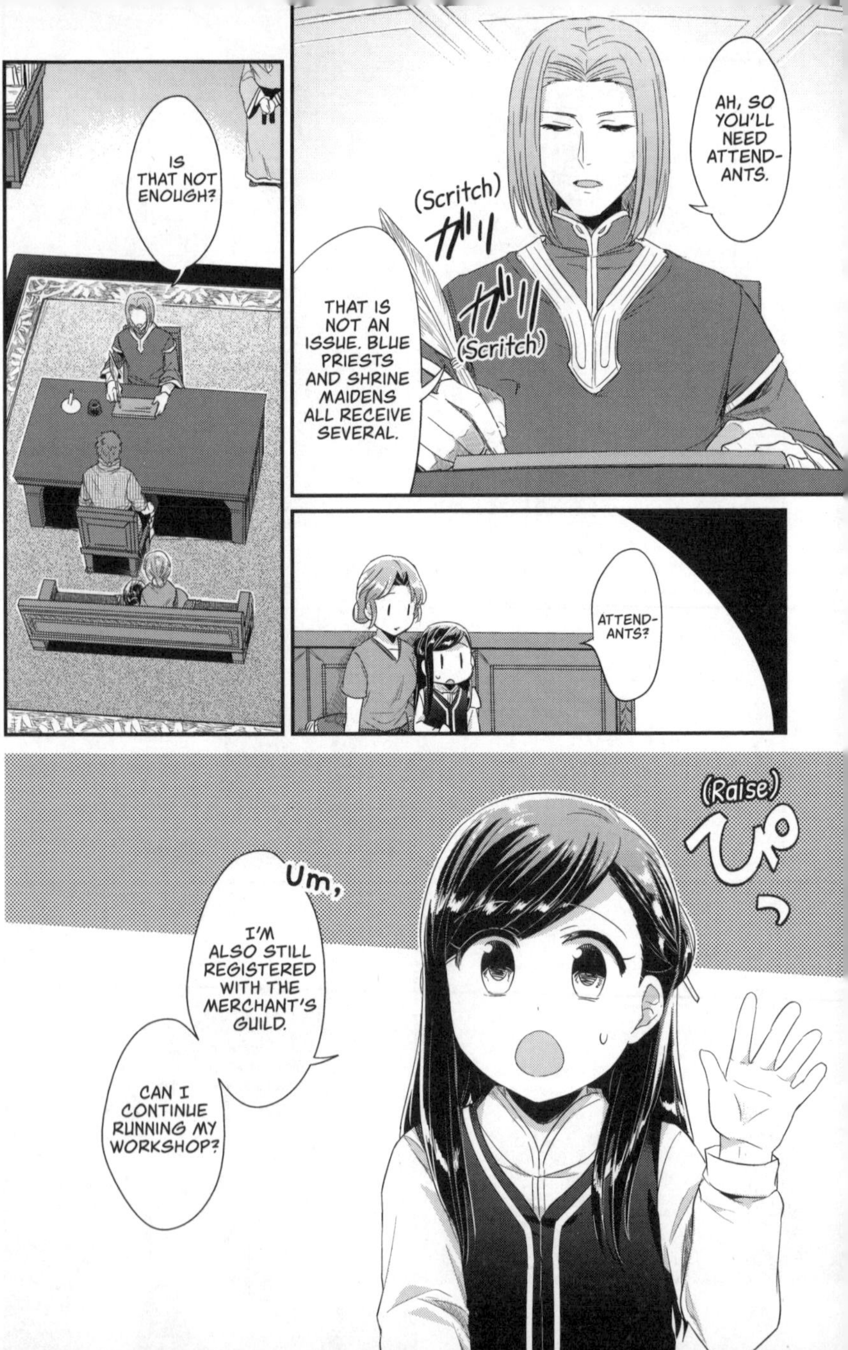
AH, SO YOU'LL NEED ATTEND-ANTS.
(Scritch)
ガリ
ガリ
(Scritch)
THAT IS NOT AN ISSUE. BLUE PRIESTS AND SHRINE MAIDENS ALL RECEIVE SEVERAL.
ATTEND-ANTS?
IS THAT NOT ENOUGH?
(Raise)
ぴっ
Um,
I'M ALSO STILL REGISTERED WITH THE MERCHANT'S GUILD.
CAN I CONTINUE RUNNING MY WORKSHOP?

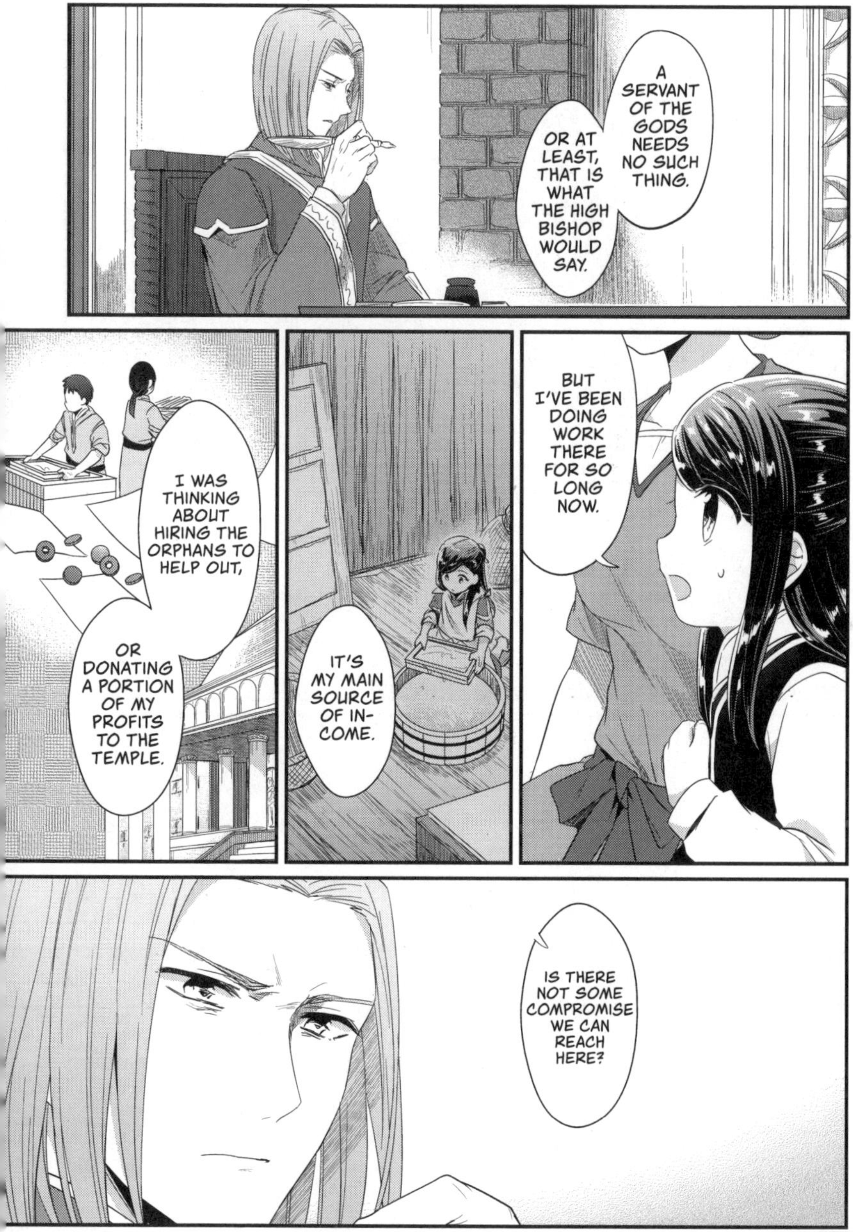
A SERVANT OF THE GODS NEEDS NO SUCH THING.
OR AT LEAST, THAT IS WHAT THE HIGH BISHOP WOULD SAY.
BUT I'VE BEEN DOING WORK THERE FOR SO LONG NOW.
IT'S MY MAIN SOURCE OF IN-COME.
I WAS THINKING ABOUT HIRING THE ORPHANS TO HELP OUT,
OR DONATING A PORTION OF MY PROFITS TO THE TEMPLE.
IS THERE NOT SOME COMPROMISE WE CAN REACH HERE?

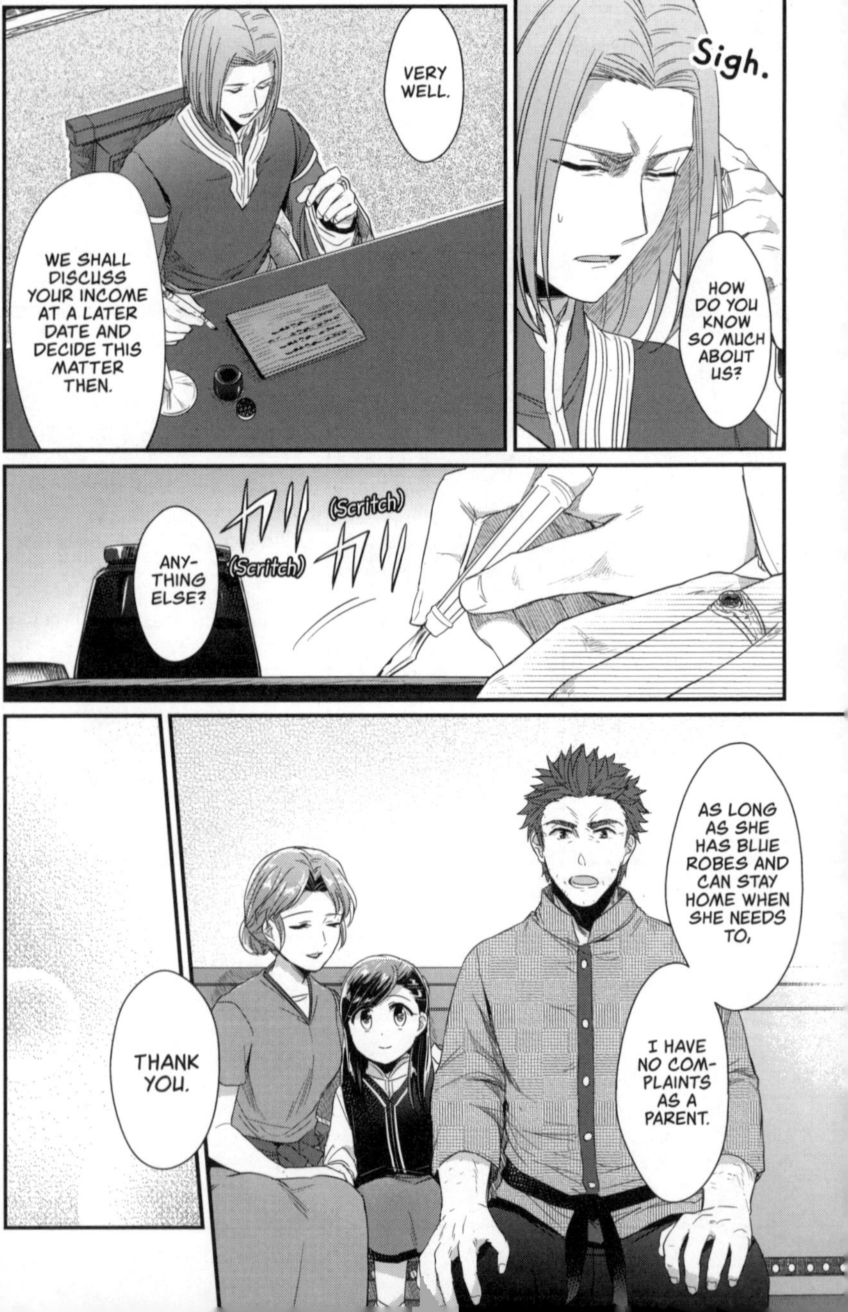
Sigh.
HOW DO YOU KNOW SO MUCH ABOUT US?
VERY WELL.
WE SHALL DISCUSS YOUR INCOME AT A LATER DATE AND DECIDE THIS MATTER THEN.
(Scritch)
(Scritch)
ANY-THING ELSE?
AS LONG AS SHE HAS BLUE ROBES AND CAN STAY HOME WHEN SHE NEEDS TO,
I HAVE NO COM-PLAINTS AS A PARENT.
THANK YOU.

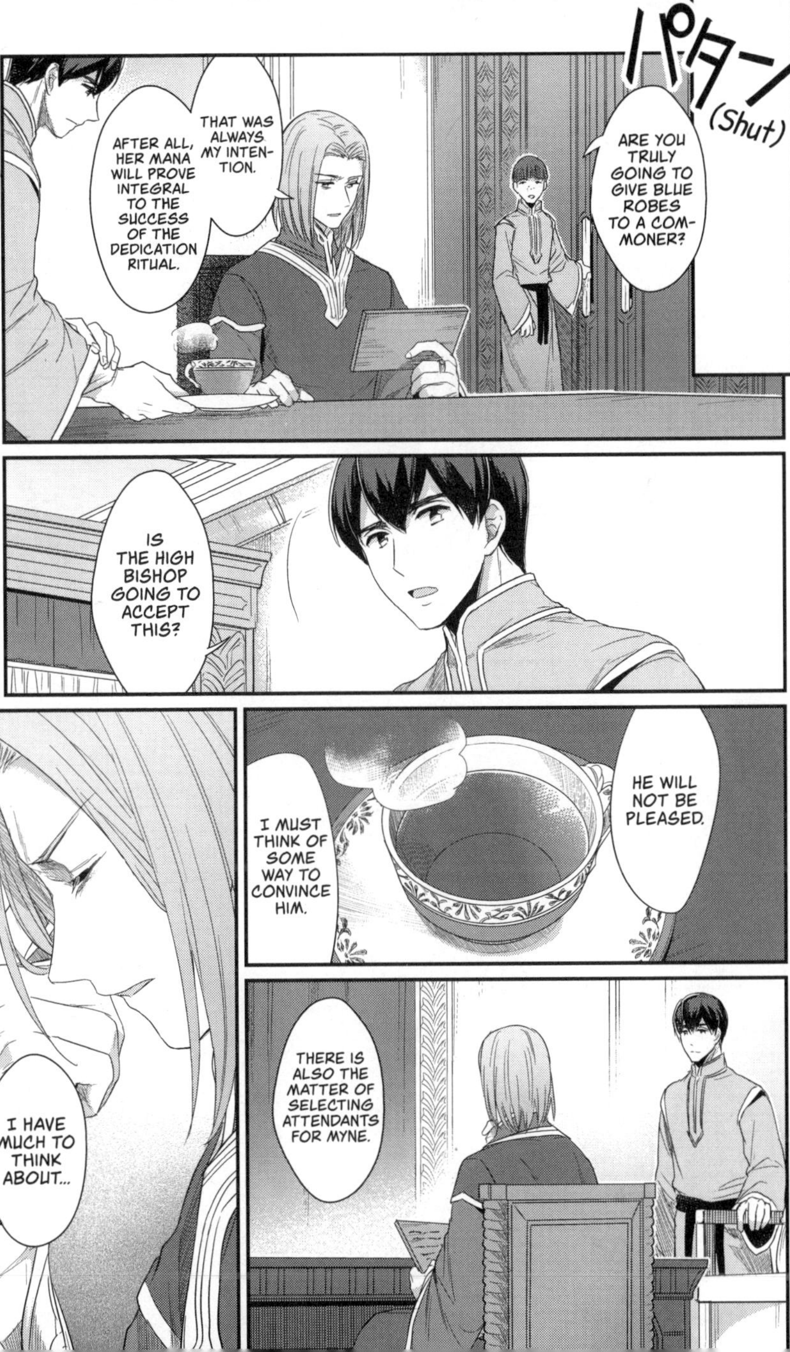
パターン
(Shut)
ARE YOU TRULY GOING TO GIVE BLUE ROBES TO A COM-MONER?
THAT WAS ALWAYS MY INTEN-TION.
AFTER ALL, HER MANA WILL PROVE INTEGRAL TO THE SUCCESS OF THE DEDICATION RITUAL.
IS THE HIGH BISHOP GOING TO ACCEPT THIS?
HE WILL NOT BE PLEASED.
I MUST THINK OF SOME WAY TO CONVINCE HIM.
THERE IS ALSO THE MATTER OF SELECTING ATTENDANTS FOR MYNE.
I HAVE MUCH TO THINK ABOUT...

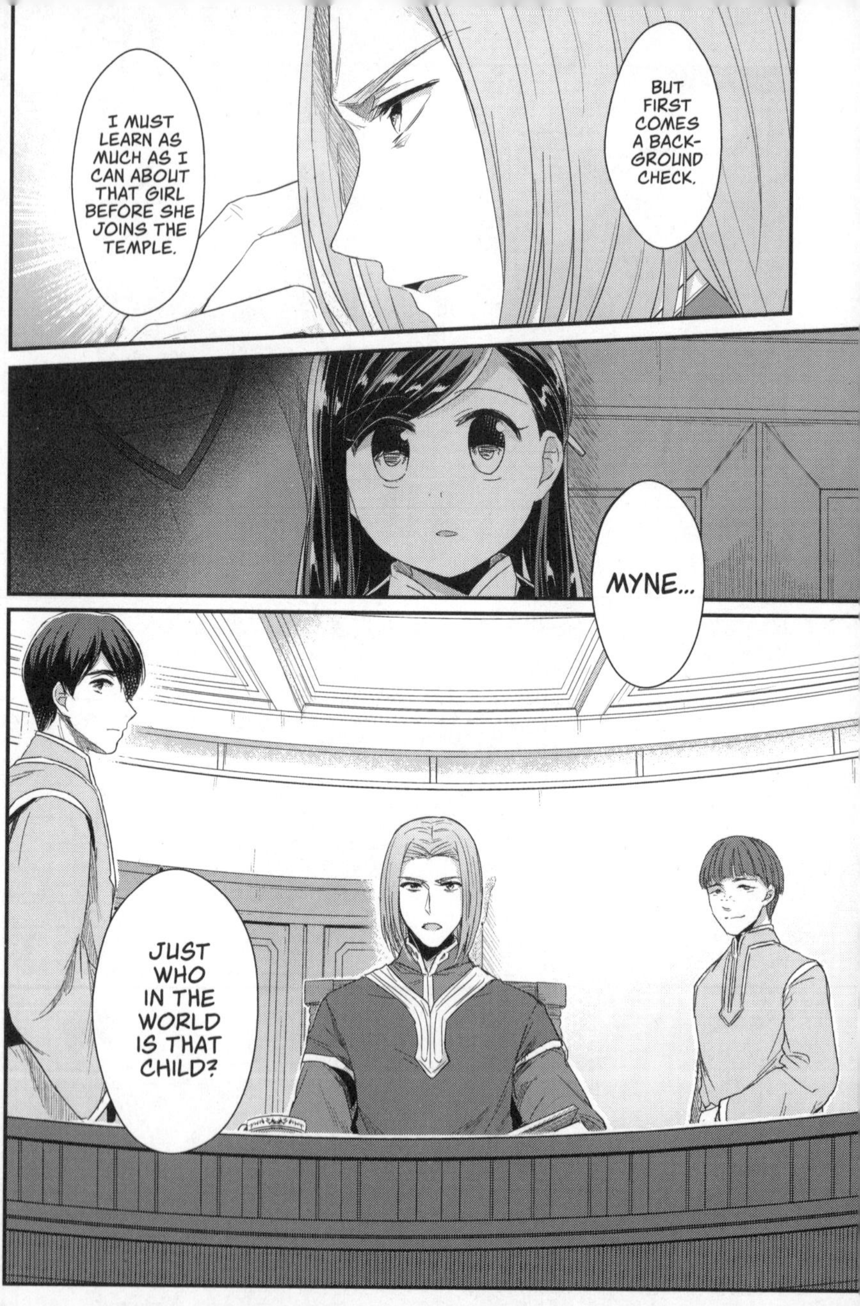
BUT FIRST COMES A BACK-GROUND CHECK.
I MUST LEARN AS MUCH AS I CAN ABOUT THAT GIRL BEFORE SHE JOINS THE TEMPLE.
MYNE...
JUST WHO IN THE WORLD IS THAT CHILD?

Ch.33.5: Negotiations in the High Priest's Chambers End

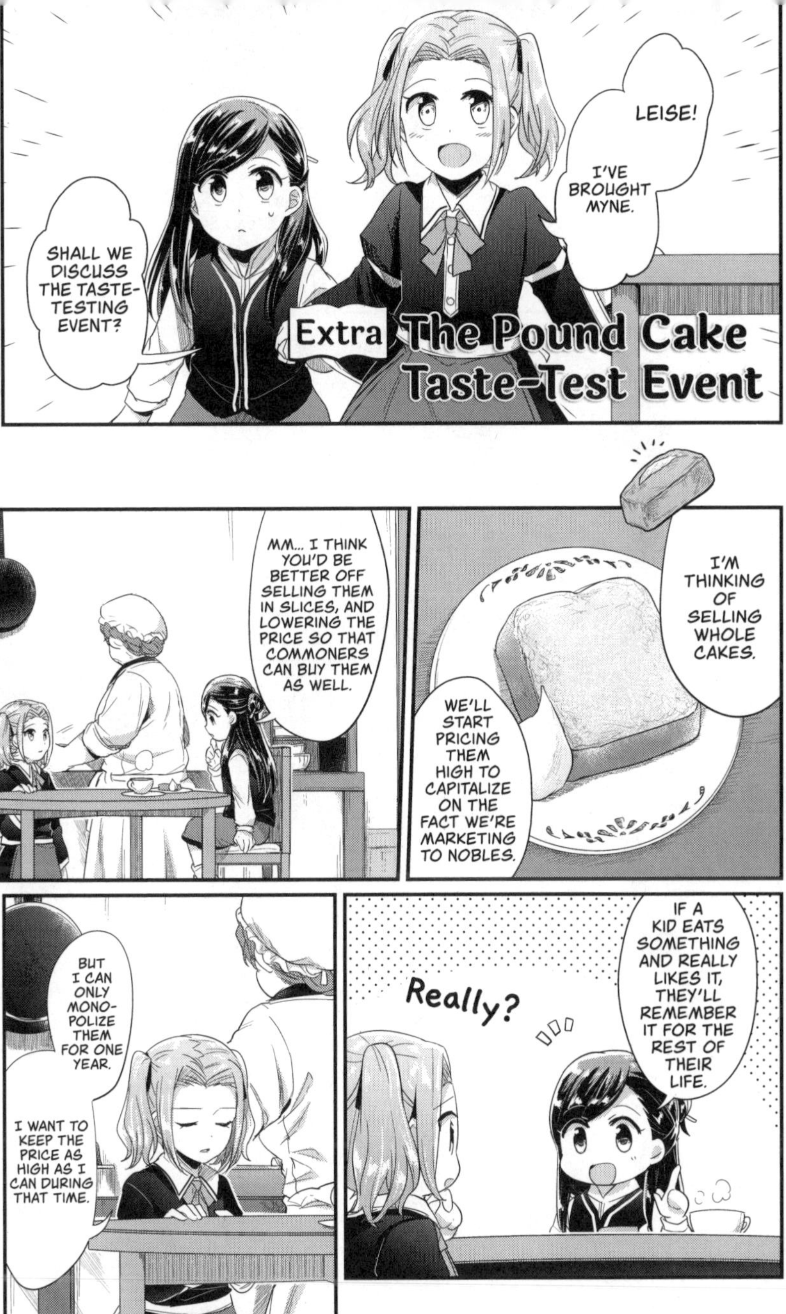
Extra The Pound Cake Taste-Test Event
LEISE!
I'VE BROUGHT MYNE.
SHALL WE DISCUSS THE TASTE-TESTING EVENT?
I'M THINKING OF SELLING WHOLE CAKES.
WE'LL START PRICING THEM HIGH TO CAPITALIZE ON THE FACT WE'RE MARKETING TO NOBLES.
MM... I THINK YOU'D BE BETTER OFF SELLING THEM IN SLICES, AND LOWERING THE PRICE SO THAT COMMONERS CAN BUY THEM AS WELL.
IF A KID EATS SOMETHING AND REALLY LIKES IT, THEY'LL REMEMBER IT FOR THE REST OF THEIR LIFE.
Really?
BUT I CAN ONLY MONO-POLIZE THEM FOR ONE YEAR.
I WANT TO KEEP THE PRICE AS HIGH AS I CAN DURING THAT TIME.

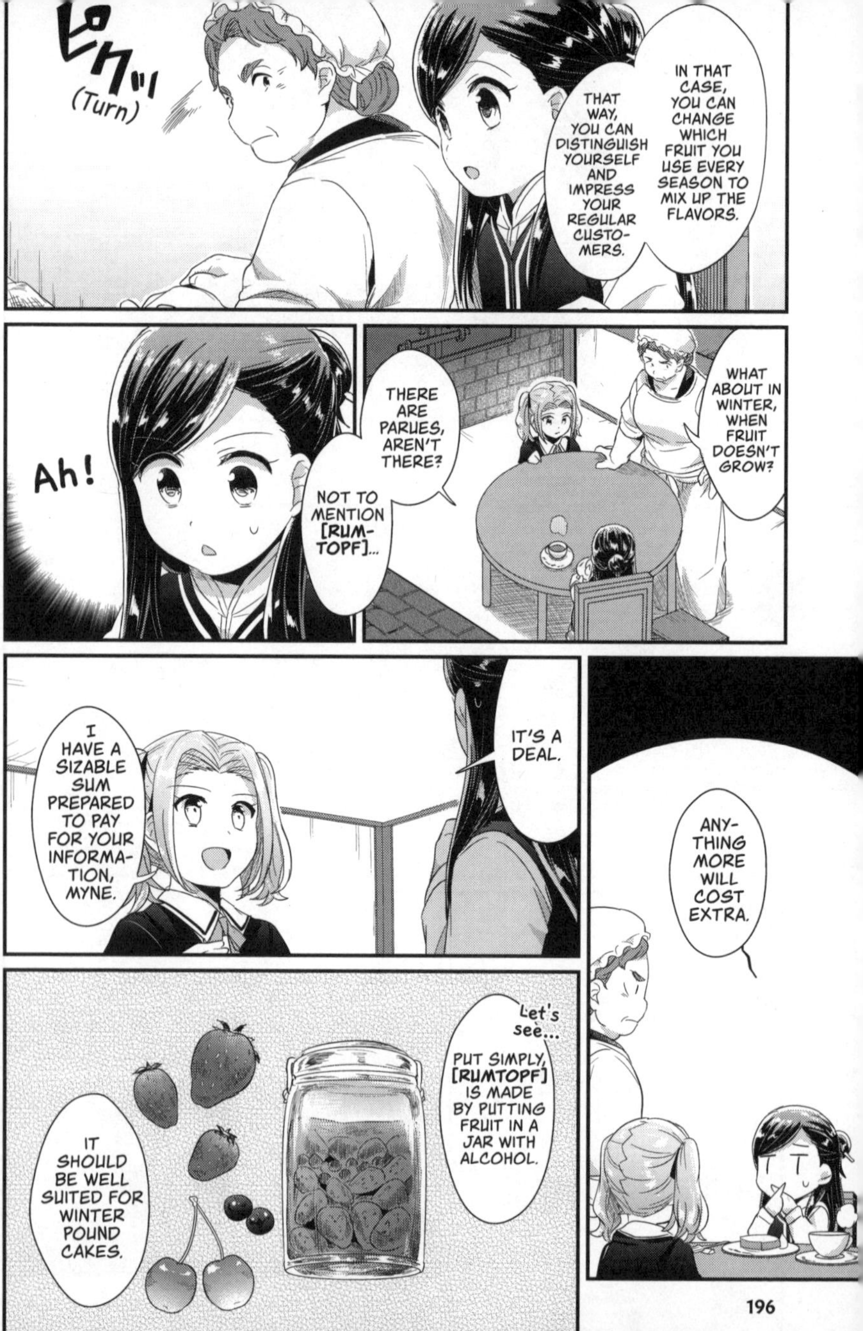
IN THAT CASE, YOU CAN CHANGE WHICH FRUIT YOU USE EVERY SEASON TO MIX UP THE FLAVORS.
THAT WAY, YOU CAN DISTINGUISH YOURSELF AND IMPRESS YOUR REGULAR CUSTO-MERS.
ピクッ
(Turn)
WHAT ABOUT IN WINTER, WHEN FRUIT DOESN'T GROW?
THERE ARE PARUES, AREN'T THERE?
NOT TO MENTION [RUMTOPF]...
Ah!
ANY-THING MORE WILL COST EXTRA.
IT'S A DEAL.
I HAVE A SIZABLE SUM PREPARED TO PAY FOR YOUR INFORMA-TION, MYNE.
Let's see...
PUT SIMPLY, [RUMTOPF] IS MADE BY PUTTING FRUIT IN A JAR WITH ALCOHOL.
IT SHOULD BE WELL SUITED FOR WINTER POUND CAKES.

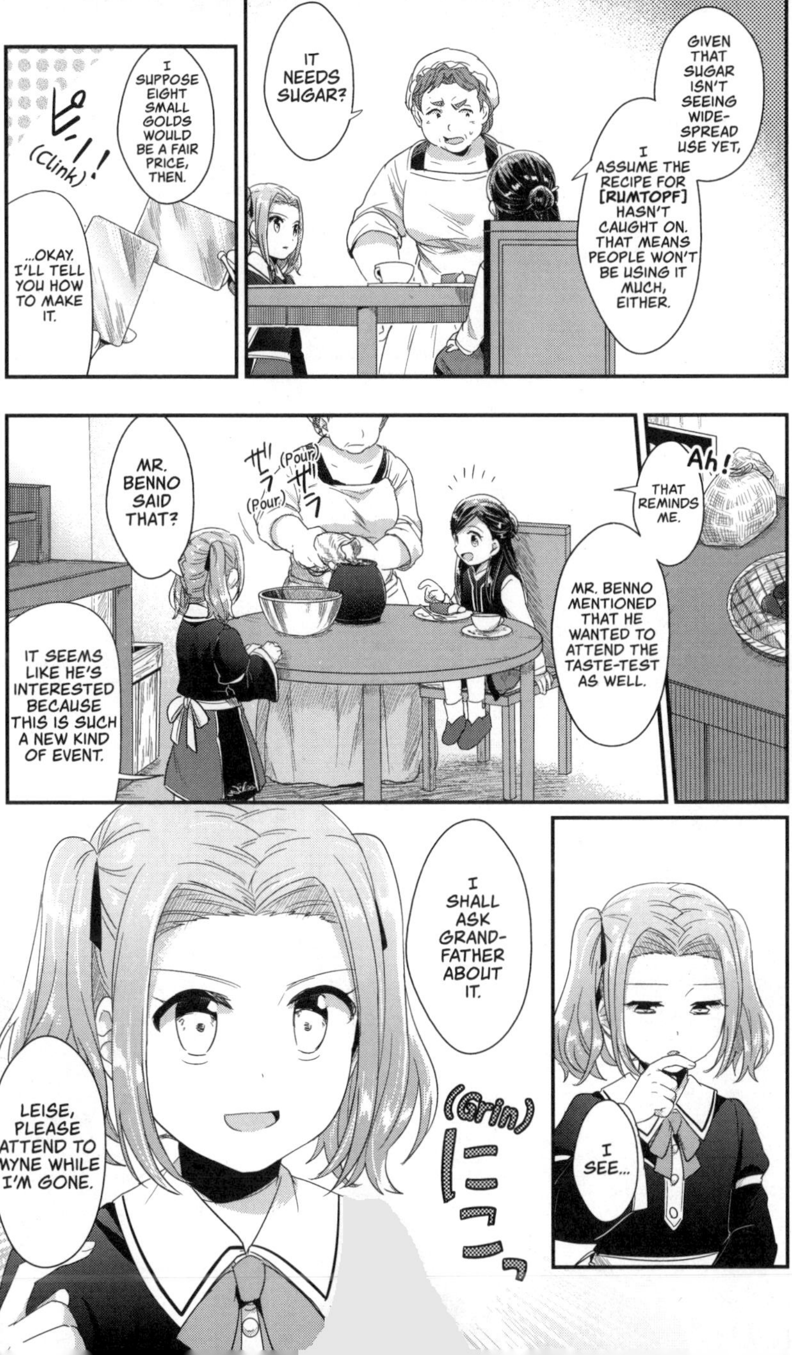

GIVEN THAT SUGAR ISN'T SEEING WIDE-SPREAD USE YET,
I ASSUME THE RECIPE FOR [RUMTOPF] HASN'T CAUGHT ON. THAT MEANS PEOPLE WON'T BE USING IT MUCH, EITHER.
IT NEEDS SUGAR?
I SUPPOSE EIGHT SMALL GOLDS WOULD BE A FAIR PRICE, THEN.
(Clink)
...OKAY. I'LL TELL YOU HOW TO MAKE IT.
Ah!
THAT REMINDS ME.
MR. BENNO MENTIONED THAT HE WANTED TO ATTEND THE TASTE-TEST AS WELL.
(Pour)
(Pour)
MR. BENNO SAID THAT?
IT SEEMS LIKE HE'S INTERESTED BECAUSE THIS IS SUCH A NEW KIND OF EVENT.
I SEE...
I SHALL ASK GRAND-FATHER ABOUT IT.
(Grin)
LEISE, PLEASE ATTEND TO MYNE WHILE I'M GONE.

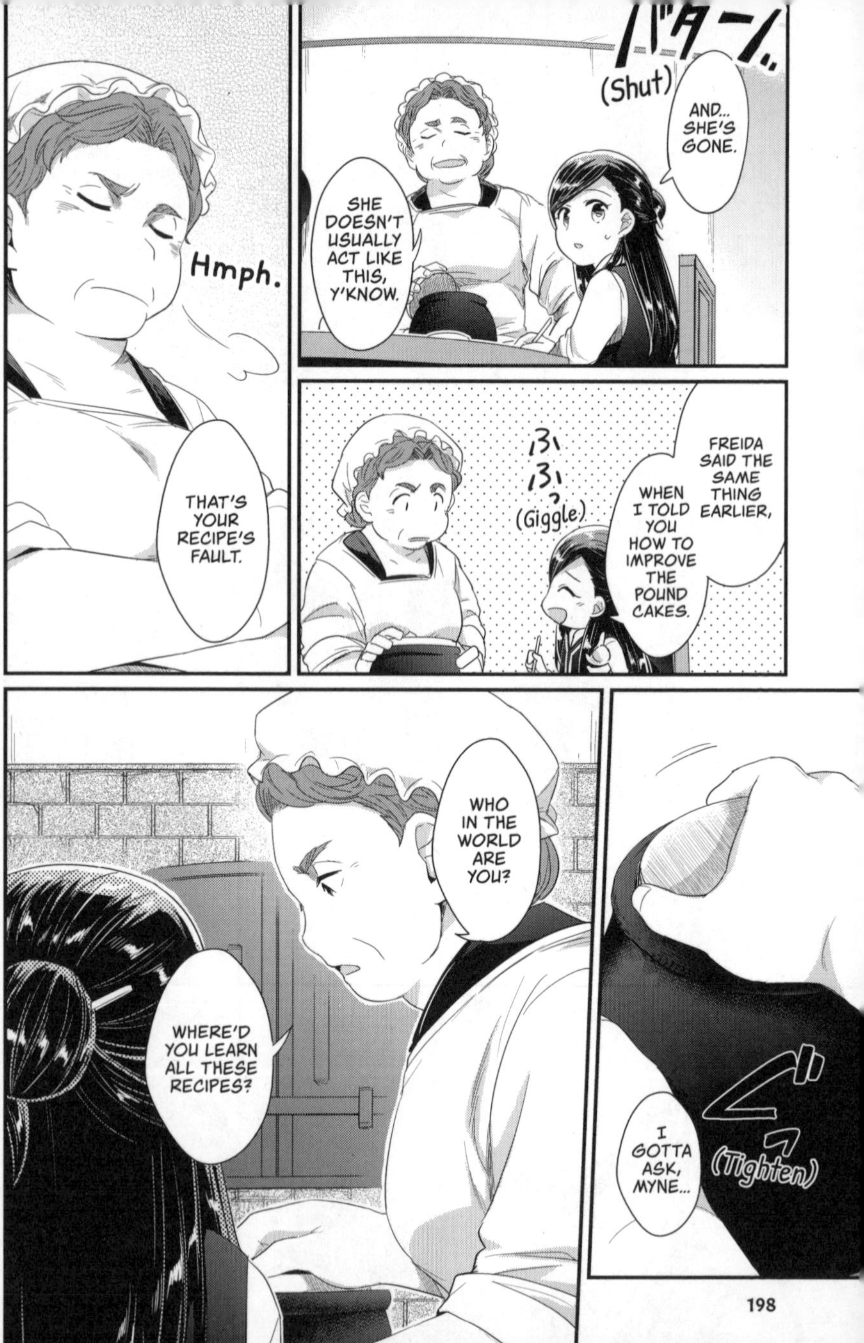
バターン
(Shut)
AND... SHE'S GONE.
SHE DOESN'T USUALLY ACT LIKE THIS, Y'KNOW.
FREIDA SAID THE SAME THING EARLIER,
WHEN I TOLD YOU HOW TO IMPROVE THE POUND CAKES.
ふふっ
(Giggle)
Hmph.
THAT'S YOUR RECIPE'S FAULT.
I GOTTA ASK, MYNE...
(Tighten)
WHO IN THE WORLD ARE YOU?
WHERE'D YOU LEARN ALL THESE RECIPES?

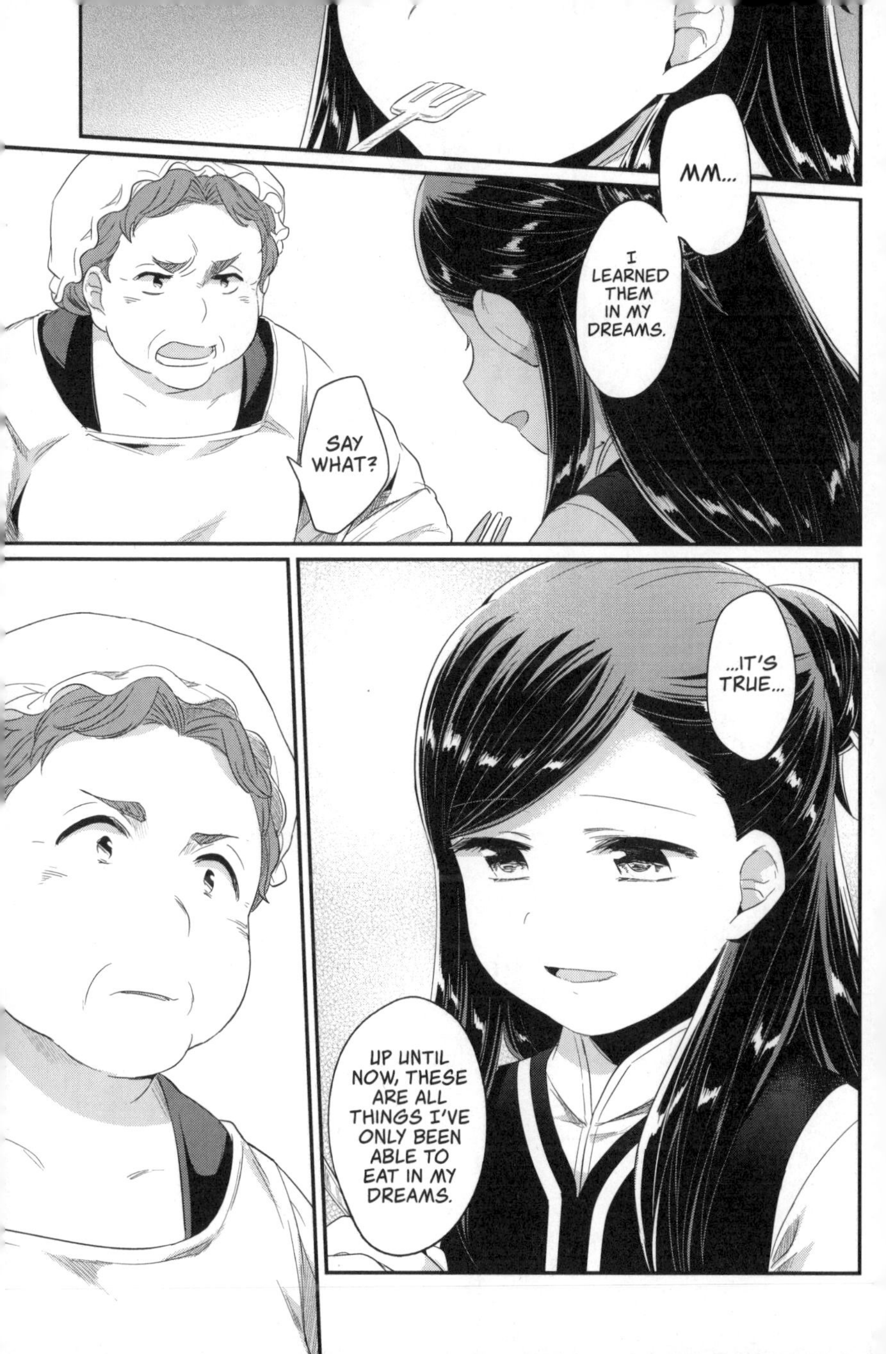
MM...
I LEARNED THEM IN MY DREAMS.
SAY WHAT?
...IT'S TRUE...
UP UNTIL NOW, THESE ARE ALL THINGS I'VE ONLY BEEN ABLE TO EAT IN MY DREAMS.

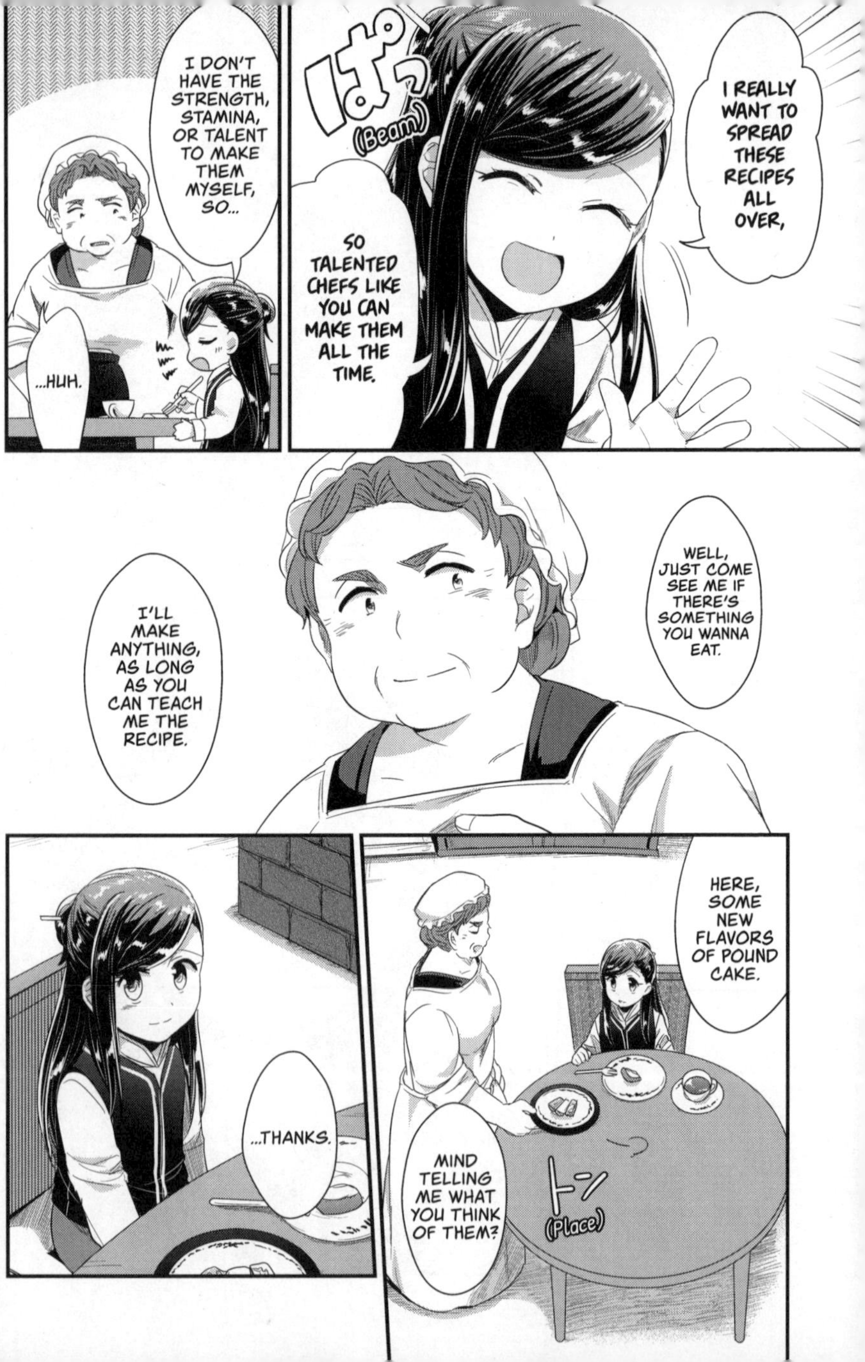
I REALLY WANT TO SPREAD THESE RECIPES ALL OVER,
ぱっ
(Beam)
SO TALENTED CHEFS LIKE YOU CAN MAKE THEM ALL THE TIME.
I DON'T HAVE THE STRENGTH, STAMINA, OR TALENT TO MAKE THEM MYSELF, SO...
...HUH.
WELL, JUST COME SEE ME IF THERE'S SOMETHING YOU WANNA EAT.
I'LL MAKE ANYTHING, AS LONG AS YOU CAN TEACH ME THE RECIPE.
HERE, SOME NEW FLAVORS OF POUND CAKE.
トン
(Place)
MIND TELLING ME WHAT YOU THINK OF THEM?
...THANKS.

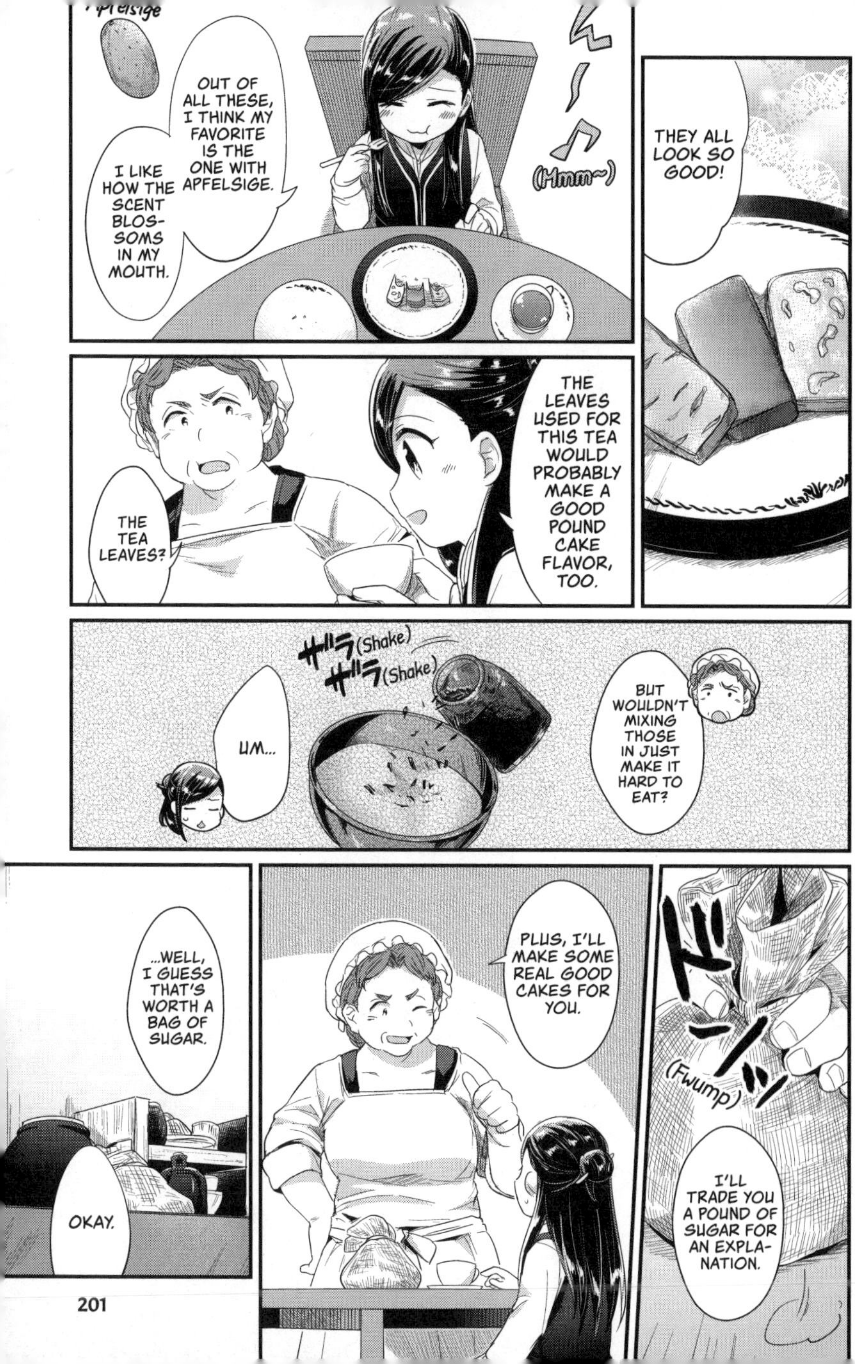
THEY ALL LOOK SO GOOD!
(Hmmm~)
Apfelsige
OUT OF ALL THESE, I THINK MY FAVORITE IS THE ONE WITH APFELSIGE.
I LIKE HOW THE SCENT BLOSSOMS IN MY MOUTH.
THE LEAVES USED FOR THIS TEA WOULD PROBABLY MAKE A GOOD POUND CAKE FLAVOR, TOO.
THE TEA LEAVES?
BUT WOULDN'T MIXING THOSE IN JUST MAKE IT HARD TO EAT?
(Shake)
(Shake)
UM...
(Fwump)
I'LL TRADE YOU A POUND OF SUGAR FOR AN EXPLANATION.
PLUS, I'LL MAKE SOME REAL GOOD CAKES FOR YOU.
...WELL, I GUESS THAT'S WORTH A BAG OF SUGAR.
OKAY.

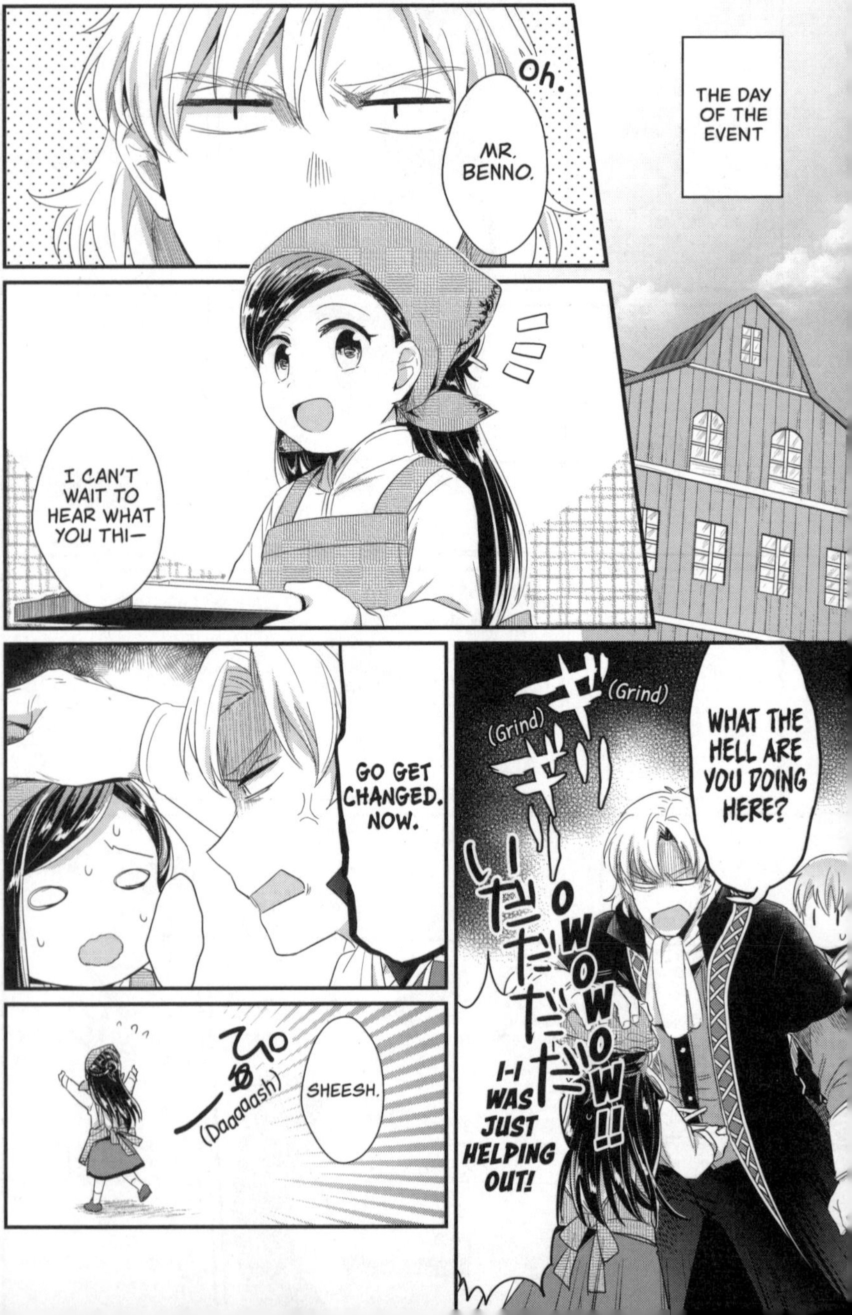
THE DAY OF THE EVENT
Oh.
MR. BENNO.
I CAN'T WAIT TO HEAR WHAT YOU THI—
WHAT THE HELL ARE YOU DOING HERE?
(Grind)
(Grind)
OWOWOWOW!!
I-I WAS JUST HELPING OUT!
GO GET CHANGED. NOW.
SHEESH.
(Daaaaash)

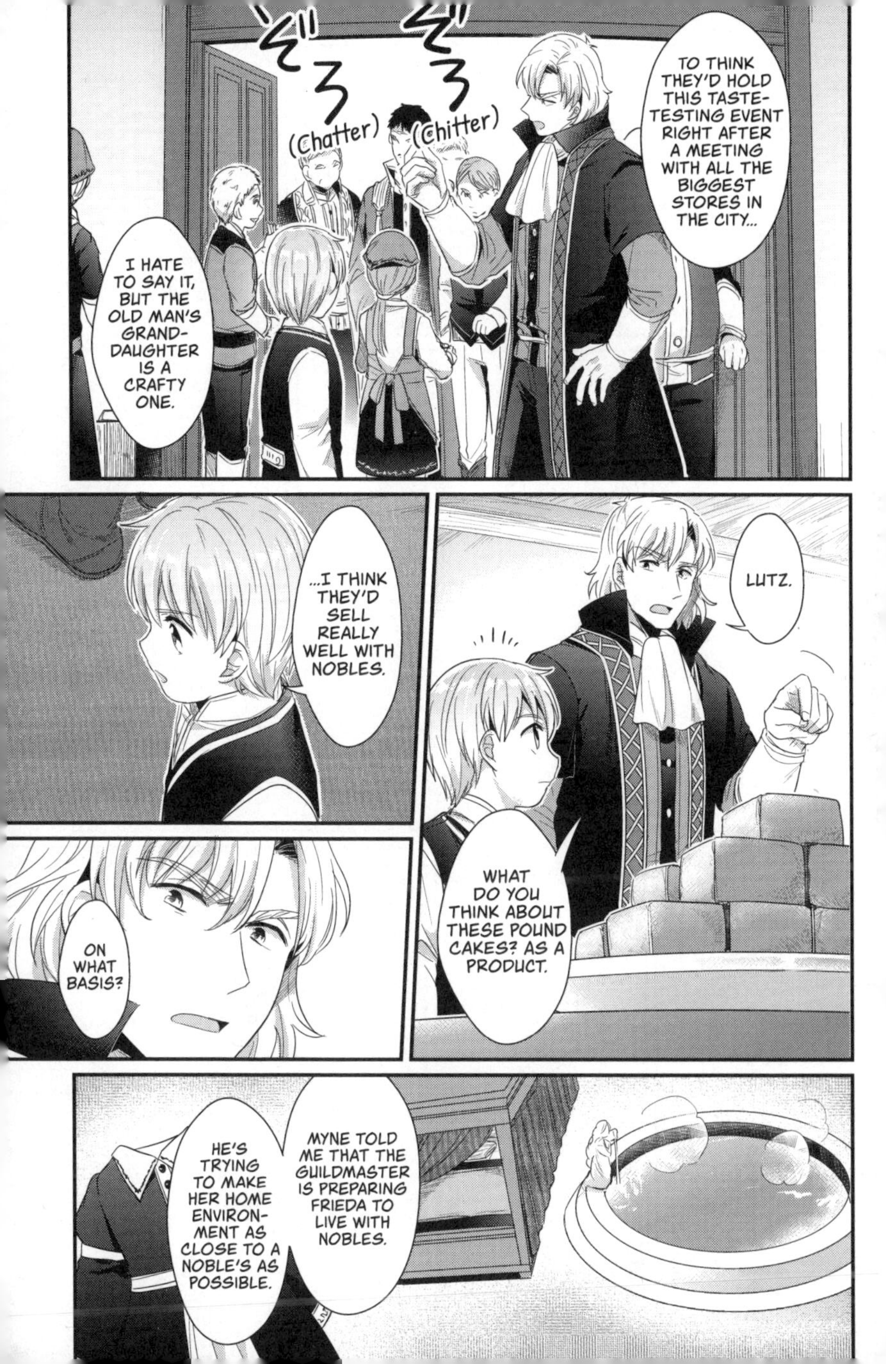
TO THINK THEY'D HOLD THIS TASTE-TESTING EVENT RIGHT AFTER A MEETING WITH ALL THE BIGGEST STORES IN THE CITY...
(Chitter)
(Chatter)
I HATE TO SAY IT, BUT THE OLD MAN'S GRAND-DAUGHTER IS A CRAFTY ONE.
LUTZ.
WHAT DO YOU THINK ABOUT THESE POUND CAKES? AS A PRODUCT.
...I THINK THEY'D SELL REALLY WELL WITH NOBLES.
ON WHAT BASIS?
MYNE TOLD ME THAT THE GUILDMASTER IS PREPARING FRIEDA TO LIVE WITH NOBLES.
HE'S TRYING TO MAKE HER HOME ENVIRON-MENT AS CLOSE TO A NOBLE'S AS POSSIBLE.

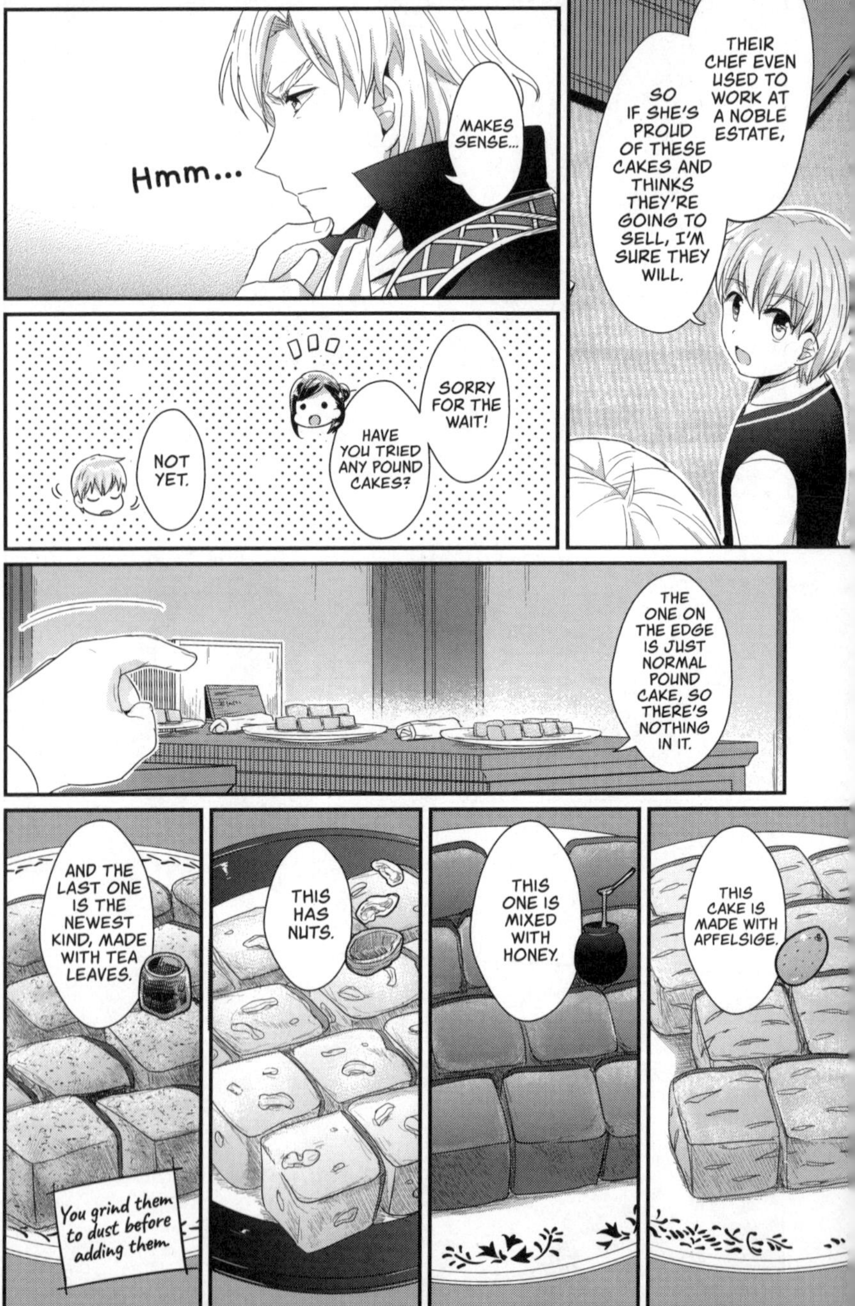

THEIR CHEF EVEN USED TO WORK AT A NOBLE ESTATE,
SO IF SHE'S PROUD OF THESE CAKES AND THINKS THEY'RE GOING TO SELL, I'M SURE THEY WILL.
MAKES SENSE...
Hmm...
SORRY FOR THE WAIT!
HAVE YOU TRIED ANY POUND CAKES?
NOT YET.
THE ONE ON THE EDGE IS JUST NORMAL POUND CAKE, SO THERE'S NOTHING IN IT.
THIS CAKE IS MADE WITH APFELSIGE.
THIS ONE IS MIXED WITH HONEY.
THIS HAS NUTS.
AND THE LAST ONE IS THE NEWEST KIND, MADE WITH TEA LEAVES.
You grind them to dust before adding them.

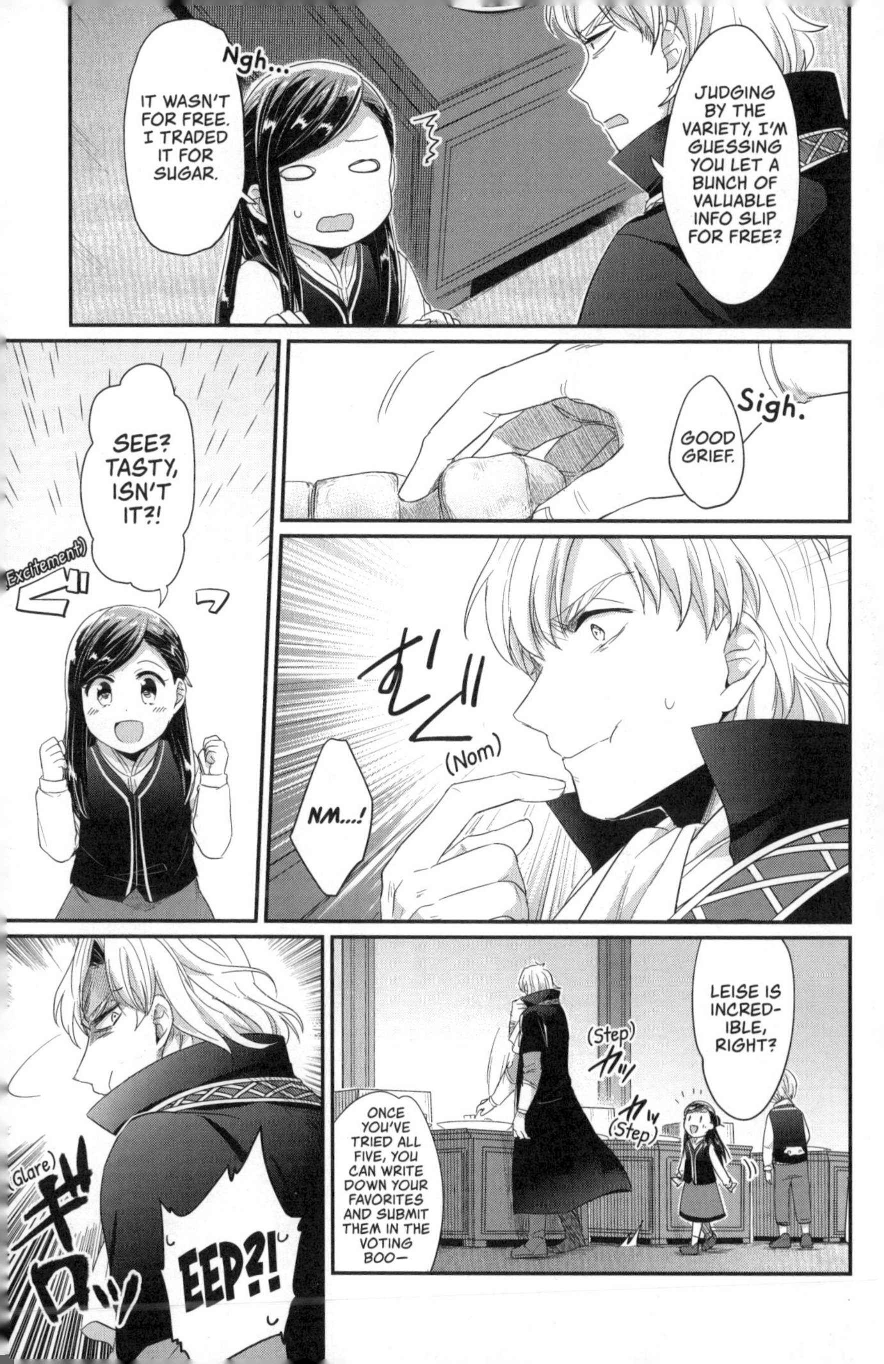
JUDGING BY THE VARIETY, I'M GUESSING YOU LET A BUNCH OF VALUABLE INFO SLIP FOR FREE?
Ngh...
IT WASN'T FOR FREE. I TRADED IT FOR SUGAR.
Sigh.
GOOD GRIEF.
(Nom)
NM...!
SEE? TASTY, ISN'T IT?!
Excitement)
LEISE IS INCRED-IBLE, RIGHT?
(Step)
(Step)
ONCE YOU'VE TRIED ALL FIVE, YOU CAN WRITE DOWN YOUR FAVORITES AND SUBMIT THEM IN THE VOTING BOO—
(Glare)
EEP?!

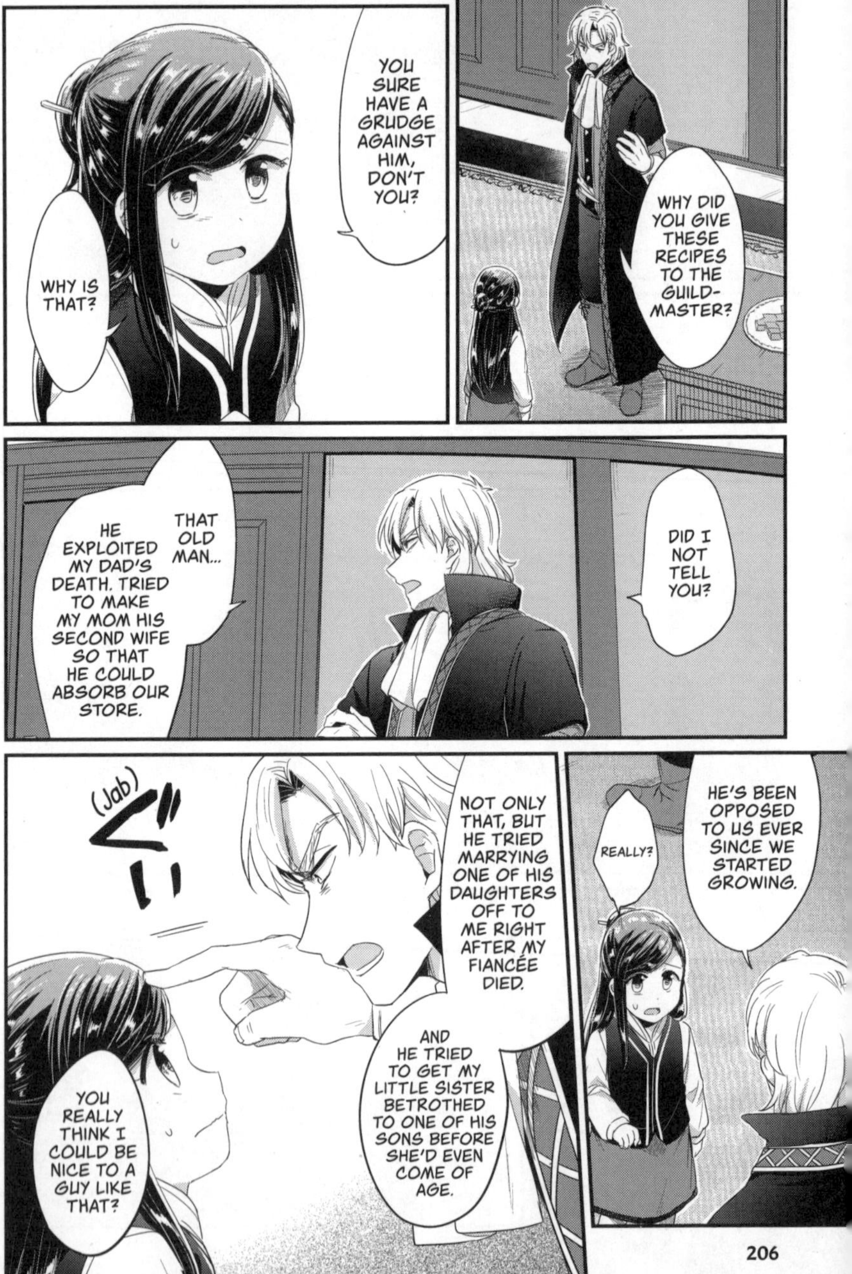
WHY DID YOU GIVE THESE RECIPES TO THE GUILD-MASTER?
YOU SURE HAVE A GRUDGE AGAINST HIM, DON'T YOU?
WHY IS THAT?
DID I NOT TELL YOU?
THAT OLD MAN...
HE EXPLOITED MY DAD'S DEATH. TRIED TO MAKE MY MOM HIS SECOND WIFE SO THAT HE COULD ABSORB OUR STORE.
HE'S BEEN OPPOSED TO US EVER SINCE WE STARTED GROWING.
REALLY?
NOT ONLY THAT, BUT HE TRIED MARRYING ONE OF HIS DAUGHTERS OFF TO ME RIGHT AFTER MY FIANCÉE DIED.
AND HE TRIED TO GET MY LITTLE SISTER BETROTHED TO ONE OF HIS SONS BEFORE SHE'D EVEN COME OF AGE.
(Jab)
YOU REALLY THINK I COULD BE NICE TO A GUY LIKE THAT?

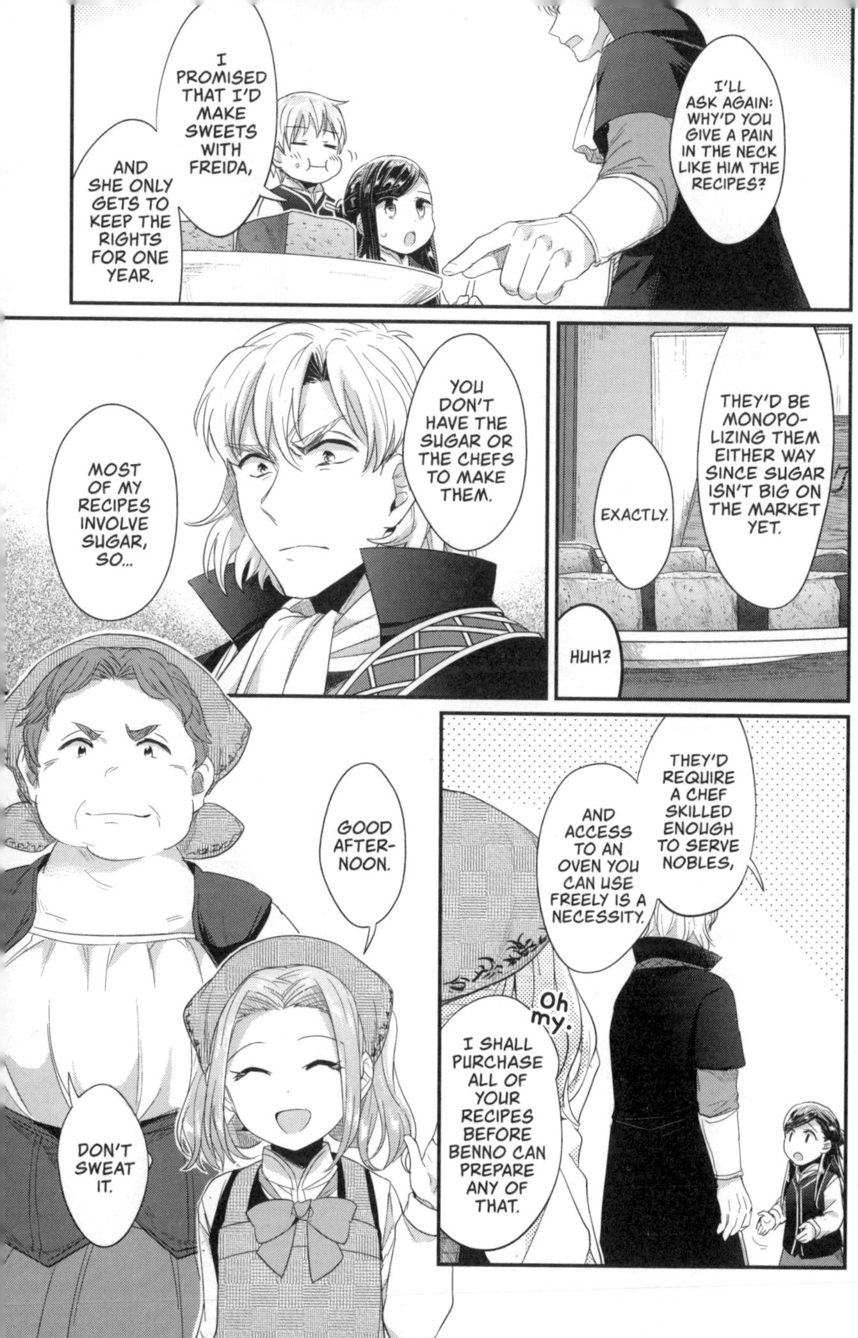
I'LL ASK AGAIN: WHY'D YOU GIVE A PAIN IN THE NECK LIKE HIM THE RECIPES?
I PROMISED THAT I'D MAKE SWEETS WITH FREIDA,
AND SHE ONLY GETS TO KEEP THE RIGHTS FOR ONE YEAR.
THEY'D BE MONOPOLIZING THEM EITHER WAY SINCE SUGAR ISN'T BIG ON THE MARKET YET.
EXACTLY.
HUH?
YOU DON'T HAVE THE SUGAR OR THE CHEFS TO MAKE THEM.
MOST OF MY RECIPES INVOLVE SUGAR, SO...
THEY'D REQUIRE A CHEF SKILLED ENOUGH TO SERVE NOBLES,
AND ACCESS TO AN OVEN YOU CAN USE FREELY IS A NECESSITY.
Oh my.
I SHALL PURCHASE ALL OF YOUR RECIPES BEFORE BENNO CAN PREPARE ANY OF THAT.
GOOD AFTERNOON.
DON'T SWEAT IT.

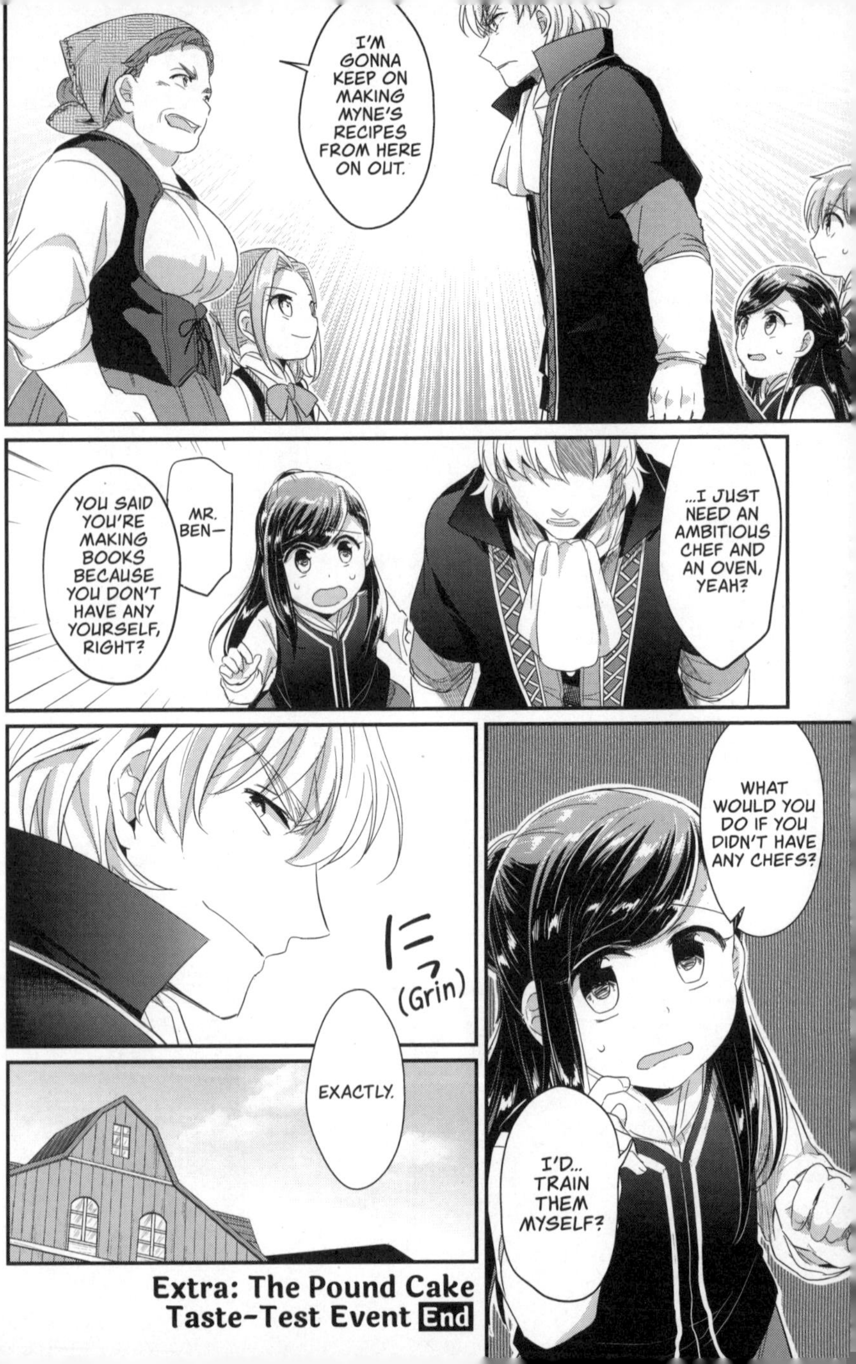
I'M GONNA KEEP ON MAKING MYNE'S RECIPES FROM HERE ON OUT.
...I JUST NEED AN AMBITIOUS CHEF AND AN OVEN, YEAH?
MR. BEN—
YOU SAID YOU'RE MAKING BOOKS BECAUSE YOU DON'T HAVE ANY YOURSELF, RIGHT?
WHAT WOULD YOU DO IF YOU DIDN'T HAVE ANY CHEFS?
I'D... TRAIN THEM MYSELF?
(Grin)
EXACTLY.

Extra: The Pound Cake Taste-Test Event End

As the Gilberta Company's Successor

As the Gilberta Company's Successor

"Corinna, got a second?" my brother asked, gesturing down the hall. He had been waiting for me to finish lunch.

"Go on ahead. I'll be right with you."

I noticed that his footsteps were light as he headed to his office, which made me sigh in relief. Today was the day that Myne was going to the temple with her parents, and since my brother always planned for the worst, he had been constantly on edge for the past two days. All the leherls who didn't know why were scared and anxious.

"The negotiations with the temple went well, I assume?" I asked upon entering his office.

"Yeah. Lutz just came with a report."

"I see... That's good. I heard from Mark that you were so worried for Myne, you thought up all sorts of plans and did whatever you could to help her."

"Hmph. The only thing I was worried about was losing the money she brings us."

"Aha. One day you'll learn to be honest, Benno," I said with a giggle.

He clicked his tongue and glared at me with his dark-red eyes, but to me, it wasn't scary at all; I knew that was the face he made when I was right on the money.

"The temple summoned Myne with the intention of making her join them, and if she has the Gilberta Company helping her, then we might end up drawing some unwanted noble attention," I continued. "If even I can see how dangerous that is, there's no way you couldn't as well. But you helped her regardless, didn't you?"

"Corinna, you..."

"As harsh as it sounds, Myne is little more than a stranger who ultimately didn't even join our store as an apprentice. Why would you go so far to help her, especially when you usually prioritize the wellbeing of our store more than anything? I want to determine whether I should stop you or help you next time, as the Gilberta Company's successor," I said, revealing the uncertainties that had been building up inside of me. Benno grimaced in response, but if something like this was going to happen again, I needed an answer sooner rather than later.

"...Did you know that Myne has the Devouring, Corinna?"

"I've heard that word before, back when she collapsed in our store," I replied. But as they hadn't told me what kind of sickness the Devouring actually was, I didn't really know anything beyond that. I had asked some others out of curiosity, but the only thing I learned was that it was extremely rare and barely anyone knew anything about it. I was honestly dying to know why Benno understood so much about such a rare disease.

"Kids born with way more mana than normal are said to have the Devouring. It's more of a constitution thing than an actual sickness."

According to Benno, for a Devouring child to survive, they needed to regularly expend their mana through the use of magic tools. But only nobles had access to such things. As such, kids with the Devouring who weren't so fortunate would inevitably die young—that is, unless they entered the temple, where magic tools were more readily available.

"I was wondering why Myne wanted to join the temple, but I never thought it would have to do with mana."

I had heard that the temple was a scary place where orphans whose parents had died before their baptisms were taken and then never allowed to leave. It was the realm of nobles, where no commoners ventured except merchants with explicit business there. At the very least, it wasn't a place I ever wanted to be.

"...But that doesn't explain why you're supporting her, Benno."

I could understand Myne wanting to go to the temple to extend her life, but that was no reason for Benno to put our store at risk for her sake.

Benno grimaced, pausing in thought for a moment before letting out a sigh. "I guess it's about time I told you. I've kept quiet about this since you were young and there's never been much point in talking about it, but... Liz died from the Devouring."

My eyes widened. Liz was my brother's late girlfriend, who had tragically passed before they could be officially engaged. She was so important to him that he was still refusing to marry anyone else. *And she had the Devouring?*

"When it happened to Liz, I didn't know anything about it. I couldn't do anything to stop it. So I wanted to do everything I could to save Myne. That's all. You can stop me next time, if you want."

I wasn't dense or foolish enough to miss the weight behind Benno's "That's all." The grimace he wore was to mask his pain, and I had grown very familiar with it since Liz's death.

My expression clouded over as well. "I won't stop you. If you can help her, you should."

"Sheesh... I knew you'd make that face. This is exactly why I didn't want to say anything in the first place. Listen, if it'll cheer you up, I did help Myne," he said, stroking my cheek before firmly poking it with a finger. "Plus, even if Liz had known there were magic tools in the temple, I don't think anything would have changed. Her parents were merchants who wouldn't have wanted their reputations tarnished by their daughter joining the temple, and if she went anyway, we wouldn't have been able to get married. I doubt she would have wanted to walk that road in life."

Now that he had all this new information, I could guess that Benno was in the middle of thinking everything through and sorting his emotions out. Liz had been an immovable rock sitting in his heart for some time now, one that I had thought could never be moved. So the fact that it was now beginning to shift made me feel both happy and sad.

"Right, that's enough of that depressing talk. Let's get to the point here. Now that the temple business is settled, Myne will be coming to show you the clothes she wore on her baptism."

Myne's baptism outfit was so frilly that she had looked like a rich child even from a distance. Its design had been unlike anything I had ever seen before, and in an instant, I recognized it as something that even noble girls would like. That was why I had asked Benno to contact Myne—so that I could see the outfit up close.

"Seems like she'll only come if you let her mom and sister accompany her, since the former made the outfit and the latter the hair stick. Thoughts?"

"I welcome them all. I was hoping to ask how exactly everything was made, but I wasn't sure whether Myne understood the sewing process," I replied. Her mother would probably be much easier to talk to in this context, anyway. "I've currently finished delivering all the Star Festival outfits and have some spare time, so I'm ready whenever they are. I cannot wait for them to arrive."

And arrive they did. Myne came into the room with her mother and sister following closely behind, both visibly tense. They were clearly poor people from the south part of town, overwhelmed by the wealthy atmosphere of the north. Myne hadn't been nervous at all during our first meeting, and her father had to deal with traveling merchants as part of his job, so I had kind of assumed that everyone in her family was relatively relaxed about status. But that ostensibly wasn't the case.

"It's nice to meet you, Mrs. Corinna. I am Myne's mother, Effa. Thank you for inviting me here today," the mother said.

"Mrs. Corinna, I'm Tuuli. I've been really looking forward to meeting you. I'm so happy to be here," her daughter added.

They were both speaking to me very formally, perhaps due to my position in the Tailor's Guild. With this in mind, I concluded it would most likely be best for me to respond in turn.

Tuuli was the quintessential normal girl. When she looked up at me, she had the same degree of respect and awe in her eyes as all the young seamstresses did when I went to the other workshops to scout out leherl apprentices to steal away. But her manner of speech and behavior were both fairly polite for a poor girl from the south part of town, so I could guess that she was used to dealing with customers at her place of work.

Her speech is polite, but still within normal bounds for a girl her age... Otto was right. Myne sticks out like a sore thumb compared to the rest of her family.

Both Effa and Tuuli had clean, glossy hair, but judging by how they drank their tea and ate the sweets offered to them, they hadn't learned proper etiquette at all. Myne, on the other hand, seemed as though she would fit right in next to a rich girl at the dinner table. It was honestly hard to believe they were actually family.

"Effa, I believe you are a dyer. Is that correct?" I asked.

Her fingers, wrapped around the teacup she was bringing to her lips, were stained with all sorts of colors. Myne's baptism outfit was visibly well made, even from afar, and since Tuuli was still just an apprentice seamstress, I concluded that Effa must have been the one responsible for it.

"Yes. I work in the Heuss Workshop."

"I often use cloth dyed by the Heuss Workshop; their prices are fair, and their dyes lovely. The blues in particular are quite nice," I said, my praise causing her to smile. She appeared to relax a little, so I continued. "When is dyeing the busiest, I wonder?"

"We're most busy in the autumn. There are more plants and fruits used for dyes available then."

It turned out that creating the dyes was much tougher work than actually using them. As we ate our snacks, I continued talking to Effa about dyeing and to Tuuli about sewing, chatting in a way that conveniently doubled as a self-introduction.

Once the tension had completely drained from my guests, we moved right onto the baptism clothes. They removed the delicately folded outfit from Myne's basket and spread it out on the table. I first noticed the frills on the sleeves, then the small decorative flowers that matched her hair stick. On closer inspection, there was also embroidery concealed within the frills. Such decoration was normal to see on sleeves, but I didn't understand the point in keeping it hidden.

"Why is such lovely embroidery hidden, I wonder?"

"Because she just altered my baptism outfit," Tuuli explained. "When I wore it, you could see the embroidery just fine. But the clothes drooped down from Myne's shoulders and stuff, since it was too long for her arms and legs, so..."

I gave an understanding nod, mentally comparing her size to Myne's. There was such a considerable height difference between them that it was hard to believe they were actually sisters. Using hand-me-downs *without* modifying them certainly wouldn't have been possible.

"They mentioned that it was normal to undo all the sewn string and recut the cloth when there's this much of a size difference, but that would have made the clothes unwearable as soon as I got even a little bigger," Myne said. "Altering it by pinching the cloth means I can slowly undo those parts as I grow."

That made sense. It was more efficient than remaking the entire outfit from scratch.

"That certainly is the rational thing to do if you intend for someone to continue wearing it as they grow," I observed. "I'm just a little surprised since, when a child normally grows, you would simply think to buy new clothes at a secondhand store."

"Clothes are of course worth less money the more you use them, but if you keep using the same outfit for years, you won't need to buy new clothes in the first place. That was why I followed Myne's suggestion," Effa said, going on to detail what she had altered and where. She had pulled up the shoulder parts and fitted them with string, pinched the hem and sleeves into folds to create frills that disguised the outfit's length, and then finally added flower-shaped decorations. It was really quite simple once explained.

But the adjustments themselves had been very precise, namely so that the frills didn't appear unnatural. Upon picking up the clothes and examining them myself, making sure to unfold the sleeves, I realized just how skilled Effa really was. I wrote down my thoughts on a board as I pondered how one would make a dress like this if they intended for the frills to be there from the start.

Like this, perhaps...?

Once I had finished outlining my own interpretation of the design in my head, I put the clothes down so that I could examine the hair stick. The tiny flowers rustled in my hands when I picked it up. They were made out of woven thread, just like the other ones, but the hair stick itself used a design entirely unlike the ones delivered to us for winter handiwork.

"I made the big white flower," Tuuli announced, proudly puffing out her chest.

"It's very nice," I replied, praising her efforts as I stroked the flower petals, all the while running calculations in my head. An apprentice seamstress with only a year's experience past her baptism had managed to create unique flowers this expertly. Had I understood how to make them myself, my own craftswomen in the workshop could no doubt mass produce them without much issue. And introducing a variety of styles to the hair sticks would allow them to become a long-term staple of our store.

Effa and Tuuli were beaming with joy, but Myne alone crossed her arms, watching me with the calculating eyes of a merchant. "I understand that you wish to make these yourself, but we of course need to consider how much you are willing to pay for them," she said coolly. I could tell that a bunch of prices and conditions were already running through her head.

"W-Wait, Myne?!" Tuuli exclaimed, her eyes wide. But Myne promptly extended a hand to stop her, keeping her gaze fixed on me.

"We make these hair sticks for our winter handiwork and they're an important source of money for us; we can't just let other people make them willy-nilly. If she really is interested in them, she would need to buy the rights and pay us the money we would lose from her competition," she said, explaining the circumstances to her family. The words "important source of money" were enough to silence Tuuli in an instant.

"In that case, I will summon Benno."

"That wouldn't be worth it at all. I would get more money selling them to Freida," Myne scoffed, turning down Benno's offer of five small golds and eight large silvers. Thus began their business discussion. Benno must have really had an influence on her, given that, despite not even being an apprentice here, she was wearing the serious face of a true merchant.

I wonder how long she'll last against Benno...?

As much as I wanted to keep watching Myne, Benno had on a truly nasty frown. I decided it would be best to take Tuuli and Effa away from the clash so that it wouldn't overwhelm them or worsen their impressions of either side.

"Effa, Tuuli—it seems that this discussion may take some time. Follow me, if you would," I said, standing up and guiding them to a table in the back, at which point I started to talk about the clothes and ornaments that were currently popular among nobles. Just as I expected, Tuuli was hanging on my every word, her eyes shining with excitement.

After talking for a while, however, she started glancing over at Myne and Benno, no doubt curious about how the business discussion was going. I used this opportunity to speak to Effa.

"I'm glad that negotiations with the temple went well. Both my brother and I were quite worried for you."

"Thank you. We were prepared for the worst-case scenario of Myne being locked in the temple and Tuuli becoming a live-in apprentice, so I can't even begin to express how pleased I am about this outcome," Effa said, revealing that both she and her husband had been prepared to die during the negotiations. Her words caused me to let out a small gasp.

"I've heard from Myne that everyone in the Gilberta Company has been very supportive," she continued. "We owe you more than we could ever say—without you, we wouldn't have even known she had the Devouring. Going to the temple to negotiate sounds innocent enough on the surface, but we didn't know anything about the place, so we were worried to death. I'm just so glad that, despite everything, we still managed to save Myne's life. I couldn't bear even the thought of watching her slowly wilt away."

She paused, tears welling up in her eyes. Her expression reminded me of how Benno looked when talking about Liz.

After a brief moment, she spoke up again. "Mrs. Corinna, why has the Gilberta Company treated Myne so well?" she asked, having apparently been wondering the same thing I had.

I glanced toward Benno and Myne as they continued verbally sparring like their lives depended on it. "Someone very important to my brother died of the Devouring... It seems he couldn't bring himself to think of Myne as just a stranger."

"I see…" Effa said, trailing off uncomfortably. She lowered her eyes as though searching for words. I had surely made a similar face when Benno revealed this same truth to me.

"Remember that this won't all end with her joining the temple. We have no idea what life Myne will lead beyond this point. But no matter what happens, both Benno and I are glad that she will survive."

"Thank you very much. I truly mean it. Thank you."

"Impressive work. How much did you settle for, in the end?" I asked once the discussions were over. "The amount will impact how much we charge for them."

Myne glanced over at Effa and Tuuli, then held up several fingers.

One large gold and seven small golds… My, how impressive indeed.

"Consider me quite impressed that you were able to squeeze that much money out of Benno," I replied. It was honestly hard to believe that she truly was a child who had just been baptized.

While I stood there in genuine awe, Tuuli also asked what price they had agreed on. Myne hesitated, looking around for any sort of escape, then gave up and whispered to her.

"Whaaat?! Did you just say *golds*?!"

"It sounds like a lot of money, but it really is the fair market price for exclusive product rights. I'm not Benno; I don't rip people off," Myne said in a desperate attempt to justify herself. But there wasn't a child in either the south or the north part of the city who engaged in such high-level business deals behind their parents' backs.

This has to be a massive surprise, even for her parents, I mused. And it seemed that Effa was indeed shocked—so much so, in fact, that she went pale. I couldn't help but feel sympathetic just from looking at her.

"You're charging the merchants who broke their backs to help us with the temple situation... a large gold and seven small golds...?" she asked, completely stunned.

"Erm, Effa... I believe that Benno settled on this knowing that it was a fair price, given that he's a merchant, so..." I began, telling her not to worry. But despite my best efforts, the price was so high that she almost seemed on the verge of collapsing from disbelief.

Something tells me that, even after she goes to the temple, Myne is going to continue shocking people in all sorts of ways, just like this.

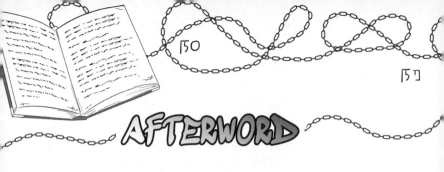

AFTERWORD

Thus concludes the entirety of Part 1! I'm Suzuka, and thank you for buying Volume 7 of *Ascendance of a Bookworm*.

I drew this series over the course of three years, and I loved how it felt like Myne's life was becoming a part of my own. I hope that even a little bit of my love for this work and its characters has carried over into my illustrations.

I'll be drawing Part 2 as well. How will Myne's life change now that she's joined the temple as an apprentice blue shrine maiden? Let's all watch what happens together. Part 3 is also currently being drawn by Ryo Namino. Please enjoy that as well.

I've finished work on the individual volumes now, so after a one-month break to recharge, I'll jump right into the start of Volume 2. Oh, and I plan to visit a Gutenberg museum in Germany during that break. In all honesty, the fact that I'm using even my time away to get material for my work is very much like me. Ahaha.

Well, that's about it from me. Thank you to the editor for helping out in all sorts of ways during the publication process; to the author, Miya Kazuki, for helping me with all my minor questions; and to everyone who read the manga adaptation of *Ascendance of a Bookworm*! Onward to Part 2!

- Suzuka -

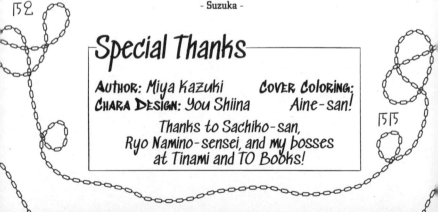

Special Thanks

Author: Miya Kazuki
Chara Design: You Shiina
Cover Coloring: Aine-san!

Thanks to Sachiko-san, Ryo Namino-sensei, and my bosses at Tinami and TO Books!

Afterword

To both those who are new to Bookworm and those who read the web novel or light novel: Thank you very much for reading Volume 7 of *Ascendance of a Bookworm*'s manga adaptation.

Part 1 is finally over. I consider the finale where Myne's whole family gathers and welcomes her home to be one of the more iconic scenes in the series, so I'm very glad to see it here once again. It's incredible!

It's been about three years since Suzuka-sama started working on this, and she's been drawing *Ascendance of a Bookworm* for that entire time. It's moving beyond words. Thank you so, so much.

This is the first manga version that TO Books has ever done, so we had no real clue what we were doing when we started. I still remember when we first begun and were floundering over where it would be published, whether it would actually start, and whether we could really keep it up. In a way, it's kind of a miracle that Part 1 finished without issue like this.

Suzuka-sama will be continuing Part 2's manga adaptation while Ryo Namino-sama draws Part 3. I'm very happy to see *Ascendance of a Bookworm* continue spreading across the world like this, and I'm looking forward to the future, too.

Part 2, drawn by Suzuka-sama, will start being published on Niconico Seiga in November. The setting moves to the temple, and many new characters appear. Suzuka-sama designed plenty of characters who never showed up in the original novels' illustrations, like Lutz's brothers, the craftsmen, the gods, and Arno. Perhaps we will also see some sections of Part 2 that never showed up in the originals.

This volume's short story, "As the Gilberta Company's Successor," was written from Corinna's perspective. There aren't many characters who can step into Benno's past and private life very much, so I actually had a surprising amount of fun writing from her point of view. I also liked writing about Myne and Benno's fierce discussion through someone else's eyes. I hope you enjoyed it as well.

Miya Kazuki

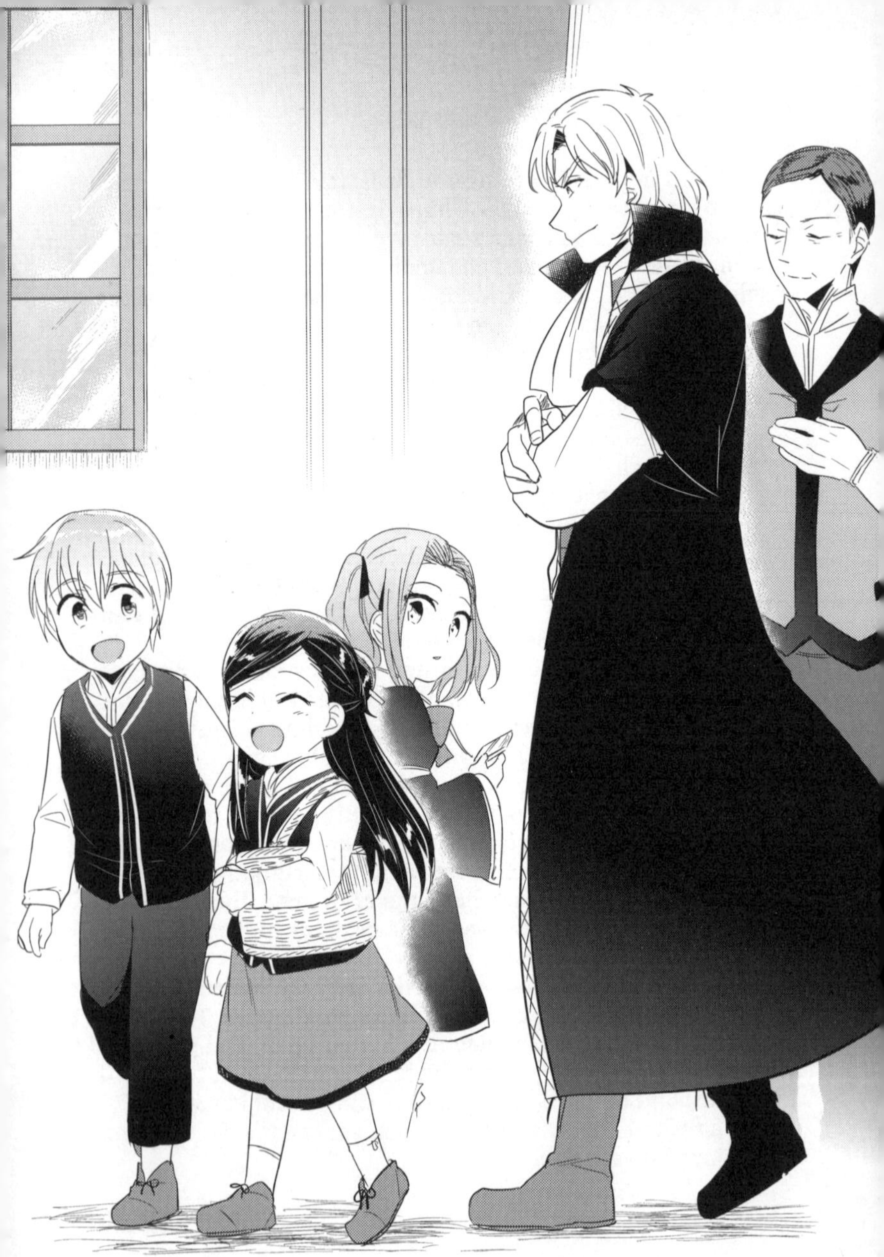

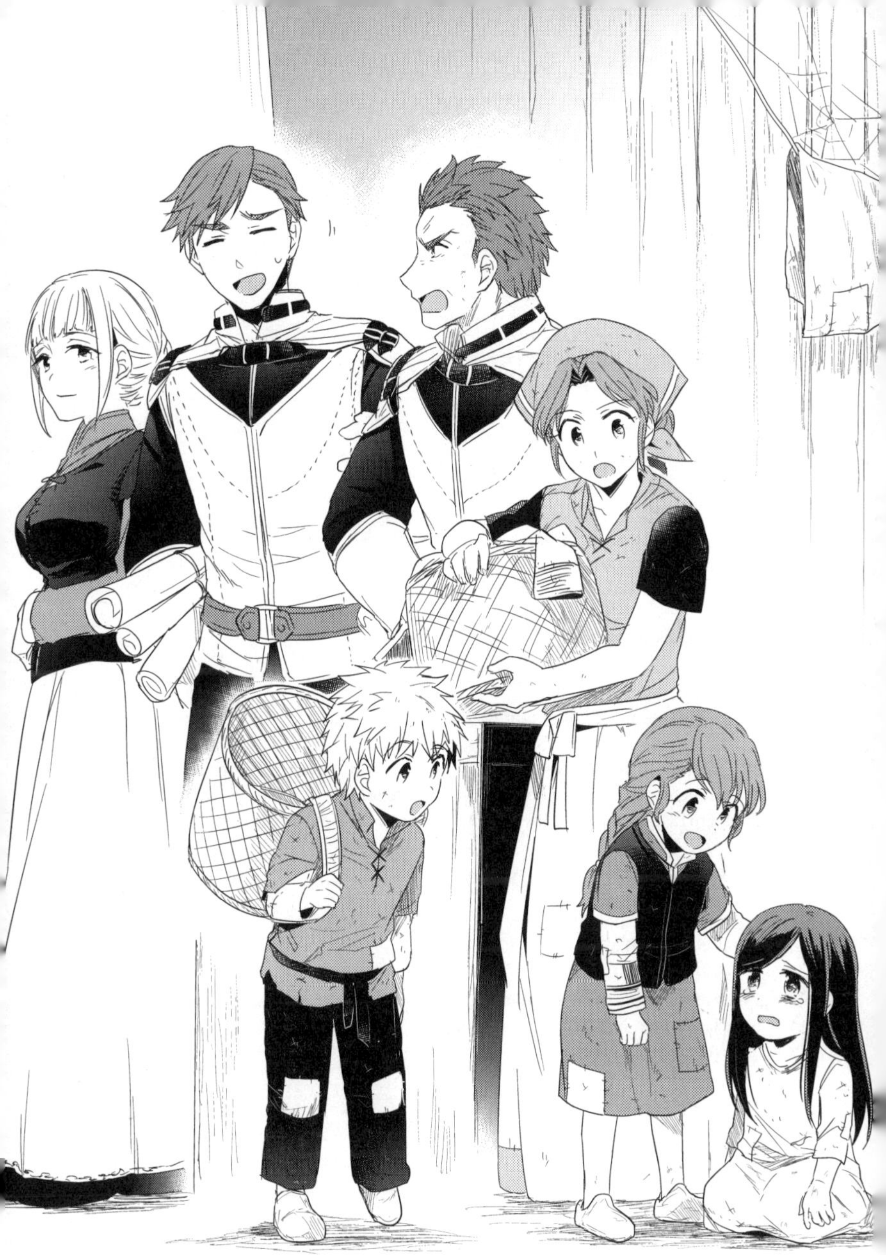

ASCENDANCE OF A BOOKWORM (MANGA)VOLUME 7
by Miya Kazuki (story) and Suzuka (artwork)
Original character designs by You Shiina

Translated by quof
Edited by Kieran Redgewell
Lettered by Meiru

This book is a work of fiction. Names, characters, places, and incidents are the product of the author's imagination or are used fictitiously. Any resemblance to actual events, locales, or persons, living or dead, is coincidental.

First published in Japan in 2018 by TO Books, Tokyo.
Publication rights for this English edition arranged through TO Books, Tokyo.

Find more books like this one at www.j-novel.club!

Managing Director: Samuel Pinansky
Manga Line Manager: J. Collis
Managing Editor: Jan Mitsuko Cash
Managing Translator: Kristi Fernandez
QA Manager: Hannah N. Carter
Marketing Manager: Stephanie Hii

ISBN: 978-1-7183-7256-6
First Printing: September 2021
Printed in Korea
10 9 8 7 6 5 4 3 2 1

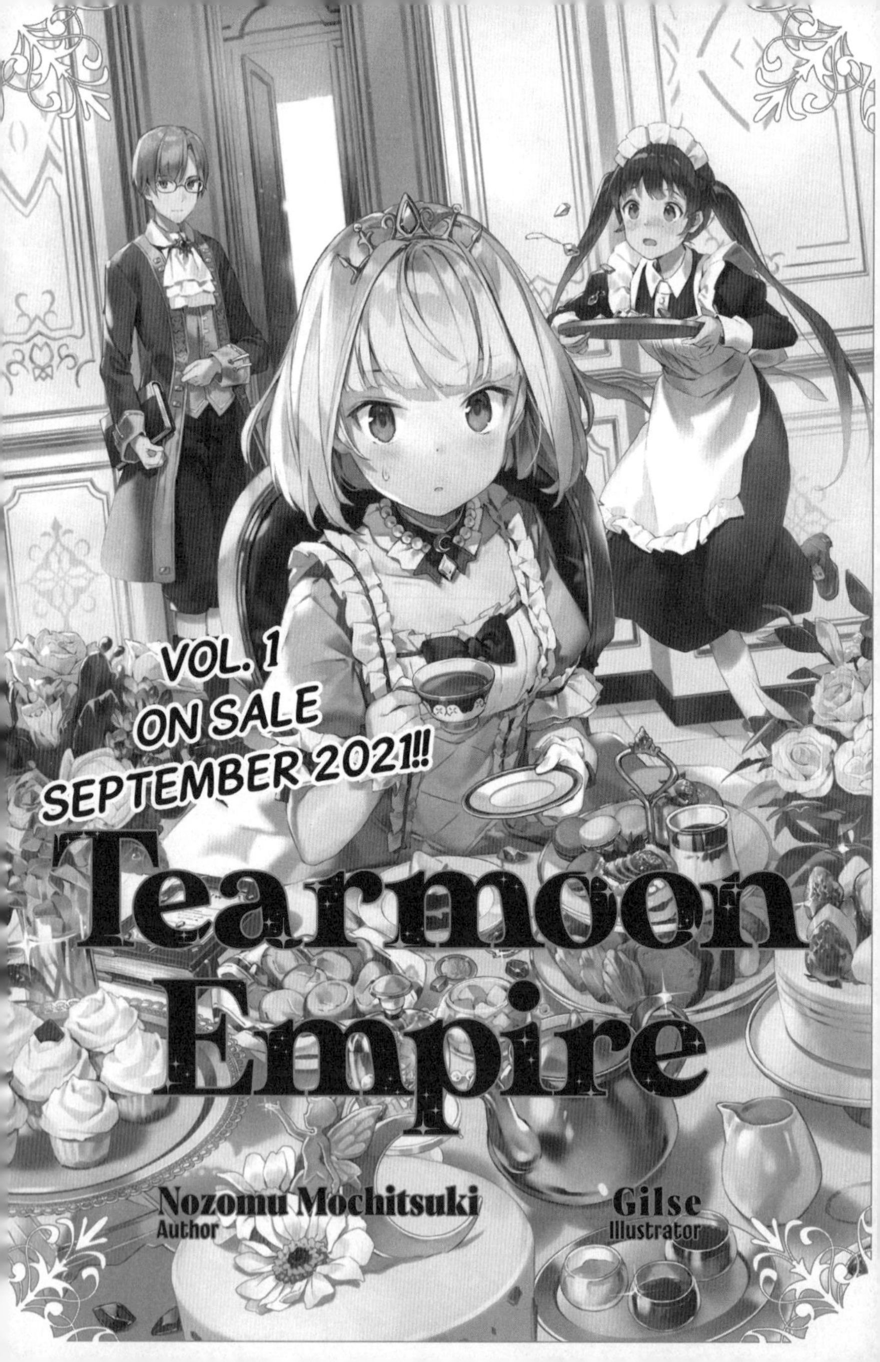

VOL. 1
ON SALE
SEPTEMBER 2021!!
Tearmoon Empire
Nozomu Mochitsuki
Author
Gilse
Illustrator

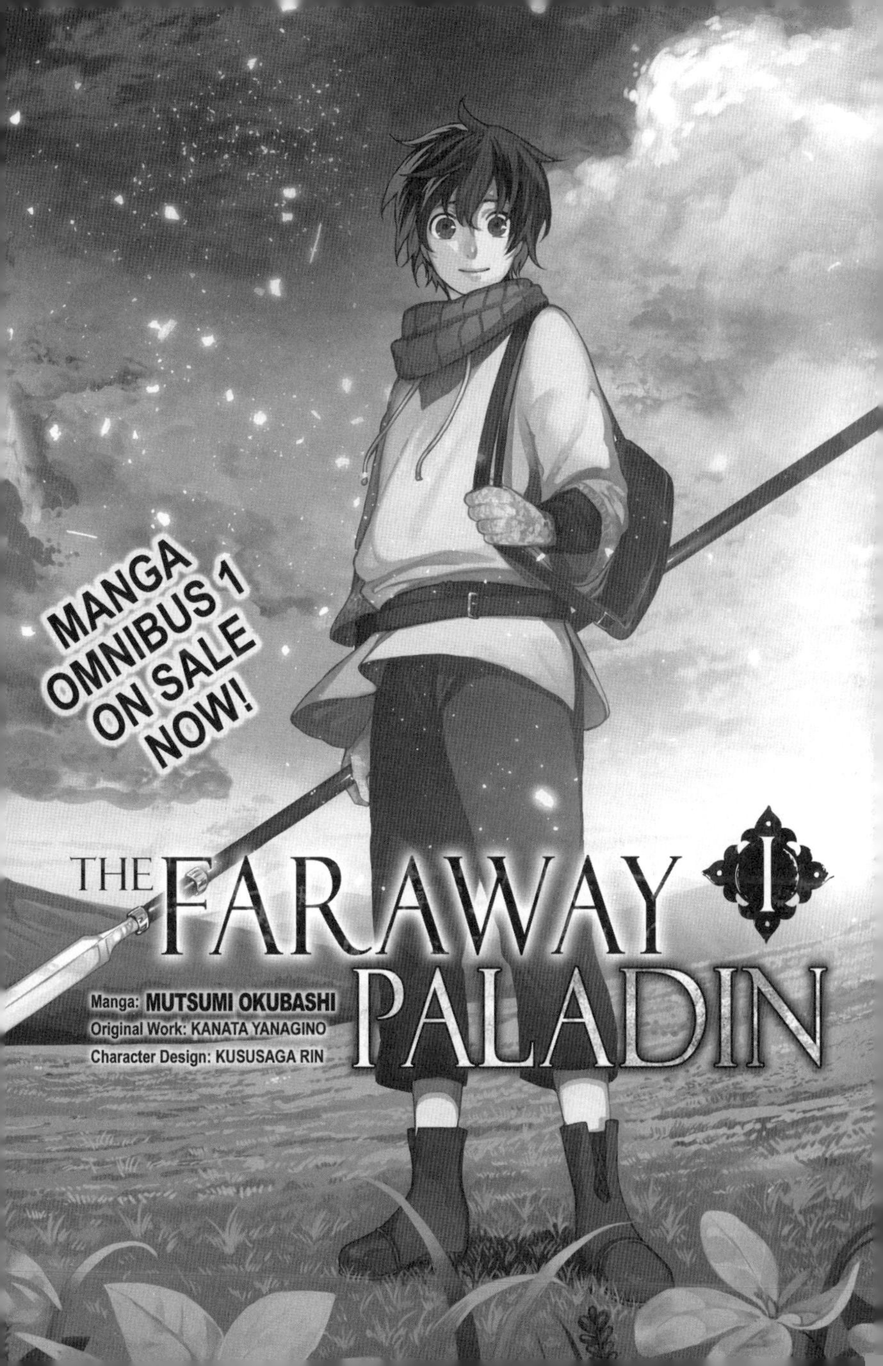
MANGA OMNIBUS 1 ON SALE NOW!
THE FARAWAY PALADIN I
Manga: MUTSUMI OKUBASHI
Original Work: KANATA YANAGINO
Character Design: KUSUSAGA RIN

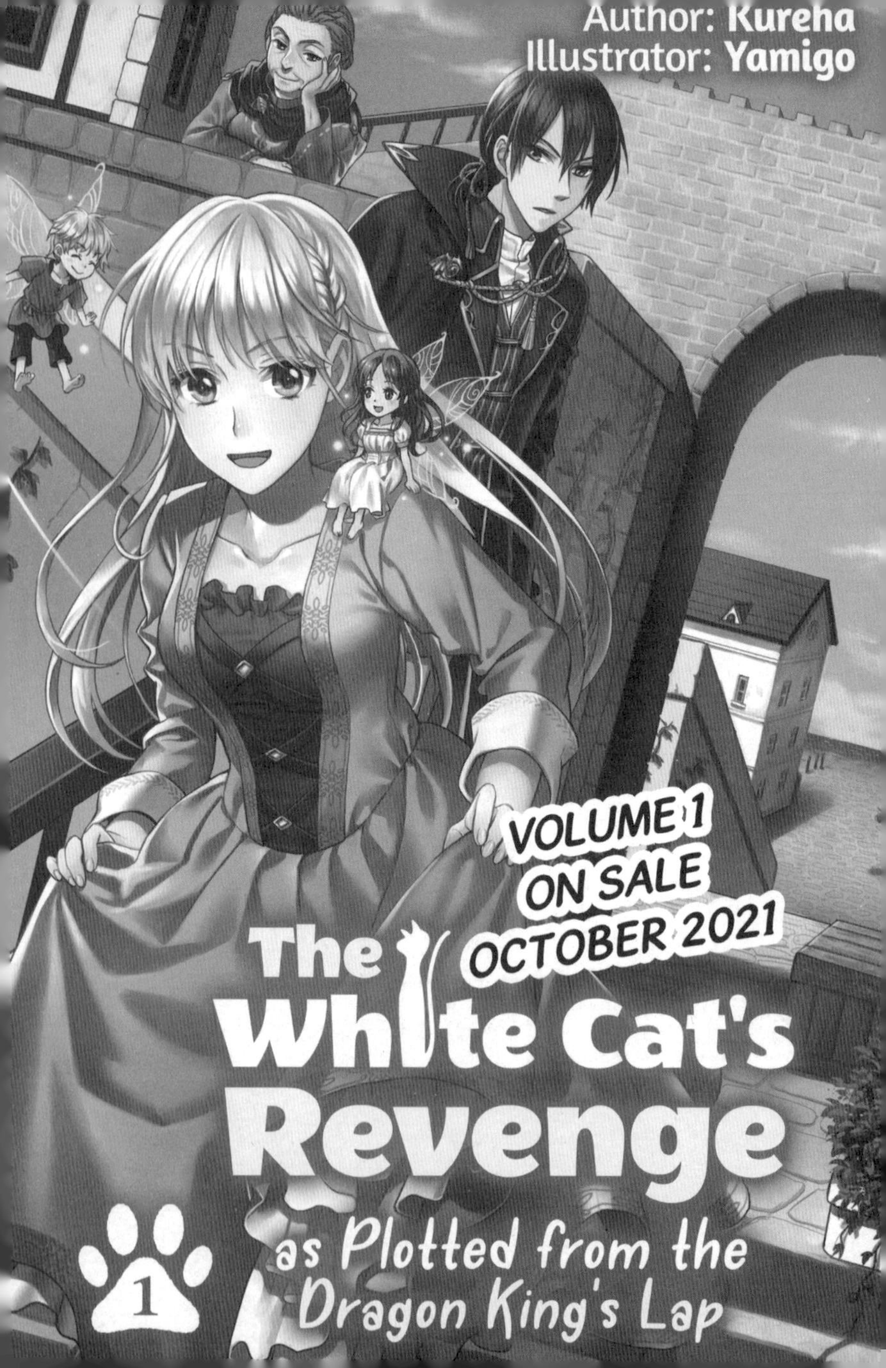
Author: Kureha
Illustrator: Yamigo
VOLUME 1
ON SALE
OCTOBER 2021
The White Cat's Revenge
as Plotted from the Dragon King's Lap
1

j-novel club

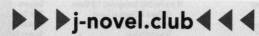

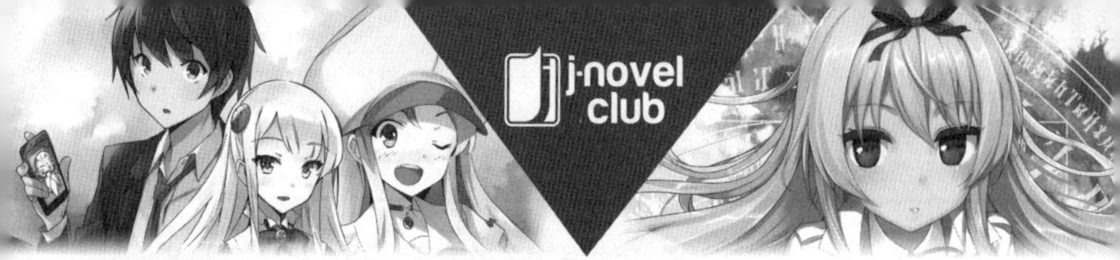

J-Novel Club Lineup

Ebook Releases Series List

A Lily Blooms in Another World
A Very Fairy Apartment**
A Wild Last Boss Appeared!
Altina the Sword Princess
Amagi Brilliant Park
An Archdemon's Dilemma: How to Love Your Elf Bride*
Animeta!**
The Apothecary Diaries
Are You Okay With a Slightly Older Girlfrienc
Arifureta: Fr
to World
Arifureta Ze
Ascendance
Banner of th
Beatless
Bibliophile P
Black Summ
The Bloodli
By the Grac
Campfire Co
World wit
Can Someone Please Explain What's Going On?!
The Combat Baker and Automaton Waitress
Cooking with Wild Game*
Deathbound Duke's Daughter
Demon King Daimaou
Demon Lord, Retry!*
Der Werwolf: The Annals of Veight*
Discommunication**
Dungeon Busters
The Economics of Prophecy
The Epic Tale of the Reincarnated Prince Herscherik
The Extraordinary, the Ordinary, and SOAP!
The Faraway Paladin*
From Truant to Anime Screenwriter: My Path to "Anohana" and "The Anthem of the Heart"
Full Metal Panic!
Fushi no Kami: Rebuilding Civilization Starts With a Village
The Great Cleric
The Greatest Magicmaster's Retirement Pla
Girls Kingdom
Grimgar of Fantasy and Ash
Her Majesty's Swa

Holmes of Kyoto
The Holy Knight's Dark Road
How a Realist Hero Rebuilt the Kingdom*
How NOT to Summon a Demon Lord
I Love Yuri and I Got Bodyswapped with a Fujoshi!**
I Refuse to Be Your Enemy!
I Saved Too Many Girls and Caused
Isekai Rebuilding Project
JK Haru is a Sex Worker in Another World
Kobold King
Kokoro Connect
Last and First Idol
Lazy Dungeon Master
The Magic in this Other World is Too Far Behind!*
The Magician Who Rose From Failure
Mapping: The Trash-Tier Skill That Got Me Into a Top-Tier Party*
Marginal Operation**
The Master of Ragnarok & Blesser of Einherjar*
Middle-Aged Businessman, Arise in Another World!
Mixed Bathing in Another Dimension
Monster Tamer
My Big Sister Lives in a Fantasy World
My Friend's Little Sister Has It
My Instant Death Ability is So
Other World Stands a Chance

My Next Life as a Villainess: All Routes Lead to Doom!
Our Crappy Social Game Club Is Gonna Make the Most Epic Game
Otherside Picnic
Outbreak Company
Outer Ragna
Record of Wortenia War*
Seirei Gensouki: Spirit Chronicles*
My Sexist Party Leader
d Me Out, So I Teamed Up
a Mythical Sorceress!
Cutest... But We're
riends!
erer's Receptionist
s Stabber Orphen*
eincarnation**
s of Marielle Clarac*
n Empire
The Underdog of the Eight Greater Tribes
The Unwanted Undead Adventurer*
WATARU!!! The Hot-Blooded Fighting Teen & His Epic Adventures After Stopping a Truck with His Bare Hands!!
Welcome to Japan, Ms. Elf!*
When the Clock Strikes Z
The White Cat's Revenge as Plotted from the Dragon King's Lap
Wild Times with a Fake Fake Princess
The World's Least Interesting Master Swordsman
Yume Nikki: I Am Not in Your Dream

* Novel and Manga Editions
** Manga Only

Keep an eye out at j-novel.club for further new title announcements!